From Enlightenment
to Romanticism

Published in our
centenary year
~ **2004** ~
MANCHESTER
UNIVERSITY
PRESS

From Enlightenment to Romanticism

ANTHOLOGY II

edited by
Carmen Lavin and Ian Donnachie

MANCHESTER UNIVERSITY PRESS
Manchester and New York

distributed exclusively in the USA by Palgrave

Published in association with

The Open University

Published by Manchester University Press
Oxford Road, Manchester M13 9NR, UK
and Room 400, 175 Fifth Avenue, New York, NY 10010, USA
www.manchesteruniversitypress.co.uk

Distributed exclusively in the USA by
Palgrave, 175 Fifth Avenue, New York, NY 10010, USA

Distributed exclusively in Canada by
UBC Press, University of British Columbia, 2029 West Mall,
Vancouver, BC, Canada, V6T 1Z2

British Library Cataloguing-in-Publication Data
A catalogue record for this book is available from the British Library

Library of Congress Cataloging-in-Publication Data applied for

ISBN 0 7190 6672 7 *hardback*
0 7190 6673 5 *paperback*

First published 2004
13 12 11 10 09 08 07 06 05 04   10 9 8 7 6 5 4 3 2 1

This publication forms part of an Open University course A207 *From Enlightenment to Romanticism, c.1780–1830*. Details of this and other Open University courses can be obtained from the Course Information and Advice Centre, PO Box 724, The Open University, Milton Keynes MK7 6ZS, United Kingdom: tel. +44 (0)1908 653231, e-mail general-enquiries@open.ac.uk. Alternatively, you may visit the Open University website at http://www.open.ac.uk where you can learn more about the wide range of courses and packs offered at all levels by The Open University.

Typeset in Sabon
by Northern Phototypesetting Co. Ltd, Bolton
Printed in Great Britain
by Biddles Ltd, Guildford and King's Lynn

*This anthology is dedicated to the memory
of our colleague Stephanie Clennell (1921–2000)*

Contents

Contents

Contents

Contents

Illustrations

Acknowledgements

The editors and publisher would like to thank the following for help in preparing this anthology: Paula James for her assistance in locating literary references in William Gilpin, *Observations, relative chiefly to Picturesque Beauty, Made in the Year 1772, On Several Parts of England; particularly the Mountains, and Lakes of Cumberland, and Westmoreland*, Vol. I. Barry Symonds for his assistance in locating literary references in William Wordsworth, *A Guide Through the District of the Lakes in the North of England, with a Description of the Scenery, etc. for the use of Tourists and Residents*. Alison Hiley for her assistance in editing Robert Owen, *A New View of Society*. Linda Walsh for preparing the *Journal of Eugène Delacroix* section.

The editors and publisher would also like to thank the following for permission to publish the enclosed texts: Edmund Burke, *A Philosophical Enquiry into the Origin of our Ideas of the Sublime and Beautiful*, J. T. Boulton, ed., Blackwell, Oxford, Revised Edition 1987. Reproduced by permission of Pollinger Limited. Jane Austen, *Northanger Abbey, Oxford World Classics Series*, Oxford University Press, 1998. Reprinted by permission of Oxford University Press. *Robert Southey: The Critical Heritage*, edited by Dr Lionel Madden, 1972, Routledge and Kegan Paul, London and Boston. Reprinted by permission of Routledge. James Sambrook, ed., *William Cowper: The Task and Selected Other Poems*, Longman, London and New York, 1994, reprinted with permission from Pearson Education Limited. Stephen Gill, ed., *William Wordsworth* in *The Oxford Authors Series*, Oxford University Press, Oxford and New York, 1987. Reprinted by permission of Oxford University Press. W. J. B. Owen and Jane Worthington Smyser, eds, *The Prose Works of William Wordsworth*, 3 vols, Oxford University Press, London, 1974, reprinted with permission. William Wordsworth and Samuel Taylor Coleridge, *Lyrical Ballads*, edited by R. L. Brett and A. R. Jones, Methuen & Co. Ltd, London, 1968, reprinted with permission from Taylor and Francis Books Ltd. Robert Owen, *A New View of Society and Other Writings*, introduction by John Butt, JM Dent, London, 1972. Helen Dorey, ed., *Visions of Ruin*, 1999, exhibition catalogue, published by Sir John Soane's Museum. Reproduced by courtesy of the Trustees of Sir John Soane's Museum. David Hume, *A Treatise of Human Nature*, L. A. Selby-Bigge and P. H. Nidditch, eds, Oxford University Press, Oxford, 1978. Reprinted by permission of Oxford University Press. Jean Le Rond D'Alembert,

Preliminary Discourse to the Encyclopaedia, translated by R. N. Schwab, University of Chicago Press, Chicago, 1995. Reprinted with permission from University of Chicago Press. Excerpts from *Wackenroder's Confessions and Fantasies*, edited and translated by M. H. Schubert, Pennsylvania University Press, Pennsylvania, 1971, pp. 118–20, 125–7, 178–81. Copyright 1971 by The Pennsylvania State University. Reproduced by permission of the publisher. Robert David MacDonald, trans., 'Gretchen am Spinnrade', from Johann Wolfgang von Goethe, *Faust*, Oberon Books, London, 1988, revised reprint 2002. Reprinted with kind permission of Oberon Books Ltd. Lord Byron, *Childe Harold's Pilgrimage*, 1816 and *Childe Harold's Pilgrimage, Preface to Cantos I and II*, 1812/13, from *Lord Byron The Major Works*, Jerome J. McGann, ed., *Oxford World's Classics*, Oxford University Press, Oxford and New York, 1986, pp. 104–5. Reprinted by permission of Oxford University Press. Leslie A. Marchand, ed., *'So late into the night'*, *Byron's Letters and Journals*, Vol. 5, John Murray, London, 1976, reprinted with permission of John Murray (Publishers) Ltd. Excerpts from *The Confessions of Jean-Jacques Rousseau*, translated by J. M. Cohen (Penguin Books, 1953). Copyright © J. M. Cohen, 1953. Reprinted with permission from Penguin Books Ltd. Andrew Rutherford, ed., *Lord Byron the Critical Heritage*, Routledge, 1985, London, reprinted with permission from Taylor and Francis Books Ltd. Maria Edgeworth, *The Absentee*, W. J. McCormack and Kim Walker, eds, *Oxford World's Classics*, Oxford University Press, Oxford and New York, 1988. Reprinted by permission of Oxford University Press. Grevel Lindop, ed., *Works of Thomas de Quincey* (18 vols, London, Pickering and Chatto, 2000), *Confessions of an English Opium Eater*, 1821/1822, Vol. 2. Reprinted with permission from the publisher. J. C. C. Mays, ed., *The Collected Works of Samuel Taylor Coleridge; Poetical Works, Vol. I*, Princeton University Press, Princeton, 2001. Reprinted with permission from the publisher.

The editors and publisher would also like to thank the following for permission to publish the enclosed illustrations: Engraving of Grasmere, from Thomas West's *A Guide to the Lakes, in Cumberland, Westmorland, and Lancashire*, 1784. Reproduced by courtesy of The British Library. Frontispiece from William Gilpin's *Observations, relative chiefly to Picturesque Beauty, Made in the Year 1772, On Several Parts of England; particularly the Mountains, and Lakes of Cumberland, and Westmoreland*, Vol. I. Reproduced by courtesy of The British Library. An explanation of the shapes and lines of mountains from William Gilpin's *Observations, relative chiefly to Picturesque Beauty, Made in the Year 1772, On Several Parts of England; particularly the Mountains, and Lakes of Cumberland, and Westmoreland*, Vol. I. Reproduced by courtesy of The British Library. An illustration of the appearance, which the shores of a lake form, when seen from its surface, in a boat, from William Gilpin's

Observations, relative chiefly to Picturesque Beauty, Made in the Year 1772, On Several Parts of England; particularly the Mountains, and Lakes of Cumberland, and Westmoreland, Vol. I. Reproduced by courtesy of The British Library. Plan of Windermere, from William Gilpin's *Observations, relative chiefly to Picturesque Beauty, Made in the Year 1772, On Several Parts of England; particularly the Mountains, and Lakes of Cumberland, and Westmoreland*, Vol. I. Reproduced by courtesy of The British Library. Plan of Keswick Lake, from William Gilpin's *Observations, relative chiefly to Picturesque Beauty, Made in the Year 1772, On Several Parts of England; particularly the Mountains, and Lakes of Cumberland, and Westmoreland*, Vol. I. Reproduced by courtesy of The British Library. Print of the kind of rocky scenery, of which Gatesgarth-dale is composed, from William Gilpin's *Observations, relative chiefly to Picturesque Beauty, Made in the Year 1772, On Several Parts of England; particulary the Mountains, and Lakes of Cumberland, and Westmoreland*, Vol. I. Reproduced by courtesy of The British Library. Thomas Rowlandson, Cartoon of Dr Syntax, from William Combe, *The Tour of Dr Syntax in Search of the Picturesque, a Poem, with Thirty-One Illustrations by Thomas Rowlandson*. Reproduced by courtesy of The British Library. Thomas Rowlandson, 'Doctor Syntax setting out on his tour to the Lakes', from William Combe, *The Tour of Dr Syntax in search of the Picturesque, a Poem, with Thirty-One Illustrations by Thomas Rowlandson*. Reproduced by courtesy of The British Library. Mrs Marcet's diagrams of the Voltaic Battery, from *Chemical Agencies of Electricity*. Reproduced by courtesy of The British Library. Mrs Marcet's diagrams showing apparatus for the decomposition of water by the Voltaic Battery, from *On Hydrogen*. Reproduced by courtesy of The British Library. Mrs Marcet's diagram for the cistern collecting oil, from On Hydrogen. Reproduced by courtesy of The British Library. Eugène Delacroix, *A Jewish Wedding in Morocco*, from *The Journal of Eugène Delacroix*. Reproduced by courtesy of The Bridgeman Art Library. Photograph by courtesy of The Bridgeman Art Library.

Every effort has been made to obtain permission to reproduce copyright material in this book. If any proper acknowledgement has not been made, copyright-holders are invited to contact the publisher.

Introduction

This is the second of two anthologies designed to accompany the Open University course *From Enlightenment to Romanticism*, an interdisciplinary second-level course exploring changes and transitions in European culture between 1780 and 1830. The course supports the Arts Faculty's acknowledged commitment to inter-disciplinary teaching and draws on the disciplines of music, philosophy, religious studies, history, literature, history of art and history of science. These different disciplines allow insights into the breadth of major cultural shifts in Europe during a period of unprecedented turbulence and change.

Momentous historical events erupted at the end of the eighteenth century and the early part of the nineteenth century. The French Revolution of 1789 and the excesses of the Terror unleashed new forces within society, and the conquests of Napoleon altered the social structure of European nations. By 1830 the last of the Bourbons had been driven from the throne of France. These political convulsions were going on at the very same time that the developments of the industrial revolution decisively changed the balance of urban and rural life and work in Britain. Meanwhile advances in social and scientific knowledge in the late eighteenth century broke down old ideas about how the world worked and how society operated. Primarily secular energies ran alongside a new evangelicalism and a quest for a different kind of transcendentalism. From all sides Enlightenment confidence in reason and empiricism was challenged in contradictory impulses. The voices of slaves were heard while at the same time colonialism was making footholds in other continents. Freedom found new forms of expression, breaking down barriers in life and in art with fresh emphasis on the spontaneous and the intuitive, and a delight in imagination and exoticism. New perceptions of human aspirations brought a significant shift in thinking of human beings first and foremost as members of society to human beings as individuals, radically altering conceptions of human nature. There was suddenly a whole different way of looking at life. Romanticism came as a reaction to the mechanistic and the urban, bringing an emphasis on wildness and the sublime in nature. The impetus came separately during this period in each European country, moving with a different momentum within the arts and within social and scientific changes. French hegemony at the beginning of this period gave way to German and British hegemony by the end of it.

The universal theme through this age is the emergence of human individuality, the essential feature of Romanticism. The spiritual, intellectual and moral conflicts – between sense and sensibility, personal aspirations and social integration – are the critical dilemmas whose repercussions are still with us today.

The collection of extracts in this anthology provides primary sources which offer perspectives to complement the course *From Enlightenment to Romanticism*. They are grouped in accordance with particular sections of the course but do not necessarily reflect the balance and arrangement of the whole course. In this second anthology you will find readings which reflect the widespread effects of the shift from Enlightenment to Romanticism in music (some of the poems by Goethe set by Schubert in his Lieder are included), in art and architecture (Romantic visions of the exotic are captured in readings relating to the Royal Pavilion at Brighton and in an excerpt from the journal of Delacroix in Morocco, while the writings by Sir John Soane reflect the continuing urge of the age to collect and display for public viewing, enjoyment and education), and in new attitudes to social, industrial and scientific developments (in Sir Humphry Davy's lectures on chemistry and in Robert Owen's great project in New Lanark). Readings on the changing concepts of the sublime, the beautiful and the picturesque relate to their expression in literature, especially in the poetry of Wordsworth and in illustrated guides to the Lake District, and the decisive impetus of German aesthetics is explored in extracts from the writings of the Schlegel brothers and their fellow-writers and thinkers in Jena, Novalis and Wackenroder, while major works of literature are represented, including selected passages from Goethe's *Faust* and Canto III from Byron's *Childe Harold's Pilgrimage*.

Like the course itself, extracts in the anthology stimulate questions rather than provide reassuring answers. The companion volume offers readings which relate to the first part of the course.

The introduction to each group of texts is intended to provide a useful context for the general reader as well as for Open University students. Editorial additions are enclosed in square brackets and deletions within the texts are indicated by an ellipsis within square brackets. Unless otherwise indicated, footnotes have been provided by the contributors and editors. Footnotes by originating authors or editors are identified by an asterisk at the close of the note.

We would like to express our thanks to the members of the course team in the preparation of these anthologies. Each anthology is a collaborative venture and the contributors to this second volume are Tim Benton, Ian Donnachie, Carmen Lavin, Robert Philip, Gerrylynn Roberts, Barry Symonds, Linda Walsh, Nicola Watson and Robert Wilkinson. We would particularly like to register our appreciation to Alison Hiley for additional support, Nancy Marten for editorial advice and guidance, Yvette Purdy for invaluable administrative support and Carol Green for secretarial assistance.

Carmen Lavin and Ian Donnachie

PART I

Industry and changing landscapes

The Lake District 1 –
The Picturesque, the Beautiful
and the Sublime

Edmund Burke's (1729–97) *A Philosophical Enquiry into the Origin of our Ideas of the Sublime and Beautiful* (1757), clearly written and methodologically explicit, became one of the most widely read and cited of the many essays and treatises on this subject that appeared in England in the course of the eighteenth century. Written by Burke as a young man of 28, it was used as a reference point by many other writers on the subject, including those debating the subject of the picturesque. One of the most important political thinkers of his time, Burke also wrote many political works, of which the best known is *Reflections on the Revolution in France* (1790). Born in Dublin, second son of an Irish Protestant attorney and a Catholic mother, educated at Trinity College Dublin, he came to London, entering the Middle Temple in 1750. He soon abandoned law for literature, making friends with many leading literary figures of the day, including Garrick and Dr Johnson. He entered politics as private assistant to the secretary for Ireland, became a Whig MP in 1765, and remained in politics for the rest of his life.

Thomas West's (c.1720–79) *Guide to the Lakes* was first published in 1778. In 1780 (after West's death) it was revised and enlarged by William Cockin (1736–1807), a schoolmaster from Kendal, and went through several more editions before the end of the century. We have reproduced here sections of the third edition, published in 1784. Thomas West was a scholar, antiquarian and historian. Many of Cockin's revisions to West's texts are stylistic, but he also added footnotes (most of which have been removed from the passages included here), illustrative plates, tables (of comparative mountain heights), a map, and, as an appendix, some earlier writings on the Lakes. Born and educated in Scotland, West trained in Liège as a Jesuit priest and became a Jesuit chaplain in Cumbria. In his later years he spent a great deal of time touring the area and accompanying visitors. He had already written a work of local interest, *The Antiquities of Furness*. His *Guide to the Lakes* inspired many other writers on the region, including William Wordsworth,

3

and helped to establish a tradition of viewing landscape as a series of picture-like or 'picturesque' compositions viewed from carefully selected 'stations' or viewpoints. It was widely used by tourists and amateur sketchers.

William Gilpin (1724–1804) was a vicar and teacher born in Cumbria. In 1772 he wrote his *Observations, relative chiefly to Picturesque Beauty, Made in the Year 1772, On Several Parts of England; particularly the Mountains, and Lakes of Cumberland, and Westmoreland* and circulated them in manuscript form. Those who read them in this form included the Royal Family. The *Observations* were first published in 1786 and went through further editions in the late eighteenth and nineteenth centuries. They were hugely influential, not only as a handbook for amateur sketchers and tourists but also in high art circles. Gilpin saw the countryside with a sense of national pride, as God's creation and as the source of the moral virtues that Rousseau had associated so powerfully with rural life. Essentially, Gilpin's *Observations* prescribed a method of picturesque composition that, like West's *Guide*, encouraged the viewing of landscape as art. The formula for the picturesque scenes Gilpin encouraged his readers to view and reproduce (with some modification) in art derived from the classical landscapes of Claude Lorrain, combined with the greater ruggedness and naturalism of the Northern landscape tradition and with the wavy, serpentine lines characteristic of the rococo style.

In a later work entitled *Essays on Picturesque Beauty* (1792) Gilpin attempted to define more precisely what he meant by 'picturesque composition' and concluded that it was made up of 'roughness', 'variety' and 'contrast'. Whereas West had attempted to locate and describe picturesque views, Gilpin offered instruction in how to recognise, classify and represent their formal qualities. After travelling extensively in England, Scotland and Wales and producing a number of tour journals illustrated by pen and wash drawings, he moved in 1777 to the New Forest, where he became vicar of Boldre.

Uvedale Price's (1747–1829) *Essays on the Picturesque, as compared with the Sublime and the Beautiful and, on the Use of studying Pictures, for the Purpose of Improving Real Landscape* (1810) take issue with Gilpin's assumption that the picturesque is a species of the beautiful. Price argues instead that it is a distinct aesthetic category, the Picturesque, equal in status to the Beautiful and the Sublime. He remodelled his estate of Foxley in Hertfordshire according to the conception of the picturesque which he outlines in the extracts, all taken from the second, enlarged edition of 1810.

William Combe's (1741–1823) satire, *The Tour of Dr Syntax in Search of the Picturesque*, was first published in 1809–11 in the *Poetical Magazine* under the title *The Schoolmaster's Tour*, richly illustrated by satirical drawings by Thomas Rowlandson (1756–1827). The poem, which tells the tale of a poor school-teacher who sets out to undertake and write up a picturesque tour, relentlessly satirises William Gilpin: by this time, his picturesque formulae were rather worn and the common butt of jokes. The collaborative production between Combe and Rowlandson was so successful that it inspired a mass of similar satires and parodies and a whole tourist industry of Syntax memorabilia, including hats, china figures, coats and wigs. Another satire of Gilpin and the picturesque was *The Lakers: A Comic Opera in Three Acts, by James Plumptre* (1770–1832). Published in 1798, it was never performed, but contained the line, spoken by Miss Beccabunga Veronique, a keen botanist and sketcher: 'I must throw a Gilpin tint over these magic scenes of beauty.' The extracts which follow in this section reproduce the first Canto of Combe's work.

Jane Austen's novel *Northanger Abbey* (written 1798, published 1818), a parody of literary and social conventions and expectations, includes, in this extract, some humorous mockery of the language of aesthetics associated with the picturesque. It comes at a point in the novel where the naïve 'heroine', Catherine Morland, staying with her aunt and uncle for a season in Bath, goes for a walk with the 'hero', Henry Tilney and his sister, and encounters the concept of the picturesque for the first time.

Edmund Burke, extracts from *A Philosophical Enquiry into the Origin of our Ideas of the Sublime and Beautiful*

Reading (A) On Beauty (i)

SECTION I
OF BEAUTY[1]

It is my design to consider beauty as distinguished from the sublime; and in the course of the enquiry, to examine how far it is consistent with it. But previous to this, we must take a short review of the opinions already entertained of this quality; which I think are hardly to be reduced to any fixed principles; because men are used to talk of beauty in a figurative manner, that is to say, in a manner extremely uncertain, and indeterminate. By beauty I mean, that quality or those qualities in bodies by which they cause love, or some passion similar to it. I confine this definition to the merely sensible qualities of things, for the sake of preserving the utmost simplicity in a subject which must always distract us, whenever we take in those various causes of sympathy which attach us to any persons or things from secondary considerations, and not from the direct force which they have merely on being viewed. I likewise distinguish love, by which I mean that satisfaction which arises to the mind upon contemplating any thing beautiful, of whatsoever nature it may be, from desire or lust; which is an energy of the mind, that hurries us on to the possession of certain objects, that do not affect us as they are beautiful, but by means altogether different. We shall have a strong desire for a woman of no remarkable beauty; whilst the greatest beauty in men, or in other animals, though it causes love, yet excites nothing at all of desire. Which shews that beauty, and the passion caused by beauty, which I call love, is different from desire, though desire may sometimes operate along with it; but it is to this latter that we must attribute those violent and tempestuous passions, and the consequent emotions of the body which attend what is called love in some of its ordinary acceptations, and not to the effects of beauty merely as it is such.

[1] *Part III. Of BEAUTY. SECTION I.* *

Reading (B) On Beauty (ii)

SECTION XIII
Beautiful objects small

The most obvious point that presents itself to us in examining any object, is its extent or quantity. And what degree of extent prevails in bodies, that are held beautiful, may be gathered from the usual manner of expression concerning it. I am told that in most languages, the objects of love are spoken of under diminutive epithets. It is so in all the languages of which I have any knowledge. In Greek the *ιον*, and other diminutive terms, are almost always the terms of affection and tenderness. These diminutives were commonly added by the Greeks to the names of persons with whom they conversed on terms of friendship and familiarity. Though the Romans were a people of less quick and delicate feelings, yet they naturally slid into the lessening termination upon the same occasions. Anciently in the English language the diminishing *ling* was added to the names of persons and things that were the objects of love. Some we retain still, as darling, (or little dear) and a few others. But to this day in ordinary conversation, it is usual to add the endearing name of *little* to every thing we love; the French and Italians make use of these affectionate diminutives even more than we. In the animal creation, out of our own species, it is the small we are inclined to be fond of; little birds, and some of the smaller kinds of beasts. A great beautiful thing, is a manner of expression scarcely ever used; but that of a great ugly thing, is very common. There is a wide difference between admiration and love. The sublime, which is the cause of the former, always dwells on great objects, and terrible; the latter on small ones, and pleasing; we submit to what we admire, but we love what submits to us; in one case we are forced, in the other we are flattered into compliance. In short, the ideas of the sublime and the beautiful stand on foundations so different, that it is hard, I had almost said impossible, to think of reconciling them in the same subject, without considerably lessening the effect of the one or the other upon the passions. So that attending to their quantity, beautiful objects are comparatively small.

SECTION XIV
SMOOTHNESS

The next property constantly observable in such objects is *Smoothness*. A quality so essential to beauty, that I do not now recollect any thing beautiful that is not smooth. In trees and flowers, smooth leaves are beautiful; smooth slopes of earth in gardens; smooth streams in the landscape; smooth coats of birds and beasts in animal beauties; in fine women, smooth skins; and in several sorts of ornamental furniture, smooth and polished surfaces. A very considerable part of the effect of beauty is owing to this quality; indeed the most considerable. For take any beautiful object, and give it a broken and rugged surface, and however well formed it may be in other respects, it pleases no longer. Whereas let it want ever so many of the other constituents, if it wants not this, it becomes more pleasing than almost all the others without it. This seems to me so evident, that I am a good deal surprised, that none who have handled the subject have made any mention of the quality of smoothness in the enumeration of those that go to the forming of beauty. For indeed any ruggedness, any sudden projection, any sharp angle, is in the highest degree contrary to that idea.

SECTION XV
Gradual VARIATION

But as perfectly beautiful bodies are not composed of angular parts, so their parts never continue long in the same right line. They vary their direction every moment, and they change under the eye by a deviation continually carrying on, but for whose beginning or end you will find it difficult to ascertain a point. The view of a beautiful bird will illustrate this observation. Here we see the head increasing insensibly to the middle, from whence it lessens gradually until it mixes with the neck; the neck loses itself in a larger swell, which continues to the middle of the body, when the whole decreases again to the tail; the tail takes a new direction; but it soon varies its new course; it blends again with the other parts; and the line is perpetually changing, above, below, upon every side. In this description I have before me the idea of a dove; it agrees very well with most of the conditions of beauty. It is smooth and downy; its parts are (to use that expression) melted into one another; you are presented with no sudden protuberance through the whole, and yet the whole is continually changing. Observe that part of a beautiful woman where she is perhaps the most beautiful, about the neck and breasts; the smoothness; the softness; the easy and insensible swell; the variety of the surface, which is never for the smallest space the same; the deceitful maze, through which the unsteady eye slides giddily, without knowing where to fix, or whither it is carried. Is not this a demonstration of that change of surface continual and yet hardly perceptible at any point which forms one of the great constituents of beauty?

[. . .]

SECTION XVI
DELICACY

An air of robustness and strength is very prejudicial to beauty. An appearance of *delicacy*, and even of fragility, is almost essential to it. Whoever examines the vegetable or animal creation, will find this observation to be founded in nature. It is not the oak, the ash, or the elm, or any of the robust trees of the forest, which we consider as beautiful; they are awful and majestic; they inspire a sort of reverence. It is the delicate myrtle, it is the orange, it is the almond, it is the jessamine, it is the vine, which we look on as vegetable beauties. It is the flowery species, so remarkable for its weakness and momentary duration, that gives us the liveliest idea of beauty, and elegance. Among animals; the greyhound is more beautiful than the mastiff; and the delicacy of a gennet, a barb, or an Arabian horse, is much more amiable than the strength and stability of some horses of war or carriage. I need here say little of the fair sex, where I believe the point will be easily allowed me. The beauty of women is considerably owing to their weakness, or delicacy, and is even enhanced by their timidity, a quality of mind analogous to it. I would not here be understood to say, that weakness betraying very bad health has any share in beauty; but the ill effect of this is not because it is weakness, but because the ill state of health which produces such weakness alters the other conditions of beauty; the parts in such a case collapse; the bright colour, the *lumen purpureum juventæ* is gone; and the fine variation is lost in wrinkles, sudden breaks, and right lines.

Reading (C) On the Sublime

SECTION I
Of the passion caused by the SUBLIME

The passion caused by the great and sublime in *nature*, when those causes operate most powerfully, is Astonishment; and astonishment is that state of the soul, in which all its motions are suspended, with some degree of horror. In this case the mind is so entirely filled with its object, that it cannot entertain any other, nor by consequence reason on that object which employs it. Hence arises the great power of the sublime, that far from being produced by them, it anticipates our reasonings, and hurries us on by an irresistible force. Astonishment, as I have said, is the effect of the sublime in its highest degree; the inferior effects are admiration, reverence and respect.

SECTION II
TERROR

No passion so effectually robs the mind of all its powers of acting and reasoning as fear. For fear being an apprehension of pain or death, it operates in a manner that resembles actual pain. Whatever therefore is terrible, with regard to sight, is sublime too, whether this cause of terror, be endued with greatness of dimensions or not; for it is impossible to look on any thing as trifling, or contemptible, that may be dangerous. There are many animals, who though far from being large, are yet capable of raising ideas of the sublime, because they are considered as objects of terror. As serpents and poisonous animals of almost all kinds. And to things of great dimensions, if we annex an adventitious idea of terror, they become without comparison greater. A level plain of a vast extent on land, is certainly no mean idea; the prospect of such a plain may be as extensive as a prospect of the ocean; but can it ever fill the mind with any thing so great as the ocean itself? This is owing to several causes, but it is owing to none more than this, that the ocean is an object of no small terror.

[. . .]

SECTION III
OBSCURITY

To make any thing very terrible, obscurity seems in general to be necessary. When we know the full extent of any danger, when we can accustom our eyes to it, a great deal of the apprehension vanishes. Every one will be sensible of this, who considers how greatly night adds to our dread, in all cases of danger, and how much the notions of ghosts and goblins, of which none can form clear ideas, affect minds, which give credit to the popular tales concerning such sorts of beings. Those despotic governments, which are founded on the passions of men, and principally upon the passion of fear, keep their chief as much as may be from the public eye. The policy has been the same in many cases of religion. Almost all the heathen temples were dark. Even in the barbarous temples of the Americans at this day, they keep their idol in a dark part of the hut, which is consecrated to his worship. For this purpose too the druids performed all their ceremonies in the bosom of the darkest woods, and in the shade of the oldest and most spreading oaks.

[. . .]

SECTION V
POWER

Besides these things which *directly* suggest the idea of danger, and those which produce a similar effect from a mechanical cause, I know of nothing sublime which is not some modification of power. And this branch rises as naturally as the other two branches, from terror, the common stock of every thing that is sublime.

[. . .]

Look at a man, or any other animal of prodigious strength, and what is your idea before reflection? Is it that this strength will be subservient to you, to your ease, to your pleasure, to your interest in any sense? No; the emotion you feel is, lest this enormous strength should be employed to the purposes of rapine and destruction. That power derives all its sublimity from the terror with which it is generally accompanied, will appear evidently from its effect in the very few cases, in which it may be possible to strip a considerable degree of strength of its ability to hurt. When you do this, you spoil it of every thing sublime, and it immediately becomes contemptible. An ox is a creature of vast strength; but he is an innocent creature, extremely serviceable, and not at all dangerous; for which reason the idea of an ox is by no means grand. A bull is strong too; but his strength is of another kind; often very destructive, seldom (at least amongst us) of any use in our business; the idea of a bull is therefore great, and it has frequently a place in sublime descriptions, and elevating comparisons. Let us look at another strong animal in the two distinct lights in which we may consider him. The horse in the light of an useful beast, fit for the plough, the road, the draft, in every social useful light the horse has nothing of the sublime; but is it thus that we are affected with him, *whose neck is cloathed with thunder, the glory of whose nostrils is terrible, who swalloweth the ground with fierceness and rage, neither believeth that it is the sound of the trumpet?* In this description the useful character of the horse entirely disappears, and the terrible and sublime blaze out together. We have continually about us animals of a strength that is considerable, but not pernicious. Amongst these we never look for the sublime: it comes upon us in the gloomy forest, and in the howling wilderness, in the form of the lion, the tiger, the panther, or rhinoceros. Whenever strength is only useful, and employed for our benefit or our pleasure, then it is never sublime; for nothing can act agreeably to us, that does not act in conformity to our will; but to act agreeably to our will, it must be subject to us; and therefore can never be the cause of a grand and commanding conception.

[. . .]

11

SECTION VI

PRIVATION

All *general* privations are great, because they are all terrible; *Vacuity, Darkness, Solitude* and *Silence*. With what a fire of imagination, yet with what severity of judgment, has Virgil amassed all these circumstances where he knows that all the images of a tremendous dignity ought to be united, at the mouth of hell! where before he unlocks the secrets of the great deep, he seems to be seized with a religious horror, and to retire astonished at the boldness of his own design.

> *Dii quibus imperium est animarum, umbræq; silentes!*
> *Et Chaos, et Phlegethon! loca nocte silentia late?*
> *Sit mihi fas audita loqui! sit numine vestro*
> *Pandere res alta terra et caligine mersas!*
> *Ibant obscuri, sola sub nocte, per umbram,*
> *Perque domos Ditis vacuas, et inania regna.*

> *Ye subterraneous gods! whose aweful sway*
> *The gliding ghosts, and silent shades obey;*
> *O Chaos hoar! and Phlegethon profound!*
> *Whose solemn empire stretches wide around;*
> *Give me, ye great tremendous powers, to tell*
> *Of scenes and wonders in the depth of hell;*
> *Give me your mighty secrets to display*
> *From those black realms of darkness to the day.*

PITT.

> Obscure *they went through dreary* shades *that led*
> *Along the* waste *dominions of the* dead.

DRYDEN.

SECTION VII

VASTNESS

Greatness of dimension, is a powerful cause of the sublime. This is too evident, and the observation too common, to need any illustration; it is not so common, to consider in what ways greatness of dimension, vastness of extent, or quantity, has the most striking effect. For certainly, there are ways, and modes, wherein the same quantity of extension shall produce greater effects than it is found to do in others. Extension is either in length, height, or depth. Of these the length strikes least; an hundred yards of even ground will never work such an effect as a tower an hundred yards high, or a rock or mountain of that altitude. I am apt to imagine likewise, that height is less grand than depth; and that we are more struck at looking down from a precipice, than at looking up at an object of equal height, but of that I am not very positive. A perpendicular has more force in forming the sublime, than an inclined plane; and the effects of a rugged and broken surface seem stronger than where it is smooth and polished. It would carry us out of our way to enter in this place into the cause of these appearances; but certain it is they afford a large and fruitful field of speculation.

[. . .]

SECTION VIII
INFINITY

Another source of the sublime, is *infinity*; if it does not rather belong to the last. Infinity has a tendency to fill the mind with that sort of delightful horror, which is the most genuine effect, and truest test of the sublime. There are scarce any things which can become the objects of our senses that are really, and in their own nature infinite. But the eye not being able to perceive the bounds of many things, they seem to be infinite, and they produce the same effects as if they were really so. We are deceived in the like manner, if the parts of some large object are so continued to any indefinite number, that the imagination meets no check which may hinder its extending them at pleasure.

Source: Edmund Burke, *A Philosophical Enquiry into the Origin of our Ideas of the Sublime and Beautiful*, J. T. Boulton ed., Blackwell, Oxford, Revised Edition 1987. Section I 'Of Beauty', p. 91, Section XIII 'Beautiful small objects', Section XIV 'Smoothness', Section XV 'Variation', pp. 113–15, Section XVI 'Delicacy', p. 116, Section I 'Sublime', Section II 'Terror', Section III 'Obscurity' pp. 57–9, Section V 'Power', pp. 64–6, Section VI 'Privation', Section VII 'Vastness', Section VIII 'Infinity', pp. 71–3.

Thomas West, extracts from *A Guide to the Lakes, in Cumberland, Westmorland, and Lancashire*

Note: the sub-headings used in this section are not those of the original author. The editors have modernised some spellings.

GRASMERE

1 Frontispiece engraving of Grasmere, from Thomas West's *A Guide to the Lakes, in Cumberland, Westmorland, and Lancashire*, 1784. By permission of the British Library, London.

Reading (A) General introduction

Since persons of genius, taste, and observation began to make the tour of their own country, and to give such pleasing accounts of the natural history, and improving state of the northern parts of the kingdom, the spirit of visiting them has diffused itself among the curious of all ranks.

Particularly, the taste for one branch of a noble art [2] (cherished under the protection of the greatest of kings and best of men) in which the

---

[2] Landscape painting.

genius of *Britain* rivals that of ancient *Greece* and modern *Rome*, induces many to visit the lakes of *Cumberland, Westmorland*, and *Lancasbire*; there to contemplate, in Alpine scenery, finished in nature's highest tints, the pastoral and rural landscape, exhibited in all their stiles, the soft, the rude, the romantic, and the sublime; and of which perhaps like instances can no where be found assembled in so small a tract of country. What may be *now* mentioned as another inducement to visit these natural beauties, is the goodness of the roads, which are much improved since Mr. *Gray*[3] made his tour in 1765, and Mr. *Pennant*[4] his, in 1772. The gentlemen of these counties have set a precedent worthy of imitation in the politest parts of the kingdom, by opening, at private expence, carriage roads for the ease and safety of such as visit the country; and the public roads are equally properly attended to. And if the entertainment at some of the inns be plain, it is accompanied with an easy charge, neatness, and attention. When the roads are more frequented, the inns may perhaps be more elegantly furnished and expensive; but the entertainment must remain much the same, as the viands at present are not excelled in any other quarter of the empire.

The design of the following sheets, is to encourage the taste of visiting the lakes, by furnishing the traveller with a Guide; and for that purpose, the writer has here collected and laid before him, all the select stations and points of view, noticed by those authors who have last made the tour of the lakes, verified by his own repeated observations. He has also added remarks on the principal objects as they appear viewed from different stations; and such other incidental information as he judged would greatly facilitate and heighten the pleasure of the tour, and relieve the traveller from the burthen of those tedious enquiries on the road, or at the inns, which generally embarrass, and often mislead.

The local knowledge here communicated, will not however injure, much less prevent the agreeable surprise that attends the first sight of scenes that surpass all description, and of objects which will always affect the spectator in the highest degree.

Such as wish to unbend the mind from anxious cares, or fatiguing studies, will meet with agreeable relaxation in making the tour of the lakes. Something new will open itself at the turn of every mountain, and

---

[3] Thomas Gray (1716–71), a well-known poet who included an account of his 1765 Lakes tour in letters written in 1769 to Dr Wharton, later collated into a *Journal*. The 1784 edition of West's *Guide* included Gray's *Journal* as an appendix.

[4] Thomas Pennant was an antiquarian and topographer. He also toured Scotland and Wales and wrote about them in his *A Tour in Scotland and Voyage to the Hebrides (1774)* and *A Tour in Wales (1778–81)*.

a succession of ideas will be supported by a perpetual change of objects, and a display of scenes behind scenes, in endless perspective. The *contemplative* traveller will be charmed with the sight of the sweet retreats, that he will observe in these enchanting regions of calm repose, and the *fanciful* may figuratively review the hurry and bustle of busy life (in all its gradations) in the variety of unshaded rills that hang on the mountains sides, the hasty brooks that warble through the dell, or the mighty torrents precipitating themselves at once with thundering noise from tremendous, rocky heights; all pursuing one general end, their increase in the vale, and their union in the ocean.

Such as spend their lives in cities, and their time in crowds will here meet with objects that will enlarge the mind, by contemplation, and raise it from nature to nature's first cause. Whoever takes a walk into these scenes must return penetrated with a sense of the creator's power in heaping mountains upon mountains, and enthroning rocks upon rocks. And such exhibitions of sublime and beautiful objects, cannot but excite at once both rapture and reverence.

When exercise and change of air are recommended for health, the convalescent will find the latter here in the purest state, and the former will be the concomitant of the tour. The many hills and mountains of various heights, separated by narrow vales, through which the air is agitated and hurried on, by a multiplicity of brooks and mountain torrents, keep it in constant circulation, which is known to add much to its purity. The water is also as pure as the air, and on that account recommends itself to the valetudinarian.

As there are few people, in easy circumstances, but may find a motive for visiting this extraordinary region, so more especially those who intend to make the continental tour should begin here; as it will give in miniature an idea of what they are to meet with there, in traversing the *Alps* and *Appenines*; to which our northern mountains are not inferior in beauty of line, or variety of summit, number of lakes, and transparency of water; not in colouring of rock, or softness of turf, but in height and extent only. The mountains here are all accessible to the summit, and furnish prospects no less surprising, and with more variety, than the *Alps* themselves. The tops of the highest *Alps* are inaccessible, being covered with everlasting snow, which commencing at regular heights above the cultivated tracts, or wooded and verdant sides, form indeed the highest contrast in nature. For there may be seen, all the variety of climate in one view. To this however we oppose the sight of the ocean from the summit of all the higher mountains as it appears intersected with promontories, decorated with islands, and animated with navigation; which adds greatly to the perfection and variety of all grand views.

16

Those who have traversed the *Alps*, visited the lake of *Geneva*, and viewed mount *Blanc*, the highest of the *Glaciers*, from the valley of *Chamouni*, in *Savoy*, may still find entertainment in this domestic tour. To trace the analogy and differences of mountainous countries, furnishes the observant traveller with amusement; and the travelled visitor of the *Cumbrian* lakes and mountains, will not be disappointed of pleasure in this particular.

This Guide will also be of use to the artist who may purpose to copy any of these views and landscapes, by directing his choice of station, and pointing out the principal objects. Yet it is not presumed positively to decide on these particulars, but only to suggest hints, that may be adopted, or rejected, at his pleasure.

The late Mr. *Gray* was a great judge of landscapes, yet whoever makes choice of his station at the three mile stone from *Lancaster*, on the *Hornby* road, will fail in taking one of the finest afternoon rural views in *England*. The station he points out is a quarter of a mile too low, and somewhat too much to the left. The more advantageous station, as I apprehend, is on the south side of the great, or Queen's road, a little higher than where Mr. *Gray* stood; for there the vale is in full display, including a longer reach of the river, and the wheel of *Lune*, forming a high crowned isthmus, fringed with tall trees, that in time past was the solitary site of a hermit. A few trees, preserved on purpose by the owner, conceal the nakedness of *Caton-moor* on the right, and render the view complete.

[...]

This Guide shall therefore take up the company at *Lancaster*, and attend them in the tour to all the lakes; pointing out (what only can be described) the *permanent* features of each scene;—the vales, the dells, the groves, the hanging woods, the scattered cots, the deep mountains, the impending cliff, the broken ridge, &c. Their *accidental* beauties depend upon a variety of circumstances; light and shade, the air, the winds, the clouds, the situation with respect to objects, and the time of the day. For though the ruling tints be permanent, yet the green and gold of the meadow and vale, and the brown and purple of the mountain, the silver grey of the rock, and the azure hue of the cloud-topt pike, are frequently varied in appearance, by an intermixture of reflection from wandering clouds, or other bodies, or a sudden stream of sunshine that harmonizes all the parts anew. The pleasure therefore arising from such scenes is in some sort accidental.

To render the tour more agreeable, the company should be provided with a telescope, for viewing the fronts and summits of inaccessible rocks, and the distant country, from the tops of the high mountains *Skiddaw* and *Helvellyn*.

The landscape mirror[5] will also furnish much amusement, in this tour. Where the objects are great and near, it removes them to a due distance, and shews them in the soft colours of nature, and in the most regular perspective the eye can perceive, or science demonstrate.

The mirror is of the greatest use in sunshine; and the person using it ought always to turn his back to the object that he views. It should be suspended by the upper part of the case, and the landscape will then be seen in the glass, by holding it a little to the right or left (as the position of the parts to be viewed require) and the face screened from the sun. A glass of four inches, or four inches and a half diameter is a proper size.

The mirror is a plano-convex glass, and should be the segment of a large circle; otherwise distant and small objects are not perceived in it; but if the glass be too flat, the perspective view of great and near objects is less pleasing, as they are represented too near. These inconveniences may be provided against by two glasses of different convexity. The dark glass answers well in sunshine; but on cloudy and gloomy days the silver foil is the better.

Whoever uses spectacles upon other occasions, must use them in viewing landscapes in these mirrors.

Reading (B) Windermere

STATION II. The views from this delicious spot are many and charming.—From the *south* side of the island[6] you look over a noble extent of water, bounded in front by waves of distant mountains, that rise from the water's edge. The two ferry points form a picturesque strait; and beyond that, the *Storrs* on one side, and *Rawlinson's-nab* on the other, shooting far into the lake, form a grand sinuosity, while the intermediate shores are beautifully indented with wooded promontories, or ornamented with elegant edgings of luxuriant trees. *Berkshire* and *Crowholme* islands break the line in this noble expanse of water. The eastern shore discovers much cultivation; and the succeeding hills are much diversified, and strangely tumbled about. Some are laid out in grass inclosures, others cut with hedges, and fringed with trees; one is crowned with wood, and skirted with the sweetest verdure; another waves with corn, and the whole is a mixture of objects that constitute the most pleas-

---

[5] This is probably a reference to the drawing mirror, a tinted mirror that was used to reflect the landscape in the mellow golden tones of the classical landscapes of Claude Lorrain, often seen as the epitome of beauty. The mirror, used by artists, would also condense and frame views and erase some of their detail in such a way that they became suitable for pictorial compositions.

[6] 'Belle Isle'.

ing of rural scenes—The upper grounds are wild, and pastured with flocks.

Reading (C) Rydal Falls

The other cascade is a small fall of water seen through the window of the summer-house, in Sir *Michael's* orchard. The first who brought this sweet scene to light, is the elegant and learned editor of Mr. *Gray's* letters. And as no one describes these views better than Mr. *Mason*,[7] the reader shall have the account of it in his own words. "Here nature has performed every thing in little that she usually executes in her larger scale; and on that account, like the miniature painter, seems to have finished every part of it in a studied manner. Not a little fragment of a rock thrown into the bason, not a single stem of brush-wood that starts from its craggy sides, but has a picturesque meaning; and the little central current dashing down a cleft of the darkest coloured stone, produces an effect of light and shadow beautiful beyond description. This little theatrical scene might be painted as large as the original, on a canvas not bigger than those usually dropped in the opera-house."

Reading (D) Keswick

This small neat town is at present renowned for nothing so much as the lake it stands near, and which is sometimes called, from the town, the lake of *Keswick*, but more properly the lake of *Derwent*; and I am inclined to think, and hope to make it appear, that the ancient name of *Keswick*, is the *Derwent Town*, or the town of *Derwent-water*. But first of the lake itself.

The whole extent of the lake is about three miles, from north to south; the form is irregular, and its greatest breadth exceeds not a mile and a half. The best method of viewing this enchanting water, is in a boat, and from the banks. Mr. *Gray* viewed it from the banks only, and Mr. *Mason*, after trying both, prefers Mr. *Gray's* choice; and where the pleasure of rowing and sailing is out of the question, it will, in general, be found the best, on account of the fore-ground, which the boat does not furnish. Every dimension of the lake however appears more extended from its bosom, than from its banks. I shall therefore point out the favourite stations round the lake, that have often been verified.

STATION I. *Cockshut-hill* is remarkable for a general view. It is covered with a motly mixture of young wood; has an easy ascent to the top,

[7] William Mason was a poet and biographer who edited Thomas Gray's descriptions of the Lakes for publication in 1775.

and from it the lake appears in great beauty. On the floor of a spacious amphitheatre, of the most picturesque mountains imaginable, an elegant sheet of water is spread out before you, shining like a mirror, and transparent as chrystal; variegated with islands adorned with wood, or cloathed with the sweetest verdure, that rise in the most pleasing forms above the watery plane. The effects all around are amazingly great; but no words can describe the surprising pleasure of this scene, on a fine day, when the sun plays upon the bosom of the lake, and the surrounding mountains are illuminated by his refulgent rays, and their rocky broken summits invertedly reflected by the surface of the water.

Reading (E) Borrowdale

STATION IV. From the top of *Castle-crag* in *Borrowdale* there is a most astonishing view of the lake and vale of *Keswick*, spread out to the north in the most picturesque manner. From the pass of *Borrowdale* is distinctly seen, every bend of the river till it joins the lake; the lake itself, spotted with islands; the most extraordinary line of shore, varied with all the surprising accompaniments of rock and wood; the village of *Grange* at the foot of the *crag*, and the white houses of *Keswick*, with *Crosthwaite* church at the lower end of the lake; behind these much cultivation, with a beautiful mixture of villages, houses, cots, and farms, standing round the skirts of *Skiddaw*, which rises in the grandest manner, from a verdant base, and closes this prospect in the noblest stile of nature's true sublime. From the summit of this rock the views are so singularly great and pleasing, that they ought never to be omitted. The ascent is by one of the narrow paths cut in the side of the mountain, for carrying down the slate, that is quarried on its top.

The view to the north, or the vale of *Keswick*, is already described; that to the south lies in *Borrowdale*. The river is seen winding upward from the lake, through the rugged pass, to where it divides and embraces a triangular vale, completely cut into inclosures of meadow enamelled with the softest verdure, and fields waving with fruitful crops. This truly secreted spot is completely surrounded by the most horrid, romantic mountains that are in this region of wonders; and whoever omits this *coup d'oeil* hath probably seen nothing equal to it.

The views here taken in the glass, when the sun shines, are amazingly fine.

This picture is reversed from the summit of *Latrigg*.

Mr. *Gray* was so much intimidated with the accounts of *Borrowdale*, that he proceeded no farther than *Grange*. But no such difficulties as he feared are now to be met with. The road into *Borrowdale* is improved since his time, at least as far as necessary for any one to proceed to see what is curious. It serpentizes through the pass above *Grange*; and, though upon the edge of a precipice that hangs over the river, it is nevertheless safe. This river brings no mixture of mud from the mountains of naked rock, and runs, in a channel of slate and granite, as clear as crystal. The water of all the lakes in these parts is clear; but the *Derwent* only is pellucid. In it the smallest pebble is seen at a great depth nearly as in the open air.

The rocky scenes in *Borrowdale* are most fantastic, and the entrance rugged. One rock elbows out, and turns the road directly against another. *Bowdar-stone*, on the right in the very pass, is a mountain of itself, and the road winds round its base. Here rock riots over rock, and mountain intersecting mountain, forms one grand semicircular sweep. Extensive woods deck their steep sides; trees grow from pointed rocks, and rocks appear like trees. Here the *Derwent*, rapid as the *Rhone*, rolls his crystal streams through all this labyrinth of embattled obstacles. Indeed, the scenes here are so sublimely terrible, the assemblage of magnificent objects so stupendously great, and the arrangement so extraordinarily curious, that they must excite the most sensible feelings of wonder and surprise, and at once impress the mind with reverential awe and admiration.

Source: Thomas West, *A Guide to the Lakes, in Cumberland, Westmorland, and Lancashire*, 1784, facsimile of third edition published in the series *Revolution and Romanticism*, 1789–1834, a series of facsimile reprints chosen and introduced by Jonathan Wordsworth, Woodstock Books, Oxford, 1989, pp. 1–7, 10–13, 61–2, 78–9, 85–6, 93–5.

William Gilpin, extracts from *Observations, relative chiefly to Picturesque Beauty, Made in the Year 1772, On Several Parts of England; particularly the Mountains, and Lakes of Cumberland, and Westmoreland*

Note: the sub-headings used in this section are not the original author's. The editors have modernised some spelling and the use of the apostrophe in it's/its.

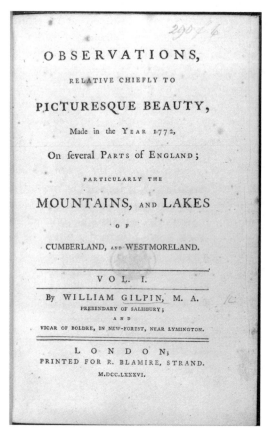

2 Title Page from William Gilpin's *Observations, relative chiefly to Picturesque Beauty, Made in the Year 1772, On Several Parts of England; particularly the Mountains, and Lakes of Cumberland, and Westmoreland*, 1786, Vol. I. By permission of the British Library, London.

Reading (A) Tourism as 'proper' amusement

The author hopes no one will be so severe, as to think a work of this kind (tho a work only of amusement) inconsistent with the profession of a clergyman. He means not to address himself to the lax notions of the age; to which he is no way apprehensive of giving offence: but he should be sorry to hurt the feelings of the most serious. How far field sports, and a variety of other diversions, which may be proper in some stations[8] are quite agreeable to the clerical one, is a subject he means not to discuss: Yet surely the study of nature, in every shape, is allowable; and affords amusement, which the severest cannot well reprehend—the study of the heavens—of the earth—of the field—of the garden, its productions, fruits, and flowers—of the bowels of the earth, containing such amazing stores of curiosity—and of animal life, through all its astonishing varieties, even to the shell, and the insect. Among these objects of rational amusement, may we not enumerate also the beautiful appearances of the face of nature?

The ground indeed, which the author hath taken, that of examining landscape by the *rules of picturesque beauty*, seems rather a deviation from *nature* to *art*. Yet, in fact, it is not so: for the *rules of picturesque beauty*, we know, are drawn from *nature*: so that to examine the face of nature by these rules, is no more than to examine nature by her own most beautiful exertions. Thus Shakespear:

> ——————————————There is an art,
> Which does mend Nature—change it rather: but
> That art itself is Nature———————————————[9]

The author however hopes, he should not greatly err, if he allowed also the amusements furnished by the three sister-arts[10] to be all very consistent with the strictest rules of the clerical profession. The only danger is, lest the *amusement*—the fascinating amusement—should press on improperly, and interfere too much with the *employment*.

Reading (B) The 'general face of the country'

In a little work of the picturesque kind,[11] which the author printed about three years ago, he gave several drawings under the character of *por-*

---

[8] Here used in the sense of social rank or profession.

[9] From *A Winter's Tale*, IV, iv 95–7. (The Shakespearean text actually begins 'This is an art'.

[10] Poetry, painting and music.

[11] Observations on the River Wye and several parts of South Wales.*

traits; rather induced by the partiality of his friends, than his own judgment. He was sensible, that sketches taken in the hasty manner, in which
those were taken, could not pretend to the accuracy necessary in portrait. He endeavoured however to guard his readers against considering
them as such, by saying, they meant only *to give some idea of the general effect of a scene; but in no degree to mark the several picturesque,
and ornamental particulars, of which it is composed.* But he himself
thought; and so, he doubts not, did the public, that this was an insufficient apology: for they were certainly not accurate enough to give even
the *general effect of a scene.*

In the drawings presented in this work, he hath followed more his own
judgment. Except a few, he hath given nothing, that pretends to the name
of *portrait*; sensible, that the hasty drawings he made in this tour, (which
were certainly made without any intention of publication,) did not
deserve it. Indeed Mr. Farington's[12] prints render any other *portraits* of
the lakes unnecessary. They are by far, in the author's opinion, the most
accurate, and beautiful views of that romantic country, which he hath
seen. The fall of Lodoar; and the view of Derwentwater, with the mountain of Skiddaw as a back-ground, from Brandelow woods, are particularly fine.—The principal drawings which are preserved in the following
work,[13] are of two kinds.

One kind is meant to *illustrate and explain picturesque ideas.* This
indeed may be considered among the most useful aids of the pencil. *Intellectual ideas* it cannot reach: but *picturesque ideas* are all cloathed in
bodily forms; and may often be explained better by a few strokes of the
pencil, than by a volume of the most laboured description.

The other sort of drawings is meant to *characterize the countries*,
through which the reader is carried. The ideas are taken from the *general
face of the country*; not from any *particular scene.* And indeed this may
perhaps be the most useful way of conveying local ideas. For a *portrait*
characterizes only a *single spot.* The idea must be relinquished, as soon
as the place is passed. But such imaginary views as give *a general idea of
a country*, spread themselves more diffusely; and are carried, in the
reader's imagination, through the *whole description.*

But whatever becomes of their *utility*, they are beyond all doubt, the
most picturesque kind of drawings. Portraits may be faithful: but they
are rarely in every part beautiful. The distance may be fine—the ruin may
be elegant; yet will there always be some awkwardness, in one part or

---

[12] Joseph Farington (1747–1821) did many landscape views, including the drawings
engraved for his 1783 series *Views of the Lakes*. His name was often associated with topographical scenes faithful to the actual appearance of a place.

[13] That is, the illustrations Gilpin himself did for his *Observations*.

other, which you would wish to remove. But truth forbids. If you are determined to call nothing a *portrait*, but what is *exactly* copied from nature, you must take it as it is; good and bad; and make the best of it.

The fact is, you may often find a *beautiful distance*. Remote objects, tho sometimes awkward, do not always strike the eye with their awkwardnesses. The obscurity, occasioned by the intervening medium, softens each line, or tint, that is harsh, or discordant. But as the landscape *advances on the eye*, the deformity grows more apparent; and on the *fore-ground*, objects are so magnified, that it is very rare indeed, if they do not in some part, offend. Their features become then so strong, that if they be not beautiful, they are disgusting.

On the other hand, he who works *from imagination*—that is, he who culls from nature the most beautiful parts of her productions —a *distance* here; and there a *fore-ground*—combines them artificially; and removing every thing offensive, admits only such parts, as are *congruous*, and *beautiful*; will in all probability, make a much better landscape, than he who takes all as it comes; and without selecting beauties, copies only what he sees presented in each particular scene.

But you wish for the representation of some *particular scene*. It is truth you desire, and not fiction.

Who objects? But even here you must allow a little to the imagination, or your scene will probably never please. What is it that you *admire*? Is it *the spot you stand on*? Or, is it the grandeur of *some lake—a cove of mountains*—an *inriched distance*—the *windings* of a noble river—or some other exhibition, which is in fact much to be admired? This noble scene, whatever it is, you wish to see set off to the best advantage. In order therefore to give this advantage to the *part you admire*, you must allow your artist to take some liberty with the *ground he stands on*; which is evidently *not* the part you admire; and probably abounds with deformities.

It is not meant to give him licence instead of liberty. Of the grand exhibition before him, which is the portrait you want, he must take a faithful copy. If *it* present any striking deformity, it is not a subject for the pencil: it should be relinquished. But if it be pure in all its parts, the foreground should be made equal to it. Yet nothing should be introduced alien to the scene presented. Such alterations only your artist should make, as the nature of the country allows, and the beauty of composition requires. Trees he may generally plant, or remove, at pleasure. If a withered stump suit the form of his landscape better than the spreading oak, which he finds in nature, he may make the exchange—or he may make it, if he wish for a spreading oak, where he finds a withered trunk: He has no right, we allow, to add a magnificent castle—an impending rock—or a river, to adorn his fore-ground. These are *new features*. But he may certainly break an ill-formed hillock; and shovel the earth about him, as he pleases, without offence. He may pull up a piece of awkward paling—he may throw down a cottage—he may even turn the course of a road, or a river, a few yards on this side, or that. These trivial alterations may greatly add to the beauty of his composition; and yet they interfere not with the truth of *portrait*. Most of these things may *in fact* be altered to-morrow; tho they disgust to-day. The road and the river, it is true, keep their station: but the change you desire, is so trifling; that the eye of truth can never be offended; tho the picturesque eye may be exceedingly gratified. There is a very beautiful scene on the banks of the Tay near Perth, which in composition is correctly picturesque; except only that the river forming two parallel lines with the sides of the picture, enters the fore-ground at right angles. So offensive a form could not but injure the beauty of any landscape. Would the truth of portrait be injured, in painting this subject, if trees were planted to hide the deformity; or a small turn given to the river, to break its disgusting regularity?

The author means not however to offer the *portraits*, and *illustrations* he hath here given, as perfect examples of the principles he hath laid down. It is a difficult matter for any artist (at least, who does not claim as a professional man) to reach his own ideas. What he represents will ever fall short of what he imagines. With regard to *figures* particularly, the author wishes to premise, that the rules laid down in the beginning of the second volume [. . .] are here little observed. Those remarks were chiefly intended for works in a larger style. Figures on so small a scale as these,[14] are not capable of receiving character. They are at best only what he calls *picturesque appendages*.

Besides, the representations here given[15] have again sustained a loss by going through a translation in so rough and unmanageable a language, as that of brass, and aquafortis. The mode of etching chosen, is the newly invented one of aqua-tinta; which is certainly the softest, and comes the nearest to the idea of drawing. But this species of etching itself, tho even managed by a masterly hand, is subject to great inconveniences; especially when a large number of prints are taken from one plate. It is impossible to make lights graduate as they ought—to keep distances pure—and to give those strong characteristic touches to objects, which may be done with a brush in *drawing*. Unavoidable defects however the candid will excuse; and may rest assured, that the author took all the

---

[14] Those that might feature in the foreground of a picturesque landscape.
[15] Gilpin refers here to his own illustrations.

pains he could, by correcting the proofs, to make the plates, what he wished them.

Reading (C) England as picturesque landscape

Before we make any observations on the picturesque beauty of particular places, it may not be amiss to take a slight view of those great features, on which picturesque beauty in landscape so much depends.

[. . .]

From whatever cause it proceeds, certain, I believe, it is, that this country exceeds most countries in the *variety* of its picturesque beauties. I should not wish to speak merely as an Englishman: the suffrages of many travellers, and foreigners, of taste, I doubt not, might be adduced.

In some or other of the *particular species* of landscape, it may probably be excelled. Switzerland may perhaps exceed it in the beauty of its wooded vallies; Germany, in its river views; and Italy, in its lake-scenes. But if it yield to some of these countries in *particular* beauties; I should suppose, that on the *whole*, it transcends them all. It exhibits perhaps more variety of hill, and dale, and level ground, than is any where to be seen in so small a compass. Its rivers assume every character, diffusive, winding and rapid. Its estuaries, and coast-views are varied, of course, from the form, and rockiness of its shores. Its mountains, and lakes, tho they cannot perhaps rival, as I have just observed, some of the choice lakes of Italy—about Tivoli especially, where the most perfect models of this kind of landscape are said to be presented; are yet in *variety*, I presume, equal to the lake-scenery of any country.

But besides the *variety* of its beauties, in some or other of which it may be rivalled; it possesses some beauties, which are *peculiar* to itself.

One of these peculiar features arises from the *intermixture* of wood and cultivation, which is found oftener in English landscape, than in the landscape of other countries. In France, in Italy, in Spain, and in most other places, cultivation, and wood have their separate limits. Trees grow in detached woods; and cultivation occupies vast, unbounded common fields. But in England, the custom of dividing property by hedges, and of planting hedge-rows, so universally prevails, that almost wherever you have cultivation, there also you have wood.

Now altho this regular intermixture produces often deformity on the nearer grounds; yet, at a distance it is the source of great beauty. On the spot, no doubt, and even in the first distances, the marks of the spade, and the plough; the hedge, and the ditch; together with all the formalities of hedge-row trees, and square divisions of property, are disgusting in a high degree. But when all these regular forms are softened by distance—when hedge-row trees begin to unite, and lengthen into streaks along the horizon—when farm-houses, and ordinary buildings lose all their vulgarity of shape, and are scattered about, in formless spots, through the several parts of a distance—it is inconceivable what richness, and beauty, this mass of deformity, when melted together, adds to landscape. One vast tract of wild, uncultivated country, unless either varied by large parts, or under some peculiar circumstances of light, cannot produce the effect. Nor is it produced by unbounded tracts of cultivation; which, without the intermixture of wood, cannot give richness to distance.—Thus English landscape affords a species of *rich distance*, which is rarely to be found in any other country.—You have likewise from this intermixture of wood and cultivation, the advantage of being sure to find a tree or two, on the foreground, to adorn any beautiful view you may meet with in the distance.

Another peculiar feature in the landscape of this country, arises from the great quantity of English oak, with which it abounds. The oak of no country has equal beauty: nor does any tree answer all the purposes of scenery so well. The oak is the noblest ornament of a fore-ground; spreading, from side to side, its tortuous branches; and foliage, rich with some autumnal tint. In a distance also it appears with equal advantage; forming itself into beautiful clumps, varied more in shape; and perhaps more in colour, than the clumps of any other tree. The pine of Italy has its beauty, hanging over the broken pediment of some ruined temple. The chesnut of Calabria is consecrated by adorning the fore-grounds of Salvator.[16] The elm, the ash, and the beech, have all their respective beauties: but no tree in the forest is adapted to all the purposes of landscape, like English oak.

Among the peculiar features of English landscape, may be added the embellished garden, and park-scene. In other countries the environs of great houses are yet under the direction of formality. The wonder-working hand of art, with its regular cascades, spouting fountains, flights of terraces, and other achievements, have still possession of the gardens of kings, and princes. In England alone the model of nature is adopted.

This is a mode of scenery intirely of the Sylvan kind. As we seek among the wild works of nature for the sublime, we seek here for the beautiful: and where there is a variety of lawn, wood, and water; and these naturally combined; and not too much decorated with buildings, nor disgraced by fantastic ornaments; we find a species of landscape, which no country, but England, can display in such perfection: not only because this just species of taste prevails no where else; but also, because no

[16] Salvator Rosa (1615–73), landscape artist from Naples.

where else are found such proper materials. The want of English oak, as we have just observed, can never be made up, in this kind of landscape especially. Nor do we any where find so close and rich a verdure. An easy swell may, every where, be given to ground: but it cannot every where be covered with a velvet turf, which constitutes the beauty of an embellished lawn.

The moisture, and vapoury heaviness of our atmosphere, which produces the rich verdure of our lawns; gives birth also to another peculiar feature in English landscape—that obscurity, which is often thrown over distance. In warmer climates especially, the air is purer. Those mists and vapours which steam from the ground at night, are dispersed with the morning-sun. Under Italian skies very remote objects are seen with great distinctness. And this mode of vision, no doubt, has its beauty; as have all the works, and all the operations of nature.—But, at best, this is only one mode of vision. Our grosser atmosphere (which likewise hath its seasons of purity) exhibits various modes; some of which are in themselves more beautiful, than the most distinct vision.

The several degrees of obscurity, which the heaviness of our atmosphere gives to landscape, may be reduced to three—*haziness, mists,* and *fogs.*

Haziness just adds that light, grey tint—that thin, dubious veil, which is often beautifully spread over landscape. It hides nothing. It only sweetens the hues of nature—it gives a consequence to every common object, by giving it a more indistinct form—it corrects the glare of colours—it softens the harshness of lines; and above all, it throws over the face of landscape that harmonizing tint, which blends the whole into unity, and repose.

Mist goes farther. It spreads still more obscurity over the face of nature. As haziness softens, and adds a beauty perhaps to the *correctest* form of landscape; mist is adapted to those landscapes, in which we want to hide much, to soften more; and to throw many parts into a greater distance, than they naturally occupy.

Even the *fog*, which is the highest degree of a gross atmosphere, is not without its beauty in landscape; especially in the mountain-scenes, which are so much the object of the following remarks. When partial, as it often is, the effect is grandest. When some vast promontory, issuing from a cloud of vapour, with which all its upper parts are blended, shoots into a lake; the imagination is left at a loss to discover, whence it comes, or to what height it aspires. The effect rises with the obscurity; and the view is sometimes wonderfully great.

To these natural features, which are, in a great degree, peculiar to the landscape of England, we may lastly add another, of the artificial kind—

the ruins of abbeys; which, being naturalized to the soil, might indeed, without much impropriety, be classed among its natural beauties.

Ruins are commonly divided into two kinds; castles, and abbeys. Of the former few countries perhaps can produce so many, as this island; for which various causes may be assigned. The feudal system, which lasted long in England, and was carried high, produced a number of castles in every part. King Stephen's reign contributed greatly to multiply them. And in the northern counties, the continued wars with Scotland had the same effect. Many of these buildings, now fallen into decay, remain objects of great beauty.

In the ruins of castles however, other countries may compare with ours. But in the remains of abbeys no country certainly can.

Where popery prevails, the abbey is still intire and inhabited; and of course less adapted to landscape.

But it is the mode of architecture, which gives such excellence to these ruins. The Gothic style[17] in which they are generally composed, is, I apprehend, unrivalled among foreign nations; and may be called a peculiar feature in English landscape.

[. . .]

Abbeys formerly abounded so much in England, that a delicious valley could scarce be found, in which one of them was not stationed. The very sites of many of these ancient edifices are now obliterated by the plough; yet still so many elegant ruins of this kind are left; that they may be called, not only one of the peculiar features of English landscape; but may be ranked also among its most picturesque beauties.

Reading (D) Mountains

We had now arrived on the confines of those romantic scenes, which were the principal inducement to this tour. Here therefore we proposed to make some pause; and pay a little more attention to the country, than a hasty passage through it, would allow.

But to render a description of these scenes more intelligible; and to shew more distinctly the sources of that kind of beauty, with which they abound; it may be proper, before we examine the scenes themselves, to take a sort of analytical view of the materials, which compose them—

---

[17] A style of architecture prevalent from the mid-twelfth century to the beginning of the fifteenth characterised by pointed arches, rib vaults and flying buttresses. The organic forms of the Gothic, similar to the spreading branches of a tree, were often contrasted with the more linear style of the classical. In the late-eighteenth and early-nineteenth centuries it was common to contrast geometric, straight-lined classicism with the more 'natural' and 'primitive' Gothic.

*mountains——lakes—broken grounds —wood—rocks—cascades—val-
lies—and rivers.*

With regard to *mountains*, it may be first premised, that, in a picturesque view, we consider them only as *distant* objects; their enormous
size disqualifying them for objects at hand. In the removed part of a
picture therefore, the mountain properly appears; where its immensity,
reduced by distance, can be taken in by the eye; and its monstrous features, losing their deformity, assume a softness which naturally belongs
not to them.

I would not however be understood to mean, that a mountain is
proper only to close an *extended* view. It may take its station in a second,
or third distance with equal propriety. And even on a fore-ground, a
rugged corner of its base may be introduced; tho its upper regions aspire
far beyond the limits of any picture.

Having thus premised the *station*, which a mountain properly occupies in landscape, we shall now examine the *mountain* itself; in which,
four things particularly strike us——its *line*—the *objects*, which adorn
its surface—its *tints*—and its *light* and *shade*.

The beauty of a distant mountain in a great measure, depends on the
line it traces along the sky; which is generally of a lighter hue. The
pyramidal shape, and easy flow of an irregular line, will be found in the
mountain, as in other delineations, the truest source of beauty.

Mountains therefore rising in regular, mathematical lines, or in whim-
sical, grotesque shapes, are displeasing. Thus *Burnswark*, a mountain on
the southern border of Scotland; *Thorp-Cloud*, near Dovedale in Der-
byshire, especially when seen from the garden at Ilam, and a mountain
in Cumberland, which from its peculiar appearance in some situations,
takes the name of *Saddle-back*, all form disagreeable lines. And thus
many of the pointed summits of the *Alps* are objects rather of singularity, than of beauty. Such forms also as suggest the idea of lumpish *heaviness* are disgusting—round, swelling forms, without any break to
disencumber them of their weight.

Indeed a continuity of line without a break, whether it be *concave,
straight*, or *convex*, will always displease, because it wants variety;
unless indeed it be well contrasted with other forms. The effect also of a
broken line is bad, if the breaks are regular.

The sources of *deformity* in the mountain line will easily suggest those
of *beauty*. If the line swell easily to an apex, and yet by irregular breaks,
which may be varied in a thousand modes, it must be pleasing.

And yet *abruptness* itself is sometimes a source of beauty, either when
it is in contrast with other parts of the line; or when rocks, or other
objects, account naturally for it.

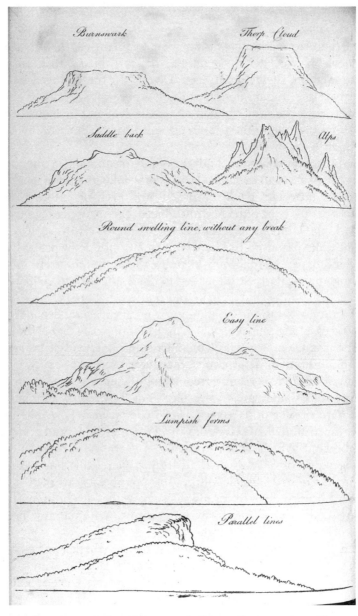

3 'An explanation of the shapes and lines of mountains. They are left unshadowed, that their forms may be more conspicuous.' William Gilpin's illustration of mountain shapes and accompanying caption from his *Observations, relative chiefly to Picturesque Beauty, Made in the Year 1772, On Several Parts of England; particularly the Mountains, and Lakes of Cumberland, and Westmoreland*, 1786, Vol. I. By permission of the British Library, London.

The same principles, on which we seek for beauty in *single* mountains, will help us to find it in a *combination* of them. Mountains *in composition* are considered as *single* objects, and follow the same rules. If they break into mathematical, or fantastic forms—if they join heavily together in lumpish shapes—if they fall into each other at right-angles—or if their lines run parrallel—in all these cases, the combination will be more or less disgusting: and a converse of these will of course be agreeable.

Having drawn the *lines*, which mountains should form, let us next fill them up, and vary them with tints.

The objects, which cover the surface of mountains, are wood, rocks, broken ground, heath, and mosses of various hues.

Ovid has very ingeniously given us the furniture of a mountain in the transformation of Atlas.

————————Jam barba, comæque
In sylvas abeunt; juga sunt humerique, manusque:
Quod caput ante fuit, summo est in monte cacumen:
Ossa lapis fiunt.————————[18]

His hair and beard become trees, and other vegetable substance; his bones, rocks; and his head, and shoulders, summits, and promontories.——But to describe minutely the *parts* of a *distant* object (for we are considering a mountain in this light) would be to invert the rules of perspective, by making that *distinct*, which should be *obscure*. I shall consider therefore all that variety, which covers the surface of distant mountains, as blended together in one mass; and made the stratum of those tints, which we often find playing upon them.

These tints, which are the most beautiful ornaments of the mountain, are of all colours; but the most prevalent are yellow, and purple. We can hardly consider *blue* as a mountain tint. It is the mere colour of the intervening air—the hue, which naturally invests all distant objects, as well as mountains. The late Dr. Brown,[19] author of the Estimate, in a description, which he printed, of the lake of Keswick, very justly calls these tints *the yellow streams of light, the purple hues, and misty azure of the*

[18] Slightly misquoted from Ovid, *Metamorphoses*, IV ll. 657–60. The story is that of Atlas being turned to stone by Medusa's head: 'His beard and head were changed to trees, his shoulders and arms to spreading ridges; what had been his head was now the mountain's top, and his bones were changed to stones.' (Trans. by H. R. Fairclough in *Satires, Epistles and Arts Poetica*, Loeb Classical Library edition, Harvard University Press, Cambridge, Massachusetts, Heinemann (London), 1961.)

[19] Dr John Brown was brought up in Cumberland and had been tutor and drawing master to William Gilpin. He had written a 'Description of the Vale of Keswick' (1753?), which was included as an addendum in the 1784 edition of West's *Guide to the Lakes*.

mountains. They are rarely permanent; but seem to be a sort of floating, silky colours—always in motion—always in harmony—and playing with a thousand changeable varieties into each other. They are literally *colours dipped in heaven.*

The variety of these tints depends on many circumstances—the season of the year—the hour of the day—a dry, or a moist atmosphere. The *lines* and *shapes* of mountains (features strongly marked) are easily caught and retained: but these meteor-forms, this rich fluctuation of airy hues, offer such a profusion of variegated splendor, that they are continually eluding the eye with breaking into each other; and are lost, as it endeavours to retain them. This airy colouring, tho in sunshine it appears most brilliant; yet in some degree it is *generally* found in those mountains, where it prevails.

In the late voyages round the world, published by Dr. Hawkesworth,[20] we have an account of the great beauty of the colouring observed on the peak of Teneriffe. "Its appearance at sun-set, says the author, was very striking. When the sun was below the horizon, and the rest of the island appeared of a deep black; the mountain still reflected his rays, and glowed with a warmth of colouring, which no painting can express."

The rays of the sun, which are the cause of all colour, no doubt, produce these tints to the eye; yet we must believe there is something peculiar in the surfaces of some mountains, which dispose them to reflect the rays with such variety of tints. On many mountains these appearances are not observable; and where the surface is uniform, the tint will be so likewise. "The effect in question, says Mr. Lock,[21] remarking on this passage, is very familiar to me. I saw it almost every evening in Savoy, when the sun shone. It is only on the tops of the highest mountains, that the effect is perfect. Mount Blanc being covered with the purest snow, and having no tint of its own, was often of the brightest rose-colour."

Having thus given the mountain a line; filled it with objects; and spread over it a beautiful assemblage of tints; it remains lastly to throw the whole into light and shade.—He who would study light and shade, must repair to the mountains. There he will see their most magnificent effects.

In every object we observe a double effect of illumination, that of the *parts*, and that of the *whole*. In a building the cornices, the pilasters, and other ornaments, *are set off*, in the language of art, with light and shade.

---

[20] Dr James Hawkesworth published his *Voyages in the Southern Hemisphere* in 1773. The work included an account of Captain Cook's 1768–71 voyage to the South Seas.

[21] Possibly William Locke of Norbury Park, Surrey. In c.1780 Locke commissioned the artist George Barret (?1732–84) to decorate a room with large landscape paintings inspired by the Lake District.

Over this *partial* effect are spread the *general* masses. It is thus in mountains.

Homer, who had a genius as picturesque as Virgil, (tho he seems to have known little of *the art of painting*) was struck with two things in his views of mountains—with those cavities and projections, which abound upon their surfaces—and with what he calls their *shadowing forms*. Of the former, he takes notice, when he speaks of a single mountain; of the latter, when he speaks of mountains in combination.[22] Now it is plain, that in both these cases he was pleased with the effect of light and shade. In one the *partial* effect is marked: in the other, the *general*.

The cavities which he observed, and which are seen only from their being the deep recesses of shade, together with the rocks, and little projections, which are visible only from catching a stronger ray of light, contribute to produce the *partial* effect—that richness, and variety on the sides of distant mountains, which would otherwise be a display of flat, fatiguing surface. The objects themselves are formless, and indistinct; yet, by presenting different surfaces for the light to rest on, the rich and variegated effect, here mentioned, is produced.

The *grand masses* are formed by one mountain's over-shadowing another—by the sun's turning round some promontory—or by the transverse position of mountains; in all which cases the shadow falls broad and deep—sweeps over all the smaller shades, to which it still gives a deeper tinge; and unites the whole in one great effect.

It is an agreeable amusement to attend these vast shadows in their slow, and solemn march over the mountains—to observe, how the morning sun sheds only a faint catching light upon the summits of the hills, through one general mass of hazy shade——in a few hours how all this confusion is dissipated——how the lights and shades begin to break, and separate, and take their form and breadth—how deep and determined the shadows are at noon—how fugitive and uncertain, as the sun declines; till its fires, glowing in the west, light up a new radiance through the landscape; and spread over it, instead of sober light and shade, all the colours of nature, in one bright, momentary gleam.

---

[22] Under the first idea he speaks of Mount Olympus, which he calls πολυπτυχου, or *many vallied*. ll. 8. 411.

Under the second, he speaks of that chain of mountains, which separate Phthia from the southern parts of Greece;

————πολλα μεταξυ————

Ουρεα τε σκιοεντα————

Many *shadowing mountains* intervene ll. I. 156.*[23]

[23] These are quotations from Homer's *Iliad*, Book 8, ll. 411 and Book 1, ll. 156–7.

It is equally amusing to observe the various shapes, which mountains assume through all this variety of illumination; rocks, knolls, and promontories, taking new forms; appearing, and disappearing, as the sun veers round; whose radiance, like varnish on a picture, (if I may use a degrading comparison,) *brings out* a thousand objects unobserved before.

To these more permanent effects of illumination may be added another species, which arises from accident—I mean those partial, flitting shades, which are occasioned by floating clouds. These may sometimes produce a good effect; but they contribute as often to disturb the repose of a land-scape. To painters however they are of great use, who are frequently obliged, by an untoward subject, to take the advantage of every proba-bility to produce an effect.

Reading (E) Lakes

Having thus considered the chief circumstances, which occur in *distant mountains*, let us now inlarge our view, and take in the *lake*, which makes the next considerable part of this romantic country.

The *fen*, the *pool*, and the *lake* would present very different ideas, tho magnitude were out of the question.

The *fen* is a plashy inundation, formed on a flat—without depth—without lineal boundary— of ambiguous texture—half water—and half land—a sort of vegetable fluid.

The *pool* is a collection of the soakings of some common; or the reser-voir of the neighbouring ditches, which deposit in its ouzy bed the soil of the country, clay, or mud; and give a correspondent tinge to the water.

In some things the *fen* and the *pool* agree. They both take every thing in, and let nothing out. Each of them is in summer a sink of putrefaction; and the receptacle of all those unclean, misshapen forms in animal life, which breed and batten in the impurities of stagnation;

> Where putrefaction into life ferments,
> And breathes destructive myriads.[24]

Very different is the origin of the *lake*. Its magnificent, and marble bed, formed in the caverns, and deep recesses of rocky mountains, received originally the pure pellucid waters of some rushing torrent, as it came first from the hand of nature—arrested its course, till the spacious, and splendid bason was filled brimfull; and then discharged the stream, unsullied, and undiminished, through some winding vale, to form other

[24] From James Thomson, *The Seasons: Summer*, ll. 1029–30.

lakes, or increase the dignity of some imperial river. Here no impurities find entrance, either of animal, or of vegetable life:

> ——————————Non illic canna palustris,
> Nec steriles ulvæ, nec acutâ cuspide junci.[25]

4 'An illustration of the appearance, which the shores of a lake form, when seen *from its surface, in a boat*. The promontories, and bays, unless very large, lose all their indentations; and the whole boundary of the lake becomes a mere thread. When you stand upon the shore, if your situation be, in any degree, elevated, the promontories appear to come forward, and all the indentations are distinct . . .' William Gilpin's illustration of a lake boundary and accompanying caption from his *Observations, relative chiefly to Picturesque Beauty, Made in the Year 1772, On Several Parts of England; particularly the Mountains, and Lakes of Cumberland, and Westmoreland*, 1786, Vol. I. By permission of the British Library, London.

From the brisk circulation of fluid through these animated bodies of water, a great master of nature has nobly styled them, *living lakes:*

> ——————————Speluncæ,
> Vivique lacus.——————————[26]

[25] From Ovid, *Metamorphoses*, IV, ll. 298–9: 'No marshy reeds grew there, no unfruitful swamp grass, nor spiky rushes.' (Loeb Classical Library translation by Frank Miller.) The description relates to the enervating pool of the naiad Salmacis whose personality is reflected in this non corporeal aspect of her identity.

[26] From Virgil, *Georgics*, II, l. 469: 'Caves and living lakes'.

and indeed nothing, which is not really alive, deserves the appellation better. For besides the vital stream, which principally feeds them, they receive a thousand little gurgling rills, which trickling through a thousand veins, give life, and spirit to every part.

The principal incidents observable in *lakes*, are, their *line of boundary*—their *islands*—and the different appearances of the *surface* of the water.

The *line of boundary* is very various. Sometimes it is boldly broken by a projecting promontory—sometimes indented by a creek—sometimes it undulates along an irregular shore —and sometimes swells into a winding bay. In each of these circumstances it is susceptible of beauty; in all, it certainly deserves attention: for as it is a line of separation between land and water, it is of course so conspicuous a boundary, that the least harshness in it is discernible. I have known many a good landscape injured by a bad water boundary.

This line, it may be further observed, varies under different circumstances. When the eye is placed *upon* the lake, the line of boundary is a *circular thread*, with little undulation; unless when some promontory of more than usual magnitude shoots into the water. All smaller irregularities are lost. The particular beauty of it under this circumstance, consists in the opposition between such a *thread*, and the irregular line formed by the summits of the mountains.

But when the eye is placed on the higher grounds, *above* the level of the lake, the line of boundary takes a new form; and what appeared to the *levelled* eye a circular thread, becomes *now* an undulating line, projecting, and retiring more or less, according to the degree of the eye's elevation. The circular thread was indebted for its principal beauty to contrast: but this, like all other elegant lines, has the additional beauty of variety.

And yet, in *some* cases the *levelled* eye has the advantage of the *elevated* one. The line, which forms an acute angle from the *higher* situation, may be softened, when seen from the water, into an easy curve.

The *islands* fall next under our view. These are either a beauty, or a deformity to the lake; as they are shaped, or stationed.

If the island be round, or of any other regular form; or if the wood upon it be thick and heavy (as I have observed some planted with a close grove of Scotch fir) it can never be an object of beauty. At *hand*, it is a heavy lump: at a *distance*, a murky spot.

Again, if the island, (however beautifully shaped, or planted;) be seated in the centre of a round lake; in the focus of an oval one; or in any other *regular* position; the beauty of it is lost, at least in some points of view.

But when its lines, and shape are both irregular—when it is ornamented with ancient oak, rich in foliage, but light and airy—and when it takes some irregular situation in the lake; then it is an object truly beautiful—beautiful in itself, as well as in composition. It must however be added, that it would be difficult to place such an object in any situation, that would be *equally* pleasing from every stand.

The *surface of the lake* offers itself last to observation. The several incidents, which arise here, are all owing to the sky, and the disposition of the water to receive its impression.

That the sky is the great regulator of the *colour* of the water, is known to all artists.

[. . .]

The effect indeed holds universally; as water in all cases, exposed to the sky, will act as a mirror to it.

In the darkness of a brooding storm, we have just seen, the *whole body* of the water will be dark: [. . .]

In clear, and windy weather, the *breezy ruffled lake*, as Thomson calls it, is a shattered mirror: It reflects the serenity; but reflects it partially. The hollow of each wave is commonly in shadow, the summit is tipped with light. The light or shadow therefore prevails, according to the position of the waves to the eye: and at a distance, when the summits of the waves, agreeably to the rules of perspective, appear in *contact*, the whole surface in that part will be light.

But when the sky is splendid, and at the same time calm, the water (being then a *perfect* mirror,) will glow all over with correspondent tints; unless other reflections, from the objects around, intervene, and form more vivid pictures.

Often you will see a spacious bay, screened by some projecting promontory, in perfect repose; while the rest of the lake, more pervious to the air, is crisped over by a gentle ripple.

Sometimes also, when the *whole* lake is tranquil, a gentle perturbation will arise in some distant part, from no apparent cause, from a breath of air, which nothing else can feel, and creeping softly on, communicate the tremulous shudder with exquisite sensibility over half the surface. In this observation I do little more than translate from Ovid:

——————————Exhorruit, æquoris instar,
Quod fremīt, exiguâ cum summum stringitur aurâ.[27]

[27] From Ovid, *Metamorphoses*, IV, ll. 135–6: 'She shuddered like the sea when its surface is ruffled by a slight breeze.' (trans. P. James). Thisbe is here described as being like the sea. In the original myth the lovers Pyramus and Thisbe had become rivers. Note: Gilpin writes 'fremit' where Ovid gives 'tremit'.

No pool, no river-bay, can present this idea in its utmost purity. In them every crystalline particle is set, as it were, in a socket of mud. Their lubricity is lost. [. . .] But the lake, like Spencer's fountain, which sprang from the limpid tears of a nymph,

————————is chast, and pure, as purest snow,
Ne lets her waves with any filth be dyed.[28]

Refined thus from every obstruction, it is *tremblingly alive* all over: the merest trifle, a frisking fly, a falling leaf, almost a sound alarms it,

————————————————that sound,
Which from the mountain, previous to the storm,
Rolls o'er the muttering earth, disturbs the flood,
And shakes the forest-leaf without a breath.[29]

This tremulous shudder is sometimes even still more partial: It will run in lengthened parallels, and separate the reflections upon the surface, which are lost on one side, and taken up on the other. This is perhaps the most picturesque form, which water assumes; as it affords the painter an opportunity of throwing in those lengthened lights and shades, which give the greatest variety and clearness to water.

There is another appearance on the surfaces of lakes, which we cannot account for on any principle either of optics, or of perspective. When there is no apparent cause in the *sky*, the *water* will sometimes appear dappled with large spots of shade. It is possible these patches may have connection with the bottom of the lake; as naturalists suppose, the shining parts of the sea are occasioned by the spawn of fish: but it is more probable, that in some way, they are connected with the sky, as they are generally esteemed in the country to be a weather-gage. The people will often say, "It will be no hay-day to day, the lake is full of shades." ——I never myself saw this appearance; or I might be able to give a better account of it: but I have heard it so often taken notice of; that I suppose there is at least some ground for the observation. Tho, after all, I think it probable these shades may be owing only to floating clouds.

From this great variety, which the surfaces of lakes assume, we may draw this conclusion, that the painter may take great liberties, in point of light and shade, in his representation of water. It is, in many cases, under no rule, that we are acquainted with; or under rules so lax, that the imagination is left very much at large.

On the subject of *lakes*, I have only farther to add, that many bodies of water, under this denomination, are found upon the *summits* of lofty

---

[28] From Edmund Spenser, *The Faerie Queen*, II, Canto ii, verse 9.
[29] Slightly misquoted from James Thomson, *The Seasons: Summer*, ll. 1117–20.

40

mountains. In this situation they are commonly mere basons; or reservoirs; and want the pleasing accompaniments, which adorn the lower lakes. Lakes of this kind are a collection of springs; and discharge themselves generally from their elevated stations in cascades.

Reading (F) Windermere

Having thus taken a view of a place abounding with so many beauties, we found our bark waiting for us at the northern point; and setting sail, instead of returning to Bowness, we stood for Ambleside. We could have wished to navigate the whole lake; but it was too great an undertaking for measured time; and we contented ourselves with going in quest of the beauties of its northern division.

As we left the island, the scene opening on every side, we found ourselves surrounded with objects of great magnificence.

On the western coast ran a continuous range of craggy mountains, thinly scattered over with trees, which had formerly overspread it. It is a part of Furness-fell; the whole of which we had before seen, in one vast combination of distant mountains, bounding our view over the bay of

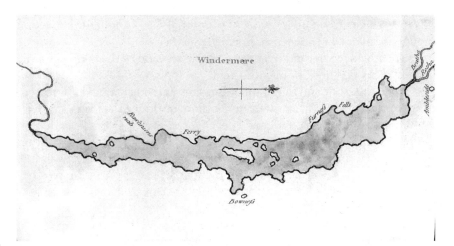

5 'This plan of Windermere is not geographically exact; but enough so to give the reader an idea of its shape, and the situation of the several places mentioned on its shores.' Outline plan of Windermere, and accompanying caption, from William Gilpin's *Observations, relative chiefly to Picturesque Beauty, Made in the Year 1772, On Several Parts of England; particularly the Mountains, and Lakes of Cumberland, and Westmoreland*, 1786, Vol. I. The general shape of Windermere, as well as the indentations of its shore, greatly exercised Gilpin's thinking on the picturesque. By permission of the British Library, London.

Cartmel. The part we now saw stretches about two leagues along the lake.

On the eastern side, we passed several small islands, some of which were well-wooded; others were mere rocks with low, twisted trees bursting from their crevices; all of them probably worth visiting, if our time had allowed. Through the openings of these islands, we had partial views of the eastern coast; till having advanced further through this little archipelago into the body of the lake, the whole eastern skreen[30] opened to the eye—This side, tho less magnificent than the mountains of Furness on the left, contains however more variety. It is broken into hills; some of which are cultivated, and others covered with wood.

But, on the whole, neither of these side screens is an object purely *picturesque*. The western shore is great indeed; but it is an unvaried mass of heavy greatness. The eastern is broken too much, and wants both unity and grandeur. When we rode through it in the morning, it made an admirable *fore-ground* in almost every part: but we now found it less qualified as a *distance*.

The side-screens however are the least essential parts of this vast scene. The front is the capital part—that part, on which the eye immediately settles. It consists of that immense body of barrier mountains, which separate the two counties of Cumberland and Westmoreland; appearing in this view to be drawn up in a sort of tumultuary array, mountain beyond mountain, as far as the eye could reach.

As we advanced in our voyage, this great division of the lake (from the islands to its northern point,) tho really oblong, assumed the form of a vast circular bason: and the rough mountains, arising round it, appeared, from so splended an area, with new grandeur. Indeed contrast gave an additional force to the character of each.

This great scene however, surveyed thus from a centre, was rather amusing, than picturesque. It was too extensive for the painter's use. A small portion of the circle, reduced to paper, or canvas, could have conveyed no idea; and a large segment would have exceeded all the powers of the pallet.

It is certainly an error in landscape-painting, to comprehend too much. It turns a picture into a map. Nothing is more delusive, than to suppose, that every view, which pleases in nature, will please in painting. In nature, the pleasure arises from the eye's roaming from one passage to another; and making its remarks on each. In painting, (as the eye is there

---

[30] A segment of scenery (here a range of wooded hills) projecting into a scene rather (in the case of 'side-skreens') like stage scenery from the wings; 'front skreens' are more centrally placed: 'that in which the eye immediately settles'.

42

confined within certain limits), it arises from seeing some select spot adorned agreeably to the rules of art. And the painter, who wishes to make a pleasing composition, must not include more than he can thus adorn. His fore-ground, and his distance must bear a proportion to each other; which cannot be the case, if he include a vast compass. For as he can only take in a *certain* quantity of fore-ground; the removed parts of his picture should bear a proper proportion to it. Well managed exceptions may be found: yet still, in general, the rule is good.

But altho the whole of the amphitheatre we are now surveying, was, in its full dimensions, no subject for a picture; yet it exhibited many parts which, as distances, were purely picturesque; and afforded an admirable collection of mountain studies for a painter. I speak particularly of the front skreen, in which the lines of the mountains were beautiful, and various—the intersections also of those lines—the promontories; with the deep shades they projected—and above all, the mountain colouring, which was the most splendid we had ever seen. Airy tints of vivid yellow, green, and purple, we could prismatically separate. Bright spots of effulgence also appeared; which could not well be denominated of any colour. Yet all, tho displayed in such rich profusion, were blended with such nice harmony; and tempered so modestly by the grey mistiness of distance; that gorgeous as these hues were, there was not a single colour, that glared, or was out of place.

> ————————For who can paint
> Like nature? Can imagination boast,
> Amidst its gay creation, hues like hers?
> Or can it mix them with that matchless skill
> And lose them in each other?[31]

We had now made a considerable progress in our voyage. The side-screen on the left, kept still the same distance; but the mountains in front, as we approached them, began now to separate into near, and distant grounds: and the rocks and woods, which, in the painter's language, *adhered* before; now *broke away* in a variety of projections; tho still o'er-spread with soft colouring, and tender shadow.

As we approached nearer, this softness of colouring took a more vivid hue; and the promontories, and rocks continued still projecting to the eye with new force of shade: while the mountains, which ranged behind, began more and more to retire. The length of the lake, tho it affected the nearer grounds, made no change in the distant mountains: so that the comparative distance between the foreground and them, was now much greater, than it had been.

[31] From James Thomson, *The Seasons: Spring*, ll. 469–73.

An appearance of this kind is beautifully described by Virgil. When Æneas came in sight of Italy, he first saw a hazy appearance of hills, and low land;

————procul obscuros colles, humilemque videmus
Italiam————————[32]

On a nearer approach, he discovered the temple of Minerva, which, being seated on high ground, seemed, as if it stood on a promontory hanging over the sea.

————Templum apparet in arce Minervæ.[33]

But as he came close in with the land, the rocks took their proper form; and the temple retreated to a distance.

————Gemino demittunt brachia muro
Turriti scopuli; refugitque a litore templum.[34]

As we approached the end of the lake, the promontories and rocks assumed new height; and almost hid the mountains, which continued to retire beyond them; while the form of the nearer grounds began also to vary. The water, which, a little before, seemed in contact with the rocks, appeared now to wash a meadow; beyond which the rocks formed a first distance.

The scenery put us in mind of Berghem;[35] who often chose a meadow, with a rock behind it, to relieve his cattle. His rock is generally left plain, and simple, almost without a single varying tint; a mere mass of tender shadow: while the cattle are touched with infinite force and spirit. We saw the picture realized. Berghem's imagination could not have formed a better back-ground, nor a more beautiful group. Such combinations are pleasing in life, in painting, and in poetry.

————————————On the grassy bank
Some ruminating lie, while others stand
Half in the flood; and often bending sip
The circling surface. In the middle rears
The strong, laborious ox his honest front,
Which incomposed he shakes; and from his side
The troublous insects lashes with his tail,

---

[32] From the *Aeneid*, III, ll. 522–3: '. . . from afar we see the shadowy hills and low lying Italy' (trans. P. James).

[33] *Aeneid* III, l. 531: 'a temple appears on Minerva's Height'.

[34] *Aeneid* III, ll. 535–6: 'turreted cliffs slope down two arms to form its walls and the temple lies back from the foreshore' (trans. Day Lewis).

[35] Nicolaes Claes Berghem (1620–83) painted landscapes influenced by the Italian Arcadian tradition.

Returning still. Amid his subjects safe,
Slumbers the monarch-swain, his careless arm
Thrown round his head, on downy moss reclined;
Here lay his scrip, with wholsome viands filled;
There, listening every noise, his faithful dog:[36]

Through the meadow at the bottom of the rocky ground, two rivers, the Bratha, and the Rotha, wind their way; and uniting before they meet the lake, enter it with a full, but quiet stream; and furnish it with large supplies.

The Rotha takes its rise from mountains about twelve miles distant; and forms the two lakes of Grasmer, and Rydal, before it enter Windermere.

The Bratha rises from the pike of Langdale, in a mountainous, and rocky country; and after a turbulent course, buries at length all its inquietude in the peaceful waters of the lake, where its name is no more remembred.

Our boatmen having conveyed us a considerable way up these united streams, landed us on the meadows, within half a mile of Ambleside.

Before we leave this grand expanse of water, I cannot forbear remarking a few circumstances, that relate to it.

In the first place we admired its extraordinary brightness. [. . .] The eye can see distinctly, in smooth water, through a medium of at least a dozen yards; and view the inhabitants of its deep recesses, as they play in shoals, and

—————————————sporting with quick glance
Shew to the sun their waved coats dropt with gold.[37]

How far the transparency of water is an addition to *a scene*, I cannot take upon me to say. Most of the lakes in Scotland, which I saw, are of a mossy-tinctured hue; and yet had their full effect in landscape.—As a *detached object* however the transparent lake is incomparably the most beautiful. I should suppose also, that the more brilliant the water is, the more brilliant are the reflections.

Reading (G) Keswick

The *lake of Derwent*, or *Keswick-lake*, as it is generally called, is contained within a circumference of about ten miles; presenting itself in a circular form, tho in fact it is rather oblong. Its area is interspersed with

---

[36] James Thomson, *Seasons: Summer*, ll. 486–97.
[37] Milton, *Paradise Lost*, VII, ll. 405–6.

four or five islands: three of which only are of consequence, *Lord's island, Vicar's island*, and *St. Herbert's island:* but none of them is comparable to the island on Windermere, in point either of size, or beauty.

If a painter were desirous of studying the whole circumference of the lake from one station, St. Herbert's island is the spot he should choose; from whence, as from a centre, he might see it in rotation. I have seen a set of drawings taken from this stand; which were hung round a circular room, and intended to give a general idea of the boundaries of the lake. But as no representation could be given of the lake itself; the idea was lost, and the drawings made but an awkward appearance.

Lord's island had its name from being the place, where once stood a pleasure-house, belonging to the unfortunate family of Derwent water, which took its title from this lake. The ancient manor-house stood on Castle-hill above Keswick; where the antiquarian traces also the vestiges of a Roman fort. But an heiress of Derwent-water marrying into the family of the Ratcliffs; the family-seat was removed from Keswick to Dilston in Northumberland.

As the boundaries of this lake are more mountainous than those of Windermere; they, of course, afford more *romantic scenery*. But tho the

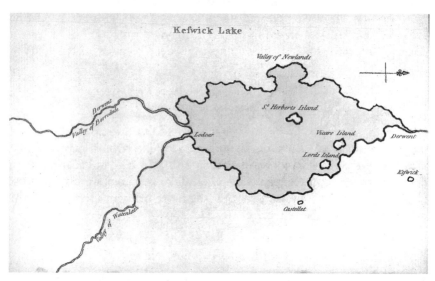

6 'This plan of Keswick-lake means only to express the general shape of it; and the relative situation of its several parts.' William Gilpin's outline plan of Keswick Lake (Derwentwater) and accompanying caption, from his *Observations, relative chiefly to Picturesque Beauty, Made in the Year 1772, On Several Parts of England; particularly the Mountains, and Lakes of Cumberland, and Westmoreland*, 1786, Vol. I. By permission of the British Library, London.

whole shore, except the spot where we stood, is incircled with mountains; they rarely fall abruptly into the water; which is girt almost round by a margin of meadow—on the western shores especially. On the eastern, the mountains approach nearer the water; and in some parts fall perpendicularly into it. But as we stood viewing the lake from its northern shores, all these marginal parts were lost; and the mountains (tho in fact they describe a circle of twenty miles, which is double the circumference of the lake) appeared universally to rise from the water's edge.

Along its western shores on the right, they rise smooth and uniform; and are therefore rather lumpish. The more removed part of this mountain-line is elegant: but, in some parts, it is disagreeably broken.

On the eastern side, the mountains are both grander, and more picturesque. The line is pleasing; and is filled with that variety of objects, broken-ground,—rocks,—and wood, which being well combined, take from the heaviness of a mountain; and give it an airy lightness.

The *front*-screen, (if we may so call a portion of a circular form,) is more formidable, than either of the sides. But its line is less elegant, than that of the eastern-screen. The fall of Lodoar, which adorns that part of the lake, is an object of no consequence at the distance we now stood. But in our intended ride we proposed to take a nearer view of it.

Of all the lakes in these romantic regions, the lake we are now examining, seems to be most generally admired. It was once admirably characterized by an ingenious person,[38] who, on his first seeing it, cryed out, *Here is beauty indeed—Beauty lying in the lap of Horrour!* We do not often find a happier illustration. Nothing conveys an idea of *beauty* more strongly, than the lake; nor of *horrour*, than the mountains; and the former *lying in the lap* of the latter, expresses in a strong manner the mode of their combination. The late Dr. Brown, who was a man of taste, and had seen every part of this country, singled out the scenery of this lake for its peculiar beauty. And unquestionably it is, in many places, very sweetly romantic; particularly along its eastern, and southern shores: but to give it *pre-eminence* may be paying it perhaps as much too high a compliment; as it would be too rigorous to make any but a few comparative objections.

In the first place, its form, which in appearance is circular, is less interesting, I think, than the winding sweep of Windermere, and some other lakes; which losing themselves in vast reaches, behind some cape or promontory, add to their other beauties the varieties of distance, and perspective. Some people object to this, as touching rather on the character of the river. But does that injure its beauty? And yet I believe

---

[38] The late Mr. Avison, organist of St. Nicolas at Newcastle upon Tyne.*

there are very few rivers, which form such reaches, as the lake of Windermere.

To the formality of its shores may be added the formality of its islands. They are round, regular, and similar spots, as they appear from most points of view; formal in their situation, as well as in their shape; and of little advantage to the scene. The islands of Windermere are in themselves better shaped; more varied; and uniting together, add a beauty, and contrast to the whole.

But among the greatest objections to this lake is the abrupt, and broken line in several of the mountains, which compose its screens, (especially on the western, and on part of the southern shore) which is more remarkable, than on any of the other lakes. We have little of the easy sweep of a mountain-line: at least the eye is hurt with too many tops of mountains, which injure the ideas of simplicity, and grandeur. Great care therefore should be taken in selecting views of this lake. If there is a littleness even amidst the grand ideas of the original, what can we expect from representations on paper, or canvas? I have seen some views of this lake, injudiciously chosen, or taken on too extensive a scale, in which the mountains appear like haycocks.—I would be understood however to speak chiefly of the appearance, which the lines of these mountains *occasionally* make. When we change our point of view, the mountain-line changes also, and may be beautiful in one point, tho it is displeasing in another.

Having thus taken a view of the *whole lake together* from its northern point, we proceeded on our rout to Borrodale, skirting the eastern coast along the edge of the water. The grand side-screen, on the left, hung over us; and we found it as beautifully romantic, and pleasing to the imagination, when its rocks, precipices, and woods became a fore-ground; as it appeared from the northern point of the lake, when we examined it in a more removed point of view.

Nor do these rocky shores recommend themselves to us only as foregrounds. We found them every where the happiest stations for obtaining the most picturesque views of the lake. The inexperienced conductor, shewing you the lake, carries you to some garish stand, where the eye may range far and wide. And such a view indeed is well calculated, as we have just seen, to obtain a general idea of the whole. But he, who is in quest of the picturesque scenes of the lake, must travel along the rough side-screens that adorn it; and catch its beauties, as they arise in smaller portions—its little bays, and winding shores—its deep recesses, and hanging promontories—its garnished rock, and distant mountain. These are, in general, the picturesque scenes, which it affords.

Part of this mountain is known by the name of Lady's-rake, from a tradition, that a young lady of the Derwentwater family, in the time of some public disturbance, escaped a pursuit by climbing a precipice, which had been thought inaccessible.——A romantic place seldom wants a romantic story to adorn it.

Detached from this *continent* of precipice, if I may so speak, stands a rocky hill, known by the name of *Castellet*. Under the beetling brow of this natural ruin we passed; and as we viewed it upwards from its base, it seemed a fabric of such grandeur, that alone it was sufficient to give dignity to any scene. We were desired to take particular notice of it for a reason, which shall afterwards be mentioned.

As we proceeded in our rout along the lake, the road grew wilder, and more romantic. There is not an idea more tremendous, than that of riding along the edge of a precipice, unguarded by any parapet, under impending rocks, which threaten above; while the surges of a flood, or the whirlpools of a rapid river, terrify below.

Many such roads there are in various parts of the world; particularly among the mountains of Norway and Sweden; where they are carried along precipices of such frightful height, that the trees at the bottom assume the azure tint of distance; and the cataracts which roar among them, cannot even be heard, unless the air be perfectly still. These tremendous roads are often not only without rail, or parapet of any kind; but so narrow, that travellers in opposite directions cannot pass, unless one of them draw himself up close to the rock. In some places, where the precipice does not afford footing even for this narrow shelf; or, where it may have foundered, a cleft pine is thrown across the chasm. The appalled traveller arriving at the spot, surveys it with dismay.—Return, he dare not—for he knows what a variety of terrors he has already passed.—Yet if his foot slip, or the plank, on which he rests, give way; he will find his death, and his grave together; and never more be heard of.

But here we had not even the miniature of these dreadful ideas, at least on the side of the lake: for in the steepest part, we were scarce raised thirty or forty feet above the water.

As we edged the precipices, we every where saw fragments of rock, and large stones scattered about, which being loosened by frosts and rains, had fallen from the cliffs above; and shew the traveller what dangers he has escaped.

Once we found ourselves in hands more capricious than the elements. We rode along the edge of a precipice, under a steep woody rock; when some large stones came rolling from the top, and rushing through the thickets above us, bounded across the road, and plunged into the lake. At that instant we had made a pause to observe some part of the scenery; and by half a dozen yards escaped mischief. The wind was loud, and we conceived the stones had been dislodged by its violence: but on riding a little further, we discovered the real cause. High above our heads, at the summit of the cliff, sat a group of mountaineer children, amusing themselves with pushing stones from the top; and watching, as they plunged into the lake.—Of us they knew nothing, who were screened from them by intervening thickets.

As we approached the head of the lake, we were desired to turn round, and take a view of Castellet, that rocky hill, which had appeared so enormous, as we stood under it. It had now shrunk into nothing in the midst of that scene of greatness, which surrounded it. I mention this circumstance, as in these wild countries, comparison is the only scale used in the mensuration of mountains. At least it was the only scale, to which we were ever referred. In countries graced by a *single* mountain, the inhabitants may be very accurate in their investigation of its height. The altitude and circumference of the *Wrekin,* I have no doubt, is accurately known in Shropshire; but in a country like this, where chain is linked to chain, exactness would be endless.

By this time we approached the head of the lake; and could now distinguish the full sound of the fall of Lodoar; which had before reached our ears, as the wind suffered, indistinctly in broken notes.

This water-fall is a noble object, both in itself, and as an ornament of the lake. It appears more as an object *connected with the lake,* as we approach by water. By land, we see it over a promontory of low ground, which, in some degree, hides its grandeur. At the distance of a mile, it begins to appear with dignity.

But of whatever advantage the fall of Lodoar may be as a piece of *distant* scenery, its effect is very noble, when examined *on the spot.* As a single object, it wants no accompaniments of offskip;[39] which would rather injure, than assist it. They would disturb its simplicity, and repose. The greatness of its parts affords scenery enough. Some instruments please in concert: others you wish to hear alone.

The stream falls through a chasm between two towering perpendicular rocks. The intermediate part, broken into large fragments, forms the rough bed of the cascade. Some of these fragments stretching out in shelves, hold a depth of soil sufficient for large trees. Among these broken rocks the stream finds its way through a fall of at least an hundred feet; and in heavy rains, the water is every way suited to the grandeur of the scene. Rocks and water in opposition can hardly produce a more animated strife. The ground at the bottom also is very much broken, and overgrown with trees, and thickets; amongst which the water is swallowed up into an abyss; and at length finds its way, through

---

[39] A landscape view adjacent and complementary to a major motif such as a castle, house or (here) waterfall.

deep channels, into the lake. We dismounted, and got as near as we could: but were not able to approach so near, as to look into the woody chasm, which receives the fall.

Having viewed this grand piece of natural ruin, we proceeded in our rout towards the mountains of Borrodale; and shaping our course along the southern shores of the lake, we came to the river Derwent, which is a little to the west of the Lodoar.

These two rivers, the Lodoar, and the Derwent, furnish the chief supplies of Derwentwater. But those of the latter are much ampler. The Lodoar accordingly is lost in the lake: while the Derwent, first giving its name to it, retains its own to the sea.

On passing this river, and turning the first great promontory on our left, we found ourselves in a vast recess of mountains. We had seen them at a distance, from the northern extremity of the lake. They were then objects of grandeur. But now they had assumed their full majestic form; surrounding us on every side with their lofty barriers; and shutting out, in appearance, every idea of an escape. Wild and various beyond conception were their shapes: but they participated rather of the desolate, than of the fantastic idea. From the bottom of the lake indeed they formed too great a combination of pointed summits. But here all these grotesque shapes disappeared. The summits receded far behind; and we only saw the bursting rocks, and bold protuberances, with which the sides of these enormous masses of solid earth are charged. Many of them are covered, like the steeps of Helvellin, with a continued pavement of craggs.

Reading (H) Figures in the landscape: 'picturesque appendages'

Moral, and picturesque ideas do not always coincide. In a moral light, cultivation, in all its parts, is pleasing; the hedge, and the furrow; the waving corn field, and the ripened sheaf. But all these, the picturesque eye, in quest of scenes of grandeur, and beauty, looks at with disgust. It ranges after nature, untamed by art, and bursting wildly into all its irregular forms.

—————————————Juvat arva videre
Non rastris hominum, non ulli obnoxia curæ.[40]

It is thus also in the introduction of figures. In a moral view, the industrious mechanic is a more pleasing object, than the loitering peasant. But

[40] Virgil, *Georgics*, II, ll. 438–9: 'it gives joy to look upon fields that owe no debt to mattocks and are not submissive to any mortal care' (trans. P. James).

in a picturesque light, it is otherwise. The arts of industry are rejected; and even idleness, if I may so speak, adds dignity to a character. Thus the lazy cowherd resting on his pole; or the peasant lolling on a rock, may be allowed in the grandest scenes; while the laborious mechanic, with his impliments of labour, would be repulsed. The fisherman, it is true, may follow his calling upon the lake: but he is indebted for this privilege, not to his art; but to the picturesque apparatus of it—his boat, and his nets, which qualify his art. *They* are the objects: *he* is but an appendage. Place him on the shore, as a single figure, with his rod, and line; and his art would ruin him. In a chearful glade, along a purling brook, near some mill, or cottage, let him angle, if he please: in such a scene the picturesque eye takes no offence. But let him take care not to introduce the vulgarity of his employment in a scene of grandeur.

Reading (I) The manners of the country

The great simplicity of this country, and that rigid temperance, and economy, which necessity injoins to all its inhabitants, may be exemplified by the following little history.

A clergyman, of the name of Mattison, was minister of this place sixty years; and died lately at the age of ninety. During the early part of his life, his benefice brought him in only twelve pounds a year. It was afterwards increased, (I suppose by the queen's bounty,) to eighteen; which it never exceeded. On this income he married—brought up four children—lived comfortably among his neighbours—educated a son, I believe, at college—and left upwards of 1000£. behind him.

With that singular simplicity, and inattention to forms which characterize a country like this; he himself read the burial-service over his mother; he married his father to a second wife; and afterwards buried him also. He published his own banns of marriage in the church, with a woman, whom he had formerly christened; and himself married all his four children.

From this specimen, the manners of the country may easily be conceived. At a distance from the refinements of the age, they are at a distance also from its vices. Many sage writers, and Montesquieu[41] in particular, have supposed these rough scenes of nature to have a great effect on the human mind: and have found virtues in mountainous countries, which were not the growth of tamer regions. Many opinions perhaps have passed current among mankind, which have less foundation

[41] Charles-Louis de Secondat, baron de La Brède et de Montesquieu (1689–1755), was famous for his *Spirit of the Laws* (1748) in which he explained the close relationship between climate and temperament.

in truth. Montesquieu is in quest chiefly of political virtue—liberty—bravery—and the arts of bold defence: but, I believe, private virtue is equally befriended by these rough scenes. It is some happiness indeed to these people, that they have no great roads among them; and that their simple villages, on the sides of lakes, and mountains, are in no line of communication with any of the busy haunts of men. Ignorance is sometimes called the mother of vice. I apprehend it to be as often the nurse of innocence.

Much have those travellers to answer for, whose casual intercourse with this innocent, and simple people tends to corrupt them; disseminating among them ideas of extravagance, and dissipation—giving them a taste for pleasures, and gratifications, of which they had no ideas—inspiring them with discontent at home—and tainting their rough, industrious manners with idleness, and a thirst after dishonest means.

If travellers would frequent this country with a view to examine its grandeur, and beauty—or to explore its varied, and curious regions with the eye of philosophy——or, if that could be hoped, to adore the great Creator in these his sublimer works—if, in their passage through it, they could be content with such fare as the country produces; or, at least reconcile themselves to it by manly exercise, and fatigue (for there is a time, when the stomach, and the plainest food will be found in perfect harmony)—if they could thus, instead of corrupting the manners of an innocent people; learn to amend their own, by seeing in how narrow a compass the wants of human life may be compressed—a journey through these wild scenes might be attended perhaps with more improvement, than a journey to Rome, or Paris. Where manners are polished into vicious refinement, simplifying is the best mode of improving; and the example of innocence is a more instructive lesson, than any that can be taught by artists, and literati.

But these scenes are too often the resort of gay company, who are under no impressions of this kind—who have no ideas, but of extending the sphere of their amusements—or, of varying a life of dissipation. The grandeur of the country is not taken into the question: or, at least it is no otherwise considered, than as affording some new mode of pleasurable enjoyment. Thus even the diversions of Newmarket are introduced——diversions, one would imagine, more foreign to the nature of this country, than any other. A number of horses are carried into the middle of a lake in a flat boat. A plug is drawn from the bottom: the boat sinks, and the horses are left floating on the surface. In different directions they make to land; and the horse, which soonest arrives, secures the prize.

Strenua nos exercet inertia: navibus atque
Quadrigis petimus bene vivere. Quod petis, hic est:
Est Ulubris; animus si te non deficit æquus.[42]

7 'This print was intended to give some idea of that kind of rocky scenery, of which Gatesgarth-dale is composed; and of that solemnity, which it assumed, when we saw the sweeping clouds pass over its summits: but I am sorry to say, it does not express the idea so well as I could wish. The proofs of this print escaped me too soon. Indeed I thought it had been brought nearer my idea, than I find it is. The clouds are ill made-out: the distant rocks are worse; and the figures, as a scale to the perspective, are twice as large as they ought to be. With these limits, however, I hope the imagination of the spectator may not be misled by the deficiencies of the print.' Illustration of rocky scenery and accompanying caption from William Gilpin, *Observations, relative chiefly to Picturesque Beauty, Made in the Year 1772, On Several Parts of England; particularly the Mountains, and Lakes of Cumberland, and Westmoreland*, 1786, Vol. I. Gilpin was at times frustrated by the process of transferring his illustrative drawings to the medium of engraving. By permission of the British Library, London.

[42] Horace, *Epistles* I, Ep. II, ll. 28–30: ''Tis a busy idleness that is our bane; with yachts and cars we seek to make life happy. What you are seeking is here. It is at Ulubrae [a decaying, marshy and foggy town], if there fail you not a mind well balanced' (trans. H.R. Fairclough, *Satires, Epistles and Arts Poetica*, Loeb Classical Library edition, Harvard University Press, Cambridge, Massachusetts, and Heineman, London, 1961).

Source: William Gilpin, *Observations on the Mountains and Lakes of Cumberland and Westmoreland*, The Richmond Publishing Co. Ltd., Richmond, Surrey, 1973, Vol. 1, pp. xxi–xxii, pp. xxii–xxxi, pp. 1–17, pp. 81–91, pp. 93–102, pp. 143–52, pp. 180–93, p. 223, Vol. II, pp. 44–5, 65–9, facsimile reprint of the first (1786) edition of Gilpin's work, *Observations, relative chiefly to Picturesque Beauty; Made in the Year 1772, On several Parts of England; particularly the Mountains, and Lakes of Cumberland, and Westmoreland.*

Uvedale Price, extracts from *Essays on the Picturesque, as compared with the Sublime and the Beautiful and, on the Use of studying Pictures, for the Purpose of Improving Real Landscape*

Reading (A)

[. . .]

According to Mr. Burke, the passion caused by the great and sublime in *nature*, when those causes operate most powerfully is astonishment; and astonishment is that state of the soul, in which all its motions are suspended with some degree of horror: the sublime also, being founded on ideas of pain and terror, like them operates by stretching the fibres beyond their natural tone. The passion excited by beauty, is love and complacency; it acts by relaxing the fibres somewhat below their natural tone, and this is accompanied by an inward sense of melting and languor. I have heard this part of Mr. Burke's book criticized, on a supposition that pleasure is more generally produced from the fibres being stimulated, than from their being relaxed. To me it appears, that Mr. Burke is right with respect to that pleasure which is the effect of beauty, or whatever has an analogy to beauty, according to the principles he has laid down.

If we examine our feelings on a warm genial day, in a spot full of the softest beauties of nature, the fragrance of spring breathing around us—pleasure then seems to be our natural state; to be received, not sought after; it is the happiness of existing to sensations of delight only; we are unwilling to move, almost to think, and desire only to feel, to enjoy. In

pursuing the same train of ideas, I may add, that the effect of the picturesque is curiosity; an effect, which, though less splendid and powerful,
has a more general influence. Those who have felt the excitement produced by the intricacies of wild romantic mountainous scenes, can tell
how curiosity, while it prompts us to scale every rocky promontory, to
explore every new recess, by its active agency keeps the fibres to their full
tone; and thus picturesqueness when mixed with either of the other characters, corrects the languor of beauty, or the tension of sublimity. But as
the nature of every corrective, must be to take off from the peculiar effect
of what it is to correct, so does the picturesque when united to either of
the others. It is the coquetry of nature; it makes beauty more amusing,
more varied, more playful, but also,

> Less winning soft, less amiably mild.

Again, by its variety, its intricacy, its partial concealments, it excites that
active curiosity which gives play to the mind, loosening those iron bonds,
with which astonishment chains up its faculties.

Where characters, however distinct in their nature, are perpetually
mixed together in such various degrees and manners, it is not always
easy to draw the exact line of separation: I think, however, we may conclude, that where an object, or a set of objects are without smoothness
or grandeur, but from their intricacy, their sudden and irregular devia-
tions, their variety of forms, tints, and lights and shadows, are interesting to a cultivated eye, they are simply picturesque. Such, for instance,
are the rough banks that often inclose a bye-road, or a hollow lane:
imagine the size of these banks, and the *space* between them to be
increased, till the lane, becomes a deep dell; the coves, large caverns; the
peeping stones, hanging rocks, so that the whole may impress an idea of
awe and grandeur;—the sublime will then be mixed with the picturesque, though the *scale* only, not the *style* of the scenery would be
changed. On the other hand, if parts of the banks were smooth and
gently sloping; or if in the middle space the turf were soft and close-
bitten; or if a gentle stream passed between them, whose clear, unbroken
surface reflected all their varieties—the beautiful and the picturesque, by
means of that softness and smoothness, would then be united.

Reading (B)

According to Mr. Burke, one of the most essential qualities of beauty
is smoothness: now as the perfection of smoothness is absolute equality
and uniformity of surface, wherever that prevails there can be but little
variety or intricacy; as, for instance, in smooth level banks, on a small,

or in open downs, on a large scale. Another essential quality of beauty is gradual variation; that is (to make use of Mr. Burke's expression) where the lines do not vary in a sudden and broken manner, and where there is no sudden protuberance: it requires but little reflection to perceive, that the exclusion of all but flowing lines cannot promote variety; and that sudden protuberances, and lines that cross each other in a sudden and broken manner, are among the most fruitful causes of intricacy.

I am therefore persuaded, that the two opposite qualities of roughness, and of sudden variation, joined to that of irregularity, are the most efficient causes of the picturesque.

This, I think, will appear very clearly, if we take a view of those objects, both natural and artificial, that are allowed to be picturesque, and compare them with those which are as generally allowed to be beautiful.

A temple or palace of Grecian architecture in its perfect entire state, and with its surface and colour smooth and even, either in painting or reality is beautiful; in ruin it is picturesque. Observe the process by which time, the great author of such changes, converts a beautiful object into a picturesque one. First, by means of weather stains, partial incrustations, mosses, &c. it at the same time takes off from the uniformity of the surface, and of the colour; that is, gives a degree of roughness, and variety of tint. Next, the various accidents of weather loosen the stones themselves; they tumble in irregular masses, upon what was perhaps smooth turf or pavement, or nicely trimmed walks and shrubberies; now mixed and overgrown with wild plants and creepers, that crawl over, and shoot among the fallen ruins. Sedums, wall-flowers, and other vegetables that bear drought, find nourishment in the decayed cement from which the stones have been detached: birds convey their food into the chinks, and yew, elder, and other berried plants project from the sides; while the ivy mantles over other parts, and crowns the top.

[. . .]

Gothic architecture is generally considered as more picturesque, though less beautiful than Grecian; and upon the same principle that a ruin is more so than a new edifice. The first thing that strikes the eye in approaching any building, is the general outline, and the effect of the openings: in Grecian buildings, the general lines of the roof are strait; and even when varied and adorned by a dome or a pediment, the whole has a character of symmetry and regularity. But symmetry, which, in works of art particularly, accords with the beautiful, is in the same degree adverse to the picturesque; and among the various causes of the superior picturesqueness of ruins compared with entire buildings, the destruction of symmetry is by no means the least powerful.

[. . .]

But among all the objects of nature, there is none in which roughness and smoothness more strongly mark the distinction between the two characters, than in water. A calm, clear lake, with the reflections of all that surrounds it, viewed under the influence of a setting sun, at the close of an evening clear and serene as its own surface, is perhaps, of all scenes, the most congenial to our ideas of beauty in its strictest, and in its most general acceptation.

Nay though the scenery around should be the most wild and picturesque (I might almost say the most savage) every thing is so softened and melted together by the reflection of such a mirror, that the prevailing idea, even then, might possibly be that of beauty, so long as the water itself was chiefly regarded. On the other hand, all water of which the surface is broken, and the motion abrupt and irregular, as universally accords with our ideas of the picturesque; and whenever the word is mentioned, rapid and stony torrents and waterfalls, and waves dashing against rocks, are among the first objects that present themselves to our imagination. The two characters also approach and balance each other, as roughness or smoothness, as gentle undulation or abruptness prevail.

[. . .]

I have now very fully stated the principal circumstances by which the picturesque is separated from the beautiful. It is equally distinct from the sublime; for though there are some qualities common to them both, yet they differ in many essential points, and proceed from very different causes. In the first place, greatness of dimension is a powerful cause of the sublime; the picturesque has no connection with dimension of any kind, and is as often found in the smallest as in the largest objects. The sublime, being founded on principles of awe and terror, never descends to any thing light or playful; the picturesque, whose characteristics are intricacy and variety, is equally adapted to the grandest, and to the gayest scenery. Infinity is one of the most efficient causes of the sublime; the boundless ocean, for that reason, inspires awful sensations: to give it picturesqueness, you must destroy that cause of its sublimity; for it is on the shape and disposition of its boundaries, that the picturesque must in great measure depend.

Uniformity, which is so great an enemy to the picturesque, is not only compatible with the sublime, but often the cause of it. That general, equal gloom which is spread over all nature before a storm, with the stillness, so nobly described by Shakspeare, is in the highest degree sublime. The picturesque requires greater variety, and does not shew itself till the dreadful thunder has rent the region, has tossed the clouds into a thousand towering forms, and opened, as it were, the recesses of the sky. A blaze of light unmixed with shade, on the same principles tends to the sublime only: Milton has placed light in its most glorious brightness, as an inaccessible barrier round the throne of the Almighty:

> *For God is light,*
> *And never but in unapproached light*
> *Dwelt from eternity.*

And such is the power he has given even to its diminished splendor,

> *That the brightest seraphim*
> *Approach not, but with both wings veil their eyes.*

In one place, indeed, he has introduced very picturesque circumstances in his sublime representation of the deity: but it is of the deity in wrath; it is when from the weakness and narrowness of our conceptions, we give the names and the effects of our passion, to the all-perfect Creator:

> *And clouds began*
> *To darken all the hill, and smoke to roll*
> *In dusky wreaths reluctant flames, the sign*
> *Of wrath awak'd.*

In general, however, where the glory, power, or majesty of God are represented, he has avoided that variety of form and of colouring, which might take off from simple and uniform grandeur; and has encompassed the divine essence with unapproached light, or with the majesty of darkness.

Again, (if we descend to earth) a perpendicular rock of vast bulk and height, though bare and unbroken; or a deep chasm under the same circumstances, are objects which produce awful sensations; but without some variety and intricacy, either in themselves or their accompaniments, they will not be picturesque. Lastly, a most essential difference between the two characters is, that the sublime, by its solemnity, takes off from the loveliness of beauty; whereas the picturesque renders it more captivating. This last difference is happily pointed out and illustrated, in the most ingenious and pleasing of all fictions, that of Venus's Cestus. Juno, however beautiful, had no captivating charms, till she had put on the magic girdle; in other words, till she had exchanged her stately dignity, for playfulness and coquetry.

Source: Malcolm Andrews, ed., *The Picturesque: Literary Sources and Documents*, vol. 2, pp. 95 sqq, Robertsbridge, Helm Information, 1994.

William Combe, *The Tour of Dr Syntax in search of the Picturesque, a Poem, with Thirty-One Illustrations by Thomas Rowlandson*

Rowlandson del.

THE REV.^D DOCTOR SYNTAX.

8 Thomas Rowlandson, cartoon of Dr Syntax, from the frontispiece of William Combe's *The Tour of Dr Syntax in Search of the Picturesque, a Poem, with Thirty-One Illustrations by Thomas Rowlandson*, seventh edition (1817). By permission of the British Library, London.

Canto I

The School was done, the bus'ness o'er,
When, tir'd of Greek and Latin lore,
Good SYNTAX sought his easy chair,
And sat in calm composure there.
His wife was to a neighbour gone
To hear the chit-chat of the town;
And left him the unfrequent power
Of brooding through a quiet hour.
Thus, while he sat, a busy train
Of images besieged his brain.
Of Church-preferment he had none,
Nay, all his hope of that was gone:
He felt that he content must be
With drudging in a Curacy.
Indeed, on ev'ry Sabbath-day,
Through eight long miles he took his way,
To preach, to grumble, and to pray;
To cheer the good, to warn the sinner,
And, if he got it,—eat a dinner:
To bury these, to christen those,
And marry such fond folks as chose
To change the tenor of their life,
And risk the matrimonial strife.
Thus were his weekly journeys made,
'Neath summer suns and wintry shade;
And all his gains, it did appear,
Where only thirty pounds a year.
Besides, th' augmenting taxes press
To aid expense and add distress:
Mutton and beef and bread and beer,
And ev'ry thing was grown so dear;
The boys too always prone to eat
Delighted less in books than meat;
So that when holy Christmas came,
His earnings ceas'd to be the same,
And now, alas! could do no more,
Than keep the wolf without the door.
E'en birch, the pedant master's boast,
Was so increas'd in worth and cost,
That oft, prudentially beguil'd,
To save the rod, he spar'd the child.
Thus, if the times refus'd to mend,
He to his school must put an end.

How hard his lot! how blind his fate!
What shall he do to mend his state?
Thus did poor Syntax ruminate.

When, as the vivid meteors fly,
And instant light the gloomy sky,
A sudden thought across him came,
And told the way to wealth and fame;
And, as th' expanding vision grew
Wider and wider to his view,
The painted fancy did beguile
His woe-worn phiz into a smile.
But, while he pac'd the room around,
Or stood immers'd in thought profound,
The Doctor, 'midst his rumination,
Was waken'd by a visitation
Which troubles many a poor man's life—
The visitation of his wife.
Good Mrs. Syntax was a lady
Ten years, perhaps, beyond her hey-day;
But though the blooming charms had flown
That grac'd her youth, it still was known
The love of power she never lost,
As Syntax found it to his cost:
For as her words were used to flow,
He but replied or, YES or NO.—
Whene'er enrag'd by some disaster,
She'd shake the boys and cuff the master:
Nay, to avenge the slightest wrong,
She could employ both arms and tongue,
And, if we list to country tales,
She sometimes would enforce her nails.
Her face was red, her form was fat,
A round-about, and rather squat;
And when in angry humour stalking,
Was like a dumpling set a-walking.
'Twas not the custom of this spouse
To suffer long a quiet house:
She was among those busy wives
Who hurry-scurry through their lives;
And make amends for fading beauty
By telling husbands of their duty.

'Twas at this moment, when, inspir'd,
And by his new ambition fir'd,
The pious man his hands uprear'd,

That Mrs. Syntax re-appear'd:
Amaz'd she look'd, and loud she shriek'd,
Or, rather like a pig she squeak'd,
To see her humble husband dare
Thus quit his sober ev'ning chair,
And pace, with varying steps, about,
Now in the room, and now without.
At first she did not find her tongue,
(A thing which seldom happen'd long,)
But soon that organ grew unquiet,
To ask the cause of all this riot.
The Doctor smil'd, and thus address'd
The secrets of his lab'ring breast——
"Sit down, my love, my dearest dear,
Nay, prithee do, and patient hear;
Let me, for once, throughout my life,
Receive this kindness from my wife;
It will oblige me so:—in troth,
It will, my dear, oblige us both;
For such a plan has come athwart me,
Which some kind sprite from heav'n has brought me,
That if you will your counsels join,
To aid this golden scheme of mine,
New days will come—new times appear,
And teeming plenty crown the year:
We then on dainty bits shall dine,
And change our home-brew'd ale for wine:
On summer days, to take the air,
We'll put our Grizzle to a chair;
While you, in silks and muslins fine,
The grocer's wife shall far outshine,
And neighb'ring folks be forc'd to own,
In this fair town you give the ton."
"Oh! tell me," cried the smiling dame,
"Tell me this golden road to same:
You charm my heart, you quite delight it."—
"*I'll make a* TOUR—*and then I'll* WRITE IT
You well know what my pen can do,
And I'll employ my pencil too:—
I'll ride and *write*, and *sketch* and *print*,
And thus create a real mint;
I'll *prose* it here, I'll *verse* it there,
And *picturesque* it ev'ry where:
I'll do what all have done before;
I think I shall—and somewhat more.
At Doctor *Pompous* give a look;

He made his fortune by a book;
And if my volume does not beat it,
When I return, I'll fry and eat it.
Next week the boys will all go home,
And I shall have a month to come.
My clothes, my cash, my all prepare;
While *Ralph* looks to the grizzle mare.
Tho' wond'ring folks may laugh and scoff
By this day fortnight I'll be off;
And when old Time a month has run,
Our bus'ness *Lovey* will be done.
I will in search of fortune roam,
While you enjoy yourself at home."

   The story told, the Doctor eas'd
Of his grand plan, and Madam pleas'd,
No pains were spar'd by night or day
To set him forward on his way:
She trimm'd his coat—she mended all
His various clothing, great and small;
And better still, a purse was found
With twenty notes of each a pound.
Thus furnish'd, and in full condition
To prosper in his expedition;
At length the ling'ring moment came
That gave the dawn of wealth and same.
Incurious *Ralph*, exact at four,
Led Grizzle, saddled, to the door;
And soon, with more than common state,
The Doctor stood before the gate.
Behind him was his faithful wife;—
"One more embrace, my dearest life!"
Then his grey palfrey he bestrode,
And gave a nod, and off he rode.
"Good luck! good luck!" she loudly cried,
"*Vale! O Vale!*" he replied.

Source: William Combe, *The Tour of Dr Syntax in Search of the Picturesque, a Poem, with thirty-one illustrations by Thomas Rowlandson*, Methuen and Co., London, 1903 based on the seventh edition of the original text published by R. Ackermann, 1817. This extract is from Canto I, pp. 1–6 plus Rowlandson's drawing, *Doctor Syntax Setting out on his Tour to the Lakes*.

9 Thomas Rowlandson, *Dr Syntax Setting out on his Journey to the Lakes,* cartoon illustration from William Combe, *The Tour of Dr Syntax in Search of the Picturesque, a Poem, with Thirty-One Illustrations by Thomas Rowlandson,* seventh edition (1817). By permission of the British Library, London.

Jane Austen, extract from *Northanger Abbey*

They [the Tilneys] were viewing the country with the eyes of persons accustomed to drawing, and decided on its capability of being formed into pictures, with all the eagerness of real taste. Here Catherine was quite lost. She knew nothing of drawing – nothing of taste: – and she listened to them with an attention which brought her little profit, for they talked in phrases which conveyed scarcely any idea to her. The little which she could understand however appeared to contradict the very few notions she had entertained on the matter before. It seemed as if a good view were no longer to be taken from the top of an high hill, and that a clear blue sky was no longer a proof of a fine day. She was heartily ashamed of her ignorance. A misplaced shame. Where people wish to attach, they should always be ignorant. To come with a well-informed mind, is to come with an inability of administering to the vanity of others, which a sensible person would always wish to avoid. A woman especially, if she have the misfortune of knowing any thing, should conceal it as well as she can.

The advantages of natural folly in a beautiful girl have been already set forth by the capital pen of a sister author; – and to her treatment of the subject I will only add in justice to men, that though to the larger and more trifling part of the sex, imbecility in females is a great enhancement of their personal charms, there is a portion of them too reasonable and too well informed themselves to desire any thing more in woman than ignorance. But Catherine did not know her own advantages – did not know that a good-looking girl, with an affectionate heart and a very ignorant mind, cannot fail of attracting a clever young man, unless circumstances are particularly untoward. In the present instance, she confessed and lamented her want of knowledge: declared that she would give any thing in the world to be able to draw; and a lecture on the picturesque immediately followed, in which his instructions were so clear that she soon began to see beauty in every thing admired by him, and her attention was so earnest, that he became perfectly satisfied of her having a great deal of natural taste. He talked of fore-grounds, distances, and second distances – side-screens and perspectives – lights and shades; and Catherine was so hopeful a scholar, that when they gained the top of Beechen Cliff, she voluntarily rejected the whole city of Bath, as unworthy to make part of a landscape. Delighted with her progress, and fearful of wearying her with too much wisdom at once, Henry suffered the subject to decline, and by an easy transition from a piece of rocky fragment and the withered oak which he had placed near its summit, to oaks in general, to forests, the inclosure of them, waste lands, crown lands and government, he shortly found himself arrived at politics; and from politics, it was an easy step to silence.

Source: Jane Austen, *Northanger Abbey, Oxford World's Classics Series*, Oxford University Press, 1998, vol. 1, pp. 86–7, chapter XIV of the novel.

The Lake District 2 –
Into the Romantic:
Wordsworth and the Lakes

Francis Jeffrey (1773–1850), in common with contemporary reviewing practice, uses his ostensible review topic, Robert Southey's long narrative poem *Thalaba the Destroyer* (1801), as a starting-point for an extended political disquisition. The supposedly radical, 'democratic' suggestions of Wordsworth's 'Preface' of 1800 and 1802 to the *Lyrical Ballads* soon become his target. Jeffrey, the founding editor of a cautiously reformist quarterly periodical, the Whig *Edinburgh Review*, generally failed to respond positively to Wordsworth in print. His sensibilities simply could not tolerate Wordsworth's idea that the experience of the common people was an exemplary frame of poetic reference.

William Hazlitt (1778–1830), like Jeffrey, is generally ranked as one of the most significant minds of the 1810s and 1820s. As his extract on the 'Lake School of Poetry' (which originally formed part of one of a series of literary lectures given at the Surrey Institution in 1818) shows, he did not share Jeffrey's view of Wordsworth. The so-called Lake School was still a current topic, the *Edinburgh Review* having resurrected the designation critically in an article of the same year, 1818. It was the apparently radical ideological impulse of *Lyrical Ballads* that appealed to him rather than, as he saw it, the conservative moralising of *The Excursion*.

Thomas De Quincey's (1785–1859) observations, from an essay on Coleridge, published just after the latter's death in July 1834, have a decidedly retrospective feel to them. One might note Francis Jeffrey's comment in the November 1822 issue of the *Edinburgh Review* that 'The Lake School of Poetry, we think, is now pretty nearly extinct.' Like Hazlitt, De Quincey was an acute cultural commentator and a Lake District neighbour, friend and early admirer of Wordsworth.

James Beattie's (1735–1803) fame as a poet was established with the publication of first book of *The Minstrel* in 1771; the second book of the unfinished poem appeared in 1774. The work tells the story of Edwin, a medieval bard, '*from the first dawning of fancy and reason*', as Beattie puts it, outlining at length his solitary wanderings through nature and the effects these have on his moral and artistic growth. The lines in the extract, set in an imaginary landscape, deal with his first experience of the '. . . beautiful, or new,/Sublime, or dreadful, in earth, sea, or sky,' and the creation of a 'romantic eye' (Book I, ll. 514–17). Wordsworth, in common with many fellow poets, drew on both the imagery and the ideas in *The Minstrel*, particularly in *The Prelude* and in *The Excursion*.

William Cowper (1731–1800) was a particular influence on Wordsworth, who read *The Task* (1785) whilst still at Hawkshead Grammar. He argued that it was an 'idyllium' (a poem dealing with various aspects of external nature), a didactic work (offering direct instruction) and a philosophical satire (on the folly and vices of humankind). The landscape of this quintessential eighteenth-century peripatetic poem, set in the south of England, is – unsurprisingly – tranquil rather than wild. What Wordsworth found particularly interesting in Cowper's poem is a conversational tone which allowed personal feeling, philosophical speculation and descriptions of nature to be combined. The extracts are taken from Book I, 'The Sofa', of the six-book poem. *The Task* opens with a mock-history of seating which contains wide digressions.

William Wordsworth's (1770–1850) *An Evening Walk*, 1793, evolved slowly towards its final shape, principally through 1788–9, during and between two summer vacations from Cambridge University, spent partly at Hawkshead, but encompassing other parts of the Lakes and the Yorkshire Dales also. The underlying impulse can be traced back to verse written when he was a schoolboy at Hawkshead Grammar. In line with the canons of the picturesque, this is a work whose poetic landscape is very much based in factual observation: as Wordsworth noted in remarks to Isabella Fenwick in 1843, 'there is not an image in it which I have not observed [. . .] I recollect the time and the place where most of them were noticed'. When the poem was first published, it showed its aesthetic background all too clearly. A cheaply bound, sizeable, if slim, book, its companion volume on publication was Wordsworth's *Descriptive Sketches* (of a continental walking tour undertaken in 1790). The original title of this second volume was *Picturesque Sketches*.

Wordsworth's 'The Sublime and the Beautiful' (1811–12) refines and extends Edmund Burke's categories of the sublime and the beautiful, looking in the process at the way the mind is either exalted or overwhelmed by an experience of the sublime. The fragment, unpublished by Wordsworth, was originally intended to form part of a full-blooded guide to the Lakes. It shows Wordsworth's particular interest in the aesthetic 'power' – the creative potential – inherent in specific aspects of landscape.

Wordsworth's 'There was a Boy' first appeared in *Lyrical Ballads* (1798), generally held to be one of the most significant collections of poems ever published. As fellow contributor Samuel Taylor Coleridge later recorded in Chapter XIV of his *Biographia Literaria* (1817), Wordsworth's aim was to 'give the charm of novelty to things of every day [by] awakening the mind's attention from the lethargy of custom and directing it to the loveliness and the wonders of the world'. It employs a sophisticated form to convey a heightened, near spiritual mode of perception. When Wordsworth incorporated it into his *Prelude* (1805, Book V, ll. 389–422), he was acknowledging the relevance of its language to the autobiographical epic on personal artistic growth that this long poem was.

Wordsworth's note to 'There was a Boy' relates to that section headed 'Poems of the Imagination' in the *Poems* (1815). The Preface sought to explain the complicated division of the poems into six categories, and hence discusses 'There was a Boy' generically.

Wordsworth's 'There is an Eminence' is the third of five numbered poems grouped in the 1800 *Lyrical Ballads* under the heading *Poems on the Naming of Places*. Wordsworth's own headnote introduces the sequence:

> By Persons resident in the country and attached to rural objects, many places will be found unnamed or of unknown names, where little Incidents will have occurred, or feelings been experienced, which will have given to such places a private and peculiar interest. From a wish to give some sort of record to such Incidents or renew the gratification of such Feelings, Names have been given to Places by the Author and some of his Friends, and the following Poems written in consequence.

The poems are, as this suggests, very personal ones, denoting as they do Grasmere walks, locations and experiences familiar to Wordsworth. As he later noted of line 3, the eminence is called Stone-Arthur, and cannot in fact be 'beheld' from the orchard seat at Dove Cottage.

Wordsworth's *The Prelude*, addressed to Coleridge, deals irregularly with formative events and experiences in his own life, with nature as the constant touchstone. A two-part version of the poem had been completed by 1799. By 1805 it ran to 13 books: the two extracts included here both come from 'Book First, Introduction – Childhood and School-time' (1805). By 1850, after much revising and remodelling, it comprised 14 books, in which form it was first published. The opening question of the first extract, 'Was it for this[?]', alludes to the poet's fruitless search for an epic poetic subject.

Wordsworth's 'Airey-Force Valley' has its origins in a visit he made to Aira Force, the sixty-foot waterfall on Aira Beck, between Matterdale and Ullswater, as he walked from Rydal Mount to Lowther Castle in September 1835. The work was written soon afterwards but not published until 1842. In mood the blank-verse poem is very different from that of Wordsworth's description of the waterfall itself in his Lakes *Guide*; here 'Aira-force thunders down the Ghyll' on the west side of Ullswater. It is worth noting that if a thundering cataract fits a Burkean category of the sublime, then no less does the 'terrible' but contradictorily soothing nature of the solitude and silence suggested by 'Airey-Force Valley'. Wordsworth captures perfectly the solitary nature and intense sequestered quality of Aira Dell, with its enveloping shroud of dark, moss-covered rocks and overhanging trees.

Aira Force also provided the locale for his poem 'The Somnambulist' (1835). In this work we read that from the nearby Lyulph's Tower on Ullswater '. . . how softly then/Doth Aira-force, that torrent hoarse,/Speak from the woody glen!/Fit music for a solemn vale!' (ll. 2–5).

Wordsworth's *A Guide through the District of the Lakes in the North of England, with a Description of the Scenery, etc. for the use of Tourists and Residents* (1835) grew out of an introduction to the Reverend Joseph Wilkinson's series of drawings, *Select Views in Cumberland, Westmoreland, and Lancashire* (1810). This work went through several editions before Wordsworth decided, in 1820, to disengage his text from Wilkinson's drawings (by which he was not very impressed), and to amend and enhance it so that, by 1835 (the fifth edition) it became a work in its own right with its changed title. The text went through several further reprints and editions. It was one of Wordsworth's most commercially successful publishing ventures and contained, for the traveller's benefit, an itinerary, descriptions of specific locations, general descriptions of Lakeland scenery and accounts of particular excursions, some of which were originally written by his sister, Dorothy. The text demonstrates many aspects of Wordsworth's attitude to the local countryside, some of which were markedly Romantic in outlook: detailed, minute observation of its appearance; a sense of nature's connection with the feelings of the wanderer and with divine powers; a respect for natural, organic developments in the landscape and a dislike of its defacement by intrusive modernisers. There is constantly a sense of closely observed landscape and, almost, of being a part of it.

Francis Jeffrey, extract from an unsigned review of Robert Southey's *Thalaba*, 1802

[This] *sect* of poets [. . .] established itself in this country within these ten or twelve years [. . .] The peculiar doctrines of this sect, it would not, perhaps, be very easy to explain; but, that they are *dissenters* from the established systems in poetry and criticism, is admitted, and proved indeed, by the whole tenor of their compositions. Though they lay claim, we believe, to a creed and a revelation of their own, there can be little doubt, that their doctrines are of *German* origin, and have been derived from some of the great modern reformers in that country.[1] Some of their leading principles, indeed, are probably of an earlier date, and seem to have been borrowed from the great apostle of Geneva.[2] [. . .]

The disciples of this school boast much of its originality, and seem to value themselves very highly, for having broken loose from the bondage of antient authority, and reasserted the independence of genius. Originality, however, we are persuaded, is rarer than mere alteration; and a man may change a good master for a bad one, without finding himself at all nearer to independence. That our new poets have abandoned the old models, may certainly be admitted; but we have not been able to discover that they have yet created any models of their own; and are very much inclined to call in question the worthiness of those to which they have transferred their admiration. The productions of this school, we conceive, are so far from being entitled to the praise of originality, that they cannot be better characterized, than by an enumeration of the sources from which their materials have been derived. The greater part of them,

---

[1] A reference to the great flowering of philosophy, aesthetic theory and creative writing in eighteenth-century Germany, which included such figures as J. W. von Goethe (1749–1832), J. C. F. von Schiller (1759–1805), and Immanuel Kant (1724–1804).

[2] The Genevan-born Jean-Jacques Rousseau (1712–78), political philosopher and man of letters. His most famous work, *The Social Contract* (1762), offers a view of society in which all work equally towards the 'general will', abandoning individual desires in the process. Behind many of Jeffrey's comments here, however, is the earlier Rousseau: the philosopher who – using the concept of the 'noble savage' – attacked private property and the 'corrupting' of innate goodness by modern society.

we apprehend, will be found to be composed of the following elements: 1. The antisocial principles, and distempered sensibility of Rousseau— his discontent with the present constitution of society—his paradoxical morality, and his perpetual hankerings after some unattainable state of voluptuous virtue and perfection. 2. The simplicity and energy (*horresco referens*)[3] of Kotzebue[4] and Schiller.[5] 3. The homeliness and harshness of some of Cowper's[6] language and versification.

[. . .]

The authors, of whom we are now speaking, have, among them, unquestionably, a very considerable portion of poetical talent, and have, consequently, been enabled to seduce many into an admiration of the false taste (as it appears to us) in which most of their productions are composed. They constitute, at present, the most formidable conspiracy that has lately been formed against sound judgment in matters poetical; and are entitled to a larger share of our censorial notice, than could be spared for an individual delinquent. [. . .]

Their most distinguishing symbol, is undoubtedly an affectation of great simplicity and familiarity of language.[7] They disdain to make use of the common poetical phraseology, or to ennoble their diction by a selection of fine or dignified expressions. There would be too much *art* in this, for that great love of nature with which they are all of them inspired; and their sentiments, they are determined shall be indebted, for their effect, to nothing but their intrinsic tenderness or elevation.

[. . .]

One of their own authors, indeed, has very ingeniously set forth, (in a kind of manifesto that preceded one of their most flagrant acts of hostility), that it was their capital object 'to adapt to the uses of poetry, the ordinary language of conversation among the middling and lower orders of the people.'[8] What advantages are to be gained by the success of this project, we confess ourselves unable to conjecture. The language of the higher and more cultivated orders may fairly be presumed to be better

---

[3] 'I shudder as I relate'; from the *Aeneid* by the Roman poet Virgil (70–19 BC).

[4] August von Kotzebue (1761–1819), German dramatist and historian, a great influence on English drama.

[5] See note 1. Schiller was a highly influential and prolific dramatist whose early play on the nature of political power, *The Robbers* (1781), proved of particular interest to British Romantic writers.

[6] William Cowper (1731–1800), English poet. Jeffrey is thinking here of such poems as *The Task* (1785), with its meditative depictions of tranquil nature.

[7] Jeffrey has Wordsworth in mind particularly here. The latter's 'Preface' to *Lyrical Ballads* argues that those living a 'low and rustic life' are daily in touch with the 'beautiful forms of nature' and thus speak a simple yet profound language suited to poetry.

[8] The 'manifesto' quoted here is Wordsworth's 'Preface' to *Lyrical Ballads*.

than that of their inferiors: at any rate, it has all those associations in its favour, by means of which, a style can ever appear beautiful or exalted, and is adapted to the purposes of poetry, by having been long consecrated to its use. The language of the vulgar, on the other hand, has all the opposite associations to contend with; and must seem unfit for poetry, (if there were no other reason), merely because it has scarcely ever been employed in it.

Source: Lionel Madden, ed., *Robert Southey: The Critical Heritage*, Routledge and Kegan Paul, London and Boston, 1972, pp. 68–71. The review first appeared in the *Edinburgh Review*, I, October 1802, pp. 63–83.

William Hazlitt on the Lake School of Poetry

Mr Wordsworth is at the head of that which has been denominated the Lake school of poetry; a school which, with all my respect for it, I do not think sacred from criticism or exempt from faults, of some of which faults I shall speak with becoming frankness; for I do not see that the liberty of the press ought to be shackled, or freedom of speech curtailed, to screen either its revolutionary or renegado extravagances.[9] This school of poetry had its origin in the French revolution, or rather in those sentiments and opinions which produced that revolution; and which sentiments and opinions were indirectly imported into this country in translations from the German about that period. Our poetical literature had, towards the close of the last century, degenerated into the most trite, insipid, and mechanical of all things, in the hands of the followers of Pope[10] and the old French school of poetry. It wanted something to stir it up, and it found that something in the principles and events of the French revolution.

[. . .]

The object was to reduce all things to an absolute level; and a singularly affected and outrageous simplicity prevailed in dress and manners, in style and sentiment. A striking effect produced where it was least expected, something new and original, no matter whether good, bad, or indifferent, whether mean or lofty, extravagant or childish, was all that

[9] An allusion to recent legal enactments limiting press freedom and freedom of speech in Britain.

[10] Alexander Pope (1688–1744), English poet, known especially for his mock epics, satires and verse epistles. Hazlitt's sentiments were shared by many writers at this time.

was aimed at, or considered as compatible with sound philosophy and an age of reason. The licentiousness grew extreme: Coryate's Crudities[11] were nothing to it. The world was to be turned topsy-turvy; and poetry, by the good will of our Adamwits,[12] was to share its fate and begin *de novo*.[13] It was a time of promise, a renewal of the world and of letters; and the Deucalions,[14] who were to perform this feat of regeneration, were the present poet-laureat[15] and the two authors of the Lyrical Ballads. The Germans, who made heroes of robbers, and honest women of cast-off mistresses, had already exhausted the extravagant and marvellous in sentiment and situation: our native writers adopted a wonderful simplicity of style and matter. The paradox they set out with was, that all things are by nature equally fit subjects for poetry; or that if there is any preference to be given, those that are the meanest and most unpromising are the best, as they leave the greatest scope for the unbounded stores of thought and fancy in the writer's own mind.

[. . .]

They founded the new school on a principle of sheer humanity, on pure nature void of art.

[. . .]

They were for bringing poetry back to its primitive simplicity and state of nature, as he [Rousseau] was for bringing society back to the savage state:[16] so that the only thing remarkable left in the world by this change, would be the persons who had produced it. A thorough adept in this school of poetry and philanthropy is jealous of all excellence but his own. He does not even like to share his reputation with his subject; for he would have it all proceed from his own power and originality of mind.

Source: William Hazlitt, from 'On the Living Poets', in *Lectures on the English Poets*, 1818. Taken from *William Hazlitt: Selected Writings*, Ronald Blythe, ed., Penguin Books Ltd, Harmondsworth, 1970, pp. 215–18.

[11] *Coryat's Crudities: Hastily gobled up in Five Moneth's Travels*, by the writer and traveller Thomas Coryate (1577–1617), an extravagant travel narrative published in 1611.

[12] In this context Hazlitt means 'innovators', not without irony.

[13] Latin, 'anew'.

[14] Deucalion is the son of Prometheus in Greek mythology. He is a Noah-like figure who repeopled the earth after a destructive flood.

[15] Robert Southey (1774–1843) had been appointed poet laureate in 1813. As with Wordsworth and Coleridge, who co-authored *Lyrical Ballads*, Southey's earlier radicalism had essentially long since mutated into conservatism.

[16] In many texts Rousseau argued that civilised society compared unfavourably with the innocent state of primitive man. Similarly, Wordsworth, Coleridge and Southey privileged what they saw as the unaffected language of rural man over the sophisticated diction of 'polite' society.

Thomas De Quincey on Wordsworth
and the Lakes School

About the close of the first revolutionary war it must have been, or in the brief interval of peace, that Coleridge resorted to the English Lakes as a place of residence.[17] Wordsworth had a natural connexion with that region by birth, breeding, and family alliances. Wordsworth attracted Coleridge to the Lakes; and Coleridge, through his affinity to Southey, eventually attracted *him*. Southey, as is known to all who take an interest in the Lake colony, married a sister of Mrs Coleridge's: and, as a singular eccentricity in the circumstances of that marriage, I may mention, that, on his wedding day, (at the very portico of the church, I have been told,) Southey left his bride, to embark for Lisbon. His uncle, Dr Herbert, was chaplain to the English factory in that city; and it was to benefit by the facilities in that way opened to him for seeing Portugal that Southey now went abroad. He extended his tour to Spain; and the result of his notices was communicated to the world in a volume of travels.[18] By such accidents of personal or family connexion as I have mentioned, was the Lake colony gathered; and the critics of the day, unaware of the real facts, supposed them to have assembled under common views in literature – particularly with regard to the true functions of poetry, and the true theory of poetic diction. Under this original blunder, laughable it is to mention, that they went on to *find* in their writings all the agreements and common characteristics which their blunder had presumed; and they incorporated the whole community under the name of the *Lake School*. Yet Wordsworth and Southey never had one principle in common.

[. . .]

And, in fact, a philosophic investigation of the difficult questions connected with this whole slang about schools, Lake schools, &c., would shew that Southey has not, nor ever had, any *peculiarities* in common with Wordsworth, beyond that of exchanging the old prescriptive diction of poetry, introduced between the periods of Milton[19] and Cowper, for the simpler and profounder forms of daily life in some instances, and of the Bible in others. The bold and uniform practice of Wordsworth was here adopted timidly by Southey.

---

[17] Coleridge lived at Greta Hall, Keswick, intermittently between 1800 to 1812; Robert Southey joined him there in 1803 and stayed for the rest of his life. The 'interval of peace' refers to the temporary ending of the war with France under the Peace of Amiens in 1802–3, fourteen months in total.

[18] *Letters written during a short residence in Spain and Portugal*, 1797.

[19] John Milton, English poet (1608–74).

Source: Thomas De Quincey, from 'Samuel Taylor Coleridge', in *Tait's Edinburgh Magazine*, I, October 1834, pp. 589–90. Taken from *Recollections of the Lakes and the Lake Poets*, David Wright, ed., Penguin Books Ltd, Harmondsworth, 1970, pp. 64–5.

James Beattie, *The Minstrel; or, The Progress of Genius*

XVII

But why should I his childish feats display?
Concourse, and noise, and toil, he ever fled;
Nor cared to mingle in the clamorous fray
Of squabbling imps; but to the forest sped,
Or roam'd at large the lonely mountain's head;
Or, where the maze of some bewilder'd stream
To deep untrodden groves his footsteps led,
There would he wander wild, 'till Phoebus' beam,[20]
Shot from the western cliff, released the weary team.   153

XVIII

Th' exploit of strength, dexterity, or speed
To him nor vanity nor joy could bring.
His heart, from cruel sport estranged, would bleed
To work the wo of any living thing,
By trap, or net; by arrow, or by sling;
These he detested, those he scorn'd to wield:
He wish'd to be the guardian, not the king,
Tyrant far less, or traitor of the field.
And sure the sylvan reign unbloody joy might yield.   162

XIX

Lo! where the stripling, wrapt in wonder, roves
Beneath the precipice o'erhung with pine;
And sees, on high, amidst th' encircling groves,
From cliff to cliff the foaming torrents shine:

---

[20] Phoebus Apollo is a god in Greek mythology sometimes associated with the sun-god, Helios, hence 'Phoebus', a conventional name for the sun itself.

While waters, woods, and winds, in concert join.
And Echo swells the chorus to the skies.
Would Edwin this majestic scene resign
For aught the huntsman's puny craft supplies?
Ah! no: he better knows great Nature's charms to prize.   171

XX

And oft he traced the uplands, to survey,
When o'er the sky advanced the kindling dawn,
The crimson cloud, blue main,[21] and mountain grey,
And lake, dim-gleaming on the smoky lawn;
Far to the west the long, long vale withdrawn,
Where twilight loves to linger for a while;
And now he faintly kens the bounding fawn,
And villager abroad at early toil.—
But, lo! the sun appears! and heaven, earth, ocean, smile.   180

XXI

And oft the craggy cliff he loved to climb,
When all in mist the world below was lost.
What dreadful pleasure! there to stand sublime,
Like shipwreck'd mariner on desert coast,
And view th' enormous waste of vapour, tost
In billows, lengthening to th' horizon round,
Now scoop'd in gulfs, with mountains now emboss'd!
And hear the voice of mirth and song rebound,
Flocks, herds, and waterfalls, along the hoar[22] profound!   189

Source: James Beattie, *Poems on Several Occasions*, W. Creech,
Edinburgh, 1776.

---

[21] The expanse of sky.
[22] Whiteness.

William Cowper, *The Task*

For I have lov'd the rural walk through lanes[23]
Of grassy swarth[24] close cropt by nibbling sheep   110
And skirted thick with intertexture[25] firm
Of thorny boughs: have lov'd the rural walk
O'er hills, through valleys, and by rivers' brink,
E'er since a truant boy I pass'd my bounds
T' enjoy a ramble on the banks of Thames.   115
And still remember, nor without regret
Of hours that sorrow since has much endear'd,
How oft, my slice of pocket store consum'd,
Still hung'ring pennyless and far from home,
I fed on scarlet hips and stoney haws,   120
Or blushing crabs,[26] or berries that imboss
The bramble, black as jet, or sloes austere.
                    [. . .]
How oft upon yon eminence[27] our[28] pace
Has slacken'd to a pause, and we have borne   155
The ruffling wind scarce conscious that it blew,
While admiration feeding at the eye,
And still unsated, dwelt upon the scene.
Thence with what pleasure have we just discern'd
The distant plough slow moving, and beside   160
His lab'ring team that swerv'd not from the track,
The sturdy swain diminish'd to a boy!
Here Ouse,[29] slow winding through a level plain
Of spacious meads with cattle sprinkled o'er,
Conducts the eye along his sinuous course   165
Delighted. There, fast rooted in his bank,
Stand, never overlook'd, our fav'rite elms,
That screen the herdsman's solitary hut;

---

[23] This is the first 'ramble' of the poem; until this section Cowper has followed his intention to 'sing the Sofa', as he puts it in line one.

[24] Poetic usage for a grassy surface.

[25] An interwoven structure.

[26] Crab-apples.

[27] The 'eminence' is a rise just west of Olney, in Buckinghamshire.

[28] The narrator is generally taken to be accompanied by Mary Unwin, the widow in whose Olney home Cowper lived.

[29] The River Ouse ran within a quarter of a mile of Olney.

While far beyond and overthwart[30] the stream
That as with molten glass inlays the vale,   170
The sloping land recedes into the clouds;
Displaying on its varied side the grace
Of hedge-row beauties numberless, square tow'r,[31]
Tall spire,[32] from which the sound of cheerful bells
Just undulates upon the list'ning ear,   175
Groves, heaths, and smoking villages remote.
                        [. . .]
Lovely indeed the mimic works of art,   420
But Nature's works far lovelier. I admire –
None more admires the painter's magic skill,
Who shews me that which I shall never see,
Conveys a distant country into mine,
And throws Italian light on English walls.[33]   425
But imitative strokes can do no more
Than please the eye, sweet Nature ev'ry sense.
The air salubrious of her lofty hills,
The chearing fragrance of her dewy vales
And music of her woods – no work of man   430
May rival these; these all bespeak a pow'r
Peculiar, and exclusively her own.
Beneath the open sky she spreads the feast;
'Tis free to all – 'tis ev'ry day renew'd,
Who scorns it starves deservedly at home.   435

Source: James Sambrook, ed., *William Cowper: The Task and Selected Other Poems*, Longman, London and New York, 1994, pp. 61–2, 63, 71.

---

[30] On the other side of.
[31] The tower of Clifton Reynes church, east of Olney.
[32] Of Olney church.
[33] A reference to the taste of Cowper's age for the sort of Italian landscape scenes by Claude Lorrain (1600–82) and Salvator Rosa (1615–73).

William Wordsworth, *An Evening Walk*

AN EVENING WALK. AN EPISTLE; IN VERSE. ADDRESSED TO A
YOUNG LADY, FROM THE LAKES OF THE NORTH OF ENGLAND.

ARGUMENT

General Sketch of the Lakes—Author's Regret of his Youth passed
amongst them—Short description of Noon—Cascade Scene—Noontide
Retreat—Precipice and Sloping Lights—Face of Nature as the Sun
declines—Mountain Farm, and the Cock—Slate Quarry—Sunset—
Superstition of the Country, connected with that Moment—Swans—
Female Beggar—Twilight Objects—Twilight Sounds—Western Lights—
Spirits—Night—Moonlight—Hope—Night Sounds—Conclusion.

> Far from my dearest friend,[34] 'tis mine to rove
> Thro' bare grey dell, high wood, and pastoral cove;
> His wizard course where hoary Derwent takes
> Thro' craggs, and forest glooms, and opening lakes,
> Staying his silent waves, to hear the roar
> That stuns the tremulous cliffs of high Lodore.[35]
> Where silver rocks the savage prospect chear
> Of giant yews that frown on Rydale's mere;[36]
> Where peace to Grasmere's lonely island leads,
> To willowy hedgerows, and to emerald meads;   10
> Leads to her bridge, rude church, and cottaged grounds,
> Her rocky sheepwalks, and her woodland bounds;
> Where, bosomed deep, the shy Winander[37] peeps
> 'Mid clust'ring isles, and holly-sprinkled steeps;
> Where twilight glens endear my Esthwaite's shore,[38]
> And memory of departed pleasures, more.
>
> Fair scenes! with other eyes, than once, I gaze,
> The ever-varying charm your round displays,

---

[34] Dorothy Wordsworth had been living apart from her brother for many years; in 1788 she
took up residence at Forncett, in Norfolk.

[35] Lodore Falls, above Derwentwater: after heavy rain, a must for the picturesque tourist.

[36] Rydal Water, one mile south-east of Grasmere.

[37] 'These lines are applicable only to the middle part of that lake'.* Windermere, largest of
the Cumbrian lakes.

[38] Esthwaite Water lies between Windermere and Hawkshead; 'endear' means to increase the
value of.

Than when, erewhile, I taught, 'a happy child,'[39]
The echoes of your rocks my carols wild: 20
Then did no ebb of chearfulness demand
Sad tides of joy from Melancholy's hand;
In youth's wild eye the livelong day was bright,
The sun at morning, and the stars of night,
Alike, when first the vales the bittern fills
Or the first woodcocks roamed the moonlight hills.[40]

Return Delights! with whom my road begun,
When Life reared laughing up her morning sun;
When Transport kissed away my april tear,
'Rocking as in a dream the tedious year;'[41]   30
When linked with thoughtless Mirth I coursed the plain,
And hope itself was all I knew of pain.
For then, ev'n then, the little heart would beat
At times, while young Content forsook her seat,
And wild Impatience, panting upward, showed
Where tipped with gold the mountain-summits glowed.
Alas! the idle tale of man is found
Depicted in the dial's moral round;
With Hope Reflexion blends her social rays
To gild the total tablet of his days;   40
Yet still, the sport of some malignant Pow'r,
He knows but from its shade the present hour.

While, Memory at my side, I wander here,
Starts at the simplest sight th' unbidden tear,
A form discovered at the well-known seat,
A spot, that angles at the riv'let's feet,
The cot the ray of morning trav'ling nigh,
And sail that glides the well-known alders by.

But why, ungrateful, dwell on idle pain?
To shew her yet some joys to me remain,   50
Say, will my friend, with soft affection's ear,
The history of a poet's ev'ning hear?

---

[39] The quotation marks are Wordsworth's own and indicate a borrowing from the sonnet 'To the South Downs' (1784, l. 1) by Charlotte Smith (1748–1806), a poet he much appreciated.

[40] 'In the beginning of winter, these mountains, in the moonlight nights, are covered with immense quantities of woodcocks; which, in the dark nights, retire into the woods'.*

[41] Wordsworth's own quotation marks denote an allusion to a passage in Milton's prose work on freedom of the press, *Areopagitica*: 'There be delights, there be recreations and jolly pastimes that will fetch the day about from sun to sun, and rock the tedious year as in a delightful dream'.

When, in the south, the wan noon brooding still,
Breathed a pale steam around the glaring hill,
And shades of deep embattled clouds[42] were seen
Spotting the northern cliffs with lights between;
Gazing the tempting shades to them denyed,
When stood the shortened herds amid the tide,
Where, from the barren wall's unsheltered end,
Long rails into the shallow lake extend;   60
When schoolboys stretched their length upon the green,
And round the humming elm, a glimmering scene!
In the brown park, in flocks, the troubled deer
Shook the still twinkling tail and glancing ear;
When horses in the wall-girt intake stood,[43]
Unshaded, eying far below the flood,
Crouded behind the swain,[44] in mute distress,
With forward neck the closing gate to press;
And long, with wistful gaze, his walk surveyed
Till dipped his pathway in the river shade;   70

—Then Quiet led me up the huddling rill,
Bright'ning with water-breaks the sombrous gill;[45]
To where, while thick above the branches close,
In dark-brown bason its wild waves repose,
Inverted shrubs, and moss of darkest green,
Cling from the rocks, with pale wood-weeds between;
Save that, atop, the subtle sunbeams shine,
On withered briars that o'er the craggs recline;
Sole light admitted here, a small cascade,
Illumes with sparkling foam the twilight shade.   80
Beyond, along the visto of the brook,
Where antique roots its bustling path o'erlook,
The eye reposes on a secret bridge[46]
Half grey, half shagged with ivy to its ridge.

[42] *deep embattled clouds*: from Charlotte Smith's 'Written September, 1791' (l. 3); it also suggests a line from James Beattie's *The Minstrel* (1771/74, II, xii).

[43] 'The word *intake* is local, and signifies a mountain-inclosure'.*

[44] *Swain*: a young rustic.

[45] 'Gill is also, I believe, a term confined to this country. Glen, gill, and dingle, have the same meaning'.* The 'huddling rill' of the previous line might be compared to Milton's 'huddling brook' (*Comus*, 1. 495).

[46] 'The reader, who has made the tour of this country, will recognize in this description the features which characterize the lower waterfall in the gardens of Rydale'.* There are two waterfalls in the grounds of Rydal Hall. Although the upper one is the higher of the two, the Lower Falls were considered the finest by the discerning picturesque tourist.

—Sweet rill, farewel! To-morrow's noon again,
Shall hide me wooing long thy wildwood[47] strain;
But now the sun has gained his western road,
And eve's mild hour invites my steps abroad.

While, near the midway cliff, the silvered kite
In many a whistling circle wheels her flight;   90
Slant wat'ry lights, from parting clouds a-pace,
Travel along the precipice's base;
Chearing its naked waste of scattered stone
By lychens grey, and scanty moss o'er-grown,
Where scarce the foxglove peeps, and thistle's beard,
And desert stone-chat, all day long, is heard.

How pleasant, as the yellowing sun declines,
And with long rays and shades the landscape shines;
To mark the birches' stems all golden light,
That lit the dark slant woods with silvery white!   100
The willows weeping trees, that twinkling hoar,
Glanced oft upturned along the breezy shore,
Low bending o'er the coloured water, fold
Their moveless boughs and leaves like threads of gold;
The skiffs with naked masts at anchor laid,
Before the boat-house peeping thro' the shade;
Th' unwearied glance of woodman's echoed stroke;
And curling from the trees the cottage smoke.

Source: Stephen Gill, ed., *William Wordsworth* in *The Oxford Authors Series*, Oxford University Press, Oxford and New York, 1987, pp. 1–4.

William Wordsworth on 'The Sublime and the Beautiful'

Let me then invite the Reader to turn his eyes with me towards that cluster of Mountains at the Head of Windermere; it is probable that they will settle ere long upon the Pikes of Langdale & the black precipice contiguous to them.—If these objects be so distant that, while we look at

---

[47] Wildwood: wild, unfrequented woodland.

them, they are only thought of as the crown of a comprehensive Landscape; if our minds be not perverted by false theories, unless those mountains be seen under some accidents of nature, we shall receive from them a grand impression, and nothing more. But if they be looked at from a point which has brought us so near that the mountain is almost the sole object before our eyes, yet not so near but that the whole of it is visible, we shall be impressed with a sensation of sublimity.—And if this is analyzed, the body of this sensation would be found to resolve itself into three component parts: a sense of individual form or forms; a sense of duration; and a sense of power. The whole complex impression is made up of these elementary parts, & the effect depends upon their co-existence.

[. . .]

And this leads me to a remark which will remove the main difficulties of this investigation. Power awakens the sublime either when it rouses us to a sympathetic energy & calls upon the mind to grasp at something towards which it can make approaches but which it is incapable of attaining—yet so that it participates[48] force which is acting upon it; or, 2dly, by producing a humiliation or prostration of the mind before some external agency which it presumes not to make an effort to participate, but is absorbed in the contemplation of the might in the external power, &, as far as it has any consciousness of itself, its grandeur subsists in the naked fact of being conscious of external Power at once awful & immeasurable; so that, in both cases, the head & the front of the sensation[49] is intense unity. But if that Power which is exalted above our sympathy impresses the mind with personal fear, so as the sensation becomes more lively than the impression or thought of the exciting cause, then self-consideration & all its accompanying littleness takes place of[50] the sublime, & wholly excludes it.

[. . .]

Whence comes it, then, that that external power, to a union or communion with which we feel that we can make no approximation while it produces humiliation & submission, reverence or adoration, & all those sensations which may be denominated passive, does nevertheless place the mind in a state that is truly sublime?[51] As I have said before, this is done by the notion or image of intense unity, with which the Soul is occu-

---

[48] *participates*: in this context, 'receives part of'.
[49] Wordsworth is saying here that thought and feeling are linked.
[50] *takes place of*: takes precedence over.
[51] The question posed here is how can the mind respond to that which it cannot really intuit or rationalise?

pied or possessed.[52] But how is this produced or supported, &, when it remits, & the mind is distinctly conscious of his own being & existence, whence comes it that it willingly & naturally relapses into the same state? The cause of this is either that our physical nature has only to a certain degree been endangered, or that our moral Nature has not in the least degree been violated.—The point beyond which apprehensions for our physical nature consistent with sublimity may be carried, has been ascertained; &, with respect to power acting upon our moral or spiritual nature, by awakening energy either that would resist or that [?hopes] to participate, the sublime is called forth.[53]

Source: W. J. B. Owen and Jane Worthington Smyser, eds, *The Prose Works of William Wordsworth*, 3 vols, Oxford University Press, London, 1974, vol. II, pp. 350–1, 354–5.

William Wordsworth, 'There was a Boy'

There was a Boy, ye knew him well, ye Cliffs
And Islands of Winander![54] many a time,
At evening, when the stars had just begun
To move along the edges of the hills,
Rising or setting, would he stand alone,
Beneath the trees, or by the glimmering lake,
And there, with fingers interwoven, both hands
Press'd closely palm to palm and to his mouth
Uplifted, he, as through an instrument,
Blew mimic hootings to the silent owls[55]   10
That they might answer him. And they would shout
Across the wat'ry vale and shout again
Responsive to his call, with quivering peals,
And long halloos, and screams, and echoes loud

---

[52] The 'unity' to which Wordsworth alludes here is an aesthetic unity, where the mind simply 'feels' that it is part of the experience it is undergoing.

[53] 'Energy' is a power of mind corresponding to – Wordsworth argues – a concomitant power latent in the landscape.

[54] Windermere, a lake which contains a number of islands, mostly in its central reaches.

[55] In a note dictated in 1843 Wordsworth remarked that 'this practice of making an instrument of their own fingers is known to most boys, though some are more skilful at it than others'.

Redoubled and redoubled, a wild scene
Of mirth and jocund din. And, when it chanced
That pauses of deep silence mock'd his skill,
Then, sometimes, in that silence, while he hung
Listening, a gentle shock of mild surprize
Has carried far into his heart the voice   20
Of mountain torrents, or the visible scene
Would enter unawares into his mind
With all its solemn imagery, its rocks,
Its woods, and that uncertain heaven, receiv'd
Into the bosom of the steady lake.[56]

    Fair are the woods, and beauteous is the spot,
The vale where he was born: the Church-yard hangs
Upon a slope above the village school,[57]
And there along that bank when I have pass'd
At evening, I believe, that near his grave   30
A full half-hour together I have stood,
Mute – for he died when he was ten years old.

Source: William Wordsworth and Samuel Taylor Coleridge, *Lyrical Ballads*, R. L. Brett and A. R. Jones, eds, Methuen & Co. Ltd, London, 1968, pp. 134–5.

William Wordsworth, note to 'There was a Boy'

I have begun with one of the earliest processes of Nature in the development of this faculty. Guided by one of my own primary consciousnesses, I have represented a commutation and transfer of internal feelings, co-operating with external accidents to plant, for immortality, images of sound and sight, in the celestial soil of the Imagination. The Boy, there introduced, is listening, with something of a feverish and restless anxiety,

---

[56] In an essay of 1839 De Quincey recounts Wordsworth's observations to him on the same subject: 'I have remarked, from my earliest days, that, if . . . the attention is energetically braced up to an act of steady observation [and] should suddenly relax . . . any beautiful object, any impressive visual object . . . falling upon the eye, is carried to the heart with a power not known under any other circumstances'.

[57] At Hawkshead, that is.

for the recurrence of the riotous sounds which he had previously excited; and, at the moment when the intenseness of his mind is beginning to remit, he is surprised into a perception of the solemn and tranquillizing images which the Poem describes.

Source: William Wordsworth and Samuel Taylor Coleridge, *Lyrical Ballads*, R. L. Brett and A. R. Jones, eds, Methuen & Co. Ltd, London, 1968, p. 299.

William Wordsworth, 'There is an Eminence'

There is an Eminence, – of these our hills
The last that parleys with the setting sun.
We can behold it from our Orchard-seat,
And, when at evening we pursue our walk
Along the public way, this Cliff, so high
Above us, and so distant in its height,
Is visible, and often seems to send
Its own deep quiet to restore our hearts.
The meteors make of it a favorite haunt:
The star of Jove,[58] so beautiful and large   10
In mid heav'ns, is never half so fair
As when he shines above it. 'Tis in truth
The loneliest place we have among the clouds.
And She[59] who dwells with me, whom I have lov'd
With such communion, that no place on earth
Can ever be a solitude to me,
Hath said, this lonesome Peak shall bear my Name.

Source: William Wordsworth and Samuel Taylor Coleridge, *Lyrical Ballads*, R. L. Brett and A. R. Jones, eds, Methuen & Co. Ltd, London, 1968, p. 222.

[58] *Star of Jove*: Jupiter, brightest of the planets.
[59] Usually taken to be the poet's sister Dorothy Wordsworth.

William Wordsworth, two extracts from
The Prelude

– Was it for this[60]
That one, the fairest of all Rivers,[61] loved
To blend his murmurs with my Nurse's song
And from his alder shades and rocky falls,
And from his fords and shallows, sent a voice
That flowed along my dreams? For this, didst Thou,
O Derwent, travelling over the green Plains
Near my 'sweet Birthplace',[62] didst thou, beauteous Stream,
Make ceaseless music through the night and day
Which with its steady cadence, tempering   280
Our human waywardness, composed my thoughts
To more than infant softness, giving me,
Among the fretful dwellings of mankind,
A knowledge, a dim earnest, of the calm
Which Nature breathes among the hills and groves?
When, having left his Mountains, to the Towers
Of Cockermouth that beauteous River came,
Behind my Father's House he passed, close by,
Along the margin of our Terrace Walk.
He was a Playmate whom we dearly loved.   290
Oh! many a time have I, a five years' Child,
A naked Boy, in one delightful Rill,
A little Mill-race severed from his stream,
Made one long bathing of a summer's day,
Basked in the sun, and plunged, and basked again
Alternate all a summer's day, or coursed
Over the sandy fields, leaping through groves
Of yellow grundsel[63] or when crag and hill,
The woods, and distant Skiddaw's lofty height,[64]

[60] This is how the 1799 two-book *Prelude* opens; the context to the question is clarified in the headnote.

[61] As a later reference shows, this is the River Derwent which flows behind the house Wordsworth was born in at Cockermouth in the north-west of Cumbria.

[62] A quote from Coleridge's poem 'Frost at Midnight', l. 28.

[63] Ragwort (or ragweed) not groundsel, as *The Prelude* of 1850 makes clear.

[64] At just over 3,000 feet Skiddaw, which lies to the north of Derwentwater, is the fourth highest peak in the Lake District.

Were bronzed with a deep radiance, stood alone   300
Beneath the sky, as if I had been born
On Indian Plains,[65] and from my Mother's hut
Had run abroad in wantonness, to sport,
A naked Savage, in the thunder shower.

[. . .]

Nor, sedulous as I have been to trace
How Nature by extrinsic passion first
Peopled my mind with beauteous forms or grand
And made me love them,[66] may I well forget
How other pleasures have been mine, and joys
Of subtler origin; how I have felt,
Not seldom, even in that tempestuous time,
Those hallowed and pure motions of the sense
Which seem, in their simplicity, to own
An intellectual[67] charm, that calm delight   580
Which, if I err not, surely must belong
To those first-born affinities that fit
Our new existence to existing things,
And, in our dawn of being, constitute
The bond of union betwixt life and joy.

Yes, I remember, when the changeful earth,
And twice five seasons on my mind had stamped
The faces of the moving year,[68] even then,
A Child, I held unconscious intercourse
With the eternal Beauty, drinking in   590
A pure organic pleasure[69] from the lines
Of curling mist, or from the level plain
Of waters coloured by the steady clouds.
The Sands of Westmorland, the Creeks and Bays
Of Cumbria's[70] rocky limits, they can tell
How when the Sea threw off his evening shade
And to the Shepherd's huts beneath the crags

---

[65] The allusion is to North American Indians.

[66] At this stage the child is heedless of the way that nature is working because he experiences it passively.

[67] As commentators point out, the word 'intellectual' is consistently used to denote spiritual experience in *The Prelude*.

[68] In other words, when he was ten years of age.

[69] Drunk in immediately through the senses.

[70] Cumberland's.

Did send sweet notice of the rising moon,
How I have stood, to fancies such as these,
Engrafted in the tenderness of thought, 600
A stranger, linking with the spectacle
No conscious memory of a kindred sight,
And bringing with me no peculiar sense
Of quietness or peace,[71] yet I have stood,
Even while mine eye has moved o'er three long leagues
Of shining water, gathering, as it seemed,
Through every hair-breath of that field of light,
New pleasure, like a bee among the flowers.

Source: Stephen Gill, ed., *William Wordsworth* in *The Oxford Authors Series*, Oxford University Press, Oxford and New York, 1987, pp. 381–2, 389–90.

William Wordsworth, 'Airey-Force Valley'

    – Not a breath of air
Ruffles the bosom of this leafy glen.
From the brook's margin, wide around, the trees
Are stedfast as the rocks; the brook itself,
Old as the hills that feed it from afar,
Doth rather deepen than disturb the calm
Where all things else are still and motionless.
And yet, even now, a little breeze, perchance
Escaped from boisterous winds that rage without,
Has entered, by the sturdy oaks unfelt, 10
But to its gentle touch how sensitive
Is the light ash! that, pendent from the brow
Of yon dim cave, in seeming silence makes
A soft eye-music of slow-waving boughs,
Powerful almost as vocal harmony
To stay the wanderer's steps and soothe his thoughts.

[71] These experiences are 'unconditioned' ones, self-contained and enjoyed as ends in themselves.

Source: Stephen Gill, ed., *William Wordsworth* in *The Oxford Authors Series*, Oxford University Press, Oxford and New York, 1987, pp. 369–70.

William Wordsworth, extracts from *A Guide Through the District of the Lakes in the North of England, with a Description of the Scenery, etc. for the use of Tourists and Residents*

Reading (A) The 'visual interest' of mountains

In the ridge that divides Eskdale from Wasdale, granite is found; but the MOUNTAINS are for the most part composed of the stone by mineralogists termed schist, which, as you approach the plain country, gives place to limestone and free-stone; but schist being the substance of the mountains, the predominant *colour* of their *rocky* parts is bluish, or hoary grey—the general tint of the lichens with which the bare stone is encrusted. With this blue or grey colour is frequently intermixed a red tinge, proceeding from the iron that interveins the stone, and impregnates the soil. The iron is the principle of decomposition in these rocks; and hence, when they become pulverized, the elementary particles crumbling down, overspread in many places the steep and almost precipitous sides of the mountains with an intermixture of colours, like the compound hues of a dove's neck. When in the heat of advancing summer, the fresh green tint of the herbage has somewhat faded, it is again revived by the appearance of the fern profusely spread over the same ground: and, upon this plant, more than upon any thing else, do the changes which the seasons make in the colouring of the mountains depend. About the first week in October, the rich green, which prevailed through the whole summer, is usually passed away. The brilliant and various colours of the fern are then in harmony with the autumnal woods; bright yellow or lemon colour, at the base of the mountains, melting gradually, through orange, to a dark russet brown towards the summits, where the plant, being more exposed to the weather, is in a more advanced state of decay. Neither heath nor furze are *generally* found upon the *sides* of these mountains, though in many places they are adorned by those plants, so beautiful when in flower. We may add, that the mountains are of height sufficient to have the surface towards the summit softened by distance, and to imbibe the finest aërial hues. In common also with other mountains, their apparent forms and colours are perpetually changed by the clouds and vapours which float round them: the effect indeed of mist or haze, in a country of this character, is like that of magic. I have seen six or seven ridges rising above each other, all created in a moment by the vapours upon the side of a mountain, which, in its ordinary appearance, shewed not a projecting point to furnish even a hint for such an operation.

I will take this opportunity of observing, that they who have studied the appearances of nature feel that the superiority, in point of visual interest, of mountainous over other countries—is more strikingly displayed in winter than in summer. This, as must be obvious, is partly owing to the *forms* of the mountains, which, of course, are not affected by the seasons; but also, in no small degree, to the greater variety that exists in their winter than their summer *colouring*. This variety is such, and so harmoniously preserved, that it leaves little cause of regret when the splendour of autumn is passed away. The oak-coppices, upon the sides of the mountains, retain russet leaves; the birch stands conspicuous with its silver stem and puce-coloured twigs; the hollies, with green leaves and scarlet berries, have come forth to view from among the deciduous trees, whose summer foliage had concealed them; the ivy is now plentifully apparent upon the stems and boughs of the trees, and upon the steep rocks. In places of the deep summer-green of the herbage and fern, many rich colours play into each other over the surface of the mountains; turf (the tints of which are interchangeably tawny-green, olive, and brown,) beds of withered fern, and grey rocks, being harmoniously blended together. The mosses and lichens are never so fresh and flourishing as in winter, if it be not a season of frost; and their minute beauties prodigally adorn the foreground. Wherever we turn, we find these productions of nature, to which winter is rather favourable than unkindly, scattered over the walls, banks of earth, rocks and stones, and upon the trunks of trees, with the intermixture of several species of small fern, now green and fresh; and, to the observing passenger, their forms and colours are a source of inexhaustable admiration. Add to this the hoar-frost and snow, with all the varieties they create, and which volumes would not be sufficient to describe. I will content myself with one instance of the colouring produced by snow, which may not be uninteresting to painters. It is extracted from the memorandum-book of a friend; and for its accuracy I can speak, having been an eye-witness of the appearance. "I observed," says he, "the beautiful effect of the drifted snow upon the mountains, and the perfect *tone* of colour. From the top of the mountains downwards a rich olive was produced by the powdery snow and the grass, which olive was warmed with a little brown, and in this way harmoniously combined, by insensible gradations, with the white. The drifting took away the monotony of snow; and the whole vale of Grasmere, seen from the terrace walk in Easedale, was as varied, perhaps more so, than even in the pomp of autumn. In the distance was Loughrigg-Fell, the basin-wall of the lake: this, from the summit downward, was a rich orange-olive; then the lake of a bright olive-green, nearly the same tint as the snow-powdered mountain tops and high slopes in Easedale; and lastly the church, with its firs, forming the centre of the view. Next to the church came nine distinguishable hills, six of them with woody sides turned towards us, all of them oak-copses with their bright red leaves and snow-powdered twigs; these hills—so variously situated in relation to each other, and to the view in general, so variously powdered, some only enough to give the herbage a rich brown tint, one intensely white and lighting up all the others—were yet so placed, as in the most inobtrusive manner to harmonise by contrast with a perfect naked, snowless bleak summit in the far distance."

Reading (B) The 'margins of these lakes'

I shall now speak of the LAKES of this country. The form of the lake is most perfect when, like Derwent-water, and some of the smaller lakes, it least resembles that of a river;—I mean, when being looked at from any given point where the whole may be seen at once, the width of it bears such proportion to the length, that, however the outline may be diversified by far-receding bays, it never assumes the shape of a river, and is contemplated with that placid and quiet feeling which belongs peculiarly to the lake—as a body of still water under the influence of no current; reflecting therefore the clouds, the light, and all the imagery of the sky and surrounding hills; expressing also and making visible the changes of the atmosphere, and motions of the lightest breeze, and subject to agitation only from the winds—

> The visible scene
> Would enter unawares into his mind
> With all its solemn imagery, its rocks,
> Its woods, and that uncertain heaven received
> Into the bosom of the *steady* lake![72]

---

[72] From Wordsworth, *The Prelude* V. ll. 409–13. 1805 version (with minor changes). These lines had appeared earlier in 'There was a Boy', in *Lyrical Ballads* (1800).

It must be noticed, as a favourable characteristic of the lakes of this country, that, though several of the largest, such as Winandermere, Ulswater, Hawswater, do, when the whole length of them is commanded from an elevated point, loose somewhat of the peculiar form of the lake, and assume the resemblance of a magnificent river; yet, as their shape is winding, (particularly that of Ulswater and Hawswater) when the view of the whole is obstructed by those barriers which determine the windings, and the spectator is confined to one reach, the appropriate feeling is revived; and one lake may thus in succession present to the eye the essential characteristic of many. But, though the forms of the large lakes have this advantage, it is nevertheless favourable to the beauty of the country that the largest of them are comparatively small; and that the same vale generally furnishes a succession of lakes, instead of being filled with one. The vales in North Wales, as hath been observed, are not formed for the reception of lakes; those of Switzerland, Scotland, and this part of the North of England, *are* so formed; but, in Switzerland and Scotland, the proportion of diffused water is often too great, as at the lake of Geneva for instance, and in most of the Scotch lakes. No doubt it sounds magnificent and flatters the imagination, to hear at a distance of expanses of water so many leagues in length and miles in width; and such ample room may be delightful to the fresh-water sailor, scudding with a lively breeze amid the rapidly-shifting scenery. But, who ever travelled along the banks of Loch-Lomond, variegated as the lower part is by islands, without feeling that a speedier termination of the long vista of blank water would be acceptable; and without wishing for an interposition of green meadows, trees, and cottages, and a sparkling stream to run by his side? In fact, a notion, of grandeur, as connected with magnitude, has seduced persons of taste into a general mistake upon this subject. It is much more desirable, for the purposes of pleasure, that lakes should be numerous, and small or middle-sized, than large, not only for communication by walks and rides, but for variety, and for recurrence of similar appearances. To illustrate this by one instance:—how pleasing is it to have a ready and frequent opportunity of watching, at the outlet of a lake, the stream pushing its way among the rocks in lively contrast with the stillness from which it has escaped; and how amusing to compare its noisy and turbulent motions with the gentle playfulness of the breezes, that may be starting up or wandering here and there over the faintly-rippled surface of the broad water! I may add, as a general remark, that, in lakes of great width, the shores cannot be distinctly seen at the same time, and therefore contribute little to mutual illustration and ornament; and, if the opposite shores are out of sight of each other, like those of the American and Asiatic lakes, then unfortunately the traveller is reminded of a nobler object; he has the blankness of a sea-prospect without the grandeur and accompanying sense of power.

As the comparatively small size of the lakes in the North of England is favourable to the production of variegated landscape their *boundary-line* also is for the most part gracefully or boldly indented. That uniformity which prevails in the primitive frame of the lower grounds among all chains or clusters of mountains where large bodies of still water are bedded, is broken by the *secondary* agents of nature, ever at work to supply the deficiencies of the mould in which things were originally cast. Using the word *deficiencies*, I do not speak with reference to those stronger emotions which a region of mountains is peculiarly fitted to excite. The bases of those huge barriers may run for a long space in straight lines, and these parallel to each other; the opposite sides of a profound vale may ascend as exact counterparts, or in mutual reflection, like the billows of a troubled sea; and the impression be, from its very simplicity, more awful and sublime. Sublimity is the result of Nature's first great dealings with the superficies of the earth; but the general tendency of her subsequent operations is towards the production of beauty; by a multiplicity of symmetrical parts uniting in a consistent whole. This is every where exemplified along the margins of these lakes. Masses of rock, that have been precipitated from the heights into the area of waters, lie in some places like stranded ships; or have acquired the compact structure of jutting piers; or project in little peninsulas crested with native wood. The smallest rivulet—one whose silent influx is scarcely noticeable in a season of dry weather—so faint is the dimple made by it on the surface of the smooth lake—will be found to have been not useless in shaping, by its deposits of gravel and soil in time of flood, a curve that would not otherwise have existed. But the more powerful brooks, encroaching upon the level of the lake, have, in course of time, given birth to ample promontories of sweeping outline that contrasts boldly with the longitudinal base of the steeps on the opposite shore; while their flat or gently-sloping surfaces never fail to introduce, into the midst of desolation and barrenness, the elements of fertility, even where the habitations of men may not have been raised. These alluvial promontories, however, threaten, in some places, to bisect the waters which they have long adorned; and, in course of ages, they will cause some of the lakes to dwindle into numerous and insignificant pools; which, in their turn, will finally be filled up. But, checking these intrusive calculations, let us rather be content with appearances as they are, and pursue in imagination the meandering shores, whether rugged steeps, admitting of no cultivation, descend into the water; or gently-sloping lawns and woods, or flat and fertile meadows stretch between the margin of the lake and the mountains. Among minuter recommendations will be noticed, especially along bays exposed to the setting-in of strong-winds, the curved rim of fine blue gravel, thrown up in course of time by the waves, half of it perhaps gleaming from under the water, and the corresponding half of a lighter hue; and in other parts bordering the lake, groves, if I may so call them, of reeds and bulrushes; or plots of water-lilies lifting up their large target-shaped leaves to the breeze, while the white flower is heaving upon the wave.

Reading (C) Mountain tarns

The *mountain* Tarns can only be recommended to the notice of the inquisitive traveller who has time to spare. They are difficult of access and naked; yet some of them are, in their permanent forms, very grand; and there are accidents of things which would make the meanest of them interesting. At all events, one of these pools is an acceptable sight to the mountain wanderer; not merely as an incident that diversifies the prospect, but as forming in his mind a centre or conspicuous point to which objects, otherwise disconnected or insubordinated, may be referred. Some few have a varied outline, with bold heath-clad promontories; and, as they mostly lie at the foot of a steep precipice, the water where the sun is not shining upon it, appears black and sullen; and, round the margin, huge stones and masses of rock are scattered; some defying conjecture as to the means by which they came thither; and others obviously fallen from on high—the contribution of ages! A not unpleasing sadness is induced by this perplexity, and these images of decay; while the prospect of a body of pure water unattended with groves and other cheerful rural images by which fresh water is usually accompanied, and unable to give furtherance to the meagre vegetation around it—excites a sense of some repulsive power strongly put forth, and thus deepens the melancholy natural to such scenes. Nor is the feeling of solitude often more forcibly or more solemnly impressed than by the side of one of these mountain pools: though desolate and forbidding, it seems a distinct place to repair to; yet where the visitants must be rare, and there can be no disturbance. Water-fowl flock hither; and the lonely Angler may here be seen; but the imagination, not content with this scanty allowance of society, is tempted to attribute a voluntary power to every change which takes place in such a spot, whether it be the breeze that wanders over the surface of the water, or the splendid lights of evening resting upon it in the midst of awful precipices.

There, sometimes does a leaping fish
Send through the tarn a lonely cheer;
The crags repeat the raven's croak
In symphony austere:
Thither the rainbow comes, the cloud,
And mists that spread the flying shroud,
And sunbeams, and the sounding blast.[73]

Reading (D) The woods

The WOODS consist chiefly of oak, ash, and birch, and here and there
Wych-elm, with underwood of hazle, the white and black thorn, and hollies; in moist places alders and willows abound; and yews among the
rocks. Formerly the whole country must have been covered with wood
to a great height up the mountains; where native Scotch firs[74] must have
grown in great profusion, as they do in the northern part of Scotland to
this day. But not one of these old inhabitants has existed, perhaps for
some hundreds of years; the beautiful traces, however, of the universal
sylvan[75] appearance the country formerly had, yet survive in the native
coppice-woods that have been protected by inclosures, and also in the
forest-trees and hollies, which, though disappearing fast, are yet scattered both over the inclosed and uninclosed parts of the mountains. The
same is expressed by the beauty and intricacy with which the fields and
coppice-woods are often intermingled: the plough of the first settlers
having followed naturally the veins of richer, dryer, or less stony soil; and
thus it has shaped out an intermixture of wood and lawn, with a grace
and wildness, which it would have been impossible for the hand of studied art to produce. Other trees have been introduced within these last
fifty years, such as beeches, larches, limes, &c. and plantations of firs,
seldom with advantage, and often with great injury to the appearance of
the country; but the sycamore (which I believe was brought into this
island from Germany, not more than two hundred years ago) has long
been the favourite of the cottagers; and, with the fir, has been chosen to
screen their dwellings: and is sometimes found in the fields whither the
winds or the waters may have carried its seeds.

---

[73] From Wordsworth, *Fidelity* (published 1807), ll. 25–31, with some minor alterations to
punctuation.

[74] This species of fir is in character much superior to the American which has usurped its
place: Where the fir is planted for ornament, let it be by all means of the aboriginal species,
which can only be procured from the Scotch nurseries.*

[75] A squirrel (so I have heard the old people of Wytheburn say) might have gone from their
chapel to Keswick without alighting on the ground.*

Reading (E) The 'most intense cravings for the tranquil, the lovely and the perfect'

It has been said that in human life there are moments worth ages. In a more subdued tone of sympathy may we affirm, that in the climate of England there are, for the lover of nature, days which are worth whole months,—I might say—even years. One of these favoured days sometimes occurs in spring-time, when the soft air is breathing over the blossoms and new-born verdure, which inspired Buchanan[76] with his beautiful Ode to the first of May; the air, which, in the luxuriance of his fancy, he likens to that of the golden age,—to that which gives motion to the funereal cypresses on the banks of Lethe,[77]—to the air which is to salute beatified spirits when expiatory fires shall have consumed the earth with all her habitations. But it is in autumn that days of such affecting influence most frequently intervene;—the atmosphere seems refined, and the sky rendered more crystalline, as the vivifying heat of the year abates; the lights and shadows are more delicate; the coloring is richer and more finely harmonized; and, in this season of stillness, the ear being unoccupied, or only gently excited, the sense of vision becomes more susceptible of its appropriate enjoyments. A resident in a country like this which we are treating of, will agree with me, that the presence of a lake is indispensable to exhibit in perfection the beauty of one of these days; and he must have experienced, while looking on the unruffled waters, that the imagination, by their aid, is carried into recesses of feeling otherwise impenetrable. The reason of this is, that the heavens are not only brought down into the bosom of the earth, but that the earth is mainly looked at, and thought of, through the medium of a purer element. The happiest time is when the equinoxial gales are departed; but their fury may probably be called to mind by the sight of a few shattered boughs, whose leaves do not differ in colour from the faded foliage of the stately oaks from which these relics of the storm depend: all else speaks of tranquillity;—not a breath of air, no restlessness of insects, and not a moving object perceptible—except the clouds gliding in the depths of the lake, or the traveller passing along, an inverted image, whose motion seems governed by the quiet of a time, to which its archetype, the living person, is, perhaps, insensible:—or it may happen, that the figure of one of the larger birds, a raven or a heron, is crossing silently among the reflected clouds, while the voice of the real bird, from the element aloft, gently awakens in the spectator the recollection of appetites and

[76] George Buchanan (1506–82), scholar and poet: the ode would have been composed in Latin.

[77] One of the rivers of the Underworld, to which Latin poets frequently referred.

instincts, pursuits and occupations, that deform and agitate the world, – yet have no power to prevent nature from putting on an aspect capable of satisfying the most intense cravings for the tranquil, the lovely, and the perfect, to which man, the noblest of her creatures, is subject.

Reading (F) Cottages

And to begin with the COTTAGES. They are scattered over the vallies, and under the hill sides, and on the rocks; and, even to this day, in the more retired dales, without any intrusion of more assuming buildings;

> Cluster'd like stars some few, but single most,
> And lurking dimly in their shy retreats,
> Or glancing on each other cheerful looks,
> Like separated stars with clouds between.   MS.[78]

The dwelling-houses, and contiguous out-houses, are, in many instances, of the colour of the native rock, out of which they have been built; but, frequently the Dwelling or Fire-house, as it is ordinarily called, has been distinguished from the barn or byer by rough-cast and white wash, which, as the inhabitants are not hasty in renewing it, in a few years acquires, by the influence of weather, a tint at once sober and variegated. As these houses have been, from father to son, inhabited by persons engaged in the same occupations, yet necessarily with changes in their circumstances, they have received without incongruity additions and accommodations adapted to the needs of each successive occupant, who, being for the most part proprietor, was at liberty to follow his own fancy: so that these humble dwellings remind the contemplative spectator of a production of nature, and may (using a strong expression) rather be said to have grown than to have been erected;—to have risen, by an instinct of their own, out of the native rock—so little is there in them of formality, such is their wildness and beauty. Among the numerous recesses and projections in the walls and in the different stages of their roofs, are seen bold and harmonious effects of contrasted sunshine and shadow. It is a favourable circumstance, that the strong winds which sweep down the vallies, induced the inhabitants, at a time when the materials for building were easily procured, to furnish many of these dwellings with substantial porches; and such as have not this defence, are seldom unprovided with a projection of two large slates over their thresholds. Nor will the singular beauty of the chimneys escape the eye of the attentive traveller. Sometimes a low chimney, almost upon a level with the

---

[78] Wordsworth, *The Recluse* (first published 1888), I, ll. 122–5.

roof, is overlaid with a slate, supported upon four slender pillars, to prevent the wind from driving the smoke down the chimney. Others are of
a quadrangular shape, rising one or two feet above the roof: which low
square is often surmounted by a tall cylinder, giving to the cottage chimney the most beautiful shape in which it is ever seen. Nor will it be too
fanciful or refined to remark, that there is a pleasing harmony between a
tall chimney of this circular form, and the living column of smoke,
ascending from it through the still air. These dwellings, mostly built, as
has been said, of rough unhewn stone, are roofed with slates, which were
rudely taken from the quarry before the present art of splitting them was
understood, and are, therefore, rough and uneven in their surface, so
that both the coverings and sides of the houses have furnished places of
rest for the seeds of lichens, mosses, ferns, and flowers. Hence buildings,
which in their very form call to mind the processes of nature, do thus,
clothed in part with a vegetable garb, appear to be received into the
bosom of the living principle of things, as it acts and exists among the
woods and fields; and, by their colour and their shape, affectingly direct
the thoughts to that tranquil course of nature and simplicity, along which
the humble-minded inhabitants have, through so many generations,
been led. Add the little garden with its shed for beehives, its small bed of
pot-herbs, and its borders and patches of flowers for Sunday posies, with
sometimes a choice of few too much prized to be plucked; an orchard of
proportioned size; a cheese-press, often supported by some tree near the
door; a cluster of embowering sycamores for summer shade; with a tall
fir, through which the winds sing when other trees are leafless; the little
rill or household spout murmuring in all seasons;—combine these incidents and images together, and you have the representative idea of a
mountain-cottage in this country so beautifully formed in itself, and so
richly adorned by the hand of nature.

Reading (G) The 'profanation' of the landscape

SUCH, as hath been said, was the appearance of things till within the
last sixty years. A practice, denominated Ornamental Gardening, was at
that time becoming prevalent over England. In union with an admiration
of this art, and in some instances in opposition to it, had been generated
a relish for select parts of natural scenery: and Travellers, instead of confining their observations to Towns, Manufactories, or Mines, began (a
thing till then unheard of) to wander over the island in search of
sequestered spots, distinguished as they might accidentally have learned,
for the sublimity or beauty of the forms of Nature there to be seen. Dr.
Brown,[79] the celebrated Author of the Estimate of the Manners and

Principles of the Times, published a letter to a friend, in which the attractions of the Vale of Keswick were delineated with a powerful pencil, and the feeling of a genuine Enthusiast. Gray,[80] the Poet, followed: he died soon after his forlorn and melancholy pilgrimage to the Vale of Keswick, and the record left behind him of what he had seen and felt in this journey, excited that pensive interest with which the human mind is ever disposed to listen to the farewell words of a man of genius. The journal of Gray feelingly showed how the gloom of ill health and low spirits had been irradiated by objects, which the Author's powers of mind enabled him to describe with distinctness and unaffected simplicity. Every reader of this journal must have been impressed with the words which conclude his notice of the Vale of Grasmere:—"Not a single red tile, no flaring gentleman's house or garden-wall, breaks in upon the repose of this little unsuspected paradise; but all is peace, rusticity, and happy poverty, in its neatest and most becoming attire."

What is here so justly said of Grasmere applied almost equally to all its sister Vales. It was well for the undisturbed pleasure of the Poet that he had no forebodings of the change which was soon to take place; and it might have been hoped that these words, indicating how much the charm of what *was*, depended upon what was *not*, would of themselves have preserved the ancient franchises of this and other kindred mountain retirements from trespass; or (shall I dare to say?) would have secured scenes so consecrated from profanation. The lakes had now become celebrated; visitors flocked hither from all parts of England; the fancies of some were smitten so deeply, that they became settlers; and the Islands of Derwentwater and Winandermere, as they offered the strongest temptation, were the first places seized upon, and were instantly defaced by the intrusion.

The venerable wood that had grown for centuries round the small house called St. Herbert's Hermitage, had indeed some years before been felled by its native proprietor, and the whole island planted anew with Scotch firs, left to spindle up by each other's side—a melancholy phalanx, defying the power of the winds, and disregarding the regret of the spectator, who might otherwise have cheated himself into a belief, that some of the decayed remains of those oaks, the place of which was in this manner usurped, had been planted by the Hermit's own hand: This sainted spot, however, suffered comparatively little injury. At the bidding of an alien improver, the Hind's Cottage, upon Vicar's island, in the same lake, with its embowering sycamores and cattle-shed, disappeared from

[79] See above, footnote 19, p. 33.
[80] See above, footnote 3, p. 15.

the corner where they stood; and right in the middle, and upon the precise point of the island's highest elevation, rose a tall square habitation, with four sides exposed like an astronomer's observatory, or a warren-house reared upon an eminence for the detection of depredators, or, like the temple of Œolus,[81] where all the winds pay him obeisance. Round this novel structure, but at a respectful distance, platoons of firs were stationed, as if to protect their commander when weather and time should somewhat have shattered his strength. Within the narrow limits of this island were typified also the state and strength of a kingdom, and its religion as it had been, and was,—for neither was the druidical circle uncreated, nor the church of the present establishment; nor the stately pier, emblem of commerce and navigation; nor the fort to deal out thunder upon the approaching invader. The taste of a succeeding proprietor rectified the mistakes as far as was practicable, and has ridded the spot of its puerilities. The church, after being docked of its steeple, is applied both ostensibly and really, to the purpose for which the body of the pile was actually erected, namely, a boat-house; the fort is demolished; and, without indignation on the part of the spirits of the ancient Druids who officiated at the circle upon the opposite hill, the mimic arrangement of stones, with its *sanctum sanctorum*, has been swept away.

The present instance has been singled out, extravagant as it is, because, unquestionably, this beautiful country has, in numerous other places, suffered from the same spirit, though not clothed exactly in the same form, nor active in an equal degree. It will be sufficient here to utter a regret for the changes that have been made upon the principal Island at Winandermere, and in its neighbourhood. What could be more unfortunate than the taste that suggested the paring of the shores, and surrounding with an embankment this spot of ground, the natural shape of which was so beautiful! An artificial appearance has thus been given to the whole, while infinite varieties of minute beauty have been destroyed. Could not the margin of this noble island be given back to nature? Winds and waves work with a careless and graceful hand: and, should they in some places carry away a portion of the soil, the trifling loss would be amply compensated by the additional spirit, dignity, and loveliness, which these agents and the other powers of nature would soon communicate to what was left behind. As to the larch-plantations upon the main shore,—they who remember the original appearance of the rocky steeps, scattered over with native hollies and ashtrees, will be prepared to agree with what I shall have to say hereafter upon plantations[82] in general.

[81] Œolus: god of the winds, in Greek mythology.
[82] These are disappearing fast, under the management of the present Proprietor, and native wood is resuming its place.*

But, in truth, no one can now travel through the more frequented tracts, without being offended, at almost every turn, by an introduction of discordant objects, disturbing that peaceful harmony of form and colour, which had been through a long lapse of ages most happily preserved.

All gross transgressions of this kind originate, doubtless, in a feeling natural and honourable to the human mind, viz, the pleasure which it receives from distinct ideas, and from the perception of order, regularity, and contrivance. Now, unpractised minds receive these impressions only from objects that are divided from each other by strong lines of demarcation; hence the delight with which such minds are smitten by formality and harsh contrast. But I would beg of those who are eager to create the means of such gratification, first carefully to study what already exists; and they will find, in a country so lavishly gifted by nature, an abundant variety of forms marked out with a precision that will satisfy their desires. Moreover, a new habit of pleasure will be formed opposite to this, arising out of the perception of the fine gradations by which in nature one thing passes away into another, and the boundaries that constitute individuality disappear in one instance only to be revived elsewhere under a more alluring form. The hill of Dunmallet, at the foot of Ulswater, was once divided into different portions, by avenues of fir-trees, with a green and almost perpendicular lane descending down the steep hill through each avenue;—contrast this quaint appearance with the image of the same hill overgrown with self-planted wood,—each tree springing up in the situation best suited to its kind, and with that shape which the situation constrained or suffered it to take. What endless melting and playing into each other of forms and colours does the one offer to a mind at once attentive and active; and how insipid and lifeless, compared with it, appear those parts of the former exhibition with which a child, a peasant perhaps, or a citizen unfamiliar with natural imagery, would have been most delighted!

The disfigurement which this country has undergone, has not, however, proceeded wholly from the common feelings of human nature which have been referred to as the primary sources of bad taste in rural imagery; another cause must be added, that has chiefly shown itself in its effect upon buildings. I mean a warping of the natural mind occasioned by a consciousness that, this country being an object of general admiration, every new house would be looked at and commented upon either for approbation or censure. Hence all the deformity and ungracefulness that ever pursue the steps of constraint or affectation. Persons, who in Leicestershire or Northamptonshire would probably have built a modest dwelling like those of their sensible neighbours, have been turned out of their course; and, acting a part, no wonder if, having had little experience, they act it ill. The craving for prospect, also, which is immoderate, particularly in new settlers, has rendered it impossible that buildings, whatever might have been their architecture, should in most instances be ornamental to the landscape; rising as they do from the summits of naked hills in staring contrast to the snugness and privacy of the ancient houses.

Reading (H) Respecting 'the spirit of the place'

The principle taken as our guide, viz. that the house should be so formed, and of such apparent size and colour, as to admit of its being gently incorporated with the works of nature, should also be applied to the management of the grounds and plantations, and is here more urgently needed; for it is from abuses in this department, far more even than from the introduction of exotics in architecture (if the phrase may be used), that this country has suffered. Larch and fir plantations have been spread, not merely with a view to profit, but in many instances for the sake of ornament. To those who plant for profit, and are thrusting every other tree out of the way, to make room for their favourite, the larch, I would utter first a regret, that they should have selected these lovely vales for their vegetable manufactory, when there is so much barren and irreclaimable land in the neighbouring moors, and in other parts of the island, which might have been had for this purpose at a far cheaper rate. And I will also beg leave to represent to them, that they ought not to be carried away by flattering promises from the speedy growth of this tree; because in rich soils and sheltered situations, the wood, though it thrives fast, is full of sap, and of little value; and is, likewise, very subject to ravage from the attacks of insects, and from blight. Accordingly, in Scotland, where planting is much better understood, and carried on upon an incomparably larger scale than among us, good soil and sheltered situations are appropriated to the oak, the ash, and other deciduous trees; and the larch is now generally confined to barren and exposed ground. There the plant, which is a hardy one, is of slower growth; much less liable to injury; and the timber is of better quality. But the circumstances of many permit, and their taste leads them, to plant with little regard to profit; and there are others, less wealthy, who have such a lively feeling of the native beauty of these scenes, that they are laudably not unwilling to make some sacrifices to heighten it. Both these classes of persons, I would entreat to enquire of themselves wherein that beauty which they admire consists. They would then see that, after the feeling has been gratified that prompts us to gather round our dwelling a few flowers and shrubs, which from the circumstance of their not being native, may, by their very looks, remind us that they owe their existence to our hands, and their prosperity to our care; they will see that, after this natural desire has been provided for, the course of all beyond has been predetermined by the spirit of the place. Before I proceed, I will remind those who are not satisfied with the restraint thus laid upon them, that they are liable to a charge of inconsistency, when they are so eager to change the face of that country, whose native attractions, by the act of erecting their habitations in it, they have so emphatically acknowledged. And surely there is not a single spot that would not have, if well managed, sufficient dignity to support itself, unaided by the productions of other climates, or by elaborate decorations which might be becoming elsewhere.

Reading (I) A sense of stability and permanence

After all, it is upon the *mind* which a traveller brings along with him that his acquisitions, whether of pleasure or profit, must principally depend.—May I be allowed a few words on this subject?

Nothing is more injurious to genuine feeling than the practice of hastily and ungraciously depreciating the face of one country by comparing it with that of another. True it is Qui *bene* distinguit bene *docet*,[83] yet fastidiousness is a wretched travelling companion; and the best guide to which, in matters of taste we can entrust ourselves, is a disposition to be pleased. For example, if a traveller be among the Alps, let him surrender up his mind to the fury of the gigantic torrents, and take delight in the contemplation of their almost irresistible violence, without complaining of the monotony of their foaming course, or being disgusted with the muddiness of the water—apparent even where it is violently agitated. In Cumberland and Westmorland, let not the comparative weakness of the streams prevent him from sympathising with such impetuosity as they possess; and, making the most of the present objects, let him, as he justly may do, observe with admiration the unrivalled brilliancy of the water, and that variety of motion, mood, and character, that arises out of the want of those resources by which the power of the streams in the Alps is supported.—Again, with respect to the mountains; though these are comparatively of diminutive size, though there is little of perpetual snow, and no voice of summer-avalanches is heard among them; and though traces left by the ravage of the elements are here comparatively rare and unimpressive, yet out of this very deficiency proceeds

[83] *Qui bene distinguit bene docet*: 'Those capable of making fine distinctions make good teachers.'

a sense of stability and permanence that is, to many minds, more grateful—

> While the course rushes to the sweeping breeze
> Sigh forth their ancient melodies.[84]

Among the Alps are few places that do not preclude this feeling of tranquil sublimity. Havoc, and ruin, and desolation, and encroachment, are everywhere more or less obtruded; and it is difficult, notwithstanding the naked loftiness of the *pikes*, and the snow-capped summits of the *mounts*, to escape from the depressing sensation, that the whole are in a rapid process of dissolution; and, were it not that the destructive agency must abate as the heights diminish, would, in time to come, be levelled with the plains. Nevertheless, I would relish to the utmost the demonstrations of every species of power at work to effect such changes.

Source: P. Bicknell, ed., *The Illustrated Wordsworth's Guide to the Lakes*, Web and Bower, Exeter, 1984. The text used here is *A Guide Through the District of the Lakes in the North of England, with a Description of the Scenery, etc. for the use of Tourists and Residents*, fifth edition, with considerable additions by William Wordsworth, Hudson and Nicholson, Kendal, 1835. Extracts taken from pp. 70–1, 75–8, 85, 87–8, 91, 105–7, 112–18, 126–8, 145.

[84] Wordsworth, *The Pass of Kirkstone* (published 1820), ll. 39–40. The poem was later entitled "Ode: The Pass of Kirkstone" and included in full later in the *Guide*.

Robert Owen,
A New View of Society

Robert Owen (1771–1858), entrepreneur and social reformer, was a controversial personality who profited enormously from his enterprise in the era of early industrialisation and then set about trying to remedy its excesses. Much of his thinking, which found best expression in the essays on *A New View of Society*, derived from his own experience managing cotton mills, most famously at New Lanark, which became a test-bed for his reforms. There and elsewhere he strongly emphasised the importance of environment, education, and ultimately, co-operation. The essays, four in number, were written at different times from 1812, initially published as pamphlets during 1813–14 and then combined into a single volume (the so-called 2nd edition of 1816). The text here, approximately half the original, tries to convey the flavour of the whole work, and by paraphrasing particularly long-winded sections provides a clear focus on Owen's main 'principles'. Many of these still have resonance for our own times, particularly the roles of the individual and government in society.

The shortened and paraphrased sections appear in italics and the editorial sub-headings are designed to emphasise the main subject matter of each section of Owen's text.

First Essay

Character Formation and Mistaken Principles

[Original Dedication of First Essay. Omitted in subsequent Editions.]
to
WILLIAM WILBERFORCE ESQ., M.P.

"Any general character, from the best to the worst, from the most ignorant to the most enlightened, may be given to any community, even to the world at large, by the application of proper means; which means are to a great extent at the command and under the control of whose [*sic*] who have influence in the affairs of men."

According to the last returns under the Population Act, the poor and working Classes of Great Britain and Ireland have been found to exceed fifteen millions of persons, or nearly three-fourths of the population of the British Islands.

The characters of these persons are now permitted to be very generally formed without proper guidance or direction, and, in many cases, under circumstances which directly impel them to a course of extreme vice and misery; thus rendering them the worst and most dangerous subjects in the empire; while the far greater part of the remainder of the community are educated upon the most mistaken principles of human nature, such, indeed, as cannot fail to produce a general conduct throughout society, totally unworthy of the character of rational beings.

The first thus unhappily situated are the poor and the uneducated profligate among the working classes, who are now trained to commit crimes, for the commission of which they are afterwards punished.

The second is the remaining mass of the population, who are now instructed to believe, or at least to acknowledge, that certain principles are unerringly true, and to act as though they were grossly false; thus filling the world with folly and inconsistency, and making society, throughout all its ramifications, a scene of insincerity and counteraction.

In this state the world has continued to the present time; its evils have been and are continually increasing; they cry aloud, for efficient corrective measures, which if we longer delay, general disorder must ensue.

Based on the fundamental principle that character formation can be governed, non-sectarian, non-partisan attempts must be made to improve society:

The chief object of these Essays is to assist and forward investigations of such vital importance to the well being of this country, and of society in general.

The view of the subject which is about to be given has arisen from extensive experience for upwards of twenty years, during which period its truth and importance have been proved by multiplied experiments. That the writer may not be charged with precipitation or presumption, he has had the principle and its consequences examined, scrutinised, and fully canvassed, by some of the most learned, intelligent, and competent characters of the present day: who, on every principle and duty as well as of interest, if they had discovered error in either, would have exposed it; – but who, on the contrary, have fairly acknowledged their incontrovertible truth and practical importance.

Assured, therefore, this his principles are true, he proceeds with confidence, and courts the most ample and free discussion of the subject;

courts it for the sake of humanity – for the sake of his fellow creatures – millions of whom experience sufferings which, were they to be unfolded, would compel those who govern the world to exclaim – "Can these things exist, and we have no knowledge of them?" But they do exist – and even the heartrending statements which were made known to the public during the discussions upon Negro slavery, do not exhibit more afflicting scenes, than those which, in various parts of the world, daily arise from the injustice of society towards itself; from the inattention of mankind to the circumstances which incessantly surround them; and from the want of a correct knowledge of human nature in those who govern and control the affairs of men.

If these circumstances did not exist to an extent almost incredible, it would be unnecessary now to contend for a principle regarding Man, which scarcely requires more than to be fairly stated to make it self-evident.

This principle is, that *"Any general character, from the best to the worst, from the most ignorant to the most enlightened, may be given to any community, even to the world at large, by the application of proper means; which means are to a great extent at the command and under the control of those who have influence in the affairs of men."*

The principle as now stated is a broad one, and, if it should be found to be true, cannot fail to give a new character to legislative proceedings, and such a character as will be most favourable to the well-being of society. The principles on which this knowledge is founded must universally prevail.

In preparing the way for the introduction of these principles, it cannot now be necessary to enter into the detail of facts to prove that children can be trained to acquire *"any language, sentiments, belief, or any bodily habits and manners, not contrary to human nature"*.

The Pursuit of Happiness via Knowledge

The lessons of history show man his duty to society – the promotion of common happiness, which self-evidently lies within his power, must be the inevitable goal:

Possessing, then, the knowledge of a power so important, which, when understood, is capable of being wielded with the certainty of a law of nature, and which would gradually remove the evils which now chiefly afflict mankind, shall we permit it to remain dormant and useless, and suffer the plagues of society perpetually to exist and increase?

No: the time is now arrived when the public mind of this country and the general state of the world, call imperatively for the introduction of this all-pervading principle, not only in theory, but into practice.

Nor can any human power now impede its rapid progress. Silence will not retard its course, and opposition will give increased celerity to its movements. The commencement of the work will, in fact, ensure its accomplishment; henceforth all the irritating angry passions arising from ignorance of the true cause of bodily and mental character, will gradually subside, and be replaced by the most frank and conciliating confidence and good-will.

Nor will it be possible hereafter for comparatively a few individuals, unintentionally to occasion the rest of mankind to be surrounded by circumstances which inevitably form such characters as they afterwards deem it a duty and a right to punish even to death; and that, too, while they themselves have been the instruments of forming those characters. Such proceedings not only create innumerable evils to the directing few, but essentially retard them and the great mass of society from attaining the enjoyment of a high degree of positive happiness. Instead of punishing crimes after they have permitted the human character to be formed so as to commit them, they will adopt the only means which can be adopted to prevent the existence of those crimes; means by which they may be most easily prevented.

Happily for poor traduced and degraded human nature, the principle for which we now contend will speedily divest it of all the ridiculous and absurd mystery with which it has been hitherto enveloped by the ignorance of preceding times: and all the complicated and counteracting motives for good conduct, which have been multiplied almost to infinity, will be reduced to one single principle of action, which, by its evident operation and sufficiency, shall render this intricate system unnecessary, and ultimately supersede it in all parts of the earth. That principle is *the happiness of self, clearly understood and uniformly practised; which can only be attained by conduct that must promote the happiness of the community.*

For that Power which governs and pervades the universe has evidently so formed man, that he must progressively pass from a state of ignorance to intelligence, the limits of which it is not for man himself to define; and in that progress to discover, that his individual happiness can be increased and extended only in proportion as he actively endeavours to increase and extend the happiness of all around him. For this state of matters, and for all the gradual changes contemplated, the extraordinary events of the present times have essentially contributed to prepare the way.

Even the late Ruler of France, although immediately influenced by the most mistaken principles of ambition, has contributed to this happy result, by shaking to its foundation that mass of superstition and bigotry, which on the continent of Europe had been accumulating for ages, until it had so overpowered and depressed the human intellect, that to attempt improvement without its removal would have been most unavailing. These transactions, in which millions have been immolated,[85] or consigned to poverty and bereft of friends, will be preserved in the records of time, and impress future ages with a just estimation of the principles now about to be introduced into practice; and will thus prove perpetually useful to all succeeding generations.

For the direful effects of Napoleon's government have created the most deep-rooted disgust at notions which could produce a belief that such conduct was glorious, or calculated to increase the happiness of even the individual by whom it was pursued.

Rational Education as the Way Forward

Owen here acknowledges the work of the contemporary educationalists, 'The Rev. Dr Bell[86] and Mr Joseph Lancaster',[87] who have proved the error of "any new exclusive system":

For it is now obvious that such a system must be destructive of the happiness of the excluded, by their seeing others enjoy what they are not permitted to possess; and also that it tends, by creating opposition, from the justly injured feelings of the excluded, in proportion to the extent of the exclusion, to diminish the happiness even of the privileged: the former therefore can have no rational motive for its continuance. It will therefore be the essence of wisdom in the privileged class to co-operate sincerely and cordially with those who desire not to touch one iota of the supposed

---

[85] *immolated*: sacrificed.

[86] Andrew Bell (1753–1832), Scottish Episcopal clergyman and founder of the monitorial 'Madras System of Education', which he developed as a chaplain in the East India Company and as superintendent of the Madras Male Orphan Asylum. Finding himself short-staffed, he enlisted the aid of the scholars themselves, under a system of mutual tuition, promoted in his pamphlet, *An Experiment in Education* (1797). Although not immediately popular the system was adapted by Lancaster. After the Church of England became concerned by the spread of Non-Conformist Lancasterian schools, it appointed Bell superintendent of its National Society for Promoting the Education of the Poor in the Principles of the Established Church, set up in 1811.

[87] Joseph Lancaster (1778–1838), a Quaker who opened a free school for the poor in London in 1798, according to the monitorial system, which he recommended in a pamphlet in 1803. The system, emphasising memorisation and largely based on Bible teaching, was non-denominational and as such attractive to Non-Conformists, adopting it. Children, sometimes numbering hundreds, were gathered together in one room and seated in rows, usually of ten. Older boys (monitors) took charge under the teacher's supervision. Corporal punishment did not feature and discipline was maintained by rewards. In 1808 the Royal Lancasterian Society was formed (later renamed the British and Foreign School Society) to promote the system.

advantages which they now possess; and whose first and last wish is to increase the particular happiness of those classes, as well as the general happiness of society. Society has hitherto been ignorant of the true means by which the most useful and valuable character may be formed.

This ignorance being removed, experience will soon teach us how to form character, individually and generally, so as to give the greatest sum of happiness to the individual and to mankind.

These principles require only to be known in order to establish themselves; the outline of our future proceedings then becomes clear and defined, nor will they permit us henceforth to wander from the right path. They direct that the governing powers of all countries should establish rational plans for the education and general formation of the characters of their subjects. *These plans must be devised to train children from their earliest infancy in good habits of every description (which will of course prevent them from acquiring those of falsehood and deception). They must afterwards be rationally educated, and their labour be usefully directed. Such habits and education will impress them with an active and ardent desire to promote the happiness of every individual, and that without the* shadow of exception *for sect, or party, or country, or climate. They will also ensure, with the fewest possible exceptions, health, strength, and vigour of body; for the happiness of man can be erected only on the foundations of health of body and peace of mind.*

Increased happiness can be effected by guiding human characteristics away from the path of evil: once every member of society has accepted the truth of the principles, then their adoption will be welcomed:

Some of the best intentioned among the various classes in society may still say, "All this is *very delightful and very beautiful in theory*, but *visionaries* alone expect to see it *realised*." To this remark only one reply *can* or *ought* to be made; that *these principles have been carried most successfully into practice.*

(The beneficial effects of this practice have been experienced for many years among a population of between two and three thousand at New Lanark, in Scotland; at Munich, in Bavaria; and in the Pauper Colonies at Fredericksoord.)[88]

The present Essays, therefore, are not brought forward as mere matter of speculation, to amuse the idle visionary who *thinks* in his closet, and never

[88] A House of Industry and other social experiments carried out in Munich by Sir Benjamin Thompson, Count Rumford (1753–1814) were well known to British philanthropists. The society which set up the pauper colonies in the Netherlands began about 1818. Only New Lanark was cited as a practical example in the first four editions published down to 1818–19, the others being added later.

acts in the world; but to create universal activity, pervade society with a knowledge of its true interests, and direct the public mind to the most important object to which it can be directed, – to a national proceeding for rationally forming the character of that immense mass of population which is now allowed to be so formed as to fill the world with crimes.

Shall questions of merely local and temporary interest, whose ultimate results are calculated only to withdraw pecuniary profits from one set of individuals and give them to others, engage day after day the attention of politicians and ministers; call forth petitions and delegates from the widely spread agricultural and commercial interests of the empire; – and shall the well-being of millions of the poor, half-naked, half-famished, untaught, and untrained hourly increasing to a most alarming extent in these islands, not call forth *one* petition, *one* delegate, or *one* rational effective legislative measure?

No! for such has been our education, that we hesitate not to devote years and expend millions in the *detection* and *punishment* of crimes, and in the attainment of objects whose ultimate results are, in comparison with this, insignificancy itself: and yet we have not moved one step in the true path to *prevent* crimes, and to diminish the innumerable evils with which mankind are now afflicted.

Are these false principles of conduct in those who govern the world to influence mankind permanently? And if not, *how*, and *when* is the change to commence?

These important considerations shall form the subject of the next Essay.

Second Essay

[Original Dedication of Second Essay. Second Dedication of the Four Essays in subsequent editions.]

TO THE BRITISH PUBLIC

The Principles of the Former Essay continued, and applied in part

To Practice.

"It is not unreasonable to hope that *hostility* may *cease*, even where *perfect agreement* cannot *be established*. If we cannot *reconcile all opinions*, let us endeavour to unite all hearts." – MR. VANSITTART'S[89] LETTER TO THE REV. DR. HERBERT MARSH.

[89] Nicholas Vansittart (1766–1851), lawyer and MP, Chancellor of the Exchequer, 1812–22. His *Letter to the Rev. Marsh* (1811) argued for greater co-operation between Anglicans and Dissenters in the cause of religious freedom, something Owen strongly favoured. Vansittart's concerns as Chancellor included the corn laws, relief of distress and tariff reform.

GENERAL principles only were developed in the First Essay. In this an attempt will be made to show the advantages which may be derived from the adoption of those principles into practice, and to explain the mode by which the practice may, without inconvenience, be generally introduced.

Society, Charity and Rational Instruction

Society's aim must be for "each man to 'have charity for *all* men'".

No feeling short of this can indeed find place in any mind which has been taught clearly to understand that children in all parts of the earth have been, are, and everlastingly will be, impressed with habits and sentiments similar to those of their parents and instructors; modified, however, by the circumstances in which they have been, are, or may be placed, and by the peculiar organisation of each individual.

Yet not one of these causes of character is at the command, or in any manner under the control, of infants, who (whatever absurdity we may have been taught to the contrary) cannot possibly be accountable for the sentiments and manners which may be given to them. And here lies the fundamental error of society; and from hence have proceeded, and do proceed, most of the miseries of mankind.

Children are, without exception, passive and wonderfully contrived compounds; which, by an accurate previous and subsequent attention, *founded on a correct knowledge of the subject,* may be formed collectively to have any human character. And although these compounds, like all the other works of nature, possess endless varieties, yet they partake of that plastic quality, which, by perseverance under judicious management, may be ultimately moulded into the very image of rational wishes and desires.

In the next place, these principles cannot fail to create feelings which, without force or the production of any counteracting motive, will irresistibly lead those who posses them to make due allowance for the difference of sentiments and manners, not only among their friends and countrymen, but also among the inhabitants of every region of the earth, even including their enemies. With this insight into the formation of character, there is no conceivable foundation for private displeasure or public enmity.

The use of reason will be essential to the application of the principles: rational instruction from infancy will teach the individual rational evaluation and this will lead naturally to charitable assessment of those whose behaviour is irrationally directed and as such "destructive of . . . comfort, pleasure, or happiness."

He will then also strongly entertain the desire "to do good to *all* men," and even to those who think themselves his enemies.

Thus *shortly*, *directly*, and *certainly* may mankind be taught the essence, and to attain the ultimate object, of all former *moral* and *religious* instruction.

These Essays, however, are intended to explain that which is *true*, and not to attack that which is *false*. For to explain that which is true may permanently improve, without creating even temporary evil; whereas to attack that, which is false, is often productive of very fatal consequences.

We cannot be held accountable for "the partial ignorance of our fore-fathers", *who had only* "some vague disjointed knowledge of the principles on which character is formed." *The true nature of these principles must therefore be carefully presented.*

The facts which by the invention of printing have gradually accumulated now show the errors of the systems of our forefathers so distinctly, that they must be, when pointed out, evident to all classes of the community, and render it absolutely necessary that new legislative measures be immediately adopted to prevent the confusion which must arise from even the most ignorant being competent to detect the absurdity and glaring injustice of many of those laws by which they are now governed.

Such are those laws which enact punishments for a very great variety of actions designated crimes; while those from whom such actions proceed are regularly trained to acquire no other knowledge than that which compels them to conclude that those actions are the best they could perform.

How much longer shall we continue to allow generation after generation to be taught crime from their infancy, and, when so taught, hunt them like beasts of the forest, until they are entangled beyond escape in the toils and nets of the law? When, if the circumstances of those poor unpitied sufferers had been reversed with those who are even surrounded with the pomp and dignity of justice, these latter would have been at the bar of the culprit, and the former would have been in the judgement seat.

Had the present Judges of these realms been born and educated among the poor and profligate of St Giles's or some similar situation, is it not certain, inasmuch as they possess native energies and abilities, that ere this they would have been at the head of their *then* profession, and, in consequence of that superiority and proficiency, would have already suffered imprisonment, transportation, or death? Can we for a moment hesitate to decide, that if some of those men whom the laws dispensed by the present Judges have doomed to suffer capital punishments, had been born, trained, and circumstanced, as these Judges were born, trained, and circumstanced, that some of those who had so suffered would have been the identical individuals who would have passed the same awful sentences on the present highly esteemed dignitaries of the law.

Owen urges his reader to visit London's prisons and "patiently inquire, with kind commiserating solicitude" **as to the lives and backgrounds of the inmates.**

They will tales unfold that *must* arrest attention, that will disclose sufferings, misery, and injustice, upon which, for obvious reasons, I will not now dwell, but which previously, I am persuaded, you could not suppose it possible to exist in any civilised state, far less that they should be permitted for centuries to increase around the very fountain of British jurisprudence." The true cause, however, of this conduct, so contrary to the general humanity of the natives of these Islands, is, that a practical remedy for the evil, on clearly defined and sound principles, had not yet been suggested. But the principles developed in this "New View of Society" *will point out a remedy which is almost simplicity itself, possessing no more practical difficulties than many of the common employments of life; and such as are readily overcome by men of very ordinary practical talents.*

That such a remedy is easily practicable, may be collected from the account of the following very partial experiment.

New Lanark – the Practical Experiment

In the year 1784, the late Mr. Dale[90], of Glasgow, founded a manufactory for spinning of cotton, near the falls of the Clyde, in the county of Lanark, in Scotland; and about that period cotton mills were first introduced into the northern part of the kingdom.

It was the power which could be obtained from the falls of water that induced Mr. Dale to erect his mills in this situation; for in other respects it was not well chosen. The country around was uncultivated; the inhabitants were poor and few in number; and the roads in the neighbourhood were so bad, that the Falls, now so celebrated, were then unknown to strangers.

It was therefore necessary to collect a new population to supply the infant establishment with labourers. This, however, was no light task; for all the regularly trained Scotch peasantry disdained the idea of working

---

[90] David Dale (1739–1806) Glasgow merchant-banker, built New Lanark, the largest cotton spinning plant of the period, in 1784. Highly religious and philanthropic he established a paternalistic regime with housing, schooling and medical care for workers. He sold out to a partnership including Owen, who married his daughter, in 1799.

early and late, day after day, within cotton mills. Two modes then only remained of obtaining these labourers; the one, to procure children from the various public charities of the country; and the other, to induce families to settle around the works.

To accommodate the first, a large house was erected, which ultimately contained about five hundred children, who were procured chiefly from workhouses and charities in Edinburgh. These children were to be fed, clothed, and educated: and these duties Mr. Dale performed with the unwearied benevolence which it is well known he possessed.

To obtain the second, a village was built; and the houses were let at a low rent to such families as could be induced to accept employment in the mills; but such was the general dislike to that occupation at the time, that, with a few exceptions, only persons destitute of friends, employment, and character, were found willing to try the experiment; and of these a sufficient number to supply a constant increase of the manufactory could not be obtained. It was therefore deemed a favour on the part even of such individuals to reside at the village, and, when taught the business, they grew so valuable to the establishment, that they became agents not to be governed contrary to their own inclinations.

Mr. Dale's principal avocations were at a distance from the works, which he seldom visited more than once for a few hours in three or four months; he was therefore under the necessity of committing the management of the establishment to various servants with more or less power.

Those who have a practical knowledge of mankind will readily anticipate the character which a population so collected and constituted would acquire. It is therefore scarcely necessary to state, that the community by degrees was formed under these circumstances into a very wretched society: every man did that which was right in his own eyes, and vice and immorality prevailed to a monstrous extent. The population lived in idleness, in poverty, in almost every kind of crime; consequently, in debt, out of health, and in misery. Yet to make matters still worse, – although the cause proceeded from the best possible motive, a conscientious adherence to principle, – the whole was under a strong sectarian influence, which gave a marked and decided preference to one set of religious opinions over all others, and the professors of the favoured opinions were the privileged of the community.

The boarding-house containing the children presented a very different scene. The benevolent proprietor spared no expense to give comfort to the poor children. The rooms provided for them were spacious, always clean, and well ventilated; the food was abundant, and of the best quality; the clothes were neat and useful; a surgeon was kept in constant pay, to direct how to prevent or cure disease; and the best instructors which the country afforded were appointed to teach such branches of education as were deemed likely to be useful to children in their situation. Kind and well-disposed persons were appointed to superintend all their proceedings. Nothing, in short, at first sight seemed wanting to render it a most complete charity.

But to defray the expense of these well-devised arrangements, and to support the establishment generally, it was absolutely necessary that the children should be employed within the mills from six o'clock in the morning till seven in the evening, summer and winter, and after these hours their education commenced. The directors of the public charities, from mistaken economy, would not consent to send the children under their care to cotton mills, unless the children were received by the proprietors at the ages of six, seven, and eight. And Mr. Dale was under the necessity of accepting them at those ages, or of stopping the manufactory which he had commenced.

It is not to be supposed that children so young could remain, with the intervals of meals only, from six in the morning until seven in the evening, in constant employment, on their feet, within cotton mills, and afterwards acquire much proficiency in education. And so it proved; for many of them became dwarfs in body and mind, and some of them were deformed. Their labour through the day and their education at night became so irksome, that numbers of them continually ran away, and almost all looked forward with impatience and anxiety to the expiration of their apprenticeship of seven, eight, and nine years, which generally expired when they were from thirteen to fifteen years old. At this period of life, unaccustomed to provide for themselves, and unacquainted with the world, they usually went to Edinburgh or Glasgow, where boys and girls were soon assailed by the innumerable temptations which all large towns present, and to which many of them fell sacrifices.

Thus Mr. Dale's arrangements, and his kind solicitude for the comfort and happiness of these children, were rendered in their ultimate effect almost nugatory. They were hired by him and sent to be employed, and without their labour he could not support them; but while under his care, he did all that any individual, circumstanced as he was, could do for his fellow-creatures. The error proceeded from the children being sent from the workhouses at an age much too young for employment. They ought to have been detained four years longer, and educated; and then some of the evils which followed would have been prevented. If such be a true picture, not overcharged, of parish apprentices to our manufacturing system, under the best and most humane regulations, in what colours must it be exhibited under the worst?

Mr. Dale was advancing in years: he had no son to succeed him; and, finding the consequences just described to be the result of all his strenuous exertions for the improvement and happiness of his fellow-creatures, it is not surprising that he became disposed to retire from the cares of the establishment. He accordingly sold it to some English merchants and manufacturers; one of whom, under the circumstances just narrated, undertook the management of the concern, and fixed his residence in the midst of the population. This individual had been previously in the management of large establishments, employing a number of work-people, in the neighbourhood of Manchester; and in every case, by the steady application of certain general principles, he succeeded in reforming the habits of those under his care, and who always, among their associates in similar employment, appeared conspicuous for their good conduct. With this previous success in remodelling English character, but ignorant of the local ideas, manner, and customs, of those now committed to his management, the stranger commenced his task.

A two year struggle between management and resentful workforce ensued, but the "stranger" kept his cool, confident that his principles would triumph.

These principles ultimately prevailed: the population could not continue to resist a firm well-directed kindness, administering justice to all. They therefore slowly and cautiously began to give him some portion of their confidence; and as this increased, he was enabled more and more to develop his plans for their amelioration. It may with truth be said, that at this period they possessed almost all the vices and very few of the virtues of a social community. Theft and the receipt of stolen goods was their trade, idleness and drunkenness their habit, falsehood and deception their garb, dissensions, civil and religious, their daily practice; they united only in a zealous systematic opposition to their employers.

Here then was a fair field on which to try the efficacy in practice of principles supposed capable of altering any characters. The manager formed his plans accordingly. He spent some time in finding out the full extent of the evil against which he had to contend, and in tracing the true causes which had produced and were continuing those effects. He found that all was distrust, disorder, and disunion; and he wished to introduce confidence, regularity, and harmony. He therefore began to bring forward his various expedients to withdraw the unfavourable circumstances by which they had hitherto been surrounded, and to replace them by others calculated to produce a more happy result. He soon discovered that theft was extended through almost all the ramifications of the community, and the receipt of stolen goods through all the country around.

To remedy this evil, not one legal punishment was inflicted, not one individual imprisoned, even for an hour; but checks and other regulations of prevention were introduced, a short plain explanation of the immediate benefits they would derive from a different conduct was inculcated by those instructed for the purpose, who had the best powers of reasoning among themselves. They were at the same time instructed how to direct their industry in legal and useful occupations, by which, without danger or disgrace, they could really earn more than they had previously obtained by dishonest practices. Thus the difficulty of committing the crime was increased, the detection afterwards rendered more easy, the habit of honest industry formed, and the pleasure of good conduct experienced.

Drunkenness was attacked in the same manner; it was discountenanced on every occasion by those who had charge of any department: its destructive and pernicious effects were frequently stated by his own more prudent comrades, at the proper moment when the individual was soberly suffering from the effects of his previous excess; pot and public houses were gradually removed from the immediate vicinity of their dwellings; the health and comfort of temperance were made familiar to them: by degrees drunkenness disappeared, and many who were habitual bacchanalians are now conspicuous for undeviating sobriety.

Falsehood and deception met with a similar fate: they were held in disgrace: their practical evils were shortly explained; and every countenance was given to truth and open conduct. The pleasure and substantial advantages derived from the latter soon overcame the impolicy, error, and consequent misery, which the former mode of acting had created.

Dissensions and quarrels were undermined by analogous expedients. When they could not be readily adjusted between the parties themselves, they were stated to the manager; and as in such cases both disputants were usually more or less in the wrong, that wrong was in as few words as possible explained, forgiveness and friendship recommended, and one simple and easily remembered precept inculcated, as the most valuable rule for their whole conduct, and the advantages of "which they would experience every moment of their lives; viz:- That in future they should endeavour to use the same active exertions to make each other happy and comfortable, as they had hitherto done to make each other miserable; and by carrying this short memorandum in their mind, and applying it on all occasions, they would soon render that place a paradise, which, from the most mistaken principle, of action, they now made the abode of misery." The experiment was tried: the parties enjoyed the gratification of this new mode of conduct; references rapidly subsided; and now serious differences are scarcely known.

An open attitude to religious differences was similarly successful. "Sectarian animosity and ignorant intolerance" *were countered via the teaching that* "true religion", *devoid of sectarianism*; "would soon form those characters which every wise and good man is anxious to see."

The same principles were applied to correct the irregular intercourse of the sexes: – such conduct was discountenanced and held in disgrace; fines were levied upon both parties for the use of the support fund of the community. (This fund arose from each individual contributing one-sixtieth part of their wages, which, under their management, was applied to support the sick, the injured by accident, and the aged.) But because they had once unfortunately offended against the established laws and customs of society, they were not forced to become vicious, abandoned, and miserable; the door was left open for them to return to the comforts of kind friends and respected acquaintances; and, beyond any previous expectation, the evil became greatly diminished.

The system of receiving apprentices from public charities was abolished; permanent settlers with large families were encouraged, and comfortable houses were built for their accommodation.

The practice of employing children in the mills, of six, seven, and eight years of age, was discontinued, and their parents advised to allow them to acquire health and education until they were ten years old. (It may be remarked, that even this age is too early to keep them at constant employment in manufactories, from six in the morning to seven in the evening. Far better would it be for the children, their parents, and for society, that the first should not commence employment until they attain the age of twelve, when their education might be finished, and their bodies would be more competent to undergo the fatigue and exertions required of them. When parents can be trained to afford this additional time to their children without inconvenience, they will, of course, adopt the practice now recommended.)

The children were taught reading, writing, and arithmetic, during five years, that is, from five to ten, in the village school, without expense to their parents. All the modern improvements in education have been adopted, or are in process of adoption. (To avoid the inconveniences which must ever arise from the introduction of a particular creed into a school, the children are taught to read in such books as inculcate those precepts of the Christian religion which are common to all denominations.) They may therefore be taught and well-trained before they engage in any regular employment. Another important consideration is, that all their instruction is rendered a pleasure and delight to them; they are much more anxious for the hour of school-time to arrive than to end; they therefore make a rapid progress; and it may be safety asserted, that if they shall not be trained to form such characters as may be most desired, the fault will not proceed from the children; the cause will be in the want of a true knowledge of human nature in those who have the management of them and their parents.

During the period that these changes were going forward, attention was given to the domestic arrangements of the community.

Their houses were rendered more comfortable, their streets were improved, the best provisions were purchased, and sold to them at low rates, yet covering the original expense, and under such regulations as taught them how to proportion their expenditure to their income. Fuel and clothes were obtained for them in the same manner; and no advantage was attempted to be taken of them, or means used to deceive them.

In consequence, their animosity and opposition to the stranger subsided, their full confidence was obtained, and they became satisfied that no evil was intended them; they were convinced that a real desire existed to increase their happiness upon those grounds alone on which it could be permanently increased. All difficulties in the way of future improvement vanished. They were taught to be rational, and they acted rationally. Thus both parties experienced the incalculable advantages of the system which had been adopted. Those employed became industrious, temperate, healthy, faithful to their employers and kind to each other; while the proprietors were deriving services from their attachment, almost without inspection, far beyond those which could be obtained by any other means than those of mutual confidence and kindness. Such was the effect of these principles on the adults; on those whose previous habits had been as ill-formed as habits could be: and certainly the application of the principles to practice was made under the most unfavourable circumstances. (It may be supposed that this community was separated from other society; but the supposition would be erroneous, for it had daily and hourly communication with a population exceeding its own number. The royal borough of Lanark is only one mile distant from the works; many individuals came daily from the former to be employed at the latter; and a general intercourse is constantly maintained between the old and new towns.)

I have thus given a detailed account of this experiment, although a partial application of the principles is of far less importance than a clear and accurate account of the principles themselves, in order that they may be so well understood as to be easily rendered applicable to practice in any community and under any circumstances. Without this, particular facts may indeed amuse or astonish, but they would not contain that substantial value which the principles will be found to possess. But if the relation of the narrative shall forward this object, the experiment cannot fail to prove the certain means of renovating the moral and religious principles of the world, by showing whence arise the various opinions, manners, vices, and virtues of mankind, and how the best or the worst of them may, with mathematical precision, be taught to the rising generation.

Let it not, therefore, be longer said that evil or injurious actions cannot be prevented, or that the most rational habits in the rising generation cannot be universally formed. In those characters which now exhibit crime, the fault is obviously not in the individual, but the defects proceed from the system in which the individual was trained. Withdraw those circumstances which tend to create crime in the human character, and crime will not be created. Replace them with such as are calculated to form habits or order, regularity, temperance, industry; and these qualities will be formed. Adopt measures of fair equity and justice, and you will readily acquire the full and complete confidence of the lower orders. Proceed systematically on principles of undeviating persevering kindness, yet retaining and using, with the least possible severity, the means of restraining crime from immediately injuring society; and by degrees even the crimes now existing in the adults will also gradually disappear: for the worst former disposition, short of incurable insanity will not long resist a firm, determined, well-directed, persevering kindness. Such a proceeding, whenever practised, will be found the most powerful and effective corrector of crime, and of all injurious and improper habits.

The experiment narrated shows that this is not hypothesis and theory. The principles may be with confidence stated to be universal, and applicable to all times, persons, and circumstances.

Reform and the Nation

These principles, applied to the community at New Lanark, at first under many of the most discouraging circumstances, but persevered in for sixteen years, effected a complete change in the general character of the village, containing upwards of two thousand inhabitants, and into which, also, there was a constant influx of new-comers. But as the promulgation of new miracles is not for present times, it is not pretended that under such circumstances one and all are become wise and good; or that they are free from error. But it may be truly stated, that they now constitute a very improved society; that their worst habits are gone, and that their minor ones will soon disappear under a continuance of the application of the same principles; that during the period mentioned, scarcely a legal punishment has been inflicted, or an application been made for parish funds by any individual among them. Drunkenness is not seen in their streets; and the children are taught and trained in the institution for forming their character without any punishment. The community exhibits the general appearance of industry, temperance, comfort, health, and happiness. These are and ever will be the sure and certain effects of the adoption of the principles explained; and these principles, applied with judgement, will effectually reform the most vicious community existing, and train the younger part of it to any character which may be desired; and that, too, much more easily on an extended than on a limited scale. To apply these principles, however, successfully to practice, both a comprehensive and a minute view must be taken of the existing state of the society on which they are intended to operate.

If the introduction of change is gradual, even barely perceptible, it will be readily accepted and the resulting improvement will in turn be rapid. Further, since ignorance of the principles must have been the sole barrier to their national application by Church and State, reform must be inevitable.

For some time to come there can be but one practicable, and therefore one rational reform, which without danger can be attempted in these realms; a reform in which all men and all parties may join – that is, a reform in the training and in the management of the poor, the ignorant, the untaught and untrained, or ill-taught and ill-trained, among the whole mass of British population; and a plain, simple, practicable plan which would not contain the least danger to any individual, or to any part of society, may be devised for that purpose.

That plan is a national, well-digested, unexclusive system for the formation of character and general amelioration of the lower orders. On the experience of a life devoted to the subject, I hesitate not to say, that the members of any community may by degrees be trained to live *without idleness, without poverty, without crime, and without punishment*; for each of these is the effect of error in the various systems prevalent throughout the world. *They are all necessary consequences of ignorance.*

Train any population rationally, and they will be rational. Furnish honest and useful employments to those so trained, and such employments they will greatly prefer to dishonest or injurious occupations. It is beyond all calculation the interest of every government to provide that training and that employment; and to provide both is easily practicable.

It would be to the detriment of both Church and State if such a programme of reform were in any way exclusive. Although the well-being of the individual must be of prime concern, the national revenue can only benefit.

Yet, important as are considerations of revenue, they must appear secondary when put in competition with the lives, liberty, and comfort of our follow-subjects; which are not hourly sacrificed for want of an *effective legislative measure to prevent crime*. And is an act of such vital importance to the well-being of all to be longer delayed? *Shall yet another year pass in which crime shall be forced on the infant, who in ten, twenty, or thirty years hence shall suffer* DEATH *for being taught that crime?* Surely it is impossible. Should it be so delayed, *the individuals of the present parliament, the legislators of this day*, ought in strict and impartial justice to be amenable to the laws for not adopting the means in their power to prevent the crime; rather than the poor, untrained, and unprotected culprit, whose previous years, if he had language to describe them, would exhibit a life of unceasing wretchedness, arising *solely* from the errors of society.

In the next Essay an account will be given of the plans which are in progress at New Lanark for the further comfort and improvement of its inhabitants; and a general *practical* system be described, by which the same advantages may be gradually introduced among the poor and working classes throughout the United Kingdom.

Third Essay

TO THE SUPERINTENDENTS OF MANUFACTORIES, AND TO THOSE INDIVIDUALS GENERALLY, WHO, BY GIVING EMPLOYMENT TO AN AGGREGATED POPULATION, MAY EASILY ADOPT THE MEANS TO FORM THE SENTIMENTS AND MANNERS OF SUCH A POPULATION

The Principles of the Former Essays applied to a Particular
Situation

"Truth must ultimately prevail over error."

The "Progress of Improvement"

That which has been hitherto done for the community at New Lanark, as described in the Second Essay, has chiefly consisted in *withdrawing some of those circumstances which tended to generate, continue, or increase early bad habits; that is to say, undoing that which society had from ignorance permitted to be done.*

To effect this, however, was a far more difficult task than to train up a child from infancy in the way he should go; for that is the most easy process for the formation of character; while to unlearn and to change long acquired habits is a proceeding directly opposed to the most tenacious feelings of human nature.

125

Nevertheless, the proper application steadily pursued did effect beneficial changes on these old habits, even beyond the most sanguine expectations of the party by whom the task was undertaken. The principles were derived from the study of human nature itself, and they could not fail of success.

Still, however, very little, comparatively speaking, had been done for them. They had not been taught the most valuable domestic and social habits: such as the most economical method of preparing food; how to arrange their dwellings with neatness, and to keep them always clean and in order; but, what was of infinitely more importance, they had not been instructed how to train their children to form them into valuable members of the community, or to know that principles existed, which, when properly applied to practice from infancy, would ensure from man to man, without chance of failure, a just, open, sincere, and benevolent conduct.

The Playground

To effect this change the "New Institution" was built, centrally located and housing the School, the Lecture Room and the Church and surrounded by an enclosed area, a supervised infant playground.

As the happiness of man chiefly, if not altogether, depends on his own sentiments and habits, as well as those of the individuals around him; and as any sentiments and habits may be given to all infants, it becomes of primary importance that those alone should be given to them which can contribute to their happiness. Each child, therefore, on his entrance into playground, is to be told in language which he can understand, that "he is never to injure his play-fellows; but that, on the contrary, he is to contribute all in his power to make them happy." This simple precept, when comprehended in all its bearings, and the habits which will arise from its early adoption into practice, *if no counteracting principle be forced upon the young mind*, will effectually supersede all the errors which have hitherto kept the world in ignorance and misery. So simple a precept, too, will be easily taught, and as easily acquired; for the chief employment of the superintendents will be to prevent any deviation from it in practice. The older children, when they shall have experienced the endless advantages from acting on this principle, will, by their example, soon enforce the practice of it on the young strangers; and the happiness which the little groups will enjoy from rational conduct, will ensure its speedy and general and willing adoption. The habit also which they will acquire at this early period of life by continually acting on the principle, will fix it firmly; it will become easy and familiar to them, or, as it is often termed, natural.

126

Thus by merely attending to the evidence of our senses respecting human nature and disregarding the wild, inconsistent, and absurd theories in which man has been hitherto trained in all parts of the earth, we shall accomplish with ease and certainty the supposed Herculean labour of forming a rational character in man, and that, too, chiefly before the child commences the ordinary course of education.

The benefits are clear:

The child will be removed, so far as it is at present practicable, from the erroneous treatment of the yet untrained and untaught parents.

The parents will be relieved from the loss of time and from the care and anxiety which are now occasioned by attendance on their children from the period when they can go alone to that at which they enter the school.

The child will be placed in a situation of safety, where, with its future school-fellows and companions, it will acquire the best habits and principles, while at meal times and at night it will return to the caresses of its parents; and the affections of each are likely to be increased by the separation.

The area is also to be a place of meeting for the children from five to ten years of age, previous to and after school-hours, and to serve for a drill ground, the object of which will be hereafter explained; and a shade will be formed, under which in stormy weather the children may retire for shelter.

These are the important purposes to which a playground attached to a school may be applied.

Relaxation and the Sabbath

Those who have derived a knowledge of human nature from observation, know, that man in every situation requires relaxation from his constant and regular occupations, whatever they be: and that if he shall not be provided with or permitted to enjoy innocent and uninjurious amusements, he must and will partake of those which he can obtain, to give him temporary relief from his exertions, although the means of gaining that relief should be most pernicious. For man, irrationally instructed, is ever influenced far more by immediate feelings than by remote considerations.

Those, then, who desire to give mankind the character which it would be for the happiness of all that they should possess, will not fail to make careful provision for their amusement and recreation.

The Sabbath was originally so intended. It was instituted to be a day of universal enjoyment and happiness to the human race. It is frequently made, however, from the opposite extremes of error, either a day of superstitious gloom and tyranny over the mind, or of the most destructive intemperance and licentiousness. The one of these has been the cause of the other; the latter the certain and natural consequences of the former. Relieve the human mind from useless and superstitious restraints; train it on those principles which facts, ascertained from the first knowledge of time to this day, demonstrate to be the only principles which are true; and intemperance and licentiousness will not exist; for such conduct in itself is neither the immediate nor the future interest of man; and he is ever governed by one or other of these considerations, according to the habits which have been given to him from infancy.

The Sabbath, in many parts of Scotland, is not a day of innocent and cheerful recreation to the labouring man; nor can those who are confined all the week to sedentary occupations, freely partake, without censure, of the air and exercise to which nature invites them, and which their health demands.

The errors of the times of superstition and bigotry still hold some sway, and compel those who wish to preserve a regard to their respectability in society, to an overstrained demeanour; and this demeanour sometimes degenerates into hypocrisy, and is often the cause of great inconsistency. It is destructive of every open, honest, generous, and manly feeling. It disgusts many, and drives them to the opposite extreme. It is sometimes the cause of insanity. It is founded on ignorance, and defeats its own object.

In order to counteract the detrimental effect of the Scottish Sabbath, it was deemed necessary to provide the villagers with week-time relaxation. In summer they could enjoy walking and tending their garden plots, but in winter they worked at the same job for 10¾ hours a day, six days a week and "experience has shown that the average health and spirits of the community are several degrees lower in winter than in summer." *A venue for* "innocent amusements and rational recreation" *was thus needed.*

Man's Character is Formed for Him, not by Him

From the earliest ages, it has been the practice of the world to act on the supposition that each individual man forms his own character, and that therefore he is accountable for all his sentiments and habits, and consequently merits reward for some and punishment for others. Every system which has been established among men has been founded on these erroneous principles. When, however, they shall be brought to the test of fair examination, they will be found not only unsupported, but in direct opposition to all experience, and to the evidence of our senses.

128

This is not a slight mistake, which involves only trivial consequences; it is a fundamental error of the highest possible magnitude; it enters into all our proceedings regarding man from his infancy; and it will be found to be the true and sole origin of evil. It generates and perpetuates ignorance, hatred, and revenge, where, without such error, only intelligence, confidence, and kindness would exist. It has hitherto been the Evil Genius of the world. It severs man from man throughout the various regions of the earth; and makes enemies of those who, but for this gross error, would have enjoyed each other's kind offices and sincere friendship. It is, in short, an error which carries misery in all its consequences.

This error cannot much longer exist; for every day will make it more and more evident *that the character of man is, without a single exception, always formed for him; that it may be, and is, chiefly, created by his predecessors; that they give him, or may give him, his ideas and habits, which are the powers that govern and direct his conduct. Man, therefore, never did, nor is it possible he ever can, form his own character.*

The knowledge of this important fact has not been derived from any of the wild and heated speculations of an ardent and ungoverned imagination; on the contrary, it proceeds from a long and patient study of the theory and practice of human nature, under many varied circumstances; it will be found to be a deduction drawn from such a multiplicity of facts, as to afford the most complete demonstration.

Ignorance and misdirected guidance have hitherto prevented man from pursuing human happiness to its full potential.

Happily for man this reign of ignorance rapidly approaches to dissolution; its terrors are already on the wing, and soon they will be compelled to take their flight, never more to return. For now the knowledge of the existing errors is not only possessed by the learned and reflecting, but it is spreading far and wide throughout society; and ere long it will be fully comprehended even by the most ignorant.

New Lanark provides a "fair test of public experiment."

It remains to be proved, whether the character of man shall continue to be formed under the guidance of the most inconsistent notions, the errors of which for centuries past have been manifest to every reflecting rational mind; or whether it shall be moulded under the direction of uniformly consistent principles, derived from the unvarying facts of the creation; principles, the truth of which no sane man will now attempt to deny.

It is then by the full and complete disclosure of these principles, that the destruction of ignorance and misery is to be effected, and the reign of reason, intelligence, and happiness is to be firmly established.

The New Institution Explained
The School and the Lecture Room

The principle instilled in the child from the age of two, "that he must endeavour to keep his companions happy", *continues as the basis of his school education from the age of five. Beyond this the children are taught basic arithmetic and to read and write with comprehension. In addition the girls learn to sew, cook and keep house. The rational basis of this instruction is emphasised:*

Can man, when possessing the full vigour of his faculties, form a rational judgement on any subject, until he has first collected all the facts respecting it which are known? Has not this been, and will not this ever remain, the only path by which human knowledge can be obtained? Then children ought to be instructed on the same principles. They should first be taught the knowledge of facts, commencing with those which are most familiar to the young mind, and gradually proceeding to the most useful and necessary to be known by the respective individuals in the rank of life in which they are likely to be placed; and in all cases the children should have as clear an explanation of each fact as their minds can comprehend, rendering those explanations more detailed as the child acquires strength and capacity of intellect.

It is in the interest of both health and happiness that the children are taught relevantly and according to their potential. Given that change can only be effected gradually since parents will continue to instil error in their children, evening lectures are proposed. These "familiar discourses" *will be given three times a week during the winter and will alternate with dancing. They will cover the training of children and the planning of personal finances and they will be designed to effect the general education of the people. Owen advocates national application across society.*

In short, these lectures may be made to convey, in an amusing and agreeable manner, highly valuable and substantial information to those who are now the most ignorant in the community; and by similar means, which at a trifling expense may be put into action over the whole kingdom, the most important benefits may be given to the labouring classes, and through them, to the whole mass of society.

For it should be considered *that the far greater part of the population belong to or have risen from the labouring classes; and by them the happiness and comfort of all ranks, not excluding the highest, are very essentially influenced:* because even much more of the character of children in all families is formed by the servants, than is ever supposed by those unaccustomed to trace with attention the human mind from *earliest infancy. It is indeed impossible that children in any situation can be correctly trained, until those who surround them from infancy shall be previously well-instructed; and the value of good servants may be duly appreciated by those who have experienced the difference between the very good and very bad.*

The Church

The Church and its doctrines are of vital significance to the New Institution:

They involve considerations of the highest interest and importance; inasmuch as a knowledge of truth on the subject of religion would permanently establish the happiness of man; for it is the inconsistencies alone, proceeding from the want of this knowledge, which have created, and still create, a great proportion of the miseries which exist in the world.

Sectarianism merely perpetuates irrationality. "Each of those systems contain some truth with more error: hence it is that no one of them has gained, or is likely to gain, universality." *Irrational systems based on a doctrine of eternal punishment and reward amount to "gross absurdities".*

The doctrines which have been and now are taught throughout the world, must necessarily create and perpetuate, and they do create and perpetuate, a total want of mental charity among men. They also generate superstitions, bigotry, hypocrisy, hatred, revenge, wars, and all their evil consequences.

Yes, my deluded fellow men, believe me, for your future happiness, that the facts around us, when you shall observe them aright, will make it evident, even to demonstration, that any such doctrines must be erroneous, because THE WILL OF MAN HAS NO POWER WHATEVER OVER HIS OPINIONS; HE MUST, AND EVER DID, AND EVER WILL BELIEVE WHAT HAS BEEN, IS OR MAY BE IMPRESSED ON HIS MIND BY HIS PREDECESSORS AND THE CIRCUMSTANCES WHICH SURROUND HIM. It becomes therefore the essence of irrationality to suppose that any human being, from the creation to this day, could deserve praise or blame, reward or punishment, for the prepossessions of early education.

Religion has thus ever been a source of human misery, but the cure will cause offence.

Shall then misery most complicated and extensive be experienced, from the prince to the peasant, in all nations throughout the world, and shall its causes and prevention be known, and yet withheld? The knowledge of this cause, however, cannot be communicated to mankind without offending against the deep-rooted prejudices of all.

The removal of sectarian prejudice will be a "high event, of unequalled magnitude in the history of humanity . . . The principle, then, on which the doctrines taught in the New Institution are proposed to be founded, is, that they shall be in unison with universally revealed facts, which cannot but be true." *Man is motivated from birth by a self-interested desire for happiness; he possesses natural, God-given inclinations and mental faculties, which direct and develop his actions and ideas; he is influenced by his surroundings and by the instruction of his elders and these in turn determine the extent of his misery or happiness. If the knowledge he gains is based on rational truth, he will enjoy happiness. He relies perforce on reason and teaching. Irrational instruction merely confuses the power of reason and causes* "inconsistencies, . . . evil and misery."

"Man's ignorance of human nature" *has been the root cause of* "fundamental errors" *on which present society is founded. Even* "accidents, disease and death" *are exacerbated by* "man's ignorance of himself." *Correct this, and the inevitable outcome will be a* "vital religion, pure and undefiled, and the only one which, without any counteracting evil, can give peace and happiness to man."

Drill Exercises for the Social Good

Having alluded to the chief uses of the playground, and exercise rooms, with the School, Lecture Room, and Church, it remains, to complete the account of the New Institution, that the object of the drill exercises, mentioned when stating the purposes of the playground, should be explained; and to this we now proceed.

Were all men trained to be rational, the art of war would be rendered useless. While, however, any part of mankind shall be taught that they form their own characters, and shall continue to be trained from infancy to think and act irrationally, – that is, to acquire feelings of enmity, and to deem it a duty to engage in war against those who have been instructed to differ from them in sentiments and habits, – even the most rational must, for their personal security, learn the means of defence; and every community of such characters, while surrounded by men who have been thus improperly taught, should acquire a knowledge of this destructive art, that they may be enabled to over-rule the actions of irrational beings, and maintain peace.

132

The playground superintendent at New Lanark will instruct all boys in drill and the use of fire-arms, which instruction will in itself produce active attentiveness and physical health and vigour. It will be impressed upon them, however, that this is only deemed essential on account of "the partial insanity of some of their fellow-creatures", *who have themselves been mistaught by their elders. If such practice were introduced throughout the British Isles, a superior, permanent force could soon be created in place of the local military, thus preventing the loss of labour hours.*

The expenditure which would be saved by this simple expedient, would be far more than competent to educate the whole of the poor and labouring classes of these kingdoms.

Provision for Old Age

All New Lanark workers already contribute to a minimal sickness and superannuation fund.

It is surely desirable that, after they have spent nearly half a century in unremitting industry, they should, if possible, enjoy a comfortable independence.

To effect this object, it is intended that in the most pleasant situation near the present village, neat and convenient dwellings should be erected, with gardens attached; that they should be surrounded and sheltered by plantations, through which public walks should be formed; and the whole arranged to give the occupiers the most substantial comforts.

By monthly, voluntary contributions for a set number of years the workers would have the opportunity to purchase these homes themselves:

This part of the arrangement would always present a prospect of rest, comfort, and happiness to those employed; in consequence, their daily occupations would be performed with more spirit and cheerfulness, and their labour would appear comparatively light and easy. Those still engaged in active operations would, of course, frequently visit their former companions and friends, who, after having spent their years of toil, were in the actual enjoyment of this simple retreat; and from this intercourse each party would naturally derive pleasure. The reflections of each would be most gratifying. The old would rejoice that they had been trained in habits of industry, temperance, and foresight, to enable them to receive and enjoy in their declining years every reasonable comfort which the present state of society will admit; the young and middle-aged, that they were pursuing the same course, and that they had not

133

been trained to waste their money, time, and health in idleness and intemperance. These and many similar reflections could not fail often to arise in their minds; and those who could look forward with confident hopes to such certain comfort and independence would, in part, enjoy by anticipation these advantages.

The Audience

Owen concludes the essay by considering to whom his proposals might best be addressed. He dismisses men of commerce, lawyers, politicians, military 'heroes', those of high fashion and society and religious leaders – all would display prejudices.

But (these principles) are to be submitted to the dispassionate and patient investigation and decision of those individuals of every rank and class and denomination of society, who have become in some degree conscious of the errors in which they exist; who have felt the thick mental darkness by which they are surrounded; who are ardently desirous of discovering and following truth wherever it may lead; and who can perceive the inseparable connection which exists between individual and general, between private and public good!

When (these principles) shall have dissipated in some degree, as they speedily will dissipate, the thick darkness in which the human mind has been and is still enveloped, the endless beneficial consequences which must follow the general introduction of them into practice may then be explained in greater detail, and urged upon minds to which they will then appear less questionable.

In the meantime we shall proceed to state, in a Fourth Essay, of what improvements the present state of the British population is susceptible in practice.

Fourth Essay

[Original Dedication of Fourth Essay. First Dedication of the Four Essays in subsequent Editions.]

to

HIS ROYAL HIGHNESS THE PRINCE REGENT OF THE BRITISH EMPIRE

The Principles of the Former Essays applied to Government

"It is beyond all comparison better to prevent than to punish crime."

"A system of government therefore which shall prevent ignorance, and consequently crime, will be infinitely superior to one, which, by encouraging the first, creates a necessity for the last, and afterwards inflicts punishment on both."

The Aim of Government: happiness without poverty, crime or punishment

The end of government is to make the governed and the governors happy.

The government, then, is the best, which in practice produces the greatest happiness to the greatest number; including those who govern, and those who obey.

In a former Essay we said, and it admits of practical demonstration, that by adopting the proper means, man may by degrees be trained to live in any part of the world without poverty, without crime, and without punishment; for all these are the effects of error in the various systems of training and governing; – error proceeding from very gross ignorance of human nature.

It is of primary importance to make this ignorance manifest, and to show what are the means which are endowed with that transcendent efficacy.

We have also said that man may be trained to acquire any sentiments and habits, or any character; and no one now, possessing pretensions to the knowledge of human nature, will deny that the government of any independent community may form the individuals of that community into the best, or into the worst characters.

If there be one duty therefore more imperative than another, on the government of every country, it is, that it should adopt, without delay, the proper means to form those sentiments and habits in the people, which shall give the most permanent and substantial advantages to the individuals and to the community.

Man does not *Form his own Character*

And yet, with all the parade of learning contained in the myriads of volumes which have been written, and which still daily pour from the press, the knowledge of the first step of the progress which leads to human happiness remains yet unknown or disregarded by the mass of mankind.

The important knowledge to which we allude is, "That the old collectively may train the young collectively, to be ignorant and miserable, or to be intelligent and happy." Fortunate will be that government which shall first acquire this knowledge in theory, and adopt it in practice.

Owen proceeds to offer his programme of reform to the "immediate governing powers of the British Empire", *in the full confidence that its*

135

reasoned consistency will bear all scrutiny, "that it may be temperately and progressively introduced, instead of those defective national practices by which the State is now governed." *Changes must be gradual, to lessen the shock of the passage from* "mental darkness" to "intellectual light".

To proceed on this plan it becomes necessary to direct our attention to the actual state of the British population, to disclose the cause of those great and leading evils of which all now complain.

It will then be seen that the foundation on which these evils have been erected is ignorance, proceeding from the errors which have been impressed on the minds of the present generation by its predecessors; and chiefly by that *greatest of all errors, the notion that individuals form their own characters.* For while this most inconsistent, and therefore most absurd, of all human conceptions shall continue to be forced upon the young mind, there will remain no foundation whatever on which to build a sincere love and extended charity from man to his fellow creatures.

But destroy this hydra of human calamity, this immolator of every principle of rationality, this monster, which hitherto has effectually guarded every avenue that can lead to true benevolence and active kindness, and human happiness will be speedily established on a rock from whence it shall never more be removed.

This enemy of humanity may now be most easily destroyed. Let it be dragged forth from beneath the dark mysterious veil by which till now it has been hid from the eyes of the world. Expose it but for an instant to the clear light of intellectual day; and, as though conscious of its own deformity, it will instantaneously vanish, never to reappear.

The Call for Legal and Church Reform

Having established the irrefutable truth of the principle, the first step must be to remove those laws which "may appear to lessen", *but in fact* "greatly increase" *current social evils*:

Some of the most prominent to which allusion is made, are such as encourage the consumption of ardent spirits, by fostering and extending those receptacles to seduce the ignorant and wretched, called gin-shops and pot-houses; those laws which sanction and legalize gambling among the poor, under the name of a State lottery; those which are insidiously destroying the real strength of the country, under the name of providing for the poor; and those of punishment, which, under the present irrational system of legislation, are supposed to be absolutely necessary to hold society together.

Owen calls for the repeal and modification of such laws; with the application of "intelligence" *and* "plain unsophisticated reason", *the causes of* "the existing evils which afflict society" *will be determined. Indeed,* "the British constitution ... is admirably adapted to effect these changes", *however, care should be taken* "that no individual of the present generation should be deprived of the emolument which he now receives, or of that which has been officially or legally promised."

The next step in national reform is to withdraw from the National Church those tenets which constitute its weakness and create its danger. Yet still, to prevent the evils of any premature change, let the Church in other respects remain as it is; because under the old established forms it may effect the most valuable purposes.

To render it truly a National Church, all tests, as they are called, that is, declarations of belief in which all cannot conscientiously join, should be withdrawn: this alteration would tend more perhaps than any other which can be devised, to give stability both to the National Church and to the State; and a conduct thus rational would at once terminate all the theological differences which now confound the intellects of men and disseminate universal discord.

Control of Alcohol and Gambling and Revision of the Poor Laws

Remove the temptation which "predisposes its victims to proceed gradually from a state of temporary insanity ... to one of madness and bodily disease" *and the path to* "private or public happiness" *is accessible. Thus the 1736 Licensing Act should be reformed and higher alcohol taxation introduced. (Owen cites a Government report for January 1736, which gave the number of liquor houses in Middlesex,* "within Westminster, Holborn, the Tower, and Finsbury division" *alone as 7,044, a figure known to be far below the real number.) Next, the State lottery, which is founded on* "neither more nor less than a law to legalize gambling, entrap the unwary, and rob the ignorant", *should be abolished. The national revenue will be much healtheir when generated by* "a State governed by laws founded on an accurate knowledge of human nature, in which the whole population are well-trained." *Finally, Owen turns to the Poor Laws, which he sees as counterproductive, irrational and deceptive. Rather than allowing such a large proportion of the population to rely on Poor Law support,* "the proper system to supersede these laws", *Owen argues, is his* "System for the Prevention of Crime, and the Formation of Character".

The fundamental principle on which all these Essays proceed is, that "children collectively may be taught any sentiments and habits"; or, in other words, "trained to acquire any character."

It is of importance that *this principle should be for ever present in the mind, and that its truth should be established beyond even the shadow of doubt.* To the superficial observer it may appear to be an abstract truth of little value; but to the reflecting and accurate reasoner, it will speedily discover itself to be a power which ultimately must destroy the ignorance and consequent prejudices that have accumulated through all preceeding ages.

History reveals the extent to which "laws and customs" *can form man: evidence can be seen in the high attributes of the ancient Spartan warrior and Greek scholar as compared to their present day descendants, who must live respectively in* "despotism" *and* "mental degradation".

Also, where formerly, the superior native American tribes roamed fearlessly through their trackless forests, uniformly exhibiting the hardy, penetrating, elevated, and sincere character, which was at a loss to comprehend how a rational being could desire to possess more than his nature could enjoy; now, on the very same soil, in the same climate, characters are formed under laws and customs so opposite, that all their bodily and mental faculties are individually exerted to obtain, if possible, ten thousand times more than any man can enjoy.

The Universality of Human Nature as the Basis for the Best Government and the Best National System of Education

Human nature, save the minute differences which are ever found in all the compounds of the creation, is one and the same in all. It is without exception universally plastic, and by judicious training *the infants of any one class in the world may be readily formed into men of any other class, even to believe and declare that conduct to be right and virtuous, and to die in its defence, which their parents had been taught to believe and say was wrong and vicious, and to oppose which, those parents would also have willingly sacrificed their lives.*

Partisan and sectarian differences and "the ideas of exclusive right and consequent superiority" stem from "mis-instructing the young mind", *and* "are indeed, in direct opposition to pure and undefiled religion". *Such a system can no longer be sustained and should be replaced by a* "system without error, . . . a system without mystery":

It becomes, then, the highest interest, and consequently the first and most important duty, of every state, to form the individual characters of which the state is composed. And if any characters, from the most ignorant and miserable to the most rational and happy, can be formed, it surely merits the deepest attention of every state to adopt those means by which the formation of the latter may be secured, and that of the former prevented.

It follows that every state, to be well-governed, ought to direct its chief attention to the formation of character; and thus the best governed state will be that which shall possess the best national system of education.

In the interest of "a well-trained, united, and happy people", *the time has come for the British Government to adopt a truly national and inclusive system of popular education,* "founded in the spirit of peace and of rationality."

Rational and Useful Education

Owen acknowledges the recent work of the educationalists, Dr Bell and Mr Lancaster, but he is also quick to point out "the errors which their respective systems assist to engrave on the ductile mind of infancy and childhood", . . . "for it is in the manner alone of giving instruction that these new systems are an improvement":

Children may be taught, by either Dr Bell's or Mr Lancaster's system, to read, write, account, and sew, and yet acquire the worst habits, and have their minds rendered irrational for life.

Reading and writing are merely instruments by which knowledge, either true or false, may be imparted; and, when given to children, are of little comparative value, unless they are also taught how to make a proper use of them. Yet the manner of giving instruction is one thing, the *instruction itself* another; and no two objects can be more distinct. The *worst* manner may be applied to give the *best* instruction, and the *best* manner to give the *worst* instruction. If, therefore, in a national system of education for the poor, it be desirable to adopt the best *manner*, it is surely so much the more desirable to adopt also the best *matter*, of instruction.

There is no point in merely educating the poor to an awareness of their "degradation"; *a state of ignorance would be preferable. Teaching doctrine and* "sectarian errors" *by rote exploits the child's natural facility for mental recall instead of instilling rationally useful facts.*

A scheme such as Mr Whitbread's,[91] *under the sole superintendence of Churchmen,* "would have created a scene of confusion over the whole

---

[91] Samuel Whitbread (1758–1815), pro-reform Whig politician, son of a London brewer. MP from 1790, he was a close friend of the Radical Whig Leader, Charles James Fox (1749–1806), and an outspoken critic both of the latter's rival, the Tory, William Pitt the Younger (1759–1806), and of the King, George III. He fought for civil and religious rights, abolition of the slave-trade, Catholic emancipation, higher agricultural wages and a national education system. In 1795 Whitbread introduced a minimum wage bill to the House of Commons and in 1807 a new Poor Law – both defeated. The latter included a proposal for the establishment of two years' free education for poor children. A supporter of the monitorial system advocated by Bell and Lancaster, Whitbread helped fund the Royal Lancasterian Society.

kingdom", *based as it would have been on* "delusive theories" *and insufficient knowledge of human nature. And yet the Church should be an obvious source of instruction:*

Let it ever be remembered that an establishment which possesses the power of propagating principles, may be rendered truly valuable when directed to inculcate a system of self-evident truth, unobstructed by inconsistencies and counteractions.

The dignitaries of the Church, and their adherents, foresaw that a national system for the education of the poor, unless it were placed under the immediate influence and management of individuals belonging to the Church, would effectually and rapidly undermine the errors, not only of their own, but of every other ecclesiastical establishment. In this foresight they evinced the superiority of their penetration over the sectaries by whom the unexclusive system is supported. The heads of the Church have wisely discovered that reason and inconsistency cannot long exist together; that the one must inevitably destroy the other, and reign paramount. They have witnessed the regular, and latterly the rapid progress which reason has made; they know that its accumulating strength cannot be much longer resisted; and, as they now see the contest is hopeless, the unsuccessful attempt to destroy the Lancastrian system of education is the last effort they will ever make to counteract the dissemination of knowledge which is now widely extending itself in every direction.

The establishment of the Rev Dr Bell's system of initiating the children of the poor in all the tenets of the Church of England, is an attempt to ward off a little longer the yet dreaded period of a change from ignorance to reason, from misery to happiness.

Let us, however, not attempt impossibilities; the task is vain and hopeless; the Church, while it adheres to the defective and injurious parts of its system, cannot be induced to act cordially in opposition to its apparent interests.

The principles here advocated give rise to no one sentiment which is not in unison with the happiness of the human race; and they impart knowledge, which renders it evident that such happiness can never be acquired until every particle of falsehood and deception shall be eradicated from the instructions which the old force upon the young.

Let us then in this spirit openly declare to the Church, that a national unexclusive plan of education for the poor, will, without the shadow of doubt, destroy all the errors which are attached to the various systems; and that, when this plan shall be fully established, not one of the tenets which is in opposition to facts can long be upheld.

This unexclusive system for the education of the poor will be speedily so improved, that by rapidly increasing strides it will firmly establish the reign of reason and happiness.

The "inconsistencies" *perpetrated by* "the present ill-taught race of men" *must be removed and replaced by* "the true, unlimited and genuine principles of mental charity".

It must surely then be the desire of every rational man, of every true friend to humanity, that a cordial co-operation and unity of action should be effected between the British Executive, the Parliament, the Church and the People, to lay a broad and firm foundation for the future happiness of themselves and the world.

Say not, my countrymen, that such an event is impracticable; for, by adopting the evident means to form a rational character in man, there is a plain and direct road opened, which, if pursued, will render its accomplishment not only possible but certain. That road, too, will be found the most safe and pleasant that human beings have ever yet travelled. It leads direct to intelligence and true knowledge, and will show the boasted acquirements of Greece, of Rome, and of all antiquity, to be the mere weakness of mental infancy. Those who travel this road will find it so straight and well-defined, that no one will be in danger of wandering from the right course. Nor is it yet a narrow or exclusive path; it admits of no exclusion; every colour of body and diversity of mind are freely and alike admitted. It is open to the human race, and it is broad and spacious enough to receive the whole, were they increased a thousand-fold.

We well know that a declaration like the one now made must sound chimerical in the ears of those who have hitherto wandered in the dark mazes of ignorance, error, and exclusion, and who have been taught folly and inconsistencies only from their cradle.

But if every known fact connected with the subject proves that, from the day in which man first saw light to that in which the sun now shines, the old collectively have taught the young collectively the sentiments and habits which the young have acquired; and that the present generation and every following generation must in like manner instruct their successors; then do we say, with a confidence founded on certainty itself, that even much more shall come to pass than has yet been foretold or promised. When these principles, derived from the unchangeable laws of nature, and equally revealed to all men, shall, as soon as they will, be publicly established in the world, no conceivable obstacle can remain to prevent a sincere and cordial union and co-operation for every wise and good purpose, not only among all the members of the same state, but also among the rulers of those kingdoms and empires whose enmity and rancour against each other have been carried to the utmost stretch of melancholy folly, and even occasionally to a high degree of madness.

The Establishment of National Seminaries

How can it be that the British Government has never yet introduced a national system of education for the poor? Legislation should be introduced to set up a Government Department to implement this. With sufficient funding it will not only be able to employ the best staff but also to establish seminaries throughout the land in which to train the teachers. The benefits will be mutual, for the State and the people.

At present there are not any individuals in the kingdom who have been trained to instruct the rising generation as it is for the interest and happiness of all that it should be instructed. The training of those who are to form the future man, becomes a consideration of the utmost magnitude; for, on due reflection, it will appear, that instruction to the young must be, of necessity, the only foundation upon which the superstructure of society can be raised.

Labour Demand

Legislation should also be implemented to address the distribution of labour. At a time of national crisis "the British Government, which, with all its errors, is among the best devised and most enlightened that have hitherto been established, makes extravagant and unnecessary waste of [human] labour." **Why support** "the idle poor"? **The regular gathering of statistics, quarterly returns from each district, would ensure a proper assessment of true labour demand. Where** "ignorance and idleness" **are allowed to continue, crime will be the inevitable result, but** "useful and productive employment" **will effect otherwise.**

All men may, by judicious and proper laws and training, readily acquire knowledge and habits which will enable them, if they be permitted, to produce far more than they need for their support and enjoyment: and thus any population, in the fertile parts of the earth, may be taught to live in plenty and in happiness, without the checks of vice and misery.

Mr Malthus[92] is, however, correct, when he says that the population of the world is ever adapting itself to the quantity of food raised for its

---

[92] Thomas Robert Malthus (1766–1834), English economist and demographer. Ordained in 1797, he published anonymously his *Essay on the Principle of Population as it effects the Future Improvement of Society, 1798*. In this he put forward the theory, which Owen here refutes, that the natural tendency of population is to increase faster than the means of subsistence. Malthus' empirical standpoint, using history as evidence, caused him on the one hand to

support; but he has not told us how much more food an intelligent and industrious people will create from the same soil, than will be produced by one ignorant and ill-governed. It is, however, as one to infinity.

Both earth and sea will cater for the world's growing population as long as man's labours are wisely directed. The working population, when properly trained and directed, will ultimately create employment for themselves and thus no longer be dependent on the rich and powerful. Incentive would be created by higher rates of pay for private labour than for public. The latter would always be in demand.

The most obvious, and, in the first place, the best source, perhaps, of employment, would be the making and repairing of roads. Such employment would be perpetual over the whole kingdom; and it will be found true national economy to keep the public roads at all times in as much higher state of repair than, perhaps, any of them are at present. If requisite, canals, harbours, docks, shipbuilding, and materials for the navy, may be afterwards resorted to: it is not, however, supposed that many of the latter resources would be necessary.

A persevering attention, without which, indeed, not anything beneficial in practice can ever be attained, will soon overcome all the difficulties which may at first appear to obstruct this plan for introducing occasional national employment into the policy of the kingdom.

In times of scarce employment labourers are forced to travel the land in search of work, often with their families and frequently without success. Whole families can thus be rendered, starving, ill-clad and ill-motivated. Application for parish support will then often lead to a loss of self-respect and a sense of degradation from which the desire to "retaliate" *naturally proceeds.*

Shall we then longer withhold national instruction from our follow-men, who, it has been shown, might easily be trained to be industrious, intelligent, virtuous, and valuable members of the State?

"The measures now proposed are only a compromise with the errors of the present systems", *but thanks to* "the force of reason", "progress" *will follow, however slowly, and* "success" *is assured.*

For such compromises bring truth and error before the public; and whenever they are fairly exhibited together, truth must ultimately prevail.

---

reject the optimistic doctrines of Rousseau and the French Revolution and on the other to systemise the views of such thinkers as his father's friend, the philosopher and sceptic, David Hume (1711–76).

As many of the inconsistencies of the present system are evident to the most intelligent and well-disposed minds, the way for the public admission of the important truths which have now been in part unfolded seems to be rendered easy; and it is confidently expected that the period is at hand, when man, through ignorance, shall not much longer inflict unnecessary misery on man; because the mass of mankind will become enlightened, and will clearly discern that by so acting they will inevitably create misery to themselves.

Reason is the remedy, but it needs careful application:

All that is now requisite, previous to withdrawing the last mental bandage by which hitherto the human race has been kept in darkness and misery is, by calm and patient reasoning to tranquillize the public mind, and thus prevent the evil effects which otherwise might arise from the too sudden prospect of freely enjoying rational liberty of mind.

To withdraw that bandage without danger, reason must be judiciously applied to lead men of every sect (for all have been in part abused), to reflect that if untold myriads of beings, formed like themselves, have been so grossly deceived as they believe them to have been, what power in nature was there to prevent *them* from being equally deceived?

Such reflections, steadily pursued by those who are anxious to follow the plain and simple path of reason, will soon make it obvious that the inconsistencies which they behold in all other sects *out of their own pale*, are precisely similar to those which all other sects can readily discover *within that pale*.

It is not, however, to be imagined, that this free and open exposure of the gross errors in which the existing generation has been instructed, should be forthwith palatable to the world; it would be contrary to reason to form any such expectations.

Yet, as evil exists, and as a man cannot be rational, nor of course happy, until the cause of it shall be removed; the writer, like a physician who feels the deepest interest in the welfare of his patient, has hitherto administered of this unpalatable restorative the smallest quantity which he deemed sufficient for the purpose. He now waits to see the effects which that may produce.

Should the application not prove of sufficient strength to remove the mental disorder, he promises that it shall be increased, until sound health to the public mind be firmly and permanently established.

Source: R. Owen (1816), *A New View of Society and Other Writings*, with introduction by John Butt, Dent, London, 1972, pp. 14–90. Based on the edition of 1837, the essays have been edited by Alison Hiley for this anthology.

PART II
New forms of knowledge

Science as public culture

Of relatively modest Cornish origins, Humphry Davy (1778–1829) became, through his work in chemistry, a lion of polite society in early-nineteenth-century England. From 1802 to 1812, he was Professor of Chemistry at the Royal Institution of Great Britain, which had been founded in 1799 with the Enlightenment ideal of applying science for profit and improvement. Davy attracted large audiences to his lectures there. Through his work with the newly developed electric battery, he discovered a number of new elements and effectively founded the science of electrochemistry. Among the applied projects associated with his name was the miners' safety lamp. In 1820, he became President of the Royal Society. The introductory lecture, which he gave to a course of lectures at the Royal Institution, is his scientific manifesto as well as a manifesto for the RI.

Jane Marcet, neé Haldimand (1769–1858), whose father was Swiss, came from a wealthy London middle-class commercial background. In keeping with Genevan practice, she was educated alongside her brothers. She married an emigré Swiss physician, Alexander Marcet, who had a wide circle of scientific friends. In 1806, she published anonymously a two-volume work entitled *Conversations on Chemistry*. The book became immensely popular. Michael Faraday, Davy's associate and later successor as Professor of Chemistry at the RI, famously credited *Conversations on Chemistry*, which he read as a bookbinder's apprentice, with attracting him to the pursuit of science.

Apparently, both Davy and Faraday assisted with the updating of the 10th edition, from which these extracts are taken. It was still published anonymously, though the 'secret' of the author's identity was widely known. Written to provide young ladies at home with sufficient background to profit from attending Davy's lectures at the Royal Institution, *Conversations* was constructed in dialogue form, a common pedagogic technique at the time. It contains charming engravings, many of them made from the author's originals. Some of the experiments and apparatus shown could not possibly have been used in a domestic context. Mrs Marcet adopted the device of a dainty hand to indicate which experiments could be done at home.

Humphry Davy,
Introductory Discourse on Chemistry

A DISCOURSE
INTRODUCTORY TO A
COURSE OF LECTURES ON CHEMISTRY.

1 Chemistry is that part of natural philosophy which relates to those intimate actions of bodies upon each other, by which their appearances are altered, and their individuality destroyed.

2 This science has for its objects all the substances found upon our globe. It relates not only to the minute alterations in the external world, which are daily coming under the cognizance of our senses, and which in consequence, are incapable of affecting the imagination, but likewise to the great changes, and convulsions in nature, which, occurring but seldom, excite our curiosity, or awaken our astonishment.

3 The phænomena of combustion, of the solution of different substances in water, of the agencies of fire; the production of rain, hail, and snow, and the conversion of dead matter into living matter by vegetable organs, all belong to chemistry; and, in their various and apparently capricious appearances, can be accurately explained only by an acquaintance with the fundamental and general chemical principles.

4 Chemistry, considered as a systematic arrangement of facts, is of later origin than most of the other sciences; yet certain of its processes and operations have been always more or less connected with them; and, lately, by furnishing new instruments and powers of investigation, it has greatly contributed to increase their perfection, and to extend their applications.

5 Mechanical philosophy, regarded as the science of the motions of the masses of matter, in its theories and practices, is, to a certain extent, dependent upon chemical laws. How in fact can the mechanic calculate with accuracy upon the powers of solids, fluids, or gases, in communicating motion to each other, unless he is previously acquainted with their particular chemical affinities, or propensities

to remain disunited, or to combine? It is to chemistry that he is indebted for the knowledge of the nature and properties of the substances he employs; and he is obliged to that science for the artificial production of the most powerful and most useful of his agents.

6 Natural history and chemistry are attached to each other by very intimate ties. For while the first of these sciences treats of the general external properties of bodies, the last unfolds their internal constitution and ascertains their intimate nature. Natural history examines the beings and substances of the external world, chiefly in their permanent and unchanging forms; whereas chemistry by studying them in the laws of their alterations, developes and explains their active powers and the particular exertions of those powers.

7 It is only in consequence of chemical discoveries that that part of natural history which relates to mineral substances has assumed the form of a science. Mineralogy, at a period not very distant from the present, consisted merely of a collection of terms badly arranged, according to certain vague external properties of substances. It is now founded upon a beautiful and methodical classification; and that chiefly in consequence of the comparison of the intimate composition of the bodies it represents with their obvious forms and appearances. The mind of the mineralogist is no longer perplexed by endeavours to discover the loose and varying analogies between the colours, the shapes, and the weights of different substances. By means of the new method of analysis, he is furnished with instruments of investigation immediately applicable, and capable of producing uniform and accurate results.

8 Even botany and zoology as branches of natural history, though independent of chemistry as to their primary classification, yet are related to it so far as they treat of the constitution and functions of vegetables and animals. How dependent in fact upon chemical processes are the nourishment and growth of organized beings; their various alterations of form, their constant production of new substances, and finally their death and decomposition, in which nature seems to take unto herself those elements and constituent principles, which for a while she had lent to a superior agent as the organs and instruments of the spirit of life!

9 And in pursuing this view of the subject, medicine and physiology, those sciences which connect the preservation of the health of the human being with the abstruse philosophy of organized nature, will be found to have derived from chemistry most of their practical applications, and many of the analogies which have contributed to give to their scattered facts order and systematic arrangement. The

art of preparing those substances which operate powerfully upon animal bodies, and which according to their different modes of exhibition are either efficient remedies or active poisons, is purely chemical. Indeed the want of an acquaintance with scientific principles in the processes of pharmacy has often been productive of dangerous consequences; and the study of the simple and unvarying agencies of dead matter ought surely to precede investigations concerning the mysterious and complicated powers of life. Knowing very little of the laws of his own existence, man has nevertheless derived some useful information from researches concerning the nature of respiration; and the composition and properties of animal organs even in their dead state. And if the connection of chemistry with physiology has given rise to some visionary and seductive theories; yet even this circumstance has been useful to the public mind in exciting it by doubt, and in leading it to new investigations. A reproach, to a certain degree just, has been thrown upon those doctrines known by the name of the chemical physiology; for in the applications of them, speculative philosophers have been guided rather by the analogies of words than of facts. Instead of slowly endeavouring to lift up the veil concealing the wonderful phænomena of living nature; full of ardent imaginations, they have vainly and presumptuously attempted to tear it asunder.

10 Though astronomy in its sublime views, and its mathematical principles, is far removed from chemistry, yet to this science it is indebted for many of its instruments of experiments. The progress of the astronomer has been in some measure commensurate with that of the chemical artist, who, indeed, by his perfection of the materials used for the astronomical apparatus, has afforded to the investigating philosopher the means of tracing the revolutions of the planets, and of penetrating into space, so as to discover the forms and appearances of the distant parts of the universe.

11 It would be unnecessary to pursue this subject to a greater extent. Fortunately for man, all the different parts of the human mind are possessed of certain harmonious relations; and it is even difficult to draw the line of distinction between the sciences; for as they have for their objects only dead and living nature, and as they consist of expressions of facts more or less analogous, they must all be possessed of certain ties of connection, and of certain dependencies on each other. The man of true genius who studies science in consequence of its application,—pointing out to himself a definite end, will make use of all the instruments of investigation which are necessary for his purposes; and in the search of discovery, he will rather

pursue the plans of his own mind than be limited by the artificial divisions of language. Following extensive views, he will combine together mechanical, chemical, and physiological knowledge, whenever this combination may be essential; in consequence his facts will be connected together by simple and obvious analogies, and in studying one class of phænomena more particularly, he will not neglect its relations to other classes.

12 But chemistry is not valuable simply in its connections with the sciences, some of which are speculative and remote from our habitual passions and desires; it applies to most of the processes and operations of common life; to those processes on which we depend for the gratification of our wants, and which in consequence of their perfection and extension by means of scientific principles, have become the sources of the most refined enjoyments and delicate pleasures of civilized society.

13 Agriculture, to which we owe our means of subsistence, is an art intimately connected with chemical science. For though the common soil of the earth will produce vegetable food, yet it can only be made to produce it in the greatest quantity, and of the best quality, in consequence of the adoption of methods of cultivation dependent upon scientific principles. The knowledge of the composition of soils, of the food of vegetables, of the modes in which their products must be treated, so as to become fit for the nourishment of animals, is essential to the cultivation of land; and his exertions are profitable and useful to society, in proportion as he is more of a chemical philosopher. Since, indeed, this truth has been understood, and since the importance of agriculture has been generally felt, the character of the agriculturist has become more dignified and more refined. No longer a mere machine of labour, he has learned to think and to reason. He is aware of his usefulness to his fellow-men; and he is become at once the friend of nature and the friend of society.

14 The working of metals is a branch of technical chemistry; and it would be a sublime though a difficult task to ascertain the effects of this art upon the progress of the human mind. It has afforded to man the powers of defence against savage animals; it has enabled him to cultivate the ground, to build houses, cities, and ships, and to model much of the surface of the earth after his own imaginations of beauty. It has furnished instruments connected not only with his sublime enjoyments, but likewise with his crimes and his miseries; it has enabled him to oppress and destroy, to conquer and protect.

15 The arts of bleaching and dyeing, which the habits and fashions of society have made important are purely chemical. To destroy and

produce colours, to define the causes of the changes they undergo, and to exhibit the modes in which they may be rendered durable, demand an intimate acquaintance with chemistry. The artist who merely labours with his hands, is obliged to theory for his discovery of the most useful of his practices; and permanent and brilliant ornamental colours which rival the most beautiful tints of nature, are artificially composed from their elements by means of human inventions.

16 Tanning and the preparation of leather are chemical processes, which, though extremely simple, are of great importance to society. The modes of impregnating skin with the tanning principle of the vegetable kingdom, so as to render it strong and insoluble in water, and the methods of preparing it for this impregnation have been reduced to scientific principles. And if the improvements resulting from new investigations have not been uniformly adopted by manufacturers, it appears to be owing rather to the difficulty occurring in inducing workmen to form new habits, to a want of certain explanations of the minutiæ of the operations, and perhaps in some measure to the common prejudice against novelties, than to any defect in the general theory of the art as laid down by chemical philosophers, and demonstrated by their experiments.

17 But amongst the chemical arts, few perhaps are more important than those of porcelain and glass making. To them we owe many of those elegant vessels and utensils which have contributed to the health and delicacy of civilized nations. They have furnished instruments of experiments for most of the sciences, and consequently have become the remote causes of some of the discoveries made in those sciences. Without instruments of glass, the gases could never have been discovered, or their combinations ascertained; the minute forms and appearances of natural objects could not have been investigated; and, lastly, the sublime researches of the moderns concerning heat and light would have been wholly lost to us.

18 This subject might be much enlarged upon; for it is difficult to examine any of our common operations or labours without finding them more or less connected with chemistry. By means of this science man has employed almost all the substances in nature either for the satisfaction of his wants or the gratification of his luxuries. Not contented with what is found upon the surface of the earth, he has penetrated into her bosom, and has even searched the bottom of the ocean for the purpose of allaying the restlessness of his desires, or of extending and increasing his power. He is to a certain extent ruler of all the elements that surround him; and he is capable of using not

only common matter according to his will and inclinations, but likewise of subjecting to his purposes the ethereal principles of heat and light. By his inventions they are elicited from the atmosphere; and under his control they become, according to circumstances, instruments of comfort and enjoyment, or of terror and destruction.

19 To be able indeed to form an accurate estimate of the effects of chemical philosophy, and the arts and sciences connected with it, upon the human mind, we ought to examine the history of society, to trace the progress of improvement, or more immediately to compare the uncultivated savage with the being of science and civilization.

20 Man, in what is called a state of nature, is a creature of almost pure sensation. Called into activity only by positive wants, his life is passed either in satisfying the cravings of the common appetites, or in apathy, or in slumber. Living only in moments he calculates but little on futurity. He has no vivid feelings of hope, or thoughts of permanent and powerful action. And unable to discover causes, he is either harassed by superstitious dreams, or quietly and passively submissive to the mercy of nature and the elements. How different is man informed through the beneficence of the Deity, by science and the arts! Knowing his wants, and being able to provide for them, he is capable of anticipating future enjoyments, and of connecting hope with an infinite variety of ideas. He is in some measure independent of chance or accident for his pleasures. Science has given to him an acquaintance with the different relations of the parts of the external world; and more than that, it has bestowed upon him powers which may be almost called creative; which have enabled him to modify and change the beings surrounding him, and by his experiments to interrogate nature with power, not simply as a scholar, passive and seeking only to understand her operations, but rather as a master, active with his own instruments.

21 But, though improved and instructed by the sciences, we must not rest contented with what has been done; it is necessary that we should likewise do. Our enjoyment of the fruits of the labours of former times should be rather an enjoyment of activity than of indolence; and, instead of passively admiring, we ought to admire with that feeling which leads to emulation.

22 Science has done much for man, but it is capable of doing still more; its sources of improvement are not yet exhausted; the benefits that it has conferred ought to excite our hopes of its capability of conferring new benefits; and in considering the progressiveness of our nature, we may reasonably look forward to a state of greater cultivation and happiness than that we at present enjoy.

23 As a branch of sublime philosophy, chemistry is far from being perfect. It consists of a number of collections of facts connected together by different relations; but as yet it is not furnished with a precise and beautiful theory. Though we can perceive, develop, and even produce, by means of our instruments of experiment, an almost infinite variety of minute phænomena, yet we are incapable of determining the general laws by which they are governed; and in attempting to define them, we are lost in obscure, though sublime imaginations concerning unknown agencies. That they may be discovered, however, there is every reason to believe. And who would not be ambitious of becoming acquainted with the most profound secrets of nature, of ascertaining her hidden operations, and of exhibiting to men that system of knowledge which relates so intimately to their own physical and moral constitution?

24 The future is composed merely of images of the past, connected in new arrangements by analogy, and modified by the circumstances and feelings of the moment; our hopes are founded upon our experience; and in reasoning concerning what may be accomplished, we ought not only to consider the immense field of research yet unexplored, but likewise to examine the latest operations of the human mind, and to ascertain the degree of its strength and activity.

25 At the beginning of the seventeenth century very little was known concerning the philosophy of the intimate actions of bodies on each other; and before this time, vague ideas, superstitious notions, and inaccurate practices, were the only effects of the first efforts of the mind to establish the foundations of chemistry. Men either were astonished and deluded by their first inventions so as to become visionaries, and to institute researches after imaginary things, or they employed them as instruments for astonishing and deluding others, influenced by their dearest passions and interests, by ambition, or the love of money. Hence arose the dreams of alchemy concerning the philosopher's stone, and the elixir of life. Hence, for a long while the other metals were destroyed or rendered useless by experiments designed to transmute them into gold; and for a long while the means of obtaining earthly immortality were sought for amidst the unhealthy vapours of the laboratory. These views of things have passed away, and a new science has gradually arisen. The dim and uncertain twilight of discovery, which gave to objects false or indefinite appearances, has been succeeded by the steady light of truth, which has shown the external world in its distinct forms, and in its true relations to human powers. The composition of the atmosphere, and the properties of the gases, have been ascertained; the phænom-

ena of electricity have been developed; the lightnings have been taken from the clouds; and lastly, a new influence has been discovered, which has enabled man to produce from combinations of dead matter effects which were formerly occasioned only by animal organs.

26 The human mind has been lately active and powerful; but there is very little reason for believing that the period of its greatest strength is passed; or even that it has attained its adult state. We find in all its exertions not only the health and vigour, but likewise the awkwardness of youth. It has gained new powers and faculties; but it is as yet incapable of using them with readiness and efficacy. Its desires are beyond its abilities; its different parts and organs are not firmly knit together, and they seldom act in perfect unity.

27 Unless any great physical changes should take place upon the globe, the permanency of the arts and sciences is rendered certain, in consequence of the diffusion of knowledge by means of the invention of printing; and those words which are the immutable instruments of thought, are become the constant and widely-diffused nourishment of the mind, the preservers of its health and energy. Individuals, in consequence of interested motives or false views, may check for a time the progress of knowledge; moral causes may produce a momentary slumber of the public spirit; the adoption of wild and dangerous theories, by ambitious or deluded men, may throw a temporary opprobrium on literature; but the influence of true philosophy will never be despised; the germs of improvement are sown in minds even where they are not perceived, and sooner or later the spring-time of their growth must arrive.

28 In reasoning concerning the future hopes of the human species, we may look forward with confidence to a state of society in which the different orders and classes of men will contribute more effectually to the support of each other than they have hitherto done. This state indeed seems to be approaching fast; for in consequence of the multiplication of the means of instruction, the man of science and the manufacturer are daily becoming more nearly assimilated to each other. The artist who formerly affected to despise scientific principles, because he was incapable of perceiving the advantages of them, is now so far enlightened, as to favour the adoption of new processes in his art, whenever they are evidently connected with a diminution of labour. And the increase of projectors, even to too great an extent, demonstrates the enthusiasm of the public mind in its search after improvement. The arts and sciences also are in a high degree cultivated, and patronized by the rich and privileged orders. The

guardians of civilization and of refinement, the most powerful and respected part of society, are daily growing more attentive to the realities of life; and, giving up many of their unnecessary enjoyments in consequence of the desire to be useful, are becoming the friends and protectors of the labouring part of the community. The unequal division of property and of labour, the difference of rank and condition amongst mankind, are the sources of power in civilized life, its moving causes, and even its very soul; and in considering and hoping that the human species is capable of becoming more enlightened and more happy, we can only expect that the great whole of society should be ultimately connected together by means of knowledge and the useful arts; that they should act as the children of one great parent, with one determinate end, so that no power may be rendered useless, no exertions thrown away. In this view we do not look to distant ages, or amuse ourselves with brilliant, though delusive dreams concerning the infinite improveability of man, the annihilation of labour, disease, and even death. But we reason by analogy from simple facts. We consider only a state of human progression arising out of its present condition. We look for a time that we may reasonably expect, for a bright day of which we already behold the dawn.

29 So far our considerations have been general; so far we have examined chemistry chiefly with regard to its great agency upon the improvement of society, as connected with the increasing perfection of the different branches of natural philosophy and the arts. At present it remains for us only to investigate the effects of the study of this science upon particular minds, and to ascertain its powers of increasing that happiness which arises out of the private feelings and interests of individuals.

30 The quantity of pleasure which we are capable of experiencing in life appears to be in a great measure connected with the number of independent sources of enjoyment in our possession. And though one great object of desire, connected with great exertions, must more or less employ the most powerful faculties of the soul; yet a certain variety of trains of feeling and of ideas is essential to its health and permanent activity. In considering the relations of the pursuit of chemistry to this part of our nature, we cannot but perceive that the contemplation of the various phænomena in the external world is eminently fitted for giving a permanent and placid enjoyment to the mind. For the relations of these phænomena are perpetually changing; and consequently they are uniformly obliging us to alter our modes of thinking. Also the theories that represent them are only

approximations to truth; and they do not fetter the mind by giving to it implicit confidence, but are rather the instruments that it employs for the purpose of gaining new ideas.

31 A certain portion of physical knowledge is essential to our existence; and all efficient exertion is founded upon an accurate and minute acquaintance with the properties of the different objects surrounding us. The germ of power indeed is native; but it can only be nourished by the forms of the external world. The food of the imagination is supplied by the senses, and all ideas existing in the human mind are representations of parts of nature accurately delineated by memory, or tinged with the glow of passion, and formed into new combinations by fancy. In this view researches concerning the phænomena of corpuscular action may be said to be almost natural to the mind, and to arise out of its instinctive feelings. The objects that are nearest to man are the first to occupy his attention: from considering their agencies on each other he becomes capable of predicting effects; in modifying these effects he gains activity; and science becomes the parent of the strength and independence of his faculties.

32 The appearances of the greater number of natural objects are originally delightful to us, and they become still more so, when the laws by which they are governed are known, and when they are associated with ideas of order and utility. The study of nature, therefore, in her various operations must be always more or less connected with the love of the beautiful and sublime; and in consequence of the extent and indefiniteness of the views it presents to us, it is eminently calculated to gratify and keep alive the more powerful passions and ambitions of the soul, which, delighting in the anticipation of enjoyment, is never satisfied with knowledge; and which is as it were nourished by futurity, and rendered strong by hope.

33 In common society, to men collected in great cities, who are wearied by the constant recurrence of similar artificial pursuits and objects, and who are in need of sources of permanent attachment, the cultivation of chemistry and the physical sciences may be eminently beneficial. For in all their applications they exhibit an almost infinite variety of effects connected with a simplicity of design. They demonstrate that every being is intended for some definite end or purpose. They attach feelings of importance even to inanimate objects; and they furnish to the mind means of obtaining enjoyment unconnected with the labour or misery of others.

34 To the man of business, or of mechanical employment, the pursuit of experimental research may afford a simple pleasure, unconnected

with the gratification of unnecessary wants, and leading to such an expansion of the faculties of the mind as must give to it dignity and power. To the refined and fashionable classes of society it may become a source of consolation and of happiness, in those moments of solitude, when the common habits and passions of the world are considered with indifference. It may destroy diseases of the imagination, owing to too deep a sensibility; and it may attach the affections to objects, permanent, important, and intimately related to the interests of the human species. Even to persons of powerful minds, who are connected with society by literary, political, or moral relations, an acquaintance with the science that represents the operations of nature cannot by wholly useless. It must strengthen their habits of minute discrimination; and by obliging them to use a language representing simple facts, may tend to destroy the influence of terms connected only with feeling. The man who has been accustomed to study natural objects philosophically, to be perpetually guarding against the delusions of the fancy, will not readily be induced to multiply words so as to forget things. From observing in the relations of inanimate things fitness and utility, he will reason with deeper reverence concerning beings possessing life; and perceiving in all the phenomena of the universe the designs of a perfect intelligence, he will be averse to the turbulence and passion of hasty innovations, and will uniformly appear as the friend of tranquillity and order.

Source: 'A discourse introductory to a course of lectures on chemistry', Humphry Davy (1802), in John Davy, ed., *Collected Works* [of Humphry Davy], vol. II, 1839, pp. 311–26.

Mrs Jane Marcet, *Conversations on Chemistry*

Preface

IN venturing to offer to the public, and more particularly to the female sex, an Introduction to Chemistry, the author, herself a woman, conceives that some explanation may be required; and she feels it the more necessary to apologize for the present undertaking, as her knowledge of the subject is but recent, and as she can have no real claims to the title of chemist.

On attending for the first time experimental lectures, the author found it almost impossible to derive any clear or satisfactory information from the rapid demonstrations which are usually, and perhaps necessarily, crowded into popular courses of this kind. But frequent opportunities having afterwards occurred of conversing with a friend on the subject of chemistry, and of repeating a variety of experiments, she became better acquainted with the principles of that science, and began to feel highly interested in its pursuit. It was then that she perceived, in attending the excellent lectures delivered at the Royal Institution, by the present Professor of Chemistry, the great advantage which her previous knowledge of the subject, slight as it was, gave her over others who had not enjoyed the same means of private instruction. Every fact or experiment attracted her attention, and served to explain some theory to which she was not a total stranger; and she had the gratification to find that the numerous and elegant illustrations, for which that school is so much distinguished, seldom failed to produce on her mind the effect for which they were intended.

Hence it was natural to infer, that familiar conversation was, in studies of this kind, a most useful auxiliary source of information; and more especially to the female sex, whose education is seldom calculated to prepare their minds for abstract ideas, or scientific language.

As, however, there are but few women who have access to this mode of instruction; and as the author was not acquainted with any book that could prove a substitute for it, she thought that it might be useful for beginners, as well as satisfactory to herself, to trace the steps by which she had acquired her little stock of chemical knowledge, and to record, in the form of dialogue, those ideas which she had first derived from conversation.

But to do this with sufficient method, and to fix upon a mode of arrangement, was an object of some difficulty. After much hesitation, and a degree of embarrassment, which, probably, the most competent chemical writers have often felt in common with the most superficial, a mode of division was adopted, which, though the most natural, does not always admit of being strictly pursued—it it that of treating first of the simplest bodies, and then gradually rising to the most intricate compounds.

[. . .]

It will, no doubt, be observed that in the course of these Conversations, remarks are often introduced, which appear much too acute for the young pupils, by whom they are supposed to be made. Of this fault the author is fully aware. But, in order to avoid it, it would have been necessary either to omit a variety of useful illustrations, or to submit to such minute explanations and frequent repetitions as would have rendered the work tedious, and therefore less suited to its intended purpose.

In writing these pages, the author was more than once checked in her progress by the apprehension that such an attempt might be considered by some, either as unsuited to the ordinary pursuits of her sex, or ill-justified by her own imperfect knowledge of the subject. But, on the one hand, she felt encouraged by the establishment of those public institutions, open to both sexes, for the dissemination of philosophical knowledge, which clearly prove that the general opinion no longer excludes women from an acquaintance with the elements of science; and, on the other, she flattered herself that whilst the impressions made upon her mind, by the wonders of Nature, studied in this new point of view, were still fresh and strong, she might, perhaps, succeed the better in communicating to others the sentiments she herself experienced.

The reader will perceive, in perusing this work, that he is supposed to have previously acquired some slight knowledge of natural philosophy, a circumstances so desirable, that the author has, since the original publication of this work, been induced to offer the public a small tract, entitled "Conversations on Natural Philosophy",[1] in which the most essential rudiments of that science are familiarly explained.

Conversation I – On the General Principles of Chemistry

MRS. B.

As you have now acquired some elementary notions of NATURAL PHILOSOPHY, I am going to propose to you another branch of science, to which I am particularly anxious that you should devote a share of your attention. This is CHEMISTRY, which is so closely connected with Natural Philosophy, that the study of the one must be incomplete without some knowledge of the other; for, it is obvious that we can derive but a very imperfect idea of bodies from the study of the general laws by which they are governed, if we remain totally ignorant of their intimate nature.

CAROLINE.

To confess the truth, Mrs. B., I am not disposed to form a very favourable idea of chemistry, nor do I expect to derive much entertainment from it. I prefer sciences which exhibit nature on a grand scale, to those that are confined to the minutiæ of petty details. Can the studies which we have lately pursued, the general properties of matter, or the revolutions of the heavenly bodies, be compared to the mixing up of a

---

[1] Physics, especially mechanics.

few insignificant drugs? I grant, however, there may be entertaining experiments in chemistry, and should not dislike to try some of them: the distilling, for instance, of lavender or rose water.

MRS. B.

I rather imagine, my dear Caroline, that your want of taste for chemistry proceeds from the very limited idea you entertain of its object. You confine the chemist's laboratory to the narrow precincts of the apothecary's and perfumer's shops, whilst it is subservient to an immense variety of higher and more useful purposes. Besides, my dear, chemistry is by no means confined to works of art. Nature also has her laboratory, which is the universe, and there she is incessantly employed in chemical operations. You are surprised, Caroline; but I assure you that the most wonderful and the most interesting phenomena of nature are almost all of them produced by chemical powers. What Bergman,[2] in the introduction to his history of chemistry, has said of this science, will give you a more just and enlarged idea of it. He observes that the knowledge of nature may be divided into three periods. The first is that in which the attention of men is occupied in learning the external forms and characters of objects, this is called *Natural History*. In the second, they consider the effects of bodies acting on each other by their mechanical power, as their weight and motion; which constitutes the science of *Natural Philosophy*. The third period is that in which the properties and mutual action of the elementary parts of bodies are investigated. This last is the science of CHEMISTRY, and I doubt not you will soon agree with me in thinking it the most interesting.

CAROLINE.

Chemical action and properties of the elements of bodies! oh! Mrs. B., that sounds alarmingly difficult.

MRS. B.

Without entering into the minute details of practical chemistry, or penetrating into the profound depths of the science, a woman may obtain such a knowledge of chemistry as will not only throw an interest on the common occurrences of life, but will enlarge the sphere of her ideas, and render the contemplation of nature a source of delightful instruction.

---

[2] Tobern Bergman (1735–84), Swedish chemist who isolated a number of new elements.

CAROLINE.

If this is the case, I have certainly been much mistaken in the notion I had formed of chemistry. I own that I thought it was chiefly confined to the knowledge and preparation of medicines.

MRS. B.

That is only a branch of chemistry which is called Pharmacy; and, though the study of it is, no doubt, of great importance to the world at large, it belongs exclusively to professional men, and is therefore the last that I should advise you to pursue.

EMILY.

Did not the chemists formerly employ themselves in search of the philosopher's stone, or the secret of making gold?

MRS. B.

These were a particular set of misguided philosophers, who dignified themselves with the name of Alchemists, to distinguish their pursuits from those of the common chemists, whose studies were confined to the knowledge of medicines.

But, since that period, chemistry has undergone so complete a revolution, that, from an obscure and mysterious art, it is now become a regular and beautiful science, to which art is entirely subservient. It is true, however, that we are indebted to the alchemists for many very useful discoveries, which sprung from their fruitless attempts to make gold, and which, undoubtedly, have proved of infinitely greater advantage to mankind than could have resulted from succeeding in their chimerical pursuits.

The modern chemists, instead of directing their ambition to the vain attempt of producing any of the original substances in nature, rather aim at analysing and imitating her combinations, and have sometimes succeeded in forming compounds, or effecting decompositions, no instances of which occur in the chemistry of Nature. They have little reason to regret their inability to make gold, whilst, by their innumerable inventions and discoveries, they have so greatly stimulated industry and facilitated labour, as prodigiously to increase the luxuries as well as the necessaries of life.

EMILY.

But I do not understand by what means chemistry can facilitate labour; is not that rather the province of the mechanic?

MRS. B.

There are many ways by which labour may be rendered more easy, independently of mechanics; but mechanical inventions themselves often derive their utility from a chemical principle. Such, for instance, as that most wonderful of all machines, the Steam-engine. In agriculture, a chemical knowledge of the nature of soils, and of vegetation, may become highly useful; and in those arts which relate to the comforts and conveniences of life, it would be endless to enumerate the advantages which result from the study of this science.

CAROLINE.

But pray, tell us more precisely in what manner the discoveries of chemists have proved so beneficial to society?

MRS. B.

That would be an injudicious anticipation; for you would not comprehend the nature of such discoveries and useful applications, so well as you will do hereafter. Without a due regard to method, we cannot expect to make any progress in chemistry. I wish to direct your observations chiefly to the chemical operations of Nature; but those of Art are certainly of too high importance to pass wholly unnoticed; we shall therefore allow them also some share of our attention.

EMILY.

Well, then, let us now set to work regularly. I am very anxious to begin.

MRS. B.

The object of chemistry is to obtain a knowledge of the intimate nature of bodies, and of their mutual action on each other. You find, therefore, Caroline, that this is no narrow or confined science, which comprehends every thing material within our sphere.

163

CAROLINE.

On the contrary it must be inexhaustible; and I am at a loss to conceive how any proficiency can be made in a science whose objects are so numerous.

MRS. B.

If every individual substance were formed of different materials, the study of chemistry would, indeed, be endless; but you must observe that the various bodies in nature are composed of certain elementary principles which are not very numerous.

CAROLINE.

Yes; – I know that all bodies are composed of fire, air, earth, and water; that I learnt many years ago.

MRS. B.

But you must now endeavour to forget it. I have already informed you what a great change chemistry has undergone since it has become a regular science. Within these thirty years especially, it has experienced an entire revolution, and it is now proved, that neither fire, air, earth, nor water, can be called elementary bodies. For an elementary body is one that has never been decomposed, that is to say, separated into other substances: and fire, air, earth, and water, are all of them susceptible of decomposition.

EMILY.

I thought that decomposing a body was dividing it into its minutest parts. And if so, I do not understand why an elementary substance is not capable of being decomposed, as well as any other.

MRS. B.

You have misconceived the idea of *decomposition*; it is very different from mere *division*. The latter simply reduces a body into parts, but the former separates it into the various ingredients, or materials, of which it is composed. If we were to take a loaf of bread, and separate the several ingredients of which it is made, the flour, the yeast, the salt, and the water, it would be very different from cuting [*sic*] or crumbling the loaf into pieces.

164

EMILY.

I understand you now very well. To decompose a body is to separate from each other the various elementary substances of which it consists.

CAROLINE.

But flour, water, and other materials of bread, according to your definition, are not elementary substances.

MRS. B.

No, my dear; I mentioned bread rather as a familiar comparison, to illustrate the idea, than as an example.

The elementary substances of which a body is composed are called the *constituent* parts of that body; in decomposing it, therefore, we separate its constituent parts. If, on the contrary, we divide a body by chopping it to pieces, or even by grinding or pounding it to the finest powder, each of these small particles will still consist of a portion of the several constituent parts of the whole body: these are called the *integrant* parts; do you understand the difference?

EMILY.

Yes, I think, perfectly. We *decompose* a body into its *constituent* parts; and *divide* it into its *integrant* parts.

MRS. B.

Exactly so. If therefore a body consists of only one kind of substance, though it may be divided into its integrant parts, it is not possible to decompose it. Such bodies are therefore called *simple* or *elementary*, as they are the elements of which all other bodies are composed. *Compound bodies* are such as consist of more than one of these elementary principles.

CAROLINE.

But do not fire, air, earth, and water, consist, each of them, but of one kind of substance?

MRS. B.

No, my dear; they are every one of them susceptible of being separated into various simple bodies. Instead of four, chemists now reckon no less than fifty-six elementary substances. The existence of most of these is

165

established by the clearest experiments; but, in regard to a few of them, particularly the most subtle agents of nature, *heat, light*, and *electricity*, there is yet much uncertainty, and I can only give you the opinions which are deduced from the latest discoveries. After I have furnished you with a list of the elementary bodies, classed according to their properties, we shall proceed to examine each of them separately, and then consider them in their combinations with each other.

[. . .]

MRS. B.

Simplicity has charms, only so far as it accords with truth. I am far from supposing the present classification of simple bodies to be perfectly correct; on the contrary, the investigation and discoveries of the most celebrated chemists shew us that occasional alterations already have been, and no doubt will continue to be required: but as long as every change brings us nearer to the truth, we have no cause to complain of their frequency. I do not mean, however, to depreciate the labours of our forefathers; we profit by their experience, both in avoiding their errors, and in following their steps when they were in the right path; and it is no small advantage to be furnished with a hand-post, which indicates *this* is the right way and *that* is the wrong one.

CAROLINE.

People are very fond of expatiating on the wisdom and experience of our ancestors, yet we must naturally be their superiors, since we have the advantage of their accumulation of knowledge to follow, and of error to avoid; and it would surely be much more rational to talk of the wisdom and experience of ourselves and our posterity, than that of our ancestors.

MRS. B.

I will admit that there is some truth in your observation, provided that you allow that it is not devoid of vanity.

MRS. B.

[. . .]

But before we proceed farther, it will be necessary to give you some idea of chemical attraction, a power on which the whole science depends.

Chemical Attraction, or the *Attraction of Composition*, consists in the peculiar tendency which bodies of a different nature have to unite with each other. It is by this force that all compositions and decompositions are effected.

[. . .]

CAROLINE.

And, pray, Mrs. B., what is the cause of the chemical attraction of bodies for each other? [. . .]

MRS. B.

Chemical attraction may, like that of cohesion or gravitation, be one of the powers inherent in matter which, in our present state of knowledge, admits of no other satisfactory explanation than an immediate reference to a divine cause. Sir H. Davy,[3] however, whose important discoveries have opened such improved views in chemistry, has suggested an hypothesis which may throw great light upon that science. He supposes that there are two kinds of electricity, with one or other of which all bodies are united. These we distinguish by the names of *positive* and *negative* electricity; those bodies are disposed to combine, which possess opposite electricities, as they are brought together by the attraction which these electricities have for each other.

EMILY.

So that we must suppose that the two electricities always attract each other, and thus compel the bodies in which they exist to combine?

[. . .]

CAROLINE.

These electricities seem to me to be a kind of chemical spirit, which animates the particles of bodies, and draws them together.

EMILY.

If it is known, then, with which of the electricities bodies are united, it can be inferred which will, and which will not, combine together?

---

[3] Sir Humphry Davy (1778–1829), Professor of Chemistry at the Royal Institution, 1802–12; President of the Royal Society 1820–7. His were the lectures for which *Conversations on Chemistry* was meant to prepare auditors. He apparently assisted with the 10th edition.

MRS. B.

Certainly. Now oxygen is always found united with the negative electricity, and the variety of bodies with which it so readily combines, are all united with the positive electricity, so that if Sir H. Davy's hypothesis be correct, their mutual attraction is thus explained.

CAROLINE.

Most clearly; oh! I am sure, Mrs. B., it must be so.
[. . .]

Conversation VI – On the Chemical Agencies of Electricity

MRS. B.

IT will now be necessary to give you some account of certain properties of electricity, which have of late years been discovered to have an essential connection with the phenomena of chemistry.

I have already informed you that the opposite states of electricity have been conjectured to be the cause of chemical attraction; what I now allude to is the influence of the voltaic battery, of which you have heard such wonders.

EMILY.

We have indeed, but without understanding them, and I should be delighted to hear them explained. [. . .]

MRS. B.

[. . .] we are as yet so ignorant of its intimate nature, that we are unable to determine, not only whether it [electricity] is simple or compound, but whether it is in fact a material agent; or as Sir H. Davy has hinted, whether it may not be merely a property inherent in matter. As, however, it is necessary to adopt some hypothesis, for the explanation of the discoveries which this agent has enabled us to make, I have chosen the opinion, at present most prevalent, which supposes the existence of two kinds of electricity, distinguished by the name of *positive* and *negative* electricity.

CAROLINE.

Well, I must confess, I do not feel nearly so interested in a science where so much uncertainty prevails, as in those which rest upon established principles. I never was fond of electricity, because, however beautiful and curious the phenomena it exhibits may be, the theories, by which they were explained, appeared to me so various, so obscure and inadequate, that I always remained dissatisfied. I was in hopes that the new discoveries in electricity had thrown so great a light on the subject, that every thing respecting it would now have been clearly explained.

MRS. B.

That is a point which we are yet far from having attained. But, in spite of the imperfection of our theories, you will be amply repaid by the importance and novelty of the subject. The number of new facts which have already been ascertained and the immense prospect of discovery which has lately been opened to us, will, I hope, ultimately lead to a perfect elucidation of this branch of natural science; but at present you must be contented with studying the effects, and in some degree explaining the phenomena, without aspiring to a precise knowledge of the remote cause of electricity.

You have already obtained some notions of electricity: in our present conversation, therefore, I shall confine myself to that part of the science which is of late discovery, and is more particularly connected with chemistry.

It was a trifling and accidental circumstance which first gave rise to this new branch of physical science. Galvani,[4] a professor of natural philosophy at Bologna, being engaged (about thirty years ago) in some experiments on muscular irritability, observed, that when a piece of metal was laid on the nerve of a frog, recently dead, whilst the limb supplied by that nerve rested upon some other metal, the limb suddenly moved, on a communication being made between the two pieces of metal.

EMILY.

How is this communication made?

MRS. B.

Either by bringing the two metals into contact, or by connecting them by means of a metallic conductor. But without subjecting a frog to any cruel experiments, I can easily make you sensible of this kind of electric action. Here is a piece of zinc, (one of the metals I mentioned in the list of elementary bodies)—put it *under* your tongue, and this piece of silver *upon* your tongue, and let both the metals project a little beyond the tip

---

[4] Luigi Galvani (1737–98), discoverer of animal electricity.

of the tongue;—very well;—now make the projecting parts of the metals touch each other, and you will instantly perceive a peculiar sensation.

EMILY.

Indeed I did; a singular taste, and I think a degree of heat; but I can hardly describe it.

MRS. B.

The action of these two pieces of metal on the tongue is, I believe, precisely similar to that made on the nerve of the frog. I shall not detain you by a detailed account of the theory by which Galvani attempted to explain this fact, as it was soon over turned by subsequent experiments, which proved that *Galvanism* (the name this new power had obtained) was nothing more than electricity. Galvani supposed that the virtue of this new agent resided in the nerves of the frog; but Volta[5] who prosecuted this subject with much greater success, showed that the phenomena did not depend on the organs of the frog, but upon the electrical agency of the metals, which is excited by the moisture of the animal, the organs of the frog being only a delicate test of the presence of electric influence.

CAROLINE.

I suppose, then, the saliva of the mouth answers the same purpose as the moisture of the frog, in exciting the electricity of the pieces of silver and zinc with which Emily tried the experiment on her tongue?

MRS. B.

Precisely. It does not appear, however, necessary that the fluid used for this purpose should be of an animal nature: water, and acids very much diluted by water, are found to be the most effectual in promoting the development of electricity in metals; and, accordingly, the original apparatus which Volta first constructed for this purpose, consisted of a pile or succession of plates of zinc and copper, each pair of which was connected by pieces of cloth or paper impregnated with water; and this instrument, from its original inconvenient structure and limited strength, has gradually arrived at its present state of power and improvement, such as is exhibited in the Voltaic battery. In this apparatus, a specimen of which you see before you (Plate IX. fig. 1.), the plates of zinc and copper are

[5] Alessandro Volta (1745–1827), Italian chemist and inventor of the electric battery, here called the 'Voltaic' battery.

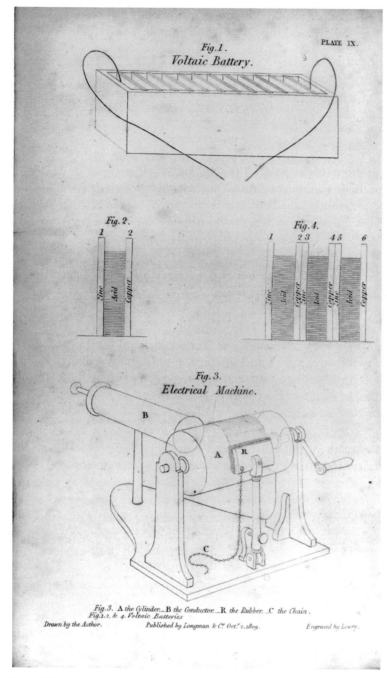

10 Plate IX Mrs Marcet's diagrams of the Voltaic Battery. By permission of the British Library, London.

soldered together in pairs, each pair being placed at regular distances in wooden troughs, and the interstices being filled with fluid.

CAROLINE.

Though you will not allow us to inquire into the precise cause of electricity, may we not ask in what manner the fluid acts on the metals so as to produce it?

MRS. B.

The action of the fluid on the metals, whether water or acid be used, is entirely of a chemical nature. But whether electricity is excited by this chemical action, or whether it is produced by the contact of the two metals, is a point upon which philosophers do not yet perfectly agree.

EMILY.

But can the mere contact of two metals, without any intervening fluid, produce electricity?

MRS. B.

Yes, if they are afterwards separated. It is an established fact, that when two metals are placed in contact, and afterwards separated, that which has the strongest attraction for oxygen exhibits signs of positive, the other of negative electricity.

CAROLINE.

It seems, then, but reasonable to infer that the power of the Voltaic battery should arise from the contact of the plates of zinc and copper.

MRS. B.

It is upon this principle that Volta and Sir H. Davy explain the phenomena of the pile: but not withstanding these two great authorities, many philosophers entertain doubts on the truth of this theory.

[. . .]

This subject, it must be owned, is involved in too much obscurity to enable us to speak very decidedly in favour of any theory. But, in order to avoid perplexing you with different explanations, I shall confine myself to one which appears to me to be least encumbered with difficulties, and most likely to accord with truth.[6]

[6] This mode of explaining the phenomena of the Voltaic pile is called the *chemical theory* of electricity, because it ascribes the cause of these phenomena to certain chemical changes which take place during their appearance.

This theory supposes the electricity to be excited by the chemical action of the acid on the zinc; but you are yet such novices in chemistry, that I think it will be necessary to give you some previous explanation of the nature of this action.

All metals have a strong attraction for oxygen; and this element is found in great abundance, both in water and in acids. The action of the diluted acid on the zinc consists, therefore, in its oxygen combining with it, and dissolving its surface. [. . .]

MRS. B.

In the Voltaic battery the diluted acid acts only on the surface of the zinc, to which it yields its oxygen, forming upon it a film or crust, which is that compound of the oxygen and the metal, we have called an oxide.

[. . .]

CAROLINE.

Does not, then, the acid act on the plates of copper, as well as on those of zinc?

MRS. B.

No: for though copper has an affinity for oxygen, it is less strong than that of zinc; and therefore the energy of the acid is only exerted upon the zinc.

It will be best, I believe, in order to render the action of the Voltaic battery more intelligible, to confine our attention at first to the effect produced on two plates only. (Plate IX. Fig. 2.)

If a plate of zinc be placed opposite to one of copper, or any other metal less attractive of oxygen, and the space between them (suppose of half an inch in thickness), be filled with an acid or any fluid capable of oxidating the zinc, the oxidated surface will have its capacity for electricity diminished, so that a quantity of electricity will be evolved from that surface. This electricity will be received by the contiguous fluid, by which it will be transmitted to the opposite metallic surface, the copper, which is not oxidated, and is therefore disposed to receive it; so that the copper plate will thus become positive, whilst the zinc plate will be in the negative state.

This evolution of electrical fluid, however, will be very limited; for as these two plates admit of but very little accumulation of electricity, and are supposed to have no communication with other bodies, the action of the acid, and further development of electricity, will be immediately stopped.

[. . .]

EMILY.

That is very clear, so far as two plates only are concerned; but I cannot say I understand how the energy of the succession of plates, or rather pairs of plates, of which the galvanic trough is composed, is propagated and accumulated throughout a battery?

MRS. B.

In order to show you how the intensity of the electricity is increased by increasing the number of plates, we will examine the action of four plates; if you understand these, you will readily comprehend that of any number whatever. In this figure (Plate IX. Fig. 4.), you will observe that the two central plates are united: they are soldered together (as we observed in describing the Voltaic trough) so as to form but one plate, which offers two different surfaces; the one of copper, the other of zinc.

Now you recollect, that, in explaining the action of two plates, we supposed that a quantity of electricity was evolved from the surface of the first zinc plate, in consequence of the action of the acid, and was conveyed by the interposed fluid to the copper plate No. 2, which thus became positive. This copper plate communicates its electricity to the contiguous zinc plate No. 3, in which, consequently, some accumulation of electricity takes place. When, therefore, the fluid in the next cell acts upon the zinc plate, electricity is extricated from it in larger quantity, and in a more concentrated form, than before. This concentrated electricity is again conveyed by the fluid to the next pair of plates, Nos. 4 and 5, when it is further increased by the action of the fluid in the third cell, and so on, to any number of plates, of which the battery may consist; so that the electrical energy will continue to accumulate in proportion to the number of double plates, the first zinc plate of the series being the most negative, and the last copper plate the most positive.

CAROLINE.

But does the battery become more and more strongly charged, merely by being allowed to stand undisturbed?

MRS. B.

No: for the action will soon stop, as was explained before, unless a vent be given to the accumulated electricities. This is easily done, however, by establishing a communication by means of the wires (Fig. 1.) between the two ends of the battery: these being brought into contact, the two electricities meet and neutralize each other, producing the shock and other effects of electricity: and the action goes on with renewed energy, being no longer obstructed by the accumulation of the two electricities which impeded its progress.

[. . .]

MRS. B.

[. . .] The great superiority of the Voltaic battery consists in the large *quantity* of electricity that passes; but in regard to the *rapidity* or *intensity* of the charge, it is greatly surpassed by the common electrical machine. It would seem that the shock or sensation depends chiefly upon the intensity; whilst, on the contrary, for chemical purposes, it is quantity which is required. In the Voltaic battery the electricity, though copious, is so weak as not to be able to force its way through the fluid which separates the plates, whilst that of a common machine will pass through any space of water.

CAROLINE.

Would it not be possible to increase the intensity of the Voltaic battery till it should equal that of the common machine?

MRS. B.

It can actually be increased till it imitates a weak electrical machine, so as to produce a visible spark when accumulated in a Leyden jar. But it can never be raised sufficiently to pass through any considerable extent of air, because of the ready communication through the fluids employed.

By increasing the number of plates of a battery, you increase its *intensity*, whilst, by enlarging the dimensions of the plates, you augment its *quantity*; and as the superiority of the battery over the common machine consists entirely in the quantity of electricity produced, it was at first supposed that it was the size, rather than the number of plates that was essential to the augmentation of power. It was, however, found upon trial, that the quantity of electricity produced by the Voltaic battery, even when of a very moderate size, was sufficiently copious, and that the chief advantage in this apparatus was obtained by increasing the intensity, which, however, still falls very short of that of the common machine.

I should not omit to mention, that a very splendid, and, at the same time, most powerful battery, was, a few years ago, constructed under the direction of Sir H. Davy, which he repeatedly exhibited in his course of electro-chemical lectures. It consists of two thousand double plates of zinc and copper, of six square inches in dimensions, arranged in troughs of Wedgwood-ware, each of which contains twenty of these plates. The troughs are furnished with a contrivance for lifting the plates out of them in a very convenient and expeditious manner.

CAROLINE.

Well, now that we understand the nature of the action of the Voltaic battery, I long to hear an account of the chemical discoveries to which it has given rise.

Conversation VIII – On Hydrogen

MRS. B.

[. . .]

HYDROGEN cannot, any more than oxygen, be obtained in a visible or palpable form. We are acquainted with it only in its gaseous state, as we are with oxygen and nitrogen.

CAROLINE.

But in its gaseous state it cannot be called a simple substance, since it is combined with heat and electricity?

MRS. B.

True, my dear: but as we do not know in nature of any substance which is not more or less combined with caloric and electricity, we are apt to say that a substance is in its pure state when united with those agents only.

Hydrogen was formerly called *inflammable air*, as it is extremely combustible, and burns with a great flame. Since the invention of the new nomenclature, it has obtained the name of hydrogen, which is derived from two Greek words, the meaning of which is *to produce water*.

EMILY.

And how does hydrogen produce water?

MRS. B.

By its combustion. Water is composed of 89 parts, by weight, of oxygen, combined with 11 parts of hydrogen; or of two parts, by bulk of hydrogen gas, to one part of oxygen gas.

CAROLINE.

Really! is it possible that water should be a combination of two gases, and that one of these should be inflammable air? Hydrogen must be a most extraordinary gas to produce both fire and water!
[. . .]

MRS. B.

The combustion of hydrogen gas certainly does; but you do not seem to have remembered the theory of combustion so well as you thought you would. Can you tell me what happens in the combustion of hydrogen gas?

CAROLINE.

The hydrogen combines with the oxygen, and their opposite electricities are disengaged in the form of caloric.—Yes, I think I understand it now—by the loss of this caloric, the gases are condensed into a liquid.
[. . .]

CAROLINE.

I should like extremely to see water decomposed.

MRS. B.

I can gratify your curiosity by a much more easy process than the oxidation of charcoal or metals: the decomposition of water by these latter means takes up a great deal of time, and is attended with much trouble; for it is necessary that the charcoal or metal should be made red hot in a furnace, that the water should pass over them in a state of vapour, that the gas formed should be collected over the water-bath, &c. In short, it is a very complicated operation. But the same effect may be produced with the greatest facility, by the action of the Voltaic battery, which this will give me an opportunity of exhibiting.

177

CAROLINE.

I am very glad of that; for I longed to see the power of this apparatus in decomposing bodies.

MRS. B.

For this purpose I fill this piece of glass-tube (Plate XI. Fig. 1.) with water, and cork it up at both ends; through one of the corks I introduce that wire of the battery which conveys the positive electricity; and the wire which conveys the negative electricity is made to pass through the other cork, so that the two wires approach each other sufficiently near to give out their respective electricities.

CAROLINE.

It does not appear to me that you approach the wires so near, as you did when you made the battery act by itself.

MRS. B.

Water being a better conductor of electricity than air, the two wires will act on each other at a greater distance in the former than in the latter case.

EMILY.

Now the electrical effect appears: I see small bubbles of air emitted from each wire.

MRS. B.

Each wire decomposes the water, the positive by attracting its oxygen which is negative, the negative by attracting its hydrogen which is positive.

CAROLINE.

That is wonderfully curious! But what are the small bubbles of air?

MRS. B.

Those which appear to proceed from the positive wire are the result of the decomposition of the water by that wire. The particles of hydrogen, having naturally the same electricity as the positive wire, are repelled by it, and pass over to the negative wire by which they are attracted.

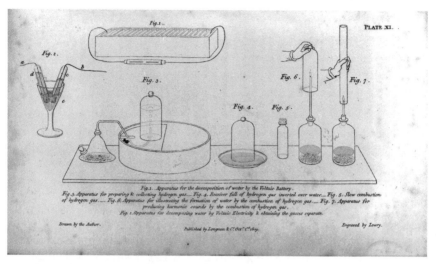

11 Plate XI Mrs Marcet's diagrams showing apparatus for the decomposition of water by the Voltaic Battery. By permission of the British Library, London.

EMILY.

And I suppose the oxygen is, on the contrary, repelled by the negative wire and attracted by the positive wire?

MRS. B.

Precisely so. Both these elements being thus separated from each other, and set at liberty, appear in the form of small bubbles of gas or air: the oxygen at the positive wire, and the hydrogen at the negative wire.

I should not forget to observe that the wires used in this experiment are made of platina, a metal which is not capable of combining with oxygen; for otherwise the wire would combine with the oxygen, and the hydrogen alone would be disengaged.

CAROLINE.

But could not water be decomposed without the electric circle being completed? If, for instance, you immersed only the positive wire in the water, would it not combine with the oxygen, and the hydrogen gas be given out?

MRS. B.

No; for as you may recollect, the battery cannot act unless the circle be completed; since the positive wire will not give out its electricity, unless attracted by that of the negative wire.

CAROLINE.

I understand it now.—But look, Mrs. B., the decomposition of the water, which has been going on for some time, does not sensibly diminish its quantity—what is the reason of that?

MRS. B.

Because the quantity decomposed is so extremely small. If you compare the density of water with that of the gases into which it is resolved, you must be aware that a single drop of water is sufficient to produce thousands of such small bubbles as those you now perceive.

CAROLINE.

But in this experiment we obtain the oxygen and hydrogen gases mixed together. Is there any means of procuring the two gases separately?

MRS. B.

They can be collected separately with great ease, by modifying a little the experiment. Thus if instead of one tube we employ two, as you see here (c, d, Plate XI. Fig. 2.), both tubes being closed at one end, and open at the other; and if after filling these tubes with water, we place them in a glass of water (e), with their open end downwards, you will see that the moment we connect the wires (a, b,) which proceed upwards from the interior of each tube, the one with one end of the battery, and the other with the other end, the water in the tubes will be decomposed; oxygen will be given out round the wire in the tube connected with the positive end of the battery, and hydrogen in the other; and these gases will be evolved exactly in the proportions which I have before mentioned, namely, two measures of hydrogen for one of oxygen. We shall now begin the experiment, but it will be some time before any sensible quantity of the gases can be collected.

EMILY.

The decomposition of water in this way, slow as it is, is certainly very wonderful; but I confess that I should be still more gratified, if you could show it us on a larger scale, and by a quicker process. [. . .]

MRS. B.

Water may be decomposed by means of metals without any difficulty; but for this purpose the intervention of an acid is required. Thus, if we add some sulphuric acid (a substance with the nature of which you are not yet acquainted) to the water which the metal is to decompose, the acid enables the metal to combine with the oxygen of the water so readily and abundantly, that no heat is required to hasten the process.

[. . .]

We shall not, suffer any to escape, as it will be wanted for experiments. I shall, therefore, collect it in a glass-receiver, by making it pass through this bent tube, which will conduct it into the water-bath. (Plate XI. Fig. 3.)

EMILY.

How very rapidly the gas escapes! it is perfectly transparent, and without any colour whatever.—Now the receiver is full——

MRS. B.

We shall, therefore, remove it, and substitute another in its place. But you must observe, that when the receiver is full, it is necessary to keep it inverted with the mouth under water, otherwise the gas would escape. And in order that it may not be in the way, I introduce within the bath, under the water, a saucer, into which I slide the receiver, so that it can be taken out of the bath and conveyed any where: the water in the saucer being equally effectual in preventing its escape as that in the bath. (Plate XI. fig. 4.)

EMILY.

I am quite surprised to see so large a quantity of hydrogen gas produced by so small a quantity of water, especially as oxygen is the principal constituent of water.

MRS. B.

In weight it is; but not in volume. For though the proportion, by weight, is nearly eight parts of oxygen to one of hydrogen, yet the proportion of the volume of the gases is about one part of oxygen to two of hydrogen; so much heavier is the former than the latter.

[. . .]

If, we allow but a very small surface of gas to burn in contact with the atmosphere, the combustion goes on quietly and gradually at the point of contact, without any detonation, because the surfaces brought together are too small for the immediate union of the gases. The experiment is a very easy one. This phial, with a narrow neck (Plate XI. fig. 5.), is full of hydrogen gas, and is carefully corked. If I take out the cork without moving the phial, and quickly place the candle at the orifice, you will see how different the result will be——

EMILY.

How prettily it burns, with a blue flame! The flame is gradually sinking within the phial—now it has entirely disappeared. But does not this combustion likewise produce water?

MRS. B.

Undoubtedly. In order to make the formation of the water sensible to you, I shall procure a fresh supply of hydrogen gas, by putting into this bottle (Plate XI. fig. 6.) iron-filings, water, and sulphuric acid, materials similar to those which we have just used for the same purpose. I shall then cork up the bottle, leaving only a small orifice in the cork, with a piece of glass-tube fixed to it, through which the gas will issue in a continued rapid stream.

CAROLINE.

I hear already the hissing of the gas through the tube, and I can feel a strong current against my hand.

MRS. B.

This current I am going to kindle with the candle—see how vividly it burns——

EMILY.

It burns like a candle with a great flame. But why does this combustion last so much longer than in the former experiment?

MRS. B.

The combustion goes on uninterruptedly, as long as the new gas continues to be produced. Now, if I invert this receiver over the flame, you will soon perceive its internal surface covered with a very fine dew, which is pure water——

CAROLINE.

Yes, indeed; the glass is now quite dim with moisture! How glad I am that we can *see* the water produced by this combustion.

EMILY.

It is exactly what I was anxious to see; for I confess I was a little incredulous.

MRS. B.

If I had not held the glass-bell over the flame, the water would have escaped in the state of vapour, as it did in the former experiment. We have here obtained but a very small quantity of water; but the difficulty of procuring a proper apparatus, with sufficient quantities of gases, prevents my showing it you on a larger scale.

The composition of water was discovered about the same period, both by Mr. Cavendish,[7] in this country, and by the celebrated French chemist, Lavoisier.[8] The latter invented a very perfect and ingenious apparatus to perform, with great accuracy, and upon a large scale, the formation of water by the combination of oxygen and hydrogen gases. Two tubes, conveying due proportions, the one of oxygen, the other of hydrogen gas, are inserted at opposite sides of a large globe of glass, previously exhausted of air; the two streams of gas are kindled within the globe, by the electrical spark, at the point where they come in contact; they burn together, that is to say, the hydrogen combines with the oxygen, the caloric is set at liberty, and a quantity of water is produced exactly equal, in weight, to that of the two gases introduced into the globe.

[. . .]

Before we take leave of hydrogen, I must not omit to mention to you a most interesting discovery of Sir H. Davy, which is connected with this subject.

[7] Henry Cavendish (1731–1810), English gentleman chemist who discovered hydrogen and also the composition of water.

[8] Antoine Laurent Lavoisier (1743–94), French chemist identified with a major theoretical shift in the understanding of chemistry towards the end of the eighteenth century. He also discovered the composition of water, independently of Cavendish.

CAROLINE.

You allude, I suppose, to the miner's lamp, which has been so much talked of? I have long been desirous of knowing what that discovery was, and what purpose it was intended to answer.

MRS. B.

It often happens in coal-mines, that quantities of the gas called by chemists *hydro-carbonat*, or by the miners *fire-damp* (the same from which the gaslights are obtained), ooze out from fissures in the beds of coal, and fill the cavities in which the men are at work: and this gas being inflammable, the consequence is, that when the men approach those places with a lighted candle, the gas takes fire, and explosions happen which destroy the men and horses employed in that part of the colliery, sometimes in great numbers.

EMILY.

What tremendous accidents these must be! But whence does that gas originate?

MRS. B.

Being the chief product of the combustion of coal, no wonder that inflammable gas should occasionally appear in situations in which this mineral abounds, since there can be no doubt that processes of combustion are frequently taking place at a great depth under the surface of the earth; and, therefore, those accumulations of gas may arise either from combustions actually going on, or from former combustions, the gas having perhaps been confined there for ages.

CAROLINE.

And how does Sir H. Davy's lamp prevent those dreadful explosions?

MRS. B.

By a contrivance equally simple and ingenious; and one which does no less credit to the philosophical views from which it was deduced, than to the philanthropic motives from which the enquiry sprung. The principle of the lamp is shortly this: It was ascertained two or three years ago, both by Mr. Tennant[9] and by Sir Humphry himself, that the combustion of

[9] Smithson Tennant (1761–1815), who died shortly after being appointed to the Chair of Chemistry at the University of Cambridge. He is best known as the discoverer of two new elements. Mrs Marcet did not update this part of her text since, in 1825, this event was more than 'two or three years ago'.

inflammable gas could not be propagated through small tubes; so that if a jet of an inflammable gaseous mixture, issuing from a bladder or any other vessel, through a small tube, be set fire to, it burns at the orifice of the tube, but the flame never penetrates into the vessel. It is upon this fact that Sir Humphry's safety lamp is founded.

EMILY.

But why does not the flame ever penetrate through the tube into the vessel from which the gas issues, so as to explode at once the whole of the gas?

MRS. B.

Because, no doubt, the inflamed gas is so much cooled in its passage through a small tube as to cease to burn before the combustion reaches the reservoir.

CAROLINE.

And how can this principle be applied to the construction of a lamp?

MRS. B.

Nothing easier. You need only suppose a lamp enclosed all round in glass or horn, but having a number of small open tubes at the bottom, and others at the top, to let the air in and out. Now, if such a lamp or lanthern be carried into an atmosphere capable of exploding, an explosion or combustion of the gas will take place *within* the lamp; and although the vent afforded by the tubes will save the lamp from bursting, yet, from the principle just explained, the combustion will not be propagated to the external air through the tubes, so that no farther consequence will ensue.

EMILY.

And is that all the mystery of that valuable lamp?

MRS. B.

No; in the early part of the enquiry a lamp of this kind was actually proposed; but it was but a rude sketch compared to its present state of improvement. Sir H. Davy, after a succession of trials, by which he brought his lamp nearer and nearer to perfection, at last conceived the happy idea that if the lamp were surrounded with a wire-work or wire-

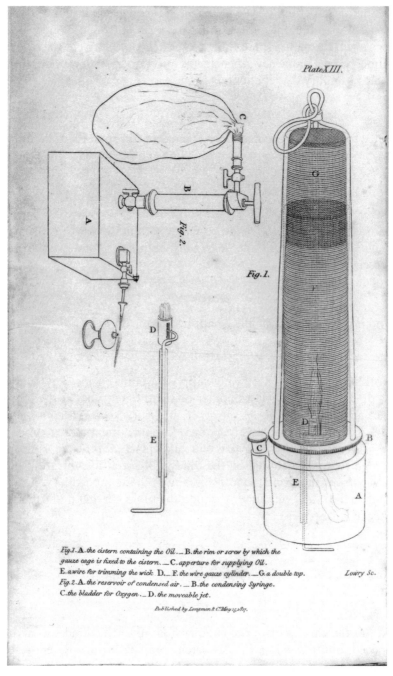

12 Plate XIII Mrs Marcet's diagram for the cistern collecting oil. By permission of the British Library, London.

gauze, of a close texture, instead of a glass or horn, the tubular contrivance I have just described would be entirely superseded, since each of the interstices of the gauze would act as a tube in preventing the propagation of explosion; so that this previous metallic covering would answer the various purposes of transparency, of permeability to air, and of protection against explosion. This idea, Sir Humphry immediately submitted to the test of experiment, and the result has answered his most sanguine expectations, both in his laboratory and in the collieries where it has already been extensively tried. And he has now the happiness of thinking that his invention is the means of saving every year a number of lives, which would have been lost in digging out of the bowels of the earth one of the most valuable necessaries of life. Here is one of these lamps, every part of which you will at once comprehend. (See Plate XIII. Fig. 1.)

CAROLINE.

How very simple and ingenious!

Source: [Mrs Jane Marcet] (1825), *Conversations on Chemistry; in which the elements of that science are familiarly explained and illustrated by experiments*, 10th edition, vol. 1, *On simple bodies* (first edition 1806). Preface, pp. v–x, Conversation I – On the General Principles of Chemistry, pp. 1–9, 16, 19, 26–8, Conversation VI – On the Chemical Agencies of Electricity, pp. 173–81, 184–6, 189–91, Conversation VIII – On Hydrogen, pp. 226–7, 229, 231–8, 241, 243, 258–61.

Sir John Soane

Sir John Soane referred to his country house, Pitzhanger Manor, as a portrait of the architect. For him, the successive transformations of his house at 12–14 Lincoln's Inn Fields were a very personal affair. The house represented for him not only a home for himself, his wife and two sons, but also his architectural office, his library and his museum. As his life changed, following his election as Professor at the Royal Academy, the departure of his sons, the death of his wife and the various successes and tribulations of his career, his house was adapted to reflect these events. The extraordinary manuscript *Crude Hints . . .*, from which extracts are printed here, mixed the intensely personal and Romantic sensibility of Soane with his persona as learned antiquarian and scholar. Just as he had constructed a fake ruin at Pitzhanger Manor to amuse his guests, so in *Crude Hints . . .* he teases the reader with a mock serious attempt to unravel the riddle of his house, imagined in ruins. That this riddle was indeed to be taken as autobiographical emerges clearly from the conclusion of the piece, where all Soane's anxieties and frustrations are allowed to pour out. A studied play on a Romantic interpretation of the house also emerges from the *Descriptions* which Soane wrote or commissioned for visitors. Soane entrusted to his good friend Mrs Barbara Hofland, a successful novelist, the task of capturing the mood of the sentimental journey expected of the visitor to Soane's house and museum. Playing on the artifice of the mysterious 'Padre Giovanni' (Sir John Soane himself in monkish form), Mrs Hofland paints a picture of scholastic and lonely seclusion, in the 'Monk's Parlour', facing onto the 'Monk's Yard', with its ruins composed of real medieval pieces salvaged from Whitehall Palace. That the lonely monk was not without some worldly pleasures, however, emerges from her wry comment about the bottle ends with which the yard is paved. And the monk's tomb turns out to be the final resting place not of Padre Giovanni, but of his wife's dog Fanny.

Extract from *Crude Hints towards an History of my House in L[incoln's] I[nn] Fields*, 1812[1]

In this age of research when the Connoisseur and the Antiquary find a lively interest in whatever relates to former times . . . so much notice has been taken of the ruins and very extensive assemblage of fragments of ancient works partly buried and in some degree attached to a building in this metropolis apparently of later date [in Lincoln's Inn Fields (del.)] – to rescue this work from its present uncertain origin and that the public should be fully [better] informed respecting these ruins and be led to have an interest in them, I shall collect together the various conjectures which have been made respecting this building and also the data on which these speculative opinions have been raised . . .

From the style of some parts of the Architecture this work has been supposed anterior to the time of Augustus [and apparently (del.)] long before Architecture had attained that high polish which the works of the Augustan Age so clearly possessed – other reasons equally plausible have been adduced . . . to establish a contrary opinion. [Soane Note: *A Votive foot & hand indicate this building to have been a temple – and the cornu ammonis*[2] *designate it as dedicated to Jupiter.*[3] *The Columns describe a Colonnade of a kind almost peculiar to Convents, and as these Cols. [sic] are of the Ionic or Feminine order it is reasonable to conclude from thence that it had been a convent of Nuns, & not a Heathen Temple.*[4]]

. . . it is to be observed that notwithstanding this building consisted of several stages or stories . . . *no vestiges remain of a staircase of any kind* . . .[5]

---

[1] Manuscript in Soane's hand, dated 30 August to 22 September 1812. Soane laid out his manuscript in several columns, with notes, alternative wordings and additions along the right hand side. Tim Benton has extracted and simplified the text. He has used the transcription in *Visions of Ruin*, a catalogue of an exhibition in 1999, published by Sir John Soane's Museum. Helen Dorey edited the text. He has included her textual notes in square brackets. His notes are presented in footnotes and are indebted to her annotations.

[2] *Cornu ammonis* – The ram's horn shape of the ammonite fossil was said to have given the name for the Temple then known as Jupiter Ammon, in Rome. In displaying an ammonite fossil in the Monument Court, Soane was making an archaeological joke.

[3] Three ammonite fossils were displayed in the Monument Court. The shape of the ammonite recalls the goat's horn taken to be the attribute of Jupiter Ammon, said to have been suckled by the goat Amalthea on the island of Crete.

[4] Two Ionic columns support a pergola in the Monument Court.

[5] This is a joke based on the fact that wooden structures perish before stone, so that antique ruins often seem to lack staircases to upper floors.

[Soane Note]. *Admitted – but at the same time there is a space, well suited for a Staircase as it would communicate most easily with the different rooms now existing in the building – I am aware it has been supposed that this very space, if a staircase, could only have been one of those Carcerian dark Staircases represented in some of Piranesi's ingenious dreams for prisons: – those who argue thus forget that a staircase may be [might have been] lighted by a Skylight . . . and after all the want of lights proves nothing – does not Pliny speak & in rapturous delight of the pleasure of writing in a Room lighted by lamps. . . .*

Those who suppose this Edifice to have been an ancient temple, reason thus: – the priests of Vesta had the care of the sacred fire and the punishment attached to neglect thereof was most exemplary [*sic*], as well as to the Vestal Virgins who were found guilty of any incontinency or human frailty:– on this supposition, it has been imagined that the place just spoken of as a Staircase, might from its retired situation and total darkness have been the very spot where was immured & left to starve to death in all the horrors of endless darkness there to pay the forfeit of a little human frailty:– here is food for meditation even to madness – particularly when made on the very spot where the unfortunate maiden breathed her last.

Whilst by some this place has been looked on as a Temple, others have supposed it to have been the residence of some Magician, & in support of this opinion they speak of a large statue placed in the centre of one of the Chapels which they say might have been this very necromancer changed into marble for having dared to destroy the statues of the Apostles formerly placed in the niches now remaining in the in the front of this building next the park.[6]

In support of this building having been a work of the Greeks it is noted that in the Cavedium[7] there are two Caryatides or female figures supporting part of the Roof of a peristyle. This is strong evidence . . . but these statues might have been brought from Greece into this Country and here placed for ornament. [Soane Note] *Lord Elgin the modern Mummius in modern times caused various parts of antique buildings to be taken from Greece into this Country and in the Staircase in Lansdowne House are several pieces of sculpture relative to Roman Cults and heathen religion.*[8] Let us now for the present leave the further consider-

---

[6] The 'park' referred to is the street called Whetstone Park on the north side. There are twelve blind (ie windowless) niches in this front, which is effectively the back entrance.

[7] *Cavedium*: courtyard.

[8] Lucius Mummius Achaicus was a Roman Consul in 146 BC known for pillaging the Greek city of Corinth and bringing its art treasures back to Rome.

ation of the interior and proceed to the exterior appearance of the fabric
. . . and as far as may be judged from its present state it must have been
raised by some fanciful *mind* smitten with the love of novelty in direct
[utter] defiance of all the established rules of the Architectural Schools,
anxious to "Sketch a grace beyond the reach of art" . . .

There is a tradition that during the progress of this [front (del.)] work
much offense [*sic*] was taken by many to the composition of this front,
doubtless from their love for pure architecture and their apprehensions
lest this example might corrupt the beautiful and simple elegance of this
mode then in use, many attempts were therefore made in conjunction to
render the whole abortive.[9] An officer yclept [called] a district Surveyor
was *pushed forward* [put in the front of the battle] on the occasion and
boldly entered his veto against this apocryphal work . . . [Soane Note.
*Some illiberal persons have asserted that the two old Women [caryatids
on the façade] are to represent [personify] the two great Architects to
whose combined talents we are indebted for the great display of fine
Architecture opposite & who are supposed to be placed here to admire
and to point out to others the beauty of that extensive pile of bricks &
mortar.*[10]]

. . . if this place has been as now premised a place of [for] public Worship a burying place would have been attached to it, accordingly we find
the ornaments with which this place is surmounted are of a kind to designate the approach to a place of sepulture, some terra santa attached to
the building . . . thus pointing out by these [ornaments (del.)] decorations and monumental mementos the intention of this place in like
manner as the terra sancta[11] at Pisa is designated . . .[12]

It is difficult to determine for what purposes such a strange and mixed
assemblage of ancient works or rather *copies of* [cast from] them, for
many are not of stone or marble, have been brought together – some
have supposed it might have been for the advancement of Architectural
knowledge by making the young Students in that noble & useful Art

---

[9] The district surveyor William Kinnard tried to force Soane to pull down the façade, which
encroached onto the pavement; Soane responded with a legal suit which was finally settled in
his favour in the House of Lords. All this was going on as Soane wrote the piece.

[10] One of two heavily sarcastic drafts of this text, referring to the Coade Stone caryatids on
Soane's house façade placed directly opposite two sculptures on the façade of the Royal College of Surgeons (still under construction) on the other side of Lincoln's Inn Fields, built by
George Dance junior (Soane's first master) and an architect called James Lewis. This was one
of the buildings criticised by Soane in his Royal Academy lectures and in other writings.

[11] *Terra Sancta*: Holy Land.

[12] The Campo Santo in Pisa was a well known thirteenth-century cloister adjoining the
Cathedral. It was visited by Grand Tourists (including Soane) because it contained large numbers of antique sarcophagi and other fragments.

who had no means of visiting Greece and Italy some better ideas of ancient Works than would be conveyed thro: the medium of drawings or prints.[13] This *proposition* [idea] is by far too visionary & absurd to be admitted for a moment, & yet it does appear in some degree to remove the obscurity & veil of darkness which at present envelopes the subject . . . Let us therefore instead of supposing the building to have been a Heathen Temple to Vesta [Soane Note. *It could not have been a temple to Vesta. They were always round.*[14]] or to some other divinity – or the palace of an Enchanter – or a Convent for Nuns – let us I say look at it merely as a dwelling, & that of an Artist, either an Architect or painter . . . and the models for Architectural decoration and the extensive Library of books on that Art which are there to be seen are circumstances indicative of the reasonableness of the latter (sic) suggestion. . . . Now if it may be presumed that this individual, this identical person, was not only an Artist but an Architect . . . do we not account most satisfactorily for that great assemblage of ancient fragments in the interior of the building which must have been placed there for the advancement and knowledge of ancient Arts & may not those varieties in the Cavedium, evidently the work of different artists have been fixed there in like manner to exemplify later changes in Architecture & to lay the foundation of an History of the Art itself – its origin – progress – meridian splendour & decline! . . . He is also recorded to have been so enthusiastically attached to his profession and so anxious to promote the knowledge of what he conceived to be its true principles that he omitted no opportunity of expressing his opinion on the works of all ages, not because he thought highly of his own discernment and acquired knowledge (for he was humble & modest, at the same time said to be of lively fancy) but in order to call forth the better & more useful observations of others, & thereby to provoke discussion on his favourite Art – but the man was a mere child in the World – he was indiscreet where policy is wont to impress restraint:– he had only one impression and that was what arose out of the thing spoken of – he never gave himself a moments time to reflect on who was the author of the work he criticised, he only considered whether it differed from what he conceived the laws of nature & the practice of antiquity justified & whether if the work passed without notice it might be quoted as an example & prove detrimental to what he thought good taste required & calculated to operate against improve-

[13] Soane did claim to open his house to students at the Royal Academy before and after his lectures (as well as to members of the public), although some students claimed that the house was not freely accessible.

[14] The antique circular Temple of Vesta at Tivoli was one of Soane's favourite buildings.

ments in Architecture.[15] . . . He did not consider his friends – his family – his kindred – his allies and the many recruits that would enlist under him from a sense of common danger – but he went on from a pure love to promote the interests of Art, until at last he had raised a nest of wasps about him sufficient to sting the strongest man to death. Revenge *levelled* [fabricated] tales of dishonour at him, which no innocence of heart or integrity of conduct could set right and to wind up the tragedy cruelty and cowardice, twin ruffians set on by malice in the dark combined together to strike at his infirmities and mistakes:- then persecutions and other misfortunes of a more direct & domestic nature preyed on his mind – he saw the views of early youth blighted – his fairest prospects utterly destroyed – his lively character became sombre – melancholy, brooding constantly over an accumulation of evils brought him into a state little short of mental derangement, his enemies perceived this – they seized the moment – they smote his rock & he fell as many had done before him and died as was generally believed of *a broken heart.*[16]

What an admirable lesson does this work furnish against the vanity of human expectations – the man who founded this place piously imagined that the fruits of his honest industry & the reward of professional appli- cation [*sic*], he was laying the foundation of a family & that the *filii filiorum*[17] of his loins should, smitten with the love of art & anxious to shew their gratitude for the benefits they thus derived from it, dwell in the place *for ages* [from generation to generation], that a race of artists would have been raised up whose efforts from the advantages they set out with, advantages the lot of the chosen few only, would have raised architecture of its meridian splendour. O man, man, how short is thy foresight. In less than half a century – in a few years – before the founder was scarcely mouldering in dust, no trace to be seen of the artist within its walls, the edifice presenting only a miserable picture of frightful dilap- idation – oh could the dead but leave for a moment their quiet mansions, & but look out of their graves what hell could equal their torments!

AN ANTIQUARY

[from an alternative ending]

Oh what a falling off do these ruins present – the subject becomes too gloomy to be pursued – the pen drops from my almost palsied hand . . .

[15] This passage refers to his violent attacks on the work of contemporary fellow Royal Aca- demicians in his fourth Lecture. The fact that he picked on buildings by George Dance junior and Henry Holland (his two masters) and Robert Smirke junior, for a brief time one of his pupils (with whom he did not get on), rather belies the force of this argument.

[16] Soane drafted three versions of this ending, clearly wallowing in the pathos of the words.

[17] *filii filiorum*: a rough translation: fruit of my loins, or, from generation to generation.

Source: Helen Dorey, ed., *Visions of Ruin*, 1999, exhibition catalogue, published by Sir John Soane's Museum.

Extract from George Soane (attrib.), 'The present low state of the Arts in England, and more particularly architecture', *The Champion*, 10 September 1815

A mercantile spirit is perhaps least of all calculated for the production of
any thing great or lasting. The mind, that has for years been employed in
the minutiae of traffic, in weighing sugar against plumbs, and reckoning
up the yearly interest of accumulated farthings, cannot easily expand
itself to the perception of what is really grand; it will measure everything
by its saleable value, or in other words, by its value in exchange for the
common necessities of life: . . . *[This explains the fact that the English
have 'no love either for Art or Science']* . . . It is indeed true that genius
sometimes has so strong a bias to art, that it overlooks these obstacles,
and to this we owe the paintings of a Lawrence[18] and an Owen, the
sculpture of a Banks, and the architecture of a Smirke; but these names
are by no means sufficient to justify the reproaches cast upon the nation
by every foreignor who has visited us; – they laugh at the heavy, lum-
bering extravagance of the Bank and the fooleries of Nash, our Chinese
pagodas and our drawing rooms built after the fashion of Grecian temples. Allowing, what in truth cannot well be denied, the vast superiority
of Grecian architecture, it yet does not follow that our parlours and bed
rooms are to be modelled after the plan of a heathen temple – because
the taste of Athens designed the figures caryatids, it surely is not requisite that ladies of stone are to be grinning at full length in the front of a
substantial, brick-built modern house – it is like decorating harlequin
with a Roman helmet; – yet all these and greater incongruities are to be
found in the capital of England: and indeed there are scarcely six buildings in the whole town that merit the attention of a moment . . . *[Then
follows an attack on the aristocratic and middle classes for their lack of
taste and the extravagance of the court. George Soane goes on to attack
the buildings of the Chelsea Hospital, not naming the architect (his
father).]* . . . To begin with Chelsea Hospital. Within the last two years,

[18] Sir Thomas Lawrence painted a portrait of Soane which now hangs in the Dining Room.

a new Infirmary, new stables and a new house for the use of the Clerk of the Works [John Soane], have been erected. Without pretending to any very great skill in architecture, it must be quite clear, that buildings so different in their nature, must require a difference of construction: the case is precisely the reverse:- not that we mean to say that there is a manager in the architect's house, or a drawing-room in the stables, but the style of architecture is the same in all, the house being rather the most awkward of the three; on the top, at the back are two large raisin jars; let us not be understood to speak jestingly; we say in all the gravity of truth, that there are two large raisin jars, fresh, to all appearance, from the grocer's shop . . .[19]

Extract from George Soane (attrib.), 'The present low state of the Arts in England, and more particularly architecture', *The Champion*, 24 September 1815

[Criticism of Chelsea Hospital continues, concluding:] There is something exquisitely ludicrous in this union of contrarities (sic), the effect of which is hardly to be conveyed in writing. Disproportion is the most striking feature in the works of this artist; he plunders from the records of antiquity things in themselves absolutely good, but which never were intended to meet in the same place. Thus in the Bank of England, the greater part of which is built by Mr SOANE, we meet with remnants of mausoleums, caryatides, pillars from temples, ornaments from the Pantheon, and all heaped together with a perversion of taste that is truly admirable. He steals a bit here, and a bit there, and in piling up these collected thefts, he imagines he has done the duty and earned the honours of an artist. Depraved as is the present taste, such follies will not pass for wisdom; the public laugh at these extravagances, which are too dull for madness, and too mad for the soberness of reason. The most extraordinary instance of this perversity of taste and dullness of invention is to be found in this artist's house in Lincoln's Inn Fields. The exterior, from its exceeding heaviness and monumental gloom, seems as if it were intended to convey a satire upon himself: it looks like a record of the departed,

---

[19] These 'raisin jars' are Soane's chimmey pots, one of which was also displayed in the Monk's Yard at Lincoln's Inn Fields.

and can only mean, that considering himself as defunct in that better part of humanity – the mind and its affections – he has reared this mausoleum for the enshrinement of his body.

The interior of this building forms a ludicrous contrast with its external appearance. The passages glow with the deepest red: the lower room, which occupies the whole length of the building, is converted into a library, a second satire upon the possessor, who must stand in the midst of these hoarded volumes like a eunuch in a seraglio;[20] the envious and impining guardian of that which he cannot enjoy. On the left is a small room intended for a study, and beyond is a narrow lofty cave, ycleped [called] the museum; it is lighted at the top by a lantern of stained glass, forming a strange medley of Gothic and Grecian taste. Its contents, in a moral point of view, are truly valuable; here are urns that once contained the ashes of the great, the wise and the good; here are relics broken from the holy temples of Greece and Italy; here is the image of the Ephesian Diana, once the object of human adoration, but now only valued as a rarity, that by its high price may feed the grovelling pride of its possessor. – We are not architects, nor do we pretend to more knowledge in the art than common observation can supply, but we aspire, however unworthily, to that higher character which unites moral feeling with those inanimate objects, and does not basely admire a column because its proportions may be just or its marble may be pure.

Somerset House and St Paul's are too well known to need discussion; but the merits of Covent-Garden Theatre have not yet been fully appreciated.[21] The exterior appearance of this building is grand and imposing; there is a unity, a harmony about the whole, which adds considerable weight to its magnificence. Nothing can excel the effect of the Pit entrance by lamp-light; it is an illusion that borders on fairy-land; the play of light and shadow upon the arches produces a feeling of mystery and extent, that must be felt to be rightly understood . . . [George goes on to criticise aspects of the interior] . . . With this reservation it is a noble building, creditable to the architect, and his country that enjoys it.[22]

[20] *seraglio*: (lit) harem, more commonly referring to a summerhouse and its garden in a Turkish palace.

[21] Sir William Chambers, Somerset House, 1776–96. Sir Christopher Wren, St Paul's Cathedral, 1667–85. The competition for Covent Garden Theatre, for which John Soane had provided an unsuccessful design, was built to the designs of Robert Smirke junior, who had been briefly articled to Soane. It was Soane's harsh criticism of this building, in his fourth Lecture 29 January 1810, which led to the Royal Academy vote to prevent Professor's criticising the work of fellow Academicians.

[22] This second instalment ends 'To be continued', but there was no further continuation.

Extract from descriptions of Soane's House written by Mrs Barbara Hofland and added to Soane's *Description of the Residence of Sir John Soane Architect*, 1835[23]

[OF THE DINING ROOM AND LIBRARY]

The general effect of these rooms is admirable: they combine the characteristics of wealth and elegance, taste and comfort, with those especial riches which belong expressly to Literature and Art – to the progressive proofs of human intellect and industry, given from age to age, in those works which most decisively evince utility and power. That which might be termed the triumph of Architecture, and which succeeding ages may adopt and complete in our metropolis (where a part only, defrauded of its fair proportions, yet appears), is seen in the beautiful model of the Board of Trade and Privy Council Offices, which we find the more admirable as a whole the longer we contemplate it. But, since every design which is truly great must possess that union of parts which constitutes the best claim to magnificence, so must we the more lament that it is left incomplete, and of course exposed to the danger of future incongruous associations.[24]

[OF THE STUDY AND DRESSING ROOM]

The fragments of Grecian and Roman sculpture, whether parts of friezes, cornices, or animals, are executed with singular elegance, and chiselled so finely, that it would be impossible for the hardest metals to represent

---

[23] Mrs Hofland was a friend of the Soanes who became a close friend after the death of Eliza Soane in 1815. Her husband was a struggling artist and illustrator, and to help make ends meet, Mrs Hofland embarked on a literary career as novelist and occasional journalist. Soane valued her romantic sensibility and willingness to listen to his more emotional outpourings. Her inserted descriptions, signed 'BH' in the 1835 *Description of the Residence of Sir John Soane Architect* have a quite different style to the rather stern antiquarian manner adopted by Soane in his publications. Soane said they were intended to 'render it more pleasing and attractive to young minds'. It is probable, however, that Mrs Hofland reflected accurately the other side of Soane's complex nature and that her insertions echo their long conversations together. I have used the edited version of her additions, compiled in a single volume by the curator of the Sir John Soane's Museum, Arthur T. Bolton, in 1919.

[24] The model is still exhibited on the mantelpiece of the Dining Room. Soane's plans for Whitehall included an extension of these buildings to include a redevelopment of Downing Street framed by triumphal arches. Soane's buildings were demolished in 1849, to be replaced by Sir Charles Barry's Treasury Building.

them with more sharpness, or the freest pencil to depict them with more flowing grace or satisfactory accuracy. . . . Contrasting small things with great ones, every person must look with interest on the sulphur casts of seals and gems, their delicate execution and classical design claiming particular attention. So will the bell-light of the recess; for it is of that soft primrose hue so peculiarly adapted for the exhibiton of marbles, imparting the tint of time to those which have not attained it, yet not increasing its effects on the more ancient.

[OF THE CORRIDOR]

Surely we have here 'sermons in stones'. If Paganism could lead the most polished people to take delight in seeing the physical energies of man devoted to the destruction of his brother-man, even by losing his own life – if murder and suicide could form amusement, not only to a debased and ferocious mob, but to the statesmen, philosophers, and ladies of Rome; well might human nature, when blest with one ray from heaven, turn from it in disgust and seek in the genius of Christianity, a power to smile even in the arms of death.

Everywhere we behold objects in perfect keeping with the sentiments they tend to awaken. Marble fragments, noble friezes, most magnificent and diversified capitals, casts of most difficult attainment, and casts from curule chairs in which have sat men who were the conquerors and rulers of the world, and whose words and actions even yet exert an influence on the destinies of mankind – by turns elicit observation. On every side are objects of deep interest alike to the antiquary, who loves to explore and retrace them through ages past; the student, who, in cultivating a classic taste, becomes enamoured of their forms; and the imaginative man, whose excursive fancy gives to each 'a local habitation and a name' in association with the most interesting events and the most noble personages the page of history has transmitted for our contemplation.

Yes! These are all feathers shed from the wings of Time, reminding us of the glories of days that are past, and of countries comparatively sunk into oblivion.

[ON THE MONK'S PARLOUR]

Whatever can be desired by a religious recluse will be found here, and much also that an age of luxury demands as essential for comfort in a certain class – and padre Giovanni is unquestionably a gentleman. He has retired from a world he was fitted to adorn, not from satiety or disgust, but from motives of piety, or a taste for retirement, aided by those sorrows inseparable from the condition of our being, and which naturally indispose us, after a certain age, to mix in the turmoil of life. His heart's dear partner has long been taken from the evil to come; the daughter whose beauty delighted, whose tenderness consoled him, has followed her to the grave; and the son, who should have supplied the place of both, is become an alien to his home and his country.[25] Whither should he go, save to a retreat where, at least, 'the wicked cease from troubling, and the weary will be soon at rest'?

Here will he find all, and more than all, his heart desires. Behold his oratoire enriched by a carved crucifix, on which his taste may expatiate, whilst his devotion kindles. Here are recesses for the relics he deems inestimable, and the missals which shall beguile his solitary hours.[26] His apartment is covered with the products of various countries on which he may meditate, and the works of various ages with which his studies have made him familiar; and his presses are stored with countless drawings of ecclesiastical edifices, dear to his memory and congenial to his tastes and pursuits; and he looks upon them through windows of painted glass, presenting subjects still more sacred. The richly tinted light descending to his apartment bestows on every object that mellow lustre which aids the all-pervading sentiment: it is light subdued, not exhausted – an autumnal, not a wintry and waning ray, and becomes about midday perfectly splendid being aided in effect by the brightness of the carpet, and chairs cushioned with crimson silk.

These luxuries do not quite accord with the simplicity and voluntary poverty demanded by conventual life; but they are far short of the princely luxuries of the Prior of Alcobaca, described with such inimitable humour by the author of 'Vathek'.[27] Our imagined padre is the last representative of an order to whom, after all, we are much indebted; for whilst learning and the arts, which followed in its train, were hidden in the cells of the monks, surely they were its preservers, and have a claim on the gratitude of those who benefit by their guardianship . . .

[ON THE BASEMENT]

Whether examining the Ante-room with its many attractions or re-entering the corridor and proceeding towards the catacombs, we are alike

---

[25] Under cover of the alias of 'Padre Giovanni' (Father John [Soane]), Mrs Hofland makes some surprising transpositions. She converts Soane's elder son John (who died in 1823) into a beautiful daughter and leaves as the only son George, the traitor. Why George Soane, the struggling playwright, should be labelled an 'alien to his country', unless it was for his imprisonment for bankruptcy, is not clear.

[26] The missals were later removed from the Monk's Parlour.

[27] William Beckford of Fonthill Abbey (1760–1844). Soane worked briefly for Beckford but saw himself supplanted by Wyatt.

sensible 'that we here attain that first of intellectual beauties, which in every production, whether of nature or art, resides in the exact correspondence between the end we propose and the means we employ'. It is evident that the hand, or rather the mind, which has arranged the beautiful fragments, massive pillars ancient sculptures, and various decorations around us, intended that sentiment to pervade our bosoms, proper to the visitants of the dead, who are not therefore the personally regretted . . .

[ON THE BELZONI SARCOPHAGUS]

If, in the hour of midday splendour, the sarcophagus appears only a superb and suitable finish to the works of art by which it is surrounded, and more calculated to complete the impression conveyed by the whole, than to claim exclusive and individual preference; it should be viewed by lamplight also.[28] . . . Deep masses of shadow, faint gleams that rise like *ignes fatui* from the adjoining crypt, lights that shone like lustrous halos round marble heads, others more vague and indistinct, yet beautiful in their revealings, present appearances beheld as in a dream of the poets' Elysium;[29] and without enlarging the objects, the scene itself, under this artificial illumination, appears considerably expanded. By degrees this space becomes peopled – figure after figure emerges from the crypt and corridors, where thay had loitered in the gloom; they assemble around the sarcophagus, which sheds from within a pale unearthly light upon the silent awe-struck beings that surround it. Fair and lovely they appear, the sons and daughters of a high-born race, exempt from the common evils of life, but awake to all its generous sensibilities and higher perceptions. Pensive is every countenance, and soft every falling footstep; yet in gentle accents many a voice breathes thanks to him who hath rolled back the current of time to show them glorious visions of the past, yet taught them to feel in the hour of pleasure itself that

The paths of glory lead but to the grave.

Such, I believe, were the feelings of all who had the gratification of witnessing this most impressive scene in the year 1825 when Sir John Soane had it thus prepared for three evenings, during which the rank and talent

---

[28] In the description which follows, Mrs Hofland recalled the three-day presentation of the Belzoni sarcophagus in March 1825 when a long list of the famous and wealthy were invited to see the Museum by lamplight. Guests included Lawrence, Turner and Coleridge, Lord and Lady Liverpool, the heir to the throne, the Duke of Sussex and Sir Robert Peel. Thousands of oil lamps were artfully deployed, some glowing through the walls of the alabaster Belzoni sarcophagus, to dramatise the objects.

[29] *Elysium*: or Elysium fields, or plain; the paradise first mentioned in Homer's *Odyssey* where heroes would live after death.

of this country, to an immense number, including many foreigners of distinction, enjoyed an exhibition as striking as it must ever be unrivalled.

Had any of that gay company been placed alone in the sepulchral chamber at the 'witching hour of night', when

Churchyards yawn and graves give up their dead

when the flickering lights become self-extinguished, and the last murmuring sounds from without ceased to speak of the living world – it is probable that even the healthiest pulse would have been affected with the darker train of emotions which a situation so unallied to common life is calculated to produce. The awe ameliorated by beauty, and softened by tender reminiscence, would be exchanged for the mysterious expectation of some terrific visitant from the invisible world; and the very strongest mind would exclaim with Hamlet

There are more things in heaven and earth, Horatio
Than are dreamt of in your philosophy.

[ON THE APOLLO BELVEDERE AND LIGHTING IN THE MUSEUM]

The beauty of this fine statue, like every other object of interest around, is considerably enhanced by that exquisite distribution of light and colour which, often from undiscovered sources, sheds the most exquisite hues, and produces the most magical effects throughout the Museum, thereby communicating the only charm in which an assemblage of marbles must be deficient . . . Life and colour are so intimately conjoined that we cannot separate them without losing one: even the most breathing sculptures 'that Art has bequeathed to Time' require some aid from those ethereal tints which at the same moment rescue them from the characteristics of death, and reveal those of life, beauty and intelligence. A writer of acknowledged genius, who has deeply studied the subject, thus speaks of colour: 'We feel as if there is a moral as well as material beauty in colour, an inherent gladness, an intention on the part of Nature to share with a pleasure felt by herself. Colours are the smiles of Nature. When they are extremely smiling, and break forth into other beauty, they are her laughs; as in the flowers.' . . . Of course, these exquisite effects vary with the time and atmosphere; but the coloured glass is so judiciously disposed (being assisted by innumerable reflections from mirrors inserted not obtrusively), that the coldness likely to arise from opaque objects nearly devoid of colour is completely avoided, and a diffusion of warm and cheerful light cast upon everything we behold.

Source: Helen Dorey, ed., *Visions of Ruin*, 1999, exhibition catalogue, published by Sir John Soane's Museum.

PART III

New conceptions of art and the artist

Two conceptions of art

The eleven extracts which follow set out some of the leading ideas in the area of aesthetics characteristic of the Enlightenment period and early Romanticism respectively. Taken together, the extracts show how great a change took place in respect of views on aesthetics between these two periods. The first extract, from the Scottish philosopher David Hume, sets out the dominant Enlightenment view of how the imagination works. The second, from the same period, by the leading French encyclopedist D'Alembert expounds the view that all the arts are forms of imitation of nature. The remaining nine extracts are taken from the works of four of the leading German theorists of Romanticism, and brief biographical details of them are given in the head notes to the relevant extracts. Taken together, these extracts set out the major ideas of Romantic aesthetics: the belief that the imagination, not the reason, is the faculty which penetrates to reality; that consequently the role of the artist becomes the same as that of the priest; that artistic genius is the most precious of human faculties; that the role of art is to lead us to knowledge of reality by stimulating our imagination without end; that good art has depth or profundity; that art is and is known by the artist to be an attempt to communicate something ultimately incommunicable, and that the art which comes closest to achieving this goal is music. In almost all areas of aesthetic thought, the views of the Enlightenment and the Romantic period about art are diametrically opposed.

Extract 1 from David Hume, *A Treatise of Human Nature*

OF THE IDEAS OF THE MEMORY AND IMAGINATION.

We find by experience, that when any impression has been present with the mind, it again makes its appearance there as an idea; and this it may do after two different ways: either when in its new appearance it retains a considerable degree of its first vivacity, and is somewhat intermediate betwixt an impression and an idea; or when it intirely loses that vivacity, and is a perfect idea. The faculty, by which we repeat our impressions in the first manner, is called the MEMORY, and the other the IMAGINA-TION. 'Tis evident at first sight, that the ideas of the memory are much more lively and strong than those of the imagination, and that the former faculty paints its objects in more distinct colours, than any which are employ'd by the latter. When we remember any past event, the idea of it flows in upon the mind in a forcible manner; whereas in the imagination the perception is faint and languid, and cannot without difficulty be pre-serv'd by the mind steddy and uniform for any considerable time. Here then is a sensible difference betwixt one species of ideas and another. But of this more fully hereafter.

There is another difference betwixt these two kinds of ideas, which is no less evident, namely that tho' neither the ideas of the memory nor imagination, neither the lively nor faint ideas can make their appearance in the mind, unless their correspondent impressions have gone before to prepare the way for them, yet the imagination is not restrain'd to the same order and form with the original impressions; while the memory is in a manner ty'd down in that respect, without any power of variation.

'Tis evident, that the memory preserves the original form, in which its objects were presented, and that where-ever we depart from it in recol-lecting any thing, it proceeds from some defect or imperfection in that faculty. An historian may, perhaps, for the more convenient carrying on of his narration, relate an event before another, to which it was in fact posterior; but then he takes notice of this disorder, if he be exact; and by that means replaces the idea in its due position. 'Tis the same case in our recollection of those places and persons, with which we were formerly acquainted. The chief exercise of the memory is not to preserve the simple ideas, but their order and position. In short, this principle is supported by such a number of common and vulgar phænomena, that we may spare ourselves the trouble of insisting on it any farther.

The same evidence follows us in our second principle, *of the liberty of the imagination to transpose and change its ideas.* The fables we meet with in poems and romances put this entirely out of question. Nature there is totally confounded, and nothing mentioned but winged horses, fiery dragons, and monstrous giants. Nor will this liberty of the fancy appear strange, when we consider, that all our ideas are copy'd from our impressions, and that there are not any two impressions which are perfectly inseparable. Not to mention, that this is an evident consequence of the division of ideas into simple and complex. Where-ever the imagination perceives a difference among ideas, it can easily produce a separation.

Source: David Hume, *A Treatise of Human Nature*, L. A. Selby-Bigge and P. H. Nidditch, eds, Oxford University Press, Oxford, 1978, pp. 8–10.

Extract 2 from Jean Le Rond D'Alembert, *Preliminary Discourse to the Encyclopaedia*

D'Alembert was the illegitimate son of the Marquise de Tencin (1685?–1749), who exposed him as an infant on the steps of the church of Saint-Jean-Le-Rond, from which he derived his Christian name. His principal intellectual interests were in the sciences, notably mathematics, astronomy and dynamics. He was one of the leading members of the group of *philosophes* and was Diderot's principal assistant in the preparation of the *Encyclopédie* until 1758. He had a Europe-wide reputation and was influential as perpetual secretary of the Académie française from 1772. Hume left him a legacy of £200. In the following extract he sets out a typical version of the theory of art as imitation as it was understood during the period of the Enlightenment.

[. . .]

Since the first operation of reflection consists in drawing together and uniting direct notions, we of necessity have begun this Discourse by looking at reflection from that point of view and reviewing the different sciences that result from it. But the notions formed by the combination of primitive ideas are not the only ones of which our minds are capable. There is another kind of reflective knowledge, and we must turn to it now. It consists of the ideas which we create for ourselves by imagining and putting together beings similar to those which are the object of our direct ideas. This is what we call the imitation of Nature, so well known and so highly recommended by the ancients. Since the direct ideas that strike us most vividly are those which we remember most easily, these are also the ones which we try most to reawaken in ourselves by the imitation of their objects. Although pleasant objects [of reality] have a greater impact on us because they are real rather than mere imitations, we are somewhat compensated for that loss of attractiveness by the pleasure which results from imitation. As for the objects which, when real, excite only sad or tumultuous sentiments, imitation of them is more pleasing than the objects themselves, because it places us at precisely that distance where we experience the pleasure of the emotion without feeling its disturbance. That imitaton of objects capable of exciting in us lively, vivid, or pleasing sentiments, whatever their nature may be, constitutes in general the imitation of *la belle Nature*, about which so many authors have written without presenting a clear idea of it. They fail to do so either because *la belle Nature* can be perceived by only an extremely delicate sensitivity, or perhaps also because in this matter the limits which distinguish the arbitrary from the true are not yet well defined and leave some area open to opinion.

Painting and Sculpture ought to be placed at the head of that knowledge which consists of imitation, because it is in those arts above all that imitation best approximates the objects represented and speaks most directly to the senses. Architecture, that art which is born of necessity and perfected by luxury, can be added to those two. Having developed by degrees from cottages to palaces, in the eyes of the philosopher it is simply the embellished mask, so to speak, of one of our greatest needs. The imitation of *la belle Nature* in Architecture is less striking and more restricted than in Painting or Sculpture. The latter express all the parts of *la belle Nature* indifferently and without restriction, portraying it as it is, uniform or varied; while Architecture, combining and uniting the different bodies it uses, is confined to imitating the symmetrical arrangement that Nature observes more or less obviously in each individual thing, and that contrasts so well with the beautiful variety of all taken together.[1]

---

[1] *La belle Nature* is defined by Jaucourt (*Encyclopédie*, XI, 42) as nature embellished and perfected by the fine arts for use and pleasure. The artist makes a choice of the most beautiful parts of nature to form an exquisite whole, which would be more beautiful than nature itself. It is not direct imitation, but rather the representation of nature as it could be.

Poetry, which comes after Painting and Sculpture, and which imitates merely by means of words disposed according to a harmony agreeable to the ear, speaks to the imagination rather than to the senses. In a touching and vivid manner it represents to the imagination the objects which make up this universe. By the warmth, the movement, and the life which it is capable of giving, it seems rather to create than to portray them. Finally, music, which speaks simultaneously to the imagination and to the senses, holds the last place in the order of imitation – not that its imitation is less perfect in the objects which it attempts to represent, but because until now it has apparently been restricted to a smaller number of images. This should be attributed less to its nature than to the lack of sufficient inventiveness and resourcefulness in most of those who cultivate it. It will not be useless to make some reflections on this subject. In its origin music perhaps was intended only to represent noise. Little by little it has become a kind of discourse, or even language, through which the different sentiments of the soul, or rather its different passions, are expressed. But why reduce this kind of expression to passions alone, and why not extend it as much as possible to the sensations themselves? Although the perceptions that we receive through various organs differ among themselves as much as their objects, we can nevertheless compare them according to another point of view which is common to them: that is, by the pleasurable or disquieting effect they have upon our soul. A frightening object, a terrible noise, each produces an emotion in us by which we can bring them somewhat together, and we can often designate both of these emotions either by the same name or by synonymous names. Thus, I do not see why a musician who had to portray a frightening object could not succeed in doing so by seeking in nature the kind of sound that can produce in us the emotion most resembling the one excited by this object. I say the same of agreeable sensations. To think otherwise would be to wish to restrict the limits of art and of our pleasures. I confess that the kind of depiction of which we are speaking here demands a subtle and profound study of the shadings which differentiate our sensations; thus it is not to be hoped that these shadings will be distinguished by an ordinary talent. Grasped by the man of genius, perceived by the man of taste, understood by the man of intelligence, they are lost on the multitude. Any music that does not portray something is only noise; and without that force of habit which denatures everything, it would hardly create more pleasure than a sequence of harmonious and sonorous words stripped of order and connection. It is true that a musician desirous of portraying everything would in many circumstances give us scenes of harmony which would not be grasped by vulgar senses. But all that can be concluded from this is that after having created an art of learning music one ought also to create an art of listening to it.

Source: Jean Le Rond D'Alembert, *Preliminary Discourse to the Encyclopaedia*, 1751, trans. R. N. Schwab, University of Chicago Press, Chicago, 1995, pp. 36–9.

Extract 3 from Novalis, *Miscellaneous Observations*

Novalis ('one who turns over new ground') is the pen-name of Friedrich, Freiherr von Hardenburg, and the name always now used to refer to him. He was born in the town of Oberwiederstedt (near Mansfeld in Thuringia) in May 1772, into a household noted for strict pietism. He was educated privately at home until he was 18. After one year at school, he went to the University of Jena, and thence to Leipzig, Wittenberg (1792) and finally to Tennstedt to learn administration. Novalis's short life was changed irrevocably when in November 1794 he met and fell in love with a thirteen year-old girl, Sophia Wilhelmine von Kühn, to whom he became engaged in March 1795. Tragically, Sophia became ill, endured appalling suffering both from abscesses on the liver and the treatment for them, and died in March 1797. Her death, which caused a serious crisis in Novalis's life, was the mainspring behind one of his best-known and most enduring sets of poems, the *Hymns to the Night (Hymnen an die Nacht)* written in 1799 and published in the leading Romantic periodical *Das Athenäum* in 1800. In 1797 Novalis entered a school of mining at Freiberg, and later took up a post as manager of a mine at Weißenfels in 1799. In 1800 he began to show symptoms of tuberculosis, and the disease killed him seven months later. Unlike the majority of the theorists of the Romantic movement, Novalis was an important creative writer as well as a theorist of Romanticism, leaving novels as well as poems at the time of his death.

[. . .]

The imagination places the world of the future either far above us, or far below, or in a relation of metempsychosis to ourselves. We dream of traveling through the universe – but is not the universe *within ourselves*? The depths of our spirit are unknown to us – the mysterious way leads inwards. Eternity with its worlds – the past and future – is in ourselves or nowhere. The external world is the world of shadows – it throws its shadow into the realm of light. At present this realm certainly seems to us so dark inside, lonely, shapeless. But how entirely different it will seem to us – when this gloom is past, and the body of shadows has moved away. We will experience greater enjoyment than ever, for our spirit has been deprived.

Source: Novalis, *Miscellaneous Observations*, 17, in Margaret Mahony Stoljar (ed. and trans.), *Novalis: Philosophical Writings*, State University of New York Press, Albany, 1997, p. 25.

Extract 4 from Novalis, *Logological² Fragments II*

As the painter sees visible objects with quite different eyes from those of the common person – so too the poet experiences the events of the outer and the inner world very differently from the ordinary person. But nowhere is it more striking than in music – that it is only the spirit that poeticizes the objects and the changes of the material, and that the beautiful, the subject of art, is not given to us nor can it be found ready in phenomena. All sounds produced by nature are rough – and empty of spirit – only the musical soul often finds the rustling of the forest – the whistling of the wind, the song of the nightingale, the babbling of the brook melodious and meaningful. The musician takes the essence of his art from within himself – not even the slightest suspicion of imitation can apply to him. To the painter, visible nature seems everywhere to be doing his preliminary work – to be entirely his unattainable model. But really the painter's art has arisen just as independently, quite as a priori, as the musician's. Only the painter uses an infinitely more difficult *symbolic language* than the musician – the painter really paints with his eye – his art is the art of seeing with order and beauty. Here seeing is quite active – entirely a formative activity. His image is only his secret sign – his expression – his reproducing tool. Suppose we compare the written

---

² The term 'logological' is a coinage by Novalis. In Greek, the term *logos* means both (a) word and (b) principle (as in all the English words which end in -logy, meaning principles of whatever it happens to be). In this neologism, Novalis is trading on both these meanings. Logology is a discourse about principles, or perhaps first principles. Certainly, the content sets out Novalis's convictions about the root or basic ideas underlying Romanticism as he understood it, the philosophy of Romanticism as we might now say.

musical *note* with this artificial sign. The musician might rather counter the painter's image with the diverse movements of the fingers, the feet, and the mouth. Really the musician too hears actively – he distinguishes by hearing. For most people this reversed use of the senses is certainly a mystery, but every artist will be more or less clearly aware of it. Almost every person is to a limited degree already an artist. In fact he sees actively and not passively – he feels actively and not passively. The main difference is this: the artist has vivified the germ of self-formative life in his sense organs – he has raised the excitability of these *for the spirit* and is thereby able to allow ideas to flow out of them at will – without external prompting – to use them as tools for such modifications of the real world *as he will.* On the other hand for the nonartist they speak only through the intervention of external prompting, and the spirit, like inert matter, seems to be governed by or to submit to the constraint of the basic laws of mechanics, namely that all changes presuppose an external cause and that effect and countereffect must equal each other at all times. At least it is some consolation to know that this mechanical behavior is unnatural to the spirit and is *transient*, like all that is spiritually unnatural.

Yet even with the most humble person the spirit does not wholly obey the law of mechanics – and hence it would be possible for everyone to develop this higher propensity and skill of the organ.

Source: Novalis, *Logological Fragments II*, 17, in Margaret Mahony Stoljar (ed. and trans.) *Novalis: Philosophical Writings*, State University of New York Press, Albany, 1997, pp. 71–2.

Extract 5 from Wilhelm Wackenroder, *Concerning Two Wonderful Languages and Their Mysterious Power*

Wihelm Heinrich Wackenroder was born in 1773, son of a high-ranking Prussian civil servant. In 1793 he went for a semester to the University of Erlangen to study law, in the company of his friend Ludwig Tieck (1773–1853), also a Berliner, member of the Romantic group and a prolific writer. His best-known work in the UK, oddly, is *Der gestiefelte Kater*, i.e. *Puss-in-Boots*). Far more than by their studies these young men were deeply moved and impressed by the landscape and towns of south Germany and Bavaria. Here for the first time they came across Baroque art and remnants of the Middle Ages. In the autumn of 1793 they moved to the University of Göttingen where – in addition to law – Wackenroder studied older German literature, together with fine art and music. These experiences resulted in Wackenroder's first book, *Confessions from the Heart of an Art-loving Friar*, 1797, from which this extract is taken. Wackenroder died, quite suddenly, in Berlin in the following year. *Fantasies on Art for Friends of Art* (*Phantasien über die Kunst, für Freunde der Kunst*) 1799, was put together by Tieck from his friend's papers.

1 The language of words is a great gift of heaven and it was a perpetual blessing of the Creator that He enabled the first human being to speak, so that he could name all the things which the Highest One had placed around him in the world and all the spiritual images which He had implanted in his soul and could exercise his mind in the diverse play with this abundance of names. We rule over the entire globe by means of words; with easy effort we acquire for ourselves through trade all the treasures of the earth by means of words. Only the invisible force which hovers over us is not drawn down into our hearts by words.

2 We have the earthly things in our hand when we speak their names;—but when we hear the infinite goodness of God mentioned, or the virtue of the saints, which are indeed subjects that ought to grip our whole being, then our ears alone become filled with empty sounds and our spirit is not elevated as it should be.

3 However, I know of two wonderful languages through which the Creator has permitted human beings to perceive and to comprehend heavenly things in their full force, as far as this (in order not to speak presumptuously) is possible, namely, for mortal creatures. They enter into our souls through entirely different ways than through the aid of words; they move our entire being suddenly in a wondrous manner, and they press their way into every nerve and every drop of blood which belongs to us. God alone speaks the first of these wonderful languages; the second is spoken only by a few Chosen Ones among men, whom He has anointed as His favorites. I mean: Nature and Art.—

4 Since my early youth, when I first became acquainted with the God of mankind from the ancient holy books of our religion, Nature always seemed to me the most fundamental and the clearest book of explanation concerning His being and His attributes. The rustling in

the treetops of the forest and the rolling of the thunder told me mysterious things about Him which I cannot set down in words. A beautiful valley surrounded by fantastic cliff formations or a calm river in which leaning trees are reflected or a pleasant green meadow, shone upon by the blue sky,—ah! these things have inspired more marvelous emotions deep within me, have filled my spirit more fervently with the omnipotence and infinite goodness of God, and have purified and elevated my entire soul far more than the language of words was ever capable of doing. It is, in my opinion, an all too earthly and clumsy instrument to handle the spiritual as well as the physical realm with it.

5 I find here a great inducement to praise the power and goodness of the Creator. Around us human beings He placed an infinite number of things, each of which has a different nature and none of which we can understand and comprehend. We do not know what a tree is; nor what a meadow nor what a cliff is; we cannot communicate with them in our language; we only understand each other. And, nevertheless, the Creator has placed in the human heart such a marvelous sympathy for these things that they bring to it by unknown pathways emotions or sentiments, or whatever one may call them, which we never acquire through the most measured words.

6 Out of a zeal for the truth which is in itself laudable, the philosophers have gone astray; they have wanted to uncover the mysteries of heaven and place them amidst the things of earth in earthly illumination and have expelled the dim intuitions of the same from their breasts with bold advocacy of their right.—Is the weak human being capable of clarifying the mysteries of heaven? Does he rashly think that he can bring to light what God has hidden with His own hand? May he, indeed, arrogantly dismiss the dim intuitions which descend to us like veiled angels?—I honor them in deep humility; for it is a great benevolence of God that He send down to us these genuine witnesses of the truth. I fold my hands and worship.—

7 Art is a language of a totally different type than Nature; but, through similar dark and mysterious ways, it also has a marvelous power over the heart of man. It speaks through pictures of human beings and, therefore, makes use of a hieroglyphic script, whose symbols we know and understand in their external aspect. But it fuses spiritual and supersensual qualities into the visible shapes in such a touching and admirable manner that, in response, our entire being and everything about us is stirred and affected deeply. Many a painting of the Passion of Christ or of our Holy Virgin or from the history of the saints has, I may indeed say it, cleansed my mind more and inspired

214

my inner consciousness with more blessedly virtuous convictions than systems of morality and spiritual meditations. Among others, I still think with fervor about a most magnificently painted picture of our Saint Sebastian, how he stands naked and bound to a tree, how an angel draws the arrow out of his breast and a second angel brings a floral wreath from heaven for his head. I am indebted to this painting for very penetrating and tenacious Christian convictions and I now can scarcely bring the same vividly back to mind without having tears well up in my eyes.

8   The teachings of the philosophers set only our brains in motion, only the one half of our beings; but the two wonderful languages whose power I am proclaiming here affect our senses as well as our minds; or, rather (I cannot express it differently), they seem thereby to fuse all parts of our nature (incomprehensible to us) into one single new organ, which perceives and comprehends the heavenly miracles in this twofold way.

9   One of the languages, which the Highest One Himself continues to speak from eternity to eternity, continuously active, infinite Nature, leads us through the vast expanses of the atmosphere directly to the godhead. Art, however, which, by means of clever mixtures of colored earth and some moisture, copies the human form in narrow, restricted space, striving for inner perfection (a type of creation as was granted to mortal beings to produce),—it discloses for us the treasures in the human breast, turns our eyes towards our inner selves, and shows us the invisible part, I mean everything that is noble, grand, and divine, in human form.—

10   Whenever I walk out of the consecrated temple of our monastery into the open air after the contemplation of Christ on the Cross and the sunshine from the blue sky embraces me warmly and vibrantly and the beautiful landscape with mountains, waters, and trees strikes my eye, then I see a special world of God arise before me and feel great things surge up in my soul in a special way.—And when I go from the open air into the temple again and reflect upon the painting of Christ on the Cross with seriousness and fervor, then I once again see another entirely different world of God before me and feel great things rise up in my soul in another special way.

11   Art represents for us the highest human perfection. Nature, to the extent that a mortal eye sees it, resembles fragmentary oracular decrees from the mouth of the deity. However, if it is permissible to speak thusly of such things, then one would perhaps like to say that God may, indeed, look upon all of Nature or the entire world in a manner similar to the manner in which we look upon a work of art.

Source: Wilhelm Heinrich Wackenroder, *Concerning Two Wonderful Languages and Their Mysterious Power* in his *Confessions from the Heart of an Art-loving Friar (Herzensergießungen eines kunstliebenden Klosterbruders)*, 1797, in M. H. Schubert (ed. and trans.) *Wackenroder's Confessions and Fantasies*, Pennsylvania University Press, Pennsylvania, 1971, pp. 118–20.

Extract 6 from Wilhelm Wackenroder, *How and in what manner one actually must regard and use the* Works of the Great Artists of Earth *for the* Well-Being of his Soul

1 I continually hear the childish and frivolous world complain that God has placed only so few truly great artists on the earth; the ordinary soul impatiently stares into the future, wondering whether the Father of Mankind will not soon let a new race of outstanding masters rise up. But I say to you, the earth has not borne too few excellent masters; indeed, some of these are so constituted that a mortal being has in one alone ample to gaze upon and contemplate throughout his entire lifetime; but indeed, far, far too few are the ones who are capable of understanding deeply and (what is essentially the same) venerating earnestly the works of these beings (fashioned from more noble clay).

2 Art galleries are regarded as annual fairs, where one evaluates, praises, and disdains new products in passing by; and they ought to be temples where, in peaceful and silent humility and in heart-lifting solitude, one might admire the great artists as the most lofty among mortals and, with long, uninterrupted contemplation of their works, might warm oneself in the sunshine of the most charming thoughts and sensations.

3 I compare the enjoyment of the more noble works of art to prayer. That one is not pleasing unto heaven who speaks thereto only in order to be rid of the daily obligation, enumerates words without thoughts, and boastfully gauges his piety according to the beads of his rosary. That one is, however, a favorite of heaven who waits with humble longing for the chosen hours when the gentle, heavenly beam comes down to him voluntarily, splits open the shell of earthly insignificance with which the mortal spirit is generally covered, and

216

releases and displays his more noble inner self; then he kneels down, turns his open heart toward the brilliance of heaven in silent rapture, and saturates it with the ethereal light; thereupon he stands up, happier and more melancholy, with a fuller and lighter heart, and applies his hand to a large, good enterprise.—I hold this to be the true meaning of prayer.

4 One would, in my opinion, have to act in just this way with the masterpieces of art in order to use them worthily for the salvation of his soul. It is to be called sacrilegious, when someone reels away from the ringing laughter of his friends in an earthly hour in order, out of habit, to communicate with God for a few minutes in a nearby church. In such an hour it is a similar sacrilege to cross the threshold of the house where the most admirable creations which could be brought forth by the hands of men are preserved for eternity, as a quiet declaration of the dignity of this species. Wait, as with prayer, for the blessed hours when the grace of heaven illuminates your soul with higher revelation; only then will your soul be united with the works of the artists in one entity. Their enchanting figures are mute and uncommunicative when you look upon them coldly; your hearts must first address them intensely, if they are to be able to speak to you and exercise all their power upon you.

5 Works of art fit into the ordinary flow of life just as little in their own way as does the thought of God; they transcend the ordinary and the usual and we must lift ourselves up to them wholeheartedly in order to make them in our eyes, which are all too often clouded over by the fog of the atmosphere, what in their exalted nature they are.

6 Everyone can learn how to read alphabetical letters; everyone can let himself be told by learned histories the stories of past ages and retell them; everyone can also study the system of a scientific discipline and comprehend theorems and truths;—for letters are only there so that the eye might recognize their form; and principles and facts are only an object of our concern as long as the eye of the mind works upon them, to grasp and understand them; as soon as they are our own, the activity of our mind is at an end and we then merely indulge, as often as it pleases us, in a lazy and unfruitful survey of our treasures.—Not so with the works of magnificent artists. They are not there for that reason, so that the eye might see them, but so that one might penetrate into them with a receptive heart and live and breathe in them. A precious painting is not a paragraph of a textbook which, when with a brief effort I have extracted the meaning of the words, I then set aside as a useless shell: rather, in superior works of art the enjoyment continues on and on without ceasing. We believe that we

are penetrating deeper and deeper into them and, nevertheless, they continuously arouse our sense anew and we foresee no boundary at which our soul would have exhausted them. There is aflame within them an eternally burning oil of life, which is never extinguished before our eyes.

7 With impatience I fly beyond the first viewing; for the surprise of newness, which many souls who snatch at constantly changing pleasures wish to expound as the principal merit of art, has always seemed to me a necessary evil of the first viewing. True enjoyment requires a silent and peaceful frame of mind and is not expressed by outcries and the clapping of hands, but solely by inner emotions. It is a sacred holiday for me, when I devote myself to the contemplation of precious art works with seriousness and with a prepared heart; I return to them frequently and endlessly: they remain firmly impressed upon my mind and, as long as I shall walk the earth, I shall carry them about with me in my imagination, as spiritual amulets, as it were, for the consolation and the inspiration of my soul and shall take them with me into the grave.

8 He whose finer nerves are once active and receptive to the secret charm which lies hidden in art is often deeply moved in his soul where another passes by indifferently; he shares in the good fortune of finding in his life more frequent occasions for a salutary agitation and excitement of his inner self. I am aware that frequently when (occupied with other thoughts) I passed through some beautiful and grand, pillared portal, the mighty, majestic columns with their lovely stateliness attracted my gaze involuntarily to themselves and filled my spirit with a special sensation, so that I bowed down inwardly before them and passed on with opened heart and with richer soul.

9 The most important factor is that one not venture to soar with rash courage beyond the spirit of exalted artists and, looking down upon them, judge them: a foolish attempt of the vain pride of men: Art is above the human being: we can only admire and esteem the magnificent works of its consecrated ones and open our entire soul before them for the liberating and cleansing of all our emotions.

Source: Wilhelm Heinrich Wackenroder, *How and in what Manner one actually must regard and use the* Works of the Great Artists of Earth for the Well-Being of his Soul *from* Confessions, in M. H. Schubert (ed. and trans.) *Wackenroder's Confessions and Fantasies*, Pennsylvania University Press, Pennsylvania, 1971, pp. 125–7.

Extract 7 from Friedrich Schlegel, *Critical Fragments*

Friedrich Schlegel was the younger brother of August Wilhelm Schlegel, and was born in Hanover in 1772. Intended by his parents for a career in commerce, Friedrich Schlegel was initially apprenticed to a banker in Leipzig, but received permission from his parents to go to university, and thereafter studied in Göttingen and Leipzig, reading first law then classics (he was an extremely gifted student of Greek and Latin). At Leipzig he met Novalis, and the two became close friends. In May 1793, Friedrich Schlegel decided that his life's work would be to answer the question: what is the nature of literature? He initiated his research on this issue by devoting himself entirely to the study of classical texts, living reclusively in Dresden for over two years while he did so. In 1796 he joined his brother August Wilhelm Schlegel in Jena, though he soon thereafter moved to Berlin. He began publishing critical and theoretical essays in the mid-1790s, and contributed to various journals, notably *Das Athenäum*. In addition he published what was for the time a novel sensational in its sexual explicitness, *Lucinde* (1799), based on his love for the woman he eventually married, Dorothea Veit. After the dissolution of the group of the early Romantics in the first decade of the nineteenth century, Friedrich Schlegel converted to Catholicism and settled in Vienna in 1808. He took service in Metternich's government, and devoted much of his later life to the administration of public affairs, though this was interspersed with a number of public lecture tours, e.g. on ancient and modern literature. It was while on one of these tours that he died of a stroke, aged 56, in January 1829. Friedrich Schlegel's theoretical writings – his essays and the important *Fragments* published in *Das Athenäum* – were extremely influential in forming the Romantic view of art.

Socratic irony is the only involuntary and yet completely deliberate dissimulation. It is equally impossible to feign it or divulge it. To a person who hasn't got it, it will remain a riddle even after it is openly confessed. It is meant to deceive no one except those who consider it a deception and who either take pleasure in the delightful roguery of making fools of the whole world or else become angry when they get an inkling they themselves might be included. In this sort of irony, everything should be playful and serious, guilelessly open and deeply hidden. It originates in

the union of *savoir vivre* and scientific spirit, in the conjunction of a perfectly instinctive and a perfectly conscious philosophy. It contains and
arouses a feeling of indissoluble antagonism between the absolute and
the relative, between the impossibility and the necessity of complete
communication. It is the freest of all licenses, for by its means one transcends oneself; and yet it is also the most lawful, for it is absolutely necessary. It is a very good sign when the harmonious bores are at a loss
about how they should react to this continuous self-parody, when they
fluctuate endlessly between belief and disbelief until they get dizzy and
take what is meant as a joke seriously and what is meant seriously as a
joke.

Source: Friedrich Schlegel, *Critical Fragments*, in P. Firchow (trans.)
Friedrich Schlegel: Philosophical Fragments, University of Minnesota Press, Minneapolis, 1991, Fragment 108.

Extract 8 from August Wilhelm Schlegel, *Course of Lectures on Dramatic Art and Literature*

August Wilhelm Schlegel was born in September 1767 in Hanover
into a family of Protestant pastors, some of whom were also minor
figures in the literary world. After schooling in Hanover and university studies at Göttingen (1786–91) August Wilhelm Schlegel
accepted an appointment as a private tutor in Amsterdam, where he
remained until 1795, in that year moving to Jena. During his time
in Holland he published a number of literary articles, and began to
translate both Dante and Shakespeare – the latter's plays were to
have a decisive effect on his literary aesthetics. In 1796 August Wilhelm Schlegel was appointed to a teaching post at the University of
Jena, and in the same year married a young widow, Caroline
Böhmer. Appointed professor at Jena in 1798, he in the same year
began to publish his new Romantic theories of literature and art in
the extremely important journal *Das Athenäum* (1798–1800),
which he co-edited with Friedrich Schlegel. The rest of August Wilhelm Schlegel's long life was taken up with lecturing, translation,
and periods of travel as advisor and tutor to Mme de Staël's children. He translated no less than seventeen of Shakespeare's plays
into German, published as an extremely successful book. He also

published translations of Italian, Spanish and Portuguese poetry with almost equivalent success. His lectures formed the basis of a number of major critical works, of which the most important published during his lifetime was the *Course of Lectures on Dramatic Art and Literature* (1809–11) from which the following extract is taken. Following the death of Mme de Staël in 1817, August Wilhelm Schlegel accepted the post of professor of oriental languages at the University of Bonn, occupying the last years of his life with Sanskrit and Indian studies. He died in Bonn in May 1845, remaining active as a critic right to the end of his life. August Wilhelm Schlegel was the most influential German critic of his generation, and a scholar of great erudition.

1 The object of the present series of Lectures will be to combine the theory of Dramatic Art with its history, and to bring before my auditors at once its principles and its models.

2 It belongs to the general philosophical theory of poetry, and the other fine arts, to establish the fundamental laws of the beautiful. Every art, on the other hand, has its own special theory, designed to teach the limits, the difficulties, and the means by which it must be regulated in its attempt to realize those laws. For this purpose, certain scientific investigations are indispensable to the artist, although they have but little attraction for those whose admiration of art is confined to the enjoyment of the actual productions of distinguished minds. The general theory, on the other hand, seeks to analyze that essential faculty of human nature—the sense of the beautiful, which at once calls the fine arts into existence, and accounts for the satisfaction which arises from the contemplation of them; and also points out the relation which subsists between this and all other sentient and cognizant faculties of man. To the man of thought and speculation, therefore, it is of the highest importance, but by itself alone it is quite inadequate to guide and direct the essays and practice of art.

3 Now, the history of the fine arts informs us what has been, and the theory teaches what ought to be accomplished by them. But without some intermediate and connecting link, both would remain independent and separate from one and other, and each by itself, inadequate and defective. This connecting link is furnished by criticism, which both elucidates the history of the arts, and makes the theory fruitful. The comparing together, and judging of the existing productions of the human mind, necessarily throws light upon the conditions which are indispensable to the creation of original and masterly works of art.

221

4 Ordinarily, indeed, men entertain a very erroneous notion of criticism, and understand by it nothing more than a certain shrewdness in detecting and exposing the faults of a work of art. As I have devoted the greater part of my life to this pursuit, I may be excused if, by way of preface, I seek to lay before my auditors my own ideas of the true genius of criticism.

5 We see numbers of men, and even whole nations, so fettered by the conventions of education and habits of life, that, even in the appreciation of the fine arts, they cannot shake them off. Nothing to them appears natural, appropriate, or beautiful, which is alien to their own language, manners, and social relations. With this exclusive mode of seeing and feeling, it is no doubt possible to attain, by means of cultivation, to great nicety of discrimination within the narrow circle to which it limits and circumscribes them. But no man can be a true critic or connoisseur without universality of mind, without that flexibility which enables him, by renouncing all personal predilections and blind habits, to adapt himself to the peculiarities of other ages and nations—to feel them, as it were, from their proper central point, and, what ennobles human nature, to recognise and duly appreciate whatever is beautiful and grand under the external accessories which were necessary to its embodying, even though occasionally they may seem to disguise and distort it. There is no monopoly of poetry for particular ages and nations; and consequently that despotism in taste, which would seek to invest with universal authority the rules which at first, perhaps, were but arbitrarily advanced, is but a vain and empty pretension. Poetry, taken in its widest acceptation, as the power of creating what is beautiful, and representing it to the eye or the ear, is a universal gift of Heaven, being shared to a certain extent even by those whom we call barbarians and savages. Internal excellence is alone decisive, and where this exists, we must not allow ourselves to be repelled by the external appearance. Everything must be traced up to the root of human nature: if it has sprung from thence, it has an undoubted worth of its own; but if, without possessing a living germ, it is merely externally attached thereto, it will never thrive nor acquire a proper growth. Many productions which appear at first sight dazzling phenomena in the province of the fine arts, and which as a whole have been honoured with the appellation of works of a golden age, resemble the mimic gardens of children: impatient to witness the work of their hands, they break off here and there branches and flowers, and plant them in the earth; everything at first assumes a noble appearance: the childish gardener struts proudly up and down among his showy

beds, till the rootless plants begin to droop, and hang their withered leaves and blossoms, and nothing soon remains but the bare twigs, while the dark forest, on which no art or care was ever bestowed, and which towered up towards heaven long before human remembrance, bears every blast unshaken, and fills the solitary beholder with religious awe.

6 Let us now apply the idea which we have been developing, of the universality of true criticism, to the history of poetry and the fine arts. This, like the so-called universal history, we generally limit (even though beyond this range there may be much that is both remarkable and worth knowing) to whatever has had a nearer or more remote influence on the present civilisation of Europe: consequently, to the works of the Greeks and Romans, and of those of the modern European nations, who first and chiefly distinguished themselves in art and literature. It is well known that, three centuries and a-half ago, the study of ancient literature received a new life, by the diffusion of the Grecian language (for the Latin never became extinct); the classical authors were brought to light, and rendered universally accessible by means of the press; and the monuments of ancient art were diligently disinterred and preserved. All this powerfully excited the human mind, and formed a decided epoch in the history of human civilisation; its manifold effects have extended to our times, and will yet extend to an incalculable series of ages. But the study of the ancients was forthwith most fatally perverted. The learned, who were chiefly in the possession of this knowledge, and who were incapable of distinguishing themselves by works of their own, claimed for the ancients an unlimited authority, and with great appearance of reason, since they are models in their kind. Maintaining that nothing could be hoped for the human mind but from an imitation of antiquity, in the works of the moderns they only valued what resembled, or seemed to bear a resemblance to, those of the ancients. Everything else they rejected as barbarous and unnatural. With the great poets and artists it was quite otherwise. However strong their enthusiasm for the ancients, and however determined their purpose of entering into competition with them, they were compelled by their independence and originality of mind, to strike out a path of their own, and to impress upon their productions the stamp of their own genius.

[. . .]

7 Those very ages, nations, and ranks; who felt least the want of a poetry of their own, were the most assiduous in their imitation of the ancients; accordingly, its results are but dull school exercises, which at best excite a frigid admiration. But in the fine arts, mere imitation

223

is always fruitless; even what we borrow from others, to assume a true poetical shape, must, as it were, be born again within us. Of what avail is all foreign imitation? Art cannot exist without nature, and man can give nothing to his fellow-men but himself.

8 Genuine successors and true rivals of the ancients, who, by virtue of congenial talents and cultivation have walked in their path and worked in their spirit, have ever been as rare as their mechanical spiritless copyists are common. Seduced by the form, the great body of critics have been but too indulgent to these servile imitators. These were held up as correct modern classics, while the great truly living and popular poets, whose reputation was a part of their nations' glory, and to whose sublimity it was impossible to be altogether blind, were at best but tolerated as rude and wild natural geniuses. But the unqualified separation of genius and taste on which such a judgment proceeds, is altogether untenable. Genius is the almost unconscious choice of the highest degree of excellence, and, consequently, it is taste in its highest activity.

9 In this state, nearly, matters continued till a period not far back, when several inquiring minds, chiefly Germans, endeavoured to clear up the misconception, and to give the ancients their due, without being insensible to the merits of the moderns, although of a totally different kind. The apparent contradiction did not intimidate them. The groundwork of human nature is no doubt everywhere the same; but in all our investigations, we may observe that, throughout the whole range of nature, there is no elementary power so simple, but that it is capable of dividing and diverging into opposite directions. The whole play of vital motion hinges on harmony and contrast. Why, then, should not this phenomenon recur on a grander scale in the history of man? In this idea we have perhaps discovered the true key to the ancient and modern history of poetry and the fine arts. Those who adopted it, gave to the peculiar spirit of *modern* art, as contrasted with the *antique* or *classical*, the name of *romantic*. The term is certainly not inappropriate; the word is derived from *romance*—the name originally given to the languages which were formed from the mixture of the Latin and the old Teutonic dialects, in the same manner as modern civilisation is the fruit of the heterogeneous union of the peculiarities of the northern nations and the fragments of antiquity; whereas the civilisation of the ancients was much more of a piece.

10 The distinction which we have just stated can hardly fail to appear well founded, if it can be shown, so far as our knowledge of antiquity extends, that the same contrast in the labours of the ancients

224

and moderns runs symmetrically, I might almost say systematically, throughout every branch of art—that it is as evident in music and the plastic arts as in poetry. This is a problem which, in its full extent, still remains to be demonstrated, though, on particular portions of it, many excellent observations have been advanced already.

[. . .]

11 By an example taken from another art, that of architecture, I shall endeavour to illustrate what I mean by this contrast. Throughout the Middle Ages there prevailed, and in the latter centuries of that æra was carried to perfection, a style of architecture, which has been called Gothic, but ought really to have been termed old German. When, on the general revival of classical antiquity, the imitation of Grecian architecture became prevalent, and but too frequently without a due regard to the difference of climate and manners or to the purpose of the building, the zealots of this new taste, passing a sweeping sentence of condemnation on the Gothic, reprobated it as tasteless, gloomy, and barbarous. This was in some degree pardonable in the Italians, among whom a love for ancient architecture, cherished by hereditary remains of classical edifices, and the similarity of their climate to that of the Greeks and Romans, might, in some sort, be said to be innate. But we Northerns are not so easily to be talked out of the powerful, solemn impressions which seize upon the mind at entering a Gothic cathedral. We feel, on the contrary, a strong desire to investigate and to justify the source of this impression. A very slight attention will convince us, that the Gothic architecture displays not only an extraordinary degree of mechanical skill, but also a marvellous power of invention; and, on a closer examination, we recognize its profound significance, and perceive that as well as the Grecian it constitutes in itself a complete and finished system.

[. . .]

12 For our present object, the justification, namely, of the grand division which we lay down in the history of art, and according to which we conceive ourselves equally warranted in establishing the same division in dramatic literature, it might be sufficient merely to have stated this contrast between the ancient, or classical, and the romantic. But as there are exclusive admirers of the ancients, who never cease asserting that all deviation from them is merely the whim of a new school of critics, who, expressing themselves in language full of mystery, cautiously avoid conveying their sentiments in a tangible shape, I shall endeavour to explain the origin and spirit of the *romantic*, and then leave the world to judge if the use of the word, and of the idea which it is intended to convey, be thereby justified.

13 The mental culture of the Greeks was a finished education in the school of Nature. Of a beautiful and noble race, endowed with susceptible senses and a cheerful spirit under a mild sky, they lived and bloomed in the full health of existence; and, favoured by a rare combination of circumstances, accomplished all that the finite nature of man is capable of. The whole of their art and poetry is the expression of a consciousness of this harmony of all their faculties. They invented the poetry of joy.

14 Their religion was the deification of the powers of nature and of the earthly life: but this worship, which, among other nations, clouded the imagination with hideous shapes, and hardened the heart to cruelty, assumed, among the Greeks, a mild, a grand, and a dignified form. Superstition, too often the tyrant of the human faculties, seemed to have here contributed to their freest development. It cherished the arts by which it was adorned, and its idols became the models of ideal beauty.

15 But however highly the Greeks may have succeeded in the Beautiful, and even in the Moral, we cannot concede any higher character to their civilisation than that of a refined and ennobled sensuality. Of course this must be understood generally. The conjectures of a few philosophers, and the irradiations of poetical inspiration, constitute an occasional exception. Man can never altogether turn aside his thoughts from infinity, and some obscure recollections will always remind him of the home he has lost; but we are now speaking of the predominant tendency of his endeavours.

16 Religion is the root of human existence. Were it possible for man to renounce all religion, including that which is unconscious, independent of the will, he would become a mere surface without any internal substance. When this centre is disturbed, the whole system of the mental faculties and feelings takes a new shape.

17 And this is what has actually taken place in modern Europe through the introduction of Christianity. This sublime and beneficent religion has regenerated the ancient world from its state of exhaustion and debasement; it is the guiding principle in the history of modern nations, and even at this day, when many suppose they have shaken off its authority, they still find themselves much more influenced by it in their views of human affairs than they themselves are aware.

18 After Christianity, the character of Europe has, since the commencement of the Middle Ages, been chiefly influenced by the Germanic race of northern conquerors, who infused new life and vigour into a degenerated people. The stern nature of the North drives man back within himself; and what is lost in the free sportive development of

the senses, must, in noble dispositions, be compensated by earnestness of mind. Hence the honest cordiality with which Christianity was welcomed by all the Teutonic tribes, so that among no other race of men has it penetrated more deeply into the inner man, displayed more powerful effects, or become more interwoven with all human feelings and sensibilities.

19 The rough, but honest heroism of the northern conquerors, by its admixture with the sentiments of Christianity, gave rise to chivalry, of which the object was, by vows which should be looked upon as sacred, to guard the practice of arms from every rude and ungenerous abuse of force into which it was so likely to sink.

20 With the virtues of chivalry was associated a new and purer spirit of love, an inspired homage for genuine female worth, which was now revered as the acmè of human excellence, and, maintained by religion itself under the image of a virgin mother, infused into all hearts a mysterious sense of the purity of love.

21 As Christianity did not, like the heathen worship, rest satisfied with certain external acts, but claimed an authority over the whole inward man and the most hidden movements of the heart; the feeling of moral independence took refuge in the domain of honour, a worldly morality, as it were, which subsisting alongside of, was often at variance with that of religion, but yet in so far resembling it that it never calculated consequences, but consecrated unconditionally certain principles of action, which like the articles of faith, were elevated far beyond the investigation of a casuistical reasoning.

22 Chivalry, love, and honour, together with religion itself, are the subjects of that poetry of nature which poured itself out in the Middle Ages with incredible fulness, and preceded the more artistic cultivation of the romantic spirit. This age had also its mythology, consisting of chivalrous tales and legends; but its wonders and its heroism were the very reverse of those of the ancient mythology.

23 Several inquirers who, in other respects, entertain the same conception of the peculiarities of the moderns, and trace them to the same source that we do, have placed the essence of the northern poetry in melancholy; and to this, when properly understood, we have nothing to object.

24 Among the Greeks human nature was in itself all sufficient; it was conscious of no defects, and aspired to no higher perfection than that which it could actually attain by the exercise of its own energies. We, however, are taught by superior wisdom that man, through a grievous transgression, forfeited the place for which he was originally destined; and that the sole destination of his earthly existence is to

struggle to regain his lost position, which, if left to his own strength, he can never accomplish. The old religion of the senses sought no higher possession than outward and perishable blessings; and immortality, so far as it was believed, stood shadow-like in the obscure distance, a faint dream of this sunny waking life. The very reverse of all this is the case with the Christian view: every thing finite and mortal is lost in the contemplation of infinity; life has become shadow and darkness, and the first day of our real existence dawns in the world beyond the grave. Such a religion must waken the vague foreboding, which slumbers in every feeling heart, into a distinct consciousness that the happiness after which we are here striving is unattainable; that no external object can ever entirely fill our souls; and that all earthly enjoyment is but a fleeting and momentary illusion. When the soul, resting as it were under the willows of exile,[3] breathes out its longing for its distant home, what else but melancholy can be the key-note of its songs? Hence the poetry of the ancients was the poetry of enjoyment, and ours is that of desire: the former has its foundation in the scene which is present, while the latter hovers betwixt recollection and hope. Let me not be understood as affirming that everything flows in one unvarying strain of wailing and complaint, and that the voice of melancholy is always loudly heard. As the austerity of tragedy was not incompatible with the joyous views of the Greeks, so that romantic poetry whose origin I have been describing, can assume every tone, even that of the liveliest joy; but still it will always, in some indescribable way, bear traces of the source from which it originated. The feeling of the moderns is, upon the whole, more inward, their fancy more incorporeal, and their thoughts more contemplative. In nature, it is true, the boundaries of objects run more into one another, and things are not so distinctly separated as we must exhibit them in order to convey distinct notions of them.

25 The Grecian ideal of human nature was perfect unison and proportion between all the powers,—a natural harmony. The moderns, on the contrary, have arrived at the consciousness of an internal discord which renders such an ideal impossible; and hence the endeavour of their poetry is to reconcile these two worlds between which we find ourselves divided, and to blend them indissolubly together. The impressions of the senses are to be hallowed, as it were, by a mysterious connexion with higher feelings; and the soul, on the other

---

[3] *Trauerweiden der Verbannung*, literally *the weeping willows of banishment*, an allusion, as every reader must know, to the 137th Psalm. Linnæus, from this Psalm, calls the weeping willow *Salix Babylonica*.—Trans.*

hand, embodies its forebodings, or indescribable intuitions of infinity, in types and symbols borrowed from the visible world.

26 In Grecian art and poetry we find an original and unconscious unity of form and matter; in the modern, so far as it has remained true to its own spirit, we observe a keen struggle to unite the two, as being naturally in opposition to each other. The Grecian executed what it proposed in the utmost perfection; but the modern can only do justice to its endeavours after what is infinite by approximation; and, from a certain appearance of imperfection, is in greater danger of not being duly appreciated.

Source: August Wilhelm Schlegel, *Course of Lectures on Dramatic Art and Literature (Vorlesungen über dramatische Kunst und Literatur)*, 1809–11, trans. J. Black, New York AMS Press reprint, 1973, pp. 17–27.

Extract 9 from Friedrich Schlegel, *Athenaeum Fragments*

116. Romantic poetry is a progressive, universal poetry. Its aim isn't merely to reunite all the separate species of poetry and put poetry in touch with philosophy and rhetoric. It tries to and should mix and fuse poetry and prose, inspiration and criticism, the poetry of art and the poetry of nature; and make poetry lively and sociable, and life and society poetical; poeticize wit and fill and saturate the forms of art with every kind of good, solid matter for instruction, and animate them with the pulsations of humor. It embraces everything that is purely poetic, from the greatest systems of art, containing within themselves still further systems, to the sigh, the kiss that the poetizing child breathes forth in artless song. It can so lose itself in what it describes that one might believe it exists only to characterize poetical individuals of all sorts: and yet there still is no form so fit for expressing the entire spirit of an author: so that many artists who started out to write only a novel ended up by providing us with a portrait of themselves. It alone can become, like the epic, a mirror of the whole circumambient world, an image of the age. And it can also—more than any other form—hover at the midpoint between the portrayed and the portrayer, free of all real and ideal self-interest, on the wings of poetic reflection, and can raise that reflection again and again

to a higher power, can multiply it in an endless succession of mirrors. It is capable of the highest and most variegated refinement, not only from within outwards, but also from without inwards; capable in that it organizes—for everything that seeks a wholeness in its effects—the parts along similar lines, so that it opens up a perspective upon an infinitely increasing classicism. Romantic poetry is in the arts what wit is in philosophy, and what society and sociability, friendship and love are in life. Other kinds of poetry are finished and are now capable of being fully analyzed. The romantic kind of poetry is still in the state of becoming; that, in fact, is its real essence: that it should forever be becoming and never be perfected. It can be exhausted by no theory and only a divinatory criticism would dare try to characterize its ideal. It alone is infinite, just as it alone is free; and it recognizes as its first commandment that the will of the poet can tolerate no law above itself. The romantic kind of poetry is the only one that is more than a kind, that is, as it were, poetry itself: for in a certain sense all poetry is or should be romantic.

Source: Friedrich Schlegel, *Athenaeum Fragments no. 116*, in P. Firchow (trans.) *Friedrich Schlegel: Philosophical Fragments*, University of Minnesota Press, Minneapolis, 1991, pp. 31–2.

Extract 10 from Wilhelm Wackenroder, *The Marvels of the Musical Art*

1 Whenever I so very fervently enjoy how a beautiful strain of sounds suddenly, in free spontaneity, extricates itself from the empty stillness and rises up like sacrificial incense, floats gently on the breezes, and then silently sinks down to earth again;—then so many new, beautiful images sprout forth and flock together in my heart that I cannot control myself out of rapture.—Sometimes music appears to me like a phoenix, which lightly and boldly raises itself for its own pleasure, floats upwards triumphantly for its own gratification, and pleases gods and men by the flapping of its wings.—At other times it seems to me as if music were like a child lying dead in the grave;—one reddish sunbeam from heaven gently draws its soul away and, transplanted in to the heavenly aether, it enjoys golden drops of eternity and embraces the original images of the most beautiful human dreams.—And sometimes,—what a magnificent fullness of images! —sometimes music is for me entirely a picture of our life:—a touch-

ingly brief joy, which arises out of the void and vanishes into the void,—which commences and passes away, why one does not know:—a little, merry, green island, with sunshine, with singing and rejoicing,—which floats upon the dark, unfathomable ocean.

2 Ask the virtuoso why he is so heartily gay upon his lyre. "Is not," he will answer, "all of life a beautiful dream? a lovely soap-bubble? My musical piece is the same."

3 Truly, it is an innocent, touching pleasure to rejoice over sounds, over pure sounds! A childlike joy!—While others deafen themselves with restless activity and, buzzed by confused thoughts as by an army of strange night birds and evil insects, finally fall to the ground unconscious;—O, then I submerge my head in the holy, cooling well-spring of sounds and the healing goddess instils the innocence of childhood in me again, so that I regard the world with fresh eyes and melt into universal, joyous reconciliation.—While others quarrel over invented troubles, or play a desperate game of wit, or brood in solitude misshapen ideas which, like the armor-clad men of the fable, consume themselves in desperation;—O, then I close my eyes to all the strife of the world—and withdraw quietly into the land of music, as into the land of belief, where all our doubts and our sufferings are lost in a resounding sea,—where we forget all the croaking of human beings, where no chattering of words and languages, no confusion of letters and monstrous hieroglyphics makes us dizzy but, instead, all the anxiety of our hearts is suddenly healed by the gentle touch.— And how? Are questions answered for us here? Are secrets revealed to us?—O, no! but, in the place of all answers and revelations, airy, beautiful cloud formations are shown to us, the sight of which calms us, we do not know how;—with brave certainty we wander through the unknown land;—we greet and embrace as friends strange spiritual beings whom we do not know, and all the incomprehensibilities which besiege our souls and which are the disease of the human race disappear before our senses, and our minds become healthy through the contemplation of marvels which are far more incomprehensible and exalted. At that moment the human being seems to want to say: "That is what I mean! Now I have found it! Now I am serene and happy!"—

4 Let the others mock and jeer, who race on through life as if on rattling wagons and do not know this land of holy peace in the soul of the human being. Let them take pride in their giddiness and boast, as if they were guiding the world with their reins. There will come times when they will suffer great want.

5 Happy the one who, when the earthly soil shakes unfaithfully under

his feet, can rescue himself serenely on airy tones and, yielding to them, now rocks himself gently, now dances away courageously and forgets his sorrows with such a pleasing diversion!

6 Happy the one who (weary of the business of splitting ideas more and more finely, which shrinks the soul) surrenders himself to the gentle and powerful currents of desire, which expand the spirit and elevate it to a beautiful faith. Such a course is the only way to universal, all-embracing love and only through such love do we come close to divine blessedness.——

7 This is the most magnificent and the most wonderful picture of the musical art which I can sketch out,—although most people will consider it to be empty dreaming.

8 But, from what sort of magic potion does the aroma of this brilliant apparition rise up?—I look,—and find nothing but a wretched web of numerical proportions, represented concretely on perforated wood, on constructions of gut strings and brass wire.—This is almost more wondrous, and I should like to believe that the invisible harp of God sounds along with our notes and contributes the heavenly power to the human web of digits.

9 And how, then, did man arrive at the marvelous idea of having wood and metal make sounds? How did he arrive at the precious invention of this most exceptional of all arts?—That is also so remarkable and extraordinary that I want to write down the story briefly, as I conceive of it.

10 The human being is initially a very innocent creature. While we are still lying in the cradle, our little minds are being nourished and educated by a hundred invisible little spirits and trained in all the polite skills. Thus, little by little, we learn to be happy by smiling; by crying, we learn to be sad; by staring wide-eyed, we learn to worship whatever is exalted. But, just as in childhood we don't yet know how to handle the toy correctly, so too, we don't rightly understand how to play with the things of the heart and, in this school of the emotions, we still mistake and confuse everything.

11 However, when we have come of age, then we understand how to employ the emotions, whether gaiety or sorrow or any other, very skillfully where they are appropriate: and sometimes we express them very beautifully, to our own satisfaction. Indeed, although these things are actually only an occasional embellishment to the events of our usual lives, yet we find so much pleasure in them that we like to separate these so-called emotions from the complex chaos and mesh of the earthly creature in whom they are entangled and elaborate them particularly into a beautiful memory and preserve

them in our individual ways. These feelings which surge up in our hearts sometimes seem to us so magnificent and grand that we lock them up like relics in expensive monstrosities, kneel down before them joyously and, in our exuberance, do not know whether we are worshipping our own human heart or the Creator, from whom all great and magnificent things come.

12 For this preservation of the emotions, various splendid inventions have been made and, thus, all the fine arts have arisen. But I consider music to be the most marvelous of these inventions, because it portrays human feelings in a superhuman way, because it shows us all the emotions of our soul above our heads in incorporeal form, clothed in golden clouds of airy harmonies,—because it speaks a language which we do not know in our ordinary life, which we have learned, we do not know where and how, and which one would consider to be solely the language of angels.

13 It is the only art which reduces the most multifarious and contradictory emotions of our souls to the same beautiful harmonies, which plays with joy and sorrow, with despair and adoration in the same harmonious tones. Therefore, it is also music which infuses in us true serenity of soul, which is the most beautiful jewel that the human being can acquire;—I mean that serenity in which everything in the world seems to us natural, true, and good, in which we find a beautiful cohesion in the wildest throng of people, in which, with sincere hearts, we feel all creatures to be related and close to us and, like children, look upon the world as through the twilight of a lovely dream.——

14 When, in my simplicity, I feel very blessed under open skies before God,—while the golden rays of the sun stretch the lofty, blue tent above me and the green earth laughs all around me,—then it is fitting that I throw myself upon the ground and, in loud jubilation, joyously thank heaven for all magnificence. But what does the so-called artist among men do thereupon? He has observed me and, internally warmed, he goes home in silence, lets his sympathetic rapture gush forth much more magnificently on a lifeless harp and preserves it in a language which no one has ever spoken, the native country of which no one knows, and which grips everyone to the core.—

15 When a brother of mine has died and, at such an event of life, I appropriately display deep sorrow, sit weeping in a narrow corner, and ask all the stars who has ever been more grieved than I.—then, —while the mocking future already stands behind my back and laughs about the quickly fleeting pain of the human being.—then the virtuoso stands before me and becomes so moved by all this woeful

wringing of the hands, that he recreates this beautiful pain on his instrument at home and beautifies and adorns the human grief with desire and love. Thus, he produces a work which arouses in all the world the deepest compassion.—But I, after I have long forgotten the anxious wringing of the hands for my dead brother and then happen to hear the product of his sorrow,—then I exult like a child over my own so magnificently glorified heart and nourish and enrich my soul with the wonderful creation.—

16 But when the angels of heaven look down upon this entire delightful play thing which we call art,—then they must smile in tender sadness over the race of children on earth and over the innocent artificiality in this art of sounds, through which the mortal creature wants to elevate himself to them.——

Source: Wilhelm Heinrich Wackenroder, *The Marvels of the Musical Art* from his *Fantasies on Art for Friends of Art*, in M. H. Schubert (ed. and trans.) *Wackenroder's Confessions and Fantasies*, Pennsylvania University Press, Pennsylvania, 1971, pp. 178–81.

Extract 11 from August Wilhelm Schlegel, *Lectures on Belles-lettres and Art*

We have seen that music occupies the dimension of time, one that is universally experienced by the inner consciousness. Time has only one dimension; it is best thought of in terms of a flowing point. Strictly speaking, variety is never experienced at one moment in time; unity must be imposed on it if it is to be experienced in this way. Basically then, music is pure succession, in which variety is experienced successively, rather than simultaneously. As such, it is an image of our restless, mutable, everchanging life. Yet nothing that is apparently simple in nature is in fact so; all reality is the product of a combination of antinomies. Part of our being derives from the unity that comprises two, three, or a multiplicity of diverse elements. The harmony made up of simultaneously sounding notes that are concordant with each other, and which, though diverse, form a unity, may well, in fact, represent in audible terms the internal structure of life. Thus harmony is the truly mystical element in music, one which does not demand some powerful reaction from progression in time, but which strives for the infinite in the indivisible instant. So we see in fact that the modern development of harmony originated in Christian worship at a time when men had lost that sense of free movement in the phenomenal world, and that energetic rhythm of the ancients, at a time when the psyche was looking inwards in its search for a higher life. The solemn church anthem expresses this striving for spiritual union in the dimension of the suprasensual. Music can express every degree of worldliness, every degree of spirituality, music ranging from the march and the dance to the chorale; the former merely excites coordinated physical movements, the latter inspires an immutable, infinite longing of reverence, altogether throwing off transient, earthly passions. In the solemn, steady movement of devotional music there is inherent in every instant a sense of harmony and perfection, a unity of existence which to Christians is an image of heavenly bliss.

Source: August Wilhelm Schlegel, *Lectures on Belles-lettres and Art* (*Vorlesungen über schöne Literatur und Kunst*), 1801, in P. LeHuray and J. Day (eds) *Music and Aesthetics in the Eighteenth and Early Nineteenth Centuries*, Cambridge University Press, Cambridge, 1988, pp. 194–5.

Goethe, *Faust Part One*

The ten thousand copies of the first edition of Mme de Staël's *De l'Allemagne*, to be translated into English as *Germany*, were destroyed in 1810 under the orders of Savary, who replaced Fouché as Napoleon's Minister of Police. This fuelled particular interest when a copy retained by Mme de Staël was used for re-publication in England in 1813, powerfully promoting her presentation of contemporary German thinking and writing as the driving influences in European culture. Mme de Staël's book was based on her travels in Germany (her account of Weimar as 'the Athens of Germany' testifies to her enthusiasm for new cultural horizons) and on her meetings with prominent German writers and artists, including Goethe, Schiller and August Wilhelm Schlegel. Her response to Goethe's recently published *Faust Part One* demonstrates her excitement about new forms of freedom of expression in contemporary German culture.

Publication of Goethe's *Faust Part One* was delayed in the turmoil of Napoleonic occupation of Weimar following the battle of Jena in 1806. Born in Frankfurt in 1749 and active in Weimar from 1775 as a statesman, scientist and director of the theatre, Goethe's novels – amongst them the bestseller, *The Sorrows of Young Werther* (1774), plays – such as *Götz of Berlichingen* (1771), and lyric poetry had already established the authority of his reputation.

Under pressure from his publisher, a fragmentary version of *Faust*, a drama on which he had been working intermittently since the 1770s, was included as *Faust. A Fragment* in collected works published in 1790, and the interest aroused in what was in effect still work in progress is evident in the responses of August Wilhelm Schlegel and his brother Friedrich.

The long-awaited appearance of *Faust Part One* in 1808 was greeted with widespread enthusiasm throughout Europe for the sweeping language and the vision of Goethe's transformation of the old legend – with its eternal punishment in hell for the man who makes his pact with the devil – into an exploration of the process of ongoing striving for greatest human potential. Even before the com-

236

pletion of *Faust Part One*, a drama in its own right, Goethe was pre-
occupied with *Faust Part Two*, which he finished just before he died
in 1832. Selected passages, from the opening Dedication, rarely
used in stage performances, to the final words of the second part of
the play, reveal the span of ideas and language in the work. Out of
the hundreds of translations into English, two – one in verse and the
other in prose – are placed, for comparison, alongside the original
German.

Madame de Staël on Weimar and the Germans

Of all the German principalities, there is none that makes us feel so much
as Weimar the advantages of a small state, of which the sovereign is a man
of strong understanding, and who is capable of endeavouring to please all
orders of his subjects, without losing any thing in their obedience. Such a
state is as a private society, where all the members are connected together
by intimate relations. The Duchess Louise of Saxe Weimar is the true
model of a woman destined by nature to the most illustrious rank; without pretension, as without weakness, she inspires in the same degree confidence and respect; and the heroism of the chivalrous ages has entered her
soul without taking from it any thing of her sex's softness. The military
talents of the duke are universally respected, and his lively and reflective
conversation continually brings to our recollection that he was formed by
the great Frederic. It is by his own and his mother's reputation that the
most distinguished men of learning have been attracted to Weimar. Germany, for the first time, possessed a literary metropolis.

[. . .]

In the same principality, in the immediate neighbourhood of this first
literary re-union of Germany, was Jena, one of the most remarkable centres of science. Thus, in a very narrow space, there seemed to be collected
together all the astonishing lights of the human understanding.

[. . .]

Weimar was called the Athens of Germany, and it was, in reality, the
only place where the fine arts inspired a national interest, which served
for a bond of fraternal union among the different ranks of society. A liberal court habitually sought the acquaintance of men of letters; and literature gained considerably in the influence of good taste which presided
there.

[. . .]

The Germans are to the human mind what pioneers are to an army; they try new roads, they attempt unknown means: how can we avoid being curious to know what they say on their return from their excursions into infinity?

Source: Baroness Staël Holstein, *Germany*. Translated from the French in three volumes, London. Printed for John Murray, Albemarle Street, 1813, vol. I *Of Germany, and the manners of the Germans*, chap. XV, 'Weimar' pp. 146–7, 148–9, 150; vol. II *On Literature and the Arts*, chap. II, 'On the Judgment formed by the English on the subject of German Literature', pp. 223–4.

Madame de Staël on Goethe

[. . .]

Goëthe never gives up the earth; even in attaining the most sublime conceptions, his mind possesses vigour not weakened by sensibility. Goëthe might be mentioned, as the representative of all German literature; not that there are no writers superior to him in different kinds of composition, but that he unites in himself all that distinguishes German genius; and no one besides is so remarkable for a peculiar species of imagination which neither Italians, English, or French have ever attained.

[. . .]

When Goëthe is induced to talk, he is admirable; his eloquence is enriched with thought; his pleasantry is, at the same time, full of grace and of philosophy; his imagination is impressed by external objects, as was that of the ancient artists; nevertheless his reason possesses but too much the maturity of our own times. Nothing disturbs the strength of his mind, and even the defects of his character, ill-humour, embarrassment, constraint, pass like clouds round the foot of that great mountain on the summit of which his genius is placed.

[. . .]

I have said, that Goëthe possessed in himself alone, all the principal features of German genius; they are all indeed found in him to an eminent degree: a great depth of ideas, that grace which springs from imagination, a grace far more original than that which is formed by the spirit of society [. . .]

238

Source: Baroness Staël Holstein, *Germany*. Translated from the French in three volumes, London. Printed for John Murray, Albemarle Street, 1813, vol. II *On Literature and the Arts*, chap. VII, 'Goëthe', pp. 265–6, 267, 271.

August Wilhelm Schlegel on *Faust, A Fragment*

REVIEW OF THE *FRAGMENT* OF 1790[1]

"Faust, a Fragment." The meaning of this dramatic poem lies too deep, is too far-reaching, and, since the piece is only a fragment, too little developed not to run the risk that a large proportion of readers will overlook it and dwell instead upon lesser works. Faust, as Goethe has heightened and expanded the folk legend for his purposes, is a man for whose understanding science and for whose stormy heart ethically moderate enjoyment are too confining, whose feelings carry within themselves the mark of inborn nobility and genuine love of nature; and whose actions are uncertain, aimless, and corruptible; a man who, at one moment, pushes himself beyond the limits of mortality in order to establish alliances with higher spirits and, at the next, surrenders himself to the devil for unrestrained sensual gratification; noble enough not to be infected by the insensitive mockery of the demon who serves him in the satisfaction of his desires, and not strong enough to master the passions which make such a guide necessary to him. Equally removed from comfortable, inactive repose and from the joy of successful activity, Faust has squandered his life in endless research. At last he tears himself free, rejects all science as the dead skeleton of nature, and hurries to embrace living nature herself. Bold enthusiasm carries him upwards into the world of spirits. New youth is given him. A girl who lives alone in modest seclusion and childish contentment attracts him and falls victim to his passion. He destroys her domestic peace: this good, weak creature perishes from love and remorse. All this is presented overpoweringly and, in Goethe's manner, tossed off with a degree of carelessness and yet with the utmost truth. But the poet takes us no further. In certain

---

[1] Schlegel (1767–1845), who subsequently emerged as the leading practical critic of European Romanticism, here offers an immediate response to the first public appearance of Goethe's drama, the *Fragment* of 1790. (From *Göttingische Anzeige von gelehrten Sachen* [1790]. Stück 154; in *Collected Works*, ed. Böcking [Leipzig, 1846], vol. 10, 16 ff.; trans. Dolores Signorl and Cyrus Hamlin.)*

respects, to be sure, Faust's fate has long since been decided: his path, once he has taken it, leads unavoidably to ruin. But will this apply only to his external condition or will it also affect the inner man? Will he remain true to himself and, even in the final instance, still deserve human compassion because he falls as a human being with great abilities? Or will the depraved spirit to whom he has surrendered himself bring him to the point where he becomes himself the creator of evil, himself a devil? – This question still remains unanswered.

Just as the design of this play is unique (for it cannot in any way be compared with any of Goethe's own works, nor with those of any other dramatic poet), so also is its treatment. No single tone, or style, or general norm holds sway, to which the particular ideas must adapt and arrange themselves. The poet has set only one law for himself: to follow the freest ranging of his mind. Hence the sudden transitions from popular simplicity to philosophical profundity, from mysterious, magical oracles to expressions of general common sense, from the sublime to the burlesque. In the versification too, one finds just as diverse an alternation: here the meter of Hans Sachs,[2] there rhymed lines of all measures and lengths; here and there also irregular lyrical rhythms. In many places one misses that polish of versification which is the work of mechanical diligence; nowhere is there a lack of energy or expression. Here too a superior mind reveals itself, which can afford to ignore discretion and yet never miss its mark.

Source: August Wilhelm Schlegel, Review of the *Fragment* of 1790 in *Göttingische Anzeige von gelehrten Sachen*, 1790. In Johann Wolfgang von Goethe, *Faust*. Translated by Walter Arndt, edited by Cyrus Hamlin 2001, 1976 by W.W. Norton & Company. Inc. pp. 552–3.

---

[2] German poet (1494–1576) and leading *Meistersinger* of the Nuremberg School, renowned for his use of the *Knittelvers*, or doggerel rhyme.*

Friedrich Schlegel on *Faust, A Fragment*

ON *HAMLET* AND *FAUST* AS PHILOSOPHICAL TRAGEDIES[3]

[. . .]

In *Hamlet* [. . .] nothing is extraneous, superfluous, or accidental in this masterpiece of artistic wisdom. [. . .] Because of his unique situation all the power of his noble nature is concentrated in his [the hero's] reason, and his power to act is completely destroyed. His spirit is divided, as if torn apart in opposite directions on the rack; it collapses and perishes from an excess of idle reason, which oppresses him more painfully than do all those with whom he comes into contact. There exists perhaps no more perfect representation of irresolvable discord, which is the true subject of philosophical tragedy, than such an utter disparity between the reflective and the active power as in the character of Hamlet. The total effect of this tragedy is one of maximum despair. All the impressions it makes, which individually seem large and important, become trivial and disappear in the face of what here appears as the final, unique result of all being and thought: the eternal, colossal dissonance which infinitely separates mankind and fate.

[. . .] Shakespeare among all artists is the one who most completely and most strikingly embodies the spirit of modern poetry.

[. . .]

The character of the aesthetic development of our age and our nation betrays itself in a remarkable and magnificent phenomenon. Goethe's poetry is the dawn of genuine art and pure beauty. – The sensual power which sustains our age and our people was only the smallest of the advantages with which he first appeared as a young man. The philosophical content, the "characteristic" truth of his later works can be compared with the inexhaustible wealth of Shakespeare. Indeed, if *Faust* were to be completed, it would probably far surpass *Hamlet*, the English poet's masterpiece, with which it seems to share a common purpose. What in *Hamlet* is only fate, event – weakness, is in *Faust* disposition, action –

---

[3] Friedrich Schlegel (1772–1829; younger brother of August Wilhelm), in his essay 'On the Study of Greek Poesy' (1795), from which the passage here included is taken (*Prosaische Jugendschriften*, ed. Jacob Minor [Vienna 1906], vol. 1, 106–8, 114; here trans. by Cyrus Hamlin), first elaborated the basic polarity between classical and Romantic poetry, which subsequently achieved European notoriety. Within this polarity Schlegel argued for a fundamental distinction between aesthetic tragedy, exemplified by the drama of Sophocles, and philosophical tragedy, here discussed with specific reference to Shakespeare's *Hamlet* as norm. Mention of *Faust*, which remains no more than that here, indicates how Goethe's play came to replace Shakespeare as the model for Romantic philosophical tragedy.*

strength. Hamlet's mood and his inclination are the result of his external situation; Faust's corresponding inclination is his natural character.

Source: Friedrich Schlegel, On *Hamlet* and *Faust* as Philosophical Tragedies in 'On the Study of Greek Poesy', 1795. In Johann Wolfgang von Goethe, *Faust*. Translated by Walter Arndt, edited by Cyrus Hamlin 2001, 1976 by W. W. Norton & Company, Inc. pp. 553–5.

Goethe, *Faust Part One*

Dedication

ZUEIGNUNG
Lines 1–32

Ihr naht euch wieder,
   schwankende Gestalten
Die früh sich einst dem trüben
   Blick gezeigt.
Versuch' ich wohl, euch diesmal
   festzuhalten?
Fühl' ich mein Herz noch jenem
   Wahn geneigt?
Ihr drängt euch zu! Nun gut, so
   mögt ihr walten,
Wie ihr aus Dunst und Nebel um
   mich steigt;
Mein Busen fühlt sich jugendlich
   erschüttert
Vom Zauberhauch, der euren
   Zug umwittert.

Ihr bringt mit euch die Bilder
   froher Tage,
Und manche liebe Schatten steigen
   auf;
Gleich einer alten,
   halbverklungnen Sage
Kommt erste Lieb' und
   Freundschaft mit herauf;

DEDICATION

Uncertain shapes, visitors from
   the past
At whom I darkly gazed so long
   ago,
My heart's mad fleeting visions –
   now at last
Shall I embrace you, must I let
   you go?
Again you haunt me: come then,
   hold me fast!
Out of the mist and murk you
   rise, who so
Besiege me, and with magic
   breath restore,
Stirring my soul, lost youth to
   me once more.

You bring back memories of
   happier days
And many a well-loved ghost
   again I greet;
As when some old half-faded
   legend plays
About our ears, lamenting strains
   repeat

Der Schmerz wird neu, es
  wiederholt die Klage
Des Lebens labyrinthisch irren
  Lauf,
Und nennt die Guten, die, um
  schöne Stunden
Vom Glück getäuscht, vor mir
  hinweggeschwunden.

Sie hören nicht die folgenden
  Gesänge,
Die Seelen, denen ich die ersten
  sang;
Zerstoben ist das freundliche
  Gedränge,
Verklungen, ach! Der erste
  Widerklang.
Mein Lied ertönt der
  unbekannten Menge,
Ihr Beifall selbst macht meinem
  Herzen bang,
Und was sich sonst an meinem
  Lied erfreuet,
Wenn es noch lebt, irrt in der
  Welt zerstreuet.

Und mich ergreift ein längst
  entwöhntes Sehnen
Nach jenem stillen, ernsten
  Geisterreich,
Es schwebet nun in
  unbestimmten Tönen
Mein lispelnd Lied, der
  Äolsharfe gleich,
Ein Schauer faßt mich, Träne
  folgt den Tränen,
Das strenge Herz, er fühlt sich
  mild und weich;
Was ich besitze, she' ich wie im
  Weiten,
Und was verschwand, wird mir
  zu Wirklichkeiten.

Old griefs revive, old friends, old
  loves I meet,
My journey through life's
  labyrinthine maze,
Those dear companions, by their
  fate's unkind
Decree cut short, who left me here
  behind.

They cannot hear my present
  music, those
Few souls who listened to my early
  song;
They are far from me now who
  were so close,
And their first answering echo has
  so long
Been silent. Now my voice is
  heard, who knows
By whom? I shudder as the
  nameless throng
Applauds it. Are they living still,
  those friends
Whom once it moved, scattered to
  the world's ends?

And am I seized by long unwonted
  yearning
For that still, solemn spirit-realm
  which then
Was mine; these hovering lisping
  tones returning
Sigh as from some Aeolian harp, as
  when
I sang them first; I tremble, and my
  burning
Tears flow, my stern heart melts to
  love again.
All that I now possess seems far
  away
And vanished worlds are real to
  me today.

David Luke

DEDICATION

You shifting figures, I remember seeing you dimly long ago, and now I find you coming back again. I wonder should I try to hold on to you this time. Have I the inclination, have I the heart for it? You draw closer out of the mist. Very well then, have your way. The magic breeze that floats along with you fills me with youthful excitement.

You bring back joyful days and joyful scenes and you recall many folk who were dear to me. Early love, early friends rise from the past like an old tale half-forgotten. The pain comes back and with it the lament that life should be so wayward, so confused, and I go over the names of those good people who left this life before me, cut off by some ill chance from further happiness.

Those that I wrote for then will not see what follows now. The friendly throng is dispersed; the early responses have died away. I write now for the unknown crowd whose very approval I dread. If there are any now alive who were pleased with my verses, they are scattered far and wide.

And a great desire seizes me – a desire I have not felt for years – to return to this solemn realm of the spirit. My song resumes hesitantly, insecurely, like an Aeolian harp. I am shaken through and through. The tears come freely and my heart is softened. All my world now seems far away, and what was lost has become real and immediate.

Barker Fairley

Two souls speech

VOR DEM TOR Lines 1112–1121	OUTSIDE THE TOWN WALL
FAUST: Zwei Seelen wohnen, ach! in meiner Brust,	In me there are two souls, alas, and their
Die eine will sich von der andern trennen;	Division tears my life in two.
Die eine hält, in derber Liebeslust,	One loves the world, it clutches her, it binds
Sich an die Welt mit klammernden Organen	Itself to her, clinging with furious lust;
Die andre hebt gewaltsam sich vom Dust	The other longs to soar beyond the dust
Zu den Gefilden hoher Ahnen.	Into the realm of high ancestral minds.

O gibt es Geister in der Luft,	Are there no spirits moving in the air,
Die zwischen Erd' und Himmel herrschend weben,	Ruling the region between earth and sky?
So steiget nieder aus dem goldnen Duft	Come down then to me from your golden mists on high,
Und führt mich weg, zu neuem, buntem Leben!	And to new, many-coloured life, oh take me there!

David Luke

OUTSIDE THE TOWN-GATE

As for myself, there are two of me, unreconciled. The one clings to the earth with its whole body sensually, while the other soars with all its might to the abodes of the blest. If there are spirits about, ranging and ruling in the atmosphere, come down to me out of this golden light, and transport me where life is rich and new.

Barker Fairley

Translation speech

STUDIERZIMMER Lines 1224–1237	FAUST'S STORY
FAUST:	
Geschrieben steht: "Im Anfang war das Wort!	'In the beginning was the Word': why, now
Hier stock' ich schon! Wer hilft mir weiter fort?	I'm stuck already! I must change that: how?
Ich kann das Wort so hoch unmöglich schätzen,	Is then 'the word' so great and high a thing?
Ich muß es anders übersetzen,	There is some other rendering,
Wenn ich vom Geiste recht erleuchtet bin.	Which with the spirit's guidance I must find.
Geschrieben steht: Im Anfang war der Sinn.	We read: 'In the beginning was the Mind.'
Bedenke wohl die erste Zeile,	Before you write this first phrase, think again;
Daß deine Feder sich nicht übereile!	Good sense eludes the overhasty pen.
Ist es der Sinn, der alles wirkt und schafft?	Does 'mind' set worlds on their creative course?

Es sollte stehn: Im Anfang war die Kraft!
Doch, auch indem ich dieses niederschreibe,
Schon warnt mich was, daß ich dabei nicht bleibe.
Mir hilft der Geist! Auf einmal seh' ich Rat
Und schreibe getrost: Im Anfang war die Tat!

It means: 'In the beginning was the Force.'
So it should be – but as I write this too,
Some instinct warns me that it will not do.
The spirit speaks! I see how it must be read,
And boldly write: 'In the beginning was the Deed!'

David Luke

The text reads: In the beginning was the word. But stop? What about this? I can't rate the word nearly as high as that. I'll have to translate it some other way. Unless I'm mistaken, the true reading is: In the beginning was the mind. But let's not be in a hurry with the first line. Can it be the mind that creates the world? Surely we ought to read: In the beginning was the energy. But no sooner do I write this than something tells me not to stop there. And now I see the light and set down confidently: In the beginning was the act.

Barker Fairley

Source: Goethe, *Faust: Der Tragödie erster und zweiter Teil*, Herausgegeben und kommentiert von Erich Trunz, Verlag C. H. Beck, München, 1999. Goethe, *Faust: Part One*. Translated with an Introduction and Notes by David Luke, Oxford World's Classics, Oxford University Press, Oxford, 1987. Goethe, *Faust*. Translated by Barker Fairley, University of Toronto Press, Toronto, 1970.

Goethe, *Faust Part Two*

Faust's last speech

PART II ACT V
GROSSER VORHOF DES
   PALASTS
Lines 11559–11586

THE GREAT FORECOURT OF
THE PALACE

FAUST:

Ein Sumpf zieht am Gebirge hin,
Verpestet alles schon Errungene,
Den faulen Pfuhl auch abzuziehn,
Das Letzte wär' das Höchsterrungene,
Eröffn' ich Räume vielen Millionen,
Nicht sicher zwar, doch tätig-frei zu wohnen.
Grün das Gefilde, fruchtbar; Mensch und Herde
Sogleich behaglich auf der neusten Erde,
Gleich angesiedelt an des Hügels Kraft,
Den aufgewälzt kühn-emsige Völkerschaft.
Im Innern hier ein paradiesisch Land,
Da rase draußen Flut bis auf dem Rand,
Und wie sie nascht, gewaltsam einzuschließen,
Gemeindrang eilt, die Lücke zu verschließen.
Ja, diesem Sinne bin ich ganz ergeben,
Das ist der Weisheit letzter Schluß:

A swamp surrounds the mountain's base,
It poisons all I have achieved till now.
I'll drain it too; that rotten place
Shall be my last great project. I see how
To give those millions a new living-space:
They'll not be safe, but active, free at last.
I see green fields, so fertile: man and beast
At once shall settle that new pleasant earth,
Bastioned by great embankments that will rise
About them, by bold labour brought to birth.
Here there shall be an inland paradise:
Outside, the sea, as high as it can reach,
May rage and gnaw; and yet a common will,
Should it intrude, will act to close the breach.
Yes! to this vision I am wedded still,
And this as wisdom's final word I teach:

247

Nur der verdient sich Freiheit wie das Leben,	Only that man earns freedom, merits life,
Der täglich sie erobern muß.	Who must reconquer both in constant daily strife.
Und so verbringt, umrungen von Gefahr,	In such a place, by danger still surrounded,
Hier Kindheit, Mann und Greis sein tüchtig Jahr.	Youth, manhood, age, their brave new world have founded.
Solch ein Gewimmel möcht' ich sehn,	I long to see that multitude, and stand
Auf freiem Grund mit freiem Volke stehn.	With a free people on free land!
Zum Augenblicke dürft' ich sagen:	Then to the moment I might say:
Verweile doch, du bist so schön!	Beautiful moment, do not pass away!
Es kann die Spur von meinen Erdetagen	Till many ages shall have passed
Nicht in Äonen untergehn.–	This record of my earthly life shall last.
Im Vorgefühl von solchem hohen Glück	And in anticipation of such bliss
Genieß' ich jetzt den höchsten Augenblick.	What moment could give me greater joy than this?

David Luke

THE GREAT COURTYARD

There is a swamp, skirting the base of the hills, a foul and filthy blot on all our work. If we could drain and cleanse this pestilence, it would crown everything we have achieved, opening up living space for many millions. Not safe from every hazard, but safe enough. Green fields and fruitful too for man and beast, both quickly domiciled on new-made land, all snug and settled under the mighty dune that many hands have built with fearless toil. Inside it life will be a paradise. Let the floods rage and mount to the dune's brink. No sooner will they nibble at it, threaten it, than all as one man run to stop the gap. Now I am wholly of this philosophy. This is the farthest wisdom goes: The man who earns his freedom every day, alone deserves it, and no other does. And, in this sense, with dangers at our door, we all, young folk and old, shall live our lives. Oh how I'd love to see that lusty throng and stand on a free soil with a free people. Now I could almost say to the passing moment: Stay, oh stay a while, you are beautiful. The mark of my endeavours will not fade. No, not in ages, not in any time. Dreaming of this incomparable happiness, I now taste and enjoy the supreme moment.

Barker Fairley

Last lines

BERGSCHLUCHTEN
Lines 12104–12111

CHORUS MYSTICUS
Alles Vergängliche
Ist nur ein Gleichnis;
Das Unzulängliche,
Hier wird's Ereignis;
Das Unbeschreibliche,
Hier ist's getan;
Das Ewig-Weibliche
Zieht uns hinan.

MOUNTAIN GORGES

All that must disappear
Is but a parable;
What lay beyond us, here
All is made visible;
Here deeds have understood
Words they were darkened by;
Eternal Womanhood
Draws us on high.

David Luke

MOUNTAIN CHASMS

Transitory things are symbolical only. Here the inadequate finds its fulfilment. The not expressible is here made manifest. The eternal in woman is the gleam we follow.

Barker Fairley

Source: Goethe, *Faust: Der Tragödie erster und zweiter Teil*, Herausgegeben und kommentiert von Erich Trunz, Verlag C. H. Beck, München, 1999. Goethe, *Faust: Part Two*. Translated with an Introduction and Notes by David Luke, Oxford World's Classics, Oxford University Press, Oxford, 1994. Goethe, *Faust*. Translated by Barker Fairley, University of Toronto Press, Toronto 1970.

Schubert's Lieder:
settings of Goethe's poems

Schubert wrote more than six hundred songs, setting to music the words of many different poets. These range from those who were internationally famous to others who were known only locally and were among his group of friends. Of all the writers he set, Goethe was the one who most consistently inspired him to write songs of startling power and originality. The first of his songs to be widely acclaimed as a masterpiece was his famous setting of Gretchen's songs at the spinning-wheel from *Faust*, composed in 1814 when he was only seventeen. 'Erlkönig', which rivals 'Gretchen' for the position of Schubert's most famous song, followed in 1815. In all, Schubert wrote more than seventy songs to words by Goethe – more than one in ten of his output.

This selection of seven texts has been chosen to show the range of poems by Goethe that Schubert set. At one extreme is the simple mock folk-song, 'Heidenröslein'. At the other is 'Ganymed', a poem of great freedom and subtlety, in which the boy Ganymede expresses his feelings as he is transported to heaven by Zeus. 'Erlkönig' and 'Gretchen am Spinnrade' were originally to be sung by actors in Goethe's dramas (though Schubert's settings take them far away from those origins). 'Wandrers Nachtlied' and 'Harfenspieler I' (from the novel *Wilhelm Meister's Apprenticeship*) are meditations. And 'Prometheus' is a dramatic monologue, originally intended for a drama that Goethe never completed. In it, Prometheus, the creator of humankind in Greek mythology, expresses his defiant disdain for the gods.

Schubert applied a range of treatments to Goethe's poems. In 'Heidenröslein', the 'folk-poem' is set to a simple tune repeating at each verse. In 'Ganymed', the freedom of Goethe's poem is matched by the extraordinary freedom of Schubert's music (it does not even begin and end in related keys, let alone the same key). Between those two extremes come 'Gretchen am Spinnrade' and 'Erlkönig'. These have repeating elements, but are not cast in verse-form. Gretchen sings of her tortured love for Faust in short breathless phrases, unable to tear herself away from the refrain 'My peace is gone' (which Schubert repeats at the end, although Goethe does not). In 'Erlkönig', the three characters in the drama have distinct musical voices, with the cries of the young boy creating the refrain. In both 'Gretchen' and 'Erlkönig', the song rides over a piano-part constructed from constantly repeating motifs: a method of scene-setting of which Schubert is the acknowledged master.

Franz Schubert, *A Selection of Schubert's Lieder and Scores*

Heidenröslein

Sah ein Knab' ein Röslein stehn,
Röslein auf der Heiden,
War so jung und morgenschön.
Lief er schnell, es nah zu sehn,
Sah's mit vielen Freuden.
Röslein, Röslein, Röslein rot,
Röslein auf der Heiden.

Knabe sprach: Ich breche dich,
Röslein auf der Heiden!
Röslein sprach: Ich steche dich,
Dass du ewig denkst an mich,
Und ich will's nicht leiden.
Röslein, Röslein, Röslein rot,
Röslein auf der Heiden.

Und der wilde Knabe brach
's Röslein auf der Heiden;
Röslein wehrte sich und stach,
Half ihm doch kein Weh und Ach,
Musst es eben leiden.

(Wild Rose)

A young boy saw a wild rose grow,
Wild rose in the heather,
It was as fresh as morning dew.
He ran to catch a closer view,
And gazed at it with pleasure.
Rose, oh rose, oh rose so red,
Wild rose in the heather.

The boy declared: 'You shall be picked,
Wild rose in the heather!'
The rose declared, 'You shall be pricked,
And think of me with more respect,
For I refuse to suffer.'
Rose, oh rose, oh rose so red,
Wild rose in the heather.

Then the reckless young boy picked
The wild rose in the heather;
And the rose fought back and pricked,
And cried with woe to no effect,
It simply had to suffer.

Röslein, Röslein, Röslein rot,
Röslein auf der Heiden.

Rose, oh rose, oh rose so red,
Wild rose in the heather.

Wandrers Nachtlied II

Über allen Gipfeln
Ist Ruh',
In allen Wipfeln
Spürest du
Kaum einen Hauch;
Die Vögelein schweigen im Walde.
Warte nur, balde
Ruhest du auch.

(Wanderer's Night Song II)

All the mountain-tops
Are still,
In all the tree-tops
You feel
Scarcely any breeze;
The birds are silent in the wood.
Wait: soon you should
Also be at peace.

Harfenspieler I

Wer sich der Einsamkeit ergibt,
Ach! der ist bald allein;
Ein jeder lebt, ein jeder liebt
Und lässt ihn seiner Pein.
Ja! Lasst mich meiner Qual!
Und kann ich nur einmal
Recht einsam sein,
Dann bin ich nicht allein.

Es schleicht ein Liebender
    lauschend sacht
Ob seine Freundin allein?
So überschleicht bei Tag und
    Nacht
Mich Einsamen die Pein,

Mich Einsamen die Qual.
Ach, werd' ich erst einmal
Einsam im Grabe sein,
Da lässt sie mich allein!

(The Harper's Songs I)

He who gives himself to solitude,
Ah, he is soon alone;
Each man lives, each man loves
And leaves him to his suffering.
Yes, leave me to my torment!
And if I can only once
Be truly lonely,
Then I shall not be alone.

There steals a lover, softly listening:

Is his sweetheart alone?
Thus there steals over me, day and
    night,
Suffering in my solitude,

Torment in my solitude.
Ah, when at last I lie
Lonely in the grave,
Then they will leave me alone.

Gretchen am Spinnrade

Meine Ruh' ist hin,
Mein Herz ist schwer;
Ich finde sie nimmer
Und nimmermehr.

Wo ich ihn nicht hab',
Ist mir das Grab,
Die ganze Welt
Ist mir vergällt.

Mein armer Kopf
Ist mir verrückt,
Mein armer Sinn
Ist mir zerstückt.

Meine Ruh' ist hin,
Mein Herz ist schwer;
Ich finde sie nimmer
Und nimmermehr.

Nach ihm nur schau' ich
Zum Fenster hinaus,
Nach ihm nur geh' ich
Aus dem Haus.

Sein hoher Gang,
Sein' edle Gestalt,
Seines Mundes Lächeln,
Seiner Augen Gewalt,

Und seine Rede
Zauberfluss,
Sein Händedruck,
Und ach, sein Kuss!

Meine Ruh' ist hin,
Mein Herz ist schwer;
Ich finde sie nimmer
Und nimmermehr.

Mein Busen drängt sich
Nach ihm hin.

(Gretchen at the Spinning-wheel)

My peace is gone,
my heart is sore,
I'll find it never,
nevermore.

Where he is not,
my world is all
a silent grave,
and turned to gall.

And my poor head
is torn apart
by thoughts of him
who has my heart.

My peace is gone,
my heart is sore,
I'll find it never,
nevermore.

I watch at the window
for him alone:
and only for him
I leave my home.

My one and only,
my North and South—
his step, his bearing,
his eyes, his mouth,

the sound of his voice,
A stream of bliss,
the touch of his hand,
and – ah! – his kiss!

My peace is gone,
my heart is sore,
I'll find it never,
nevermore.

My poor heart races,
To feel him near:

Ach dürft' ich fassen Und halten ihn.	ah! Just to clasp him and hold him here.
Und küssen ihn, So wie ich wollt', An seinen Küssen Vergehen sollt'!	And kiss and kiss again, till I under his kisses, sink and die.
(O könnt' ich ihn küssen, So wie ich wollt', An seinen Küssen Vergehen sollt'!)	(And kiss him and kiss him again, till I under his kisses, sink and die.)
(Meine Ruh' ist hin, Mein Herz ist schwer)	(My peace is gone, my heart is sore)

Erlkönig

(The Erl-King)

Wer reitet so spät durch Nacht und Wind? Es ist der Vater mit seinem Kind; Er hat den Knaben wohl in dem Arm, Er fasst ihn sicher, er hält ihn warm.	Who rides at a gallop through night so wild? It is the father with his dear child. He grips the boy firmly in his arms, He holds him safe, he keeps him warm.
'Mein Sohn, was birgst du so bang dein Gesicht?' 'Siehst, Vater, du den Erlkönig nicht? Den Erlenkönig mit Kron und Schweif?' 'Mein Sohn, es ist ein Nebelstreif.'	'Son, why do you cower so fearfully?' 'Father, the Erl-king! Can you not see? The dreadful Erl-king with crown and tail?' 'My son, it is mist blown by the gale.'
'Du liebes Kind, komm, geh mit mir! Gar schöne Spiele spiel ich mit dir; Manch bunte Blumen sind an dem Strand, Meine Mutter hat manch gülden Gewand.'	'You lovely child, come away with me, We'll play together down by the sea; Such pretty flowers grow on the shore, My mother has golden robes in store.'

'Mein Vater, mein Vater, und hörest du nicht,
Was Erlenkönig mir leise verspricht?'
'Sei ruhig, bleibe ruhig, mein Kind;
In dürren Blättern säuselt der Wind.'

'Willst, feiner Knabe, du mit mir gehn?
Meine Töchter sollen dich warten schön;
Meine Töchter führen die nächtlichen Reihn
Und wiegen und tanzen und singen dich ein.'

'Mein Vater, mein Vater, und siehst du nicht dort
Erlkönigs Töchter am düstern Ort?'
'Mein Sohn, mein Sohn, ich seh es genau:
Es scheinen die alten Weiden so grau.'

'Ich liebe dich, mich reizt deine schöne Gestalt;
Und bist du nicht willig, so brauch ich Gewalt.'
'Mein Vater, mein Vater, jetzt fasst er mich an!
Erlkönig hat mir ein Leids getan!'

Dem Vater grauset's, er reitet geschwind,
Er hält in Armen das ächzende Kind,
Erreicht den Hof mit Mühe und Not:
In seinen Armen das Kind war tot.

'My father, my father, oh do you not hear
What the Erl-king whispers into my ear?'
'Be calm, stay calm, it's nothing my child
But dry leaves blown by the wind so wild.'

'My fine young lad, won't you come away?
My daughters are waiting for you to play;
My daughters will lead the dance through the night,
And sing and rock you until you sleep tight.'

'My father, my father, can you still not see
The Erl-king's daughters waiting for me?'
'My son, my son, I can see quite clear
The moon on the willows, there's nothing else there.'

'I love you my boy, you are such a delight;
And I'll take you by force if you put up a fight.'
'My father, my father, he's gripping me fast!
The Erl-king is hurting! Help me, I'm lost!'

The father shudders, and speeds through the night,
In his arms he holds the moaning boy tight;
At last he arrives, to home and bed:
In the father's arms the child was dead.

Prometheus

Bedecke deinen Himmel, Zeus,	Cover your heaven, Zeus,
Mit Wolkendunst	With a gauze of cloud.
Und übe, dem Knaben gleich,	And, like a boy beheading thistles,
Der Disteln köpft,	Practise on oak-trees
An Eichen dich und Bergeshöhn;	And mountain-peaks;
Musst mir meine Erde	But you will have to leave
Doch lassen stehn	My world standing,
Und meine Hütte, die du nicht	And my hut, which you did not
gebaut,	build,
Und meine Herd,	And my fireside,
Um dessen Glut	Whose glow
Du mich beneidest.	You envy me.
Ich kenne nichts Ärmeres	I know nothing more wretched
Unter der Sonn' als euch, Götter!	Beneath the sun than you gods!
Ihr nähret kümmerlich	Meagrely you nourish
Von Opfersteuern	Your majesty
Und Gebetshauch	With offerings
Eure Majestät	And the breath of prayer,
Und darbtet, wären	And would starve,
Nicht Kinder und Bettler	If children and beggars were not
Hoffnungsvolle Toren.	Ever-hopeful fools.
Da ich ein Kind war,	When I was a child,
Nicht wusste, wo aus noch ein,	And did not know a thing,
Kehrt' ich mein verirrtes Auge	I turned my perplexed gaze
Zur Sonne, als wenn drüber wär'	To the sun, as if beyond it
Ein Ohr, zu hören meine	There were an ear to listen to my
Klage,	lament
Ein Herz wie meins,	And a heart like mine
Sich des Bedrängten zu erbarmen.	To pity the distressed.
Wer half mir	Who helped me
Wider der Titanen	Against the overweening pride of
Übermut?	the Titans?
Wer rettete vom Tode mich,	Who saved me from death
Von Sklaverei?	And from slavery?
Hast du nicht alle selbst	Did you not accomplish it all
vollendet	yourself,
Heilig glühend Herz?	Sacred, ardent heart?
Und glühtest jung und	And, deceived in your youthful
gut,	goodness,

Betrogen,	Were you not fired with gratitude
Rettungsdank,	for your deliverance
Dem Schlafenden da droben?	To the sleeper up above?
Ich dich ehren? Wofür?	I honour you? What for?
Hast du die Schmerzen gelindert	Have you ever eased the suffering
Je des Beladenen?	Of him who is oppressed?
Hast du die Tränen gestillet	Have you ever dried the tears
Je des Geängsteten?	Of him who is troubled?
Hat nicht mich zum Manne	Did not almighty
geschmiedet	Time
Die allmächtige Zeit	And eternal Fate,
Und das ewige Schicksal,	My masters and yours,
Meine Herrn und deine?	Forge me into a man?
Wähntest du etwa,	Did you perhaps imagine
Ich sollte das Leben hassen,	That I would hate life,
In Wüsten fliehen,	Flee into the wilderness,
Weil nicht alle	Because not all
Blütenträume reiften?	My blossoming dreams bore fruit?
Hier sitz' ich, forme Menschen	Here I sit, forming men
Nach meinem Bilde,	In my own image,
Ein Geschlecht, das mir gleich sei,	A race that shall be like me,
Zu leiden, zu weinen,	That shall suffer, weep,
Zu geniessen und zu freuen sich,	Enjoy and rejoice,
Und dein nicht zu achten,	And ignore you,
Wie ich!	As I do!

Ganymed	(Ganymede)
Wie im Morgenglanze	How your glow envelops me
Du rings mich anglühst,	In the morning radiance,
Frühling, Geliebter!	Spring. My beloved!
Mit tausendfacher Liebeswonne	With love's thousandfold joy
Sich an mein Herz drängt	The hallowed sensation
Deiner ewigen Wärme	Of your eternal warmth
Heilig Gefühl,	Floods my heart,
Undendliche Schöne!	Infinite beauty!
Dass ich dich fassen möcht	O that I might clasp you
In diesen Arm!	In my arms!
Ach, an deinen Busen	Ah, on your breast
Lieg ich, schmachte,	I lie languishing,

Und deine Blumen, dein Gras	And your flowers, your grass
Drängen sich an mein Herz.	Press close to my heart.
Du kühlst den brennenden	You cool the burning
Durst meines Busens,	Thirst within my breast,
Lieblicher Morgenwind!	Sweet morning breeze,
Ruft drein die Nachtigall	As the nightingale calls
Liebend nach mir aus dem	Tenderly to me from the misty
Nebeltal.	valley.
Ich komm, ich komme!	I come, I come!
Wohin? Ach, wohin?	But whither? Ah whither?
Hinauf! Hinauf strebt's.	Upwards! Strive upwards!
Es schweben die Wolken	The clouds drift
Abwärts, die Wolken	Down, yielding
Neigen sich der sehnenden Liebe,	To yearning love,
Mir! Mir!	To me! To me!
In eurem Schosse	In your lap,
Aufwärts!	Upwards,
Umfangend umfangen!	Embracing and embraced!
Aufwärts an deinen Busen,	Upwards to your bosom,
Alliebender Vater!	All-loving father!

Source: The translation of 'Gretchen am Spinnrade' is from Johann Wolfgang von Goethe, *Faust*, translated by Robert David MacDonald, Oberon Books, London, 1988, revised reprint 2002. Translations of 'Prometheus' and 'Ganymed' are from *Schubert: the complete song texts*, translated by Richard Wigmore, London, 1988, from which all the German texts were also taken. Other translations are by Robert Philip.

Lord Byron, *Childe Harold's Pilgrimage, III*

George Gordon, Lord Byron, composed and published Canto III of his poem *Childe Harold's Pilgrimage* in 1816. Fuelled by the scandal surrounding his departure from England earlier that year – a hasty and messy divorce and well-founded rumours of incest with his half-sister Augusta Leigh – sales soared. The poem caught the spirit of the time in its tone of melancholy and ennui, and definitively constituted Byron as the most important poet in Britain and Europe for the next decade and beyond. Some of Byron's early ambitions for the poem are set out in his Preface to Cantos I and II (published in 1812 to instant acclaim) which are here reprinted for reference, although it will readily become clear that Byron's conception of the poem as a whole had changed markedly by the time he was writing Canto III.

A very large and celebrated portion of the poem is taken up with Byron's meditations upon the phenomenon of Napoleon and the import of Waterloo. The poem's language and self-positioning in relation to Waterloo are here highlighted in the first instance by Byron's letter to his friend John Cam Hobhouse describing his visit to the battlefield in the summer of 1816, and by two accounts of the battle and the battlefield given by his friend and rival the poet and novelist Sir Walter Scott. Scott writes at length to his patron the Earl of Buccleuch about the experience of being a tourist to the field of Waterloo in the summer of 1815, a letter that provides an instructive contrast both to Byron's tone, and to Scott's own very successful account of Waterloo, his poem *The Field of Waterloo* (1815). This poem was written following his visit and set the agenda for the majority of subsequent poetic treatments of the victory. Dedicated to royalty, it is emphatically an establishment poem, from its dedication to royalty to its quasi-official statements of patriotism.

If Byron is fascinated by Napoleon in the early part of Canto III, the figure that most intrigues him in the later part of the poem is undoubtedly that of Jean-Jacques Rousseau. Byron sees in him the political theorist who fathered the French Revolution, the writer of the celebrated sentimental novel *La Nouvelle Héloïse*, and the autobiographer in his *Confessions* (completed 1770, and published posthumously in 1782). Arguably the first exercise in modern auto-biography, and remarkable for its interest in psychological self-analysis and its astonishing sexual frankness, the *Confessions* provided a model for the exhaustive analysis of the self characteris-tic of *Childe Harold's Pilgrimage, III*. An extract is reprinted here to illustrate how closely Byron's own language and narrative con-cerning Rousseau mirrors Rousseau's own. Next in this section comes Byron's own prose account of his journey from Dover to Geneva in 1816, told in a number of letters to various correspon-dents, including Augusta Leigh. They are included to emphasise how carefully Byron crafts his account and tone to suit his reader, whether private or public, and to caution the reader against con-struing the 'Byron' of *Childe Harold* as more – or less – authentic than the Byron of the letters.

Contemporaries did, however, identify the poet fully with the sen-timents expressed – as inexpressible – in the poem, and this is evi-dent from the last item here reprinted, an extract from Sir Walter Scott's long review of Canto III, and of Byron's career to date, in the *Quarterly Review* of 1817. In addition to taking issue with Byron's view of Waterloo (of interest as a further instalment of the debate between the two men outlined above), Scott also ventures personal and moral advice to the poet, a move that would become familiar, the more intimately connected Byron's life and work were seen to be. This intimate connection, realised explicitly for the first time by Canto III, arguably made Byron into the first Romantic celebrity.

Lord Byron, *Childe Harold's Pilgrimage, Canto the Third*, 1816

Notes marked with an asterisk are Byron's own.

Afin que cette application vous forçât à penser à autre chose. Il n'y a en vérité de remède que celui-là et le temps.[1]
> *Lettre du Roi de Prusse à D'Alembert, Sept. 7, 1776.*

---

[1] Canto III epigraph: 'So that this work will force you to think of something else. Truly, that and time are the only remedies'.

1

Is thy face like thy mother's, my fair child!
Ada! sole daughter of my house and heart?[2]
When last I saw thy young blue eyes they smiled,
And then we parted,—not as now we part,
But with a hope.—
　　　　　　Awaking with a start,
The waters heave around me; and on high
The winds lift up their voices; I depart,
Whither I know not; but the hour's gone by,
When Albion's lessening shores could grieve or glad mine eye.[3]

2

Once more upon the waters! yet once more!　　　　　10
And the waves bound beneath me as a steed
That knows his rider. Welcome, to their roar!
Swift be their guidance, wheresoe'er it lead!
Though the strain'd mast should quiver as a reed,
And the rent canvas fluttering strew the gale,
Still must I on; for I am as a weed,
Flung from the rock, on Ocean's foam, to sail
Where'er the surge may sweep, or tempest's breath prevail.

3

In my youth's summer I did sing of One,[4]
The wandering outlaw of his own dark mind;　　　　20
Again I seize the theme then but begun,
And bear it with me, as the rushing wind
Bears the cloud onwards: in that Tale I find
The furrows of long thought, and dried-up tears,
Which, ebbing, leave a sterile track behind,
O'er which all heavily the journeying years
Plod the last sands of life,—where not a flower appears.

---

[2] l. 2 *Ada*: Augusta Ada Byron, Byron's daughter (b. 10 December 1815) by his wife Annabella née Milbanke, who left her husband when the child was five weeks old; Byron never saw his daughter again.

[3] l. 9 *Albion*: Britain.

[4] l. 19 *In my youth's summer I did sing of One*: referring to the hero of Cantos I and II of *Childe Harold's Pilgrimage*.

4

Since my young days of passion—joy, or pain,
Perchance my heart and harp have lost a string,
And both may jar: it may be, that in vain   30
I would essay as I have sung to sing.
Yet, though a dreary strain, to this I cling;
So that it wean me from the weary dream
Of selfish grief or gladness—so it fling
Forgetfulness around me—it shall seem
To me, though to none else, a not ungrateful theme.

5

He, who grown aged in this world of woe,
In deeds, not years, piercing the depths of life,
So that no wonder waits him, nor below
Can love, or sorrow, fame, ambition, strife,   40
Cut to his heart again with the keen knife
Of silent, sharp endurance: he can tell
Why thought seeks refuge in lone caves, yet rife
With airy images, and shapes which dwell
Still unimpair'd, though old, in the soul's haunted cell.

6

'Tis to create, and in creating live
A being more intense, that we endow
With form our fancy, gaining as we give
The life we imagine, even as I do now.
What am I? Nothing; but not so art thou,   50
Soul of my thought! with whom I traverse earth,
Invisible but gazing, as I glow
Mix'd with thy spirit, blended with thy birth,
And feeling still with thee in my crush'd feelings' dearth.

7

Yet must I think less wildly:—I *have* thought
Too long and darkly, till my brain became,
In its own eddy boiling and o'erwrought,
A whirling gulf of phantasy and flame:
And thus, untaught in youth my heart to tame,
My springs of life were poison'd. 'Tis too late!   60

262

Yet am I chang'd; though still enough the same
In strength to bear what time can not abate,
And feed on bitter fruits without accusing Fate.

8

Something too much of this:—but now 'tis past,
And the spell closes with its silent seal.
Long absent HAROLD re-appears at last;
He of the breast which fain no more would feel,
Wrung with the wounds which kill not, but ne'er heal;
Yet Time, who changes all, had altered him
In soul and aspect as in age: years steal   70
Fire from the mind as vigour from the limb;
And life's enchanted cup but sparkles near the brim.

9

His had been quaff'd too quickly, and he found
The dregs were wormwood; but he fill'd again,[5]
And from a purer fount, on holier ground,[6]
And deem'd its spring perpetual; but in vain!
Still round him clung invisibly a chain
Which gall'd for ever, fettering though unseen,
And heavy though it clank'd not; worn with pain,
Which pined although it spoke not; and grew keen,   80
Entering with every step, he took, through many a scene.

10

Secure in guarded coldness, he had mix'd
Again in fancied safety with his kind,
And deem'd his spirit now so firmly fix'd
And sheath'd with an invulnerable mind,
That, if no joy, no sorrow lurk'd behind;
And he, as one, might midst the many stand
Unheeded, searching through the crowd to find
Fit speculation! such as in strange land
He found in wonder-works of God and Nature's hand.   90

---

[5] l. 74 *wormwood:* purgative herbal remedy proverbial for its bitterness.
[6] l. 75 *purer fount:* Greece, to which Childe Harold in earlier cantos travels in search of personal renewal.

11

But who can view the ripened rose, nor seek
To wear it? who can curiously behold
The smoothness and the sheen of beauty's cheek,
Nor feel the heart can never all grow old?
Who can contemplate Fame through clouds unfold
The star which rises o'er her steep, nor climb?
Harold, once more within the vortex, roll'd
On with the giddy circle, chasing Time,
Yet with a nobler aim than in his youth's fond prime.

12

But soon he knew himself the most unfit   100
Of men to herd with Man; with whom he held
Little in common; untaught to submit
His thoughts to others, though his soul was quell'd
In youth by his own thoughts; still uncompell'd,
He would not yield dominion of his mind
To spirits against whom his own rebell'd;
Proud though in desolation; which could find
A life within itself, to breathe without mankind.

13

Where rose the mountains, there to him were friends;
Where roll'd the ocean, thereon was his home;   110
Where a blue sky, and glowing clime, extends,
He had the passion and the power to roam;
The desart, forest, cavern, breaker's foam,
Were unto him companionship; they spake
A mutual language, clearer than the tome[7]
Of his land's tongue, which he would oft forsake
For Nature's pages glass'd by sunbeams on the lake.

14

Like the Chaldean, he could watch the stars,[8]
Till he had peopled them with beings bright
As their own beams; and earth, and earth-born jars,   120

---

[7] l. 115 *tome*: archaic term for book.
[8] l. 118 *the Chaldean*: the Chaldees were famous Babylonian astronomers.

And human frailties, were forgotten quite:
Could he have kept his spirit to that flight
He had been happy; but this clay will sink
Its spark immortal, envying it the light
To which it mounts as if to break the link
That keeps us from yon heaven which woos us to its brink.

15

But in Man's dwellings he became a thing
Restless and worn, and stern and wearisome,
Droop'd as a wild-born falcon with clipt wing,
To whom the boundless air alone were home: 130
Then came his fit again, which to o'ercome,
As eagerly the barr'd-up bird will beat
His breast and beak against his wiry dome
Till the blood tinge his plumage, so the heat
Of his impeded soul would through his bosom eat.

16

Self-exiled Harold wanders forth again,
With nought of hope left, but with less of gloom;
The very knowledge that he lived in vain,
That all was over on this side the tomb,
Had made Despair a smilingness assume,   140
Which, though 'twere wild,—as on the plundered wreck
When mariners would madly meet their doom
With draughts intemperate on the sinking deck,[9]
Did yet inspire a cheer, which he forbore to check.

17

Stop!—for thy tread is on an Empire's dust![10]
An Earthquake's spoil is sepulchred below!
Is the spot mark'd with no colossal bust?
Nor column trophied for triumphal show?
None; but the moral's truth tells simpler so,

---

[9] l. 143 *draughts intemperate:* the allusion is to the contemporary commonplace that sailors, seeing certain death in shipwreck approaching, would break out the ship's store of spirits and become roaring drunk to keep up their courage.

[10] l. 145 *an Empire's dust:* The first French empire (1804–15) was overthrown at Waterloo.

As the ground was before, thus let it be;— 150
How that red rain hath made the harvest grow!
And is this all the world has gained by thee,
Thou first and last of fields! king-making Victory?[11]

18

And Harold stands upon this place of skulls,
The grave of France, the deadly Waterloo!
How in an hour the power which gave annuls
Its gifts, transferring fame as fleeting too!
In 'pride of place' here last the eagle flew,[12]
Then tore with bloody talon the rent plain,
Pierced by the shaft of banded nations through;[13] 160
Ambition's life and labours all were vain;
He wears the shattered links of the world's broken chain.

19

Fit retribution! Gaul may champ the bit
And foam in fetters;—but is Earth more free?
Did nations combat to make *One* submit;
Or league to teach all kings true sovereignty?
What! shall reviving Thraldom again be
The patched-up idol of enlightened days?
Shall we, who struck the Lion down, shall we
Pay the Wolf homage? proffering lowly gaze 170
And servile knees to thrones? No; *prove* before ye praise![14]

20

If not, o'er one fallen despot boast no more!
In vain fair cheeks were furrowed with hot tears
For Europe's flowers long rooted up before
The trampler of her vineyards; in vain years
Of death, depopulation, bondage, fears,

---

[11] l. 153 *king-making Victory*: Waterloo resulted in the wholesale restoration of European monarchies through the offices of the 'king-making' Congress of Vienna (1815).

[12] l. 158 'Pride of place' is a term of falconry, and means the highest pitch of flight.—See *Macbeth*, etc.

A Falcon towering in her pride of place
Was by a mousing Owl hawked at and killed.*

[13] l. 160 *banded nations*: the allied forces of the British and the Prussians, principally.

[14] l. 171 *prove*: here, to test the value of something.

Have all been borne, and broken by the accord
Of roused-up millions: all that most endears
Glory, is when the myrtle wreathes a sword
Such as Harmodius drew on Athens' tyrant lord.[15, 16]   180

21

There was a sound of revelry by night,
And Belgium's capital had gathered then
Her Beauty and her Chivalry, and bright
The lamps shone o'er fair women and brave men;
A thousand hearts beat happily; and when
Music arose with its voluptuous swell,
Soft eyes look'd love to eyes which spake again,
And all went merry as a marriage-bell;[17, 18]
But hush! hark! a deep sound strikes like a rising knell!

22

Did ye not hear it?—No; 'twas but the wind,   190
Or the car rattling o'er the stony street,
On with the dance! let joy be unconfined;
No sleep till morn, when Youth and Pleasure meet
To chase the glowing Hours with flying feet—
But, hark!—that heavy sound breaks in once more,
As if the clouds its echo would repeat;
And nearer, clearer, deadlier than before!
Arm! Arm! and out—it is—the cannon's opening roar!

[15] l. 180 See the famous Song on Harmodius and Aristogiton.—The best English translation is in Bland's Anthology, by Mr Denham.
   With myrtle my sword will I wreathe, etc.*
[16] l. 180 *Harmodius*. Herodotus tells the story of how in 514 BC Harmodius and his fellow-conspirator Aristogiton attempted to assassinate the tyrants of Athens, Hippias and Hipparchus, in the event killing only Hipparchus. They wreathed their daggers in myrtle to conceal them, and thereafter the sword wreathed with myrtle became a symbol of liberty.
[17] l. 188 On the night previous to the action, it is said that a ball was given in Brussels.*
[18] l. 181ff. the ball given by the Duchess of Richmond on 15 June, the night before the inconclusive battle of Quatre-Bras. Waterloo, which was conclusive of Napoleon's campaign, was fought on 18 June.

23

Within a windowed niche of that high hall
Sate Brunswick's fated chieftain; he did hear[19]   200
That sound the first amidst the festival,
And caught its tone with Death's prophetic ear;
And when they smiled because he deem'd it near,
His heart more truly knew that peal too well
Which stretch'd his father on a bloody bier,
And roused the vengence blood alone could quell:
He rush'd into the field, and, foremost fighting, fell.

24

Ah! then and there was hurrying to and fro,
And gathering tears, and tremblings of distress,
And cheeks all pale, which but an hour ago   210
Blush'd at the praise of their own loveliness;
And there were sudden partings, such as press
The life from out young hearts, and choking sighs
Which ne'er might be repeated; who could guess
If ever more should meet those mutual eyes,
Since upon nights so sweet such awful morn could rise?

25

And there was mounting in hot haste: the steed,
The mustering squadron, and the clattering car,
Went pouring forward in impetuous speed,
And swiftly forming in the ranks of war;   220
And the deep thunder peal on peal afar;
And near, the beat of the alarming drum
Roused up the soldier ere the morning star;
While throng'd the citizens with terror dumb,
Or whispering, with white lips—'The foe! They come! they come!'

---

[19] l. 200 *Brunswick's fated chieftain:* Frederick Duke of Brunswick (1771–1815), nephew to
George III, was killed at Quatre-Bras. Much was made at the time of his vow of vengeance on
Napoleon for his father's death at Auerstadt in 1806.

26

And wild and high the 'Cameron's gathering' rose![20]
The war-note of Lochiel, which Albyn's hills[21]
Have heard, and heard, too, have her Saxon foes:—
How in the noon of night that pibroch thrills,
Savage and shrill! But with the breath which fills   230
Their mountain-pipe, so fill the mountaineers
With the fierce native daring which instils
The stirring memory of a thousand years,
And Evan's, Donald's fame rings in each clansman's ears![22, 23]

27

And Ardennes waves above them her green leaves,[24]
Dewy with nature's tear-drops, as they pass,
Grieving, if aught inanimate e'er grieves,
Over the unreturning brave,—alas!
Ere evening to be trodden like the grass
Which now beneath them, but above shall grow   240
In its next verdure, when this fiery mass
Of living valour, rolling on the foe
And burning with high hope, shall moulder cold and low.

28

Last noon beheld them full of lusty life,
Last eve in Beauty's circle proudly gay,
The midnight brought the signal-sound of strife,
The morn the marshalling in arms,—the day
Battle's magnificently-stern array!
The thunder-clouds close o'er it, which when rent

[20] l. 226 *Cameron's gathering*: the clan song and war-cry of the Camerons whose chieftain is titled 'Lochiel'.

[21] l. 227 *Albyn*. Gaelic name for Scotland.

[22] l. 234 Sir Evan Cameron, and his descendant Donald, the 'gentle Lochiel' of the 'forty-five'.*

[23] l. 234 *Evan, Donald's fame*: Sir Evan Cameron (1629–1719) resisted Cromwell on behalf of the Stuart dynasty and fought on behalf of James II at Killiecrankie (1689); his grandson, Donald Cameron (1695–1748), was wounded fighting for the exiled Charles Stuart at Culloden (1746).*

[24] l. 235 The wood of Soignies is supposed to be a remnant of the 'forest of Ardennes', famous in Boiardo's *Orlando*, and immortal in Shakespeare's 'As you like it'. It is also celebrated in Tacitus as being the spot of successful defence by the Germans against the Roman encroachments.—I have ventured to adopt the name connected with nobler associations than those of mere slaughter.*

The earth is covered thick with other clay,   250
Which her own clay shall cover, heaped and pent,
Rider and horse,—friend, foe,—in one red burial blent!

29

Their praise is hymn'd by loftier harps than mine;[25]
Yet one I would select from that proud throng,[26]
Partly because they blend me with his line,
And partly that I did his sire some wrong,
And partly that bright names will hallow song;
And his was of the bravest, and when shower'd
The death-bolts deadliest the thinn'd files along,
Even where the thickest of war's tempest lower'd,   260
They reach'd no nobler breast than thine, young, gallant Howard!

30

There have been tears and breaking hearts for thee,
And mine were nothing, had I such to give,
But when I stood beneath the fresh green tree,
Which living waves where thou didst cease to live,
And saw around me the wide field revive
With fruits and fertile promise; and the Spring
Come forth her work of gladness to contrive,
With all her reckless birds upon the wing,
I turn'd from all she brought to those she could not bring.[27,28]   270

[25] l. 253 *loftier harps than mine*: reference to Sir Walter Scott's *The Field of Waterloo* (1815).

[26] l. 254 *one I would select*: the Hon. Frederick Howard (1785–1815) was Byron's cousin.

[27] l. 270 My guide from Mont St Jean over the field seemed intelligent and accurate. The place where Major Howard fell was not far from two tall and solitary trees (there was a third cut down, or shivered in the battle) which stand a few yards from each other at a pathway's side.—Beneath these he died and was buried. The body has since been removed to England. A small hollow for the present marks where it lay, but will probably soon be effaced; the plough has been upon it, and the grain is.

After pointing out the different spots where Picton and other gallant men had perished; the guide said, 'here Major Howard lay; I was near him when wounded'. I told him my relationship, and he seemed then still more anxious to point out the particular spot and circumstances. The place is one of the most marked in the field from the peculiarity of the two trees above mentioned.

I went on horseback twice over the field, comparing it with my recollection of similar scenes. As a plain, Waterloo seems marked out for the scene of some great action, though this may be mere imagination: I have viewed with attention those of Platea, Troy, Mantinea, Leuctra, Chaeronea, and Marathon; and the field around Mont St Jean and Hougoumont appears to

3 1

I turn'd to thee, to thousands, of whom each
And one as all a ghastly gap did make
In his own kind and kindred, whom to teach
Forgetfulness were mercy for their sake;
The Archangel's trump, not Glory's, must awake[29]
Those whom they thirst for; though the sound of Fame
May for a moment soothe, it cannot slake
The fever of vain longing, and the name
So honoured but assumes a stronger, bitterer claim.

3 2

They mourn, but smile at length; and, smiling, mourn: 280
The tree will wither long before it fall;
The hull drives on, though mast and sail be torn;
The roof-tree sinks, but moulder on the hall
In massy hoariness; the ruined wall
Stands when its wind-worn battlements are gone;
The bars survive the captive they enthrall;
The day drags through though storms keep out the sun;
And thus the heart will break, yet brokenly live on:

3 3

Even as a broken mirror, which the glass
In every fragment multiplies; and makes   290
A thousand images of one that was,

---

want little but a better cause, and that undefinable but impressive halo which the lapse of ages throws around a celebrated spot, to vie in interest with any or all of these, except perhaps the last mentioned.[28]*

[28] *Byron's note to l. 270: Platea, Troy, Mantinea, Leuctra, Chaeronea, and Marathon:* Plataea was a battle fought with Athenian troops to beat back the invading Persians in 479 BC; Troy was the scene of the ten-year conflict between the Greeks and the Trojans; Mantinea was the scene of a decisive Spartan victory in 418 BC; Leuctra (371 BC) was a victory by the Mantineans over the Spartans; Chaeronea saw an important defeat of the Athenians and the Thebans in 338 BC, Marathon saw the defeat of the Persians by the Athenians. Byron's point seems to be that all these battles were fought on plains and were world-historical events in the classical world and therefore in world-history, and that they were on the whole nobler in their causes and outcomes than that fought on Waterloo plain.

[29] l. 275 *the Archangel's trump:* referring to the Christian belief that at the end of the world there will be a general resurrection of the dead heralded by the 'last trump', a trumpet-blast blown by the Archangel. 1 Corinthians 15:52.

The same, and still the more, the more it breaks;
And thus the heart will do which not forsakes,
Living in shattered guise, and still, and cold,
And bloodless, with its sleepless sorrow aches,
Yet withers on till all without is old,
Showing no visible sign, for such things are untold.

34

There is a very life in our despair,
Vitality of poison,—a quick root
Which feeds these deadly branches; for it were   300
As nothing did we die; but Life will suit
Itself to Sorrow's most detested fruit,
Like to the apples on the Dead Sea's shore,[30]
All ashes to the taste: Did man compute[31]
Existence by enjoyment, and count o'er
Such hours 'gainst years of life,—say, would he name threescore?

35

The Psalmist numbered out the years of man:
They are enough; and if thy tale be *true*,[32]
Thou, who didst grudge him even that fleeting span,
More than enough, thou fatal Waterloo!   310
Millions of tongues record thee, and anew
Their children's lips shall echo them, and say—
'Here, where the sword united nations drew,
Our countrymen were warring on that day!'
And this is much, and all which will not pass away.

36

There sunk the greatest, nor the worst of men,[33]
Whose spirit antithetically mixt
One moment of the mightiest, and again
On little objects with like firmness fixt,
Extreme in all things! hadst thou been betwixt,   320

[30] l. 303 The (Fabled) apples on the brink of the lake Asphaltes were said to be fair without, and within ashes.—*Vide* Tacitus, *Historia* [Book 5, sec. 7].*
[31] l. 304ff. *Did man . . . the years of man:* 'the days of man are three-score and ten' Psalms, 90 : 10.
[32] l. 308 *tale:* a pun meaning at once 'story' and 'tally' or account.
[33] l. 316 *the greatest, nor the worst of men:* Napoleon.

Thy throne had still been thine, or never been;
For daring made thy rise as fall: thou seek'st
Even now to re-assume the imperial mien,
And shake again the world, the Thunderer of the scene!

37

Conqueror and captive of the earth art thou!
She trembles at thee still, and thy wild name
Was ne'er more bruited in men's minds than now
That thou art nothing, save the jest of Fame,
Who wooed thee once, thy vassal, and became
The flatterer of thy fierceness, till thou wert   330
A god unto thyself; nor less the same
To the astounded kingdoms all inert,
Who deem'd thee for a time whate'er thou didst assert.

38

Oh, more or less than man—in high or low,
Battling with nations, flying from the field;
Now making monarchs' necks thy footstool, now
More than thy meanest soldier taught to yield,
An empire thou couldst crush, command, rebuild,
But govern not thy pettiest passion, nor,
However deeply in men's spirits skill'd,   340
Look through thine own, nor curb the lust of war,
Nor learn that tempted Fate will leave the loftiest star.

39

Yet well thy soul hath brook'd the turning tide
With that untaught innate philosophy,
Which, be it wisdom, coldness, or deep pride,
Is gall and wormwood to an enemy.
When the whole host of hatred stood hard by,
To watch and mock thee shrinking, thou hast smiled
With a sedate and all-enduring eye;—
When Fortune fled her spoil'd and favourite child,   350
He stood unbowed beneath the ills upon him piled.

40

Sager than in thy fortunes; for in them
Ambition steel'd thee on too far to show
That just habitual scorn which could contemn
Men and their thoughts; 'twas wise to feel, not so
To wear it ever on thy lip and brow,
And spurn the instruments thou wert to use
Till they were turn'd unto thine overthrow:
'Tis but a worthless world to win or lose;
So hath it proved to thee, and all such lot who choose.   360

41

If, like a tower upon a headlong rock,
Thou hadst been made to stand or fall alone,
Such scorn of man had help'd to brave the shock;
But men's thoughts were the steps which paved thy throne,
Their admiration thy best weapon shone;
The part of Philip's son was thine, not then[34]
(Unless aside thy purple had been thrown)
Like stern Diogenes to mock at men;
For sceptred cynics earth were far too wide a den.[35, 36]

42

But quiet to quick bosoms is a hell,   370
And *there* hath been thy bane; there is a fire
And motion of the soul which will not dwell
In its own narrow being, but aspire
Beyond the fitting medium of desire;
And, but once kindled, quenchless evermore,
Preys upon high adventure, nor can tire
Of aught but rest; a fever at the core,
Fatal to him who bears, to all who ever bore.

---

[34] l. 366 *Philip's son*: Alexander the Great, Philip of Macedon's son.

[35] l. 369 The great error of Napoleon, 'if we have writ our annals true', was a continued obtrusion on mankind of his want of all community of feeling for or with them, perhaps more offensive to human vanity than the active cruelty of more trembling and suspicious tyranny.

Such were his speeches to public assemblies as well as individuals: and the single expression which he is said to have used on returning to Paris after the Russian winter had destroyed his army, rubbing his hands over a fire, 'This is pleasanter than Moscow', would probably alienate more favour from his cause than the destruction and reverses which led to the remark.[*36]

[36] Byron's note to l. 369: *if we have writ our annals true*: *Coriolanus*, V, vi, 114.

43

This makes the madmen who have made men mad
By their contagion; Conquerors and Kings,   380
Founders of sects and systems, to whom add
Sophists, Bards, Statesmen, all unquiet things
Which stir too strongly the soul's secret springs,
And are themselves the fools to those they fool;
Envied, yet how unenviable! what stings
Are theirs! One breast laid open were a school
Which would unteach mankind the lust to shine or rule:

44

Their breath is agitation, and their life
A storm whereon they ride, to sink at last,
And yet so nurs'd and bigotted to strife,   390
That should their days, surviving perils past,
Melt to calm twilight, they feel overcast
With sorrow and supineness, and so die;
Even as a flame unfed, which runs to waste
With its own flickering, or a sword laid by
Which eats into itself, and rusts ingloriously.

45

He who ascends to mountain-tops, shall find
The loftiest peaks most wrapt in clouds and snow;
He who surpasses or subdues mankind,
Must look down on the hate of those below.   400
Though high *above* the sun of glory glow,
And far *beneath* the earth and ocean spread,
Round him are icy rocks, and loudly blow
Contending tempests on his naked head,
And thus reward the toils which to those summits led.

46

Away with these! true Wisdom's world will be
Within its own creation, or in thine,
Maternal Nature! for who teems like thee,
Thus on the banks of thy majestic Rhine?
There Harold gazes on a work divine,   410
A blending of all beauties; streams and dells,

Fruit, foliage, crag, wood, cornfield, mountain, vine,
And chiefless castles breathing stern farewells
From grey but leafy walls, where Ruin greenly dwells.

47

And there they stand, as stands a lofty mind,
Worn, but unstooping to the baser crowd,
All tenantless, save to the crannying wind,
Or holding dark communion with the cloud.
There was a day when they were young and proud,
Banners on high, and battles pass'd below;   420
But they who fought are in a bloody shroud,
And those which waved are shredless dust ere now,
And the bleak battlements shall bear no future blow.

48

Beneath these battlements, within those walls,
Power dwelt amidst her passions; in proud state
Each robber chief upheld his armed halls,
Doing his evil will, nor less elate
Than mightier heroes of a longer date.
What want these outlaws conquerors should have[37]
But History's purchased page to call them great?   430
A wider space, an ornamented grave?
Their hopes were not less warm, their souls were full as brave.

49

In their baronial feuds and single fields,
What deeds of prowess unrecorded died!
And Love, which lent a blazon to their shields,
With emblems well devised by amorous pride,
Through all the mail of iron hearts would glide;
But still their flame was fierceness, and drew on

[37] l. 429 What wants that knave
         That a king should have?
was King James's question on meeting Johnny Armstrong and his followers in full accoutre-
ments.—See the Ballad.[38]*

[38] Byron's note to l. 429: *see the Ballad*: in 1532 Johnnie Armstrong, Laird of Gliknockie,
surrendered in such splendid clothing that the king had him hanged for insolence. The quotation is derived from Sir Walter Scott's edition of ballads, *Minstrelsy of the Scottish Border* (4th
edn) (1810), I, 127.

Keen contest and destruction near allied,
And many a tower for some fair mischief won,   440
Saw the discoloured Rhine beneath its ruin run.

50

But Thou, exulting and abounding river!
Making thy waves a blessing as they flow
Through banks whose beauty would endure for ever
Could man but leave thy bright creation so,
Nor its fair promise from the surface mow
With the sharp scythe of conflict,—then to see
Thy valley of sweet waters, were to know
Earth paved like Heaven; and to seem such to me
Even now what wants thy stream?—that it should Lethe be.[39]   450

51

A thousand battles have assail'd thy banks,
But these and half their same have pass'd away,
And Slaughter heap'd on high his weltering ranks;
Their very graves are gone, and what are they?
Thy tide wash'd down the blood of yesterday,
And all was stainless, and on thy clear stream
Glass'd with its dancing light the sunny ray;
But o'er the blackened memory's blighting dream
Thy waves would vainly roll, all sweeping as they seem.

52

Thus Harold inly said, and pass'd along,   460
Yet not insensibly to all which here
Awoke the jocund birds to early song
In glens which might have made even exile dear:
Though on his brow were graven lines austere,
And tranquil sternness which had ta'en the place
Of feelings fierier far but less severe,
Joy was not always absent from his face,
But o'er it in such scenes would steal with transient trace.

[39] l. 450 *Lethe*: in classical mythology a river in hell, of which the souls of the dead about to be reincarnated were supposed to drink and whose waters conferred entire forgetfulness of their previous lives.

53

Nor was all love shut from him, though his days
Of passion had consumed themselves to dust.　　　470
It is in vain that we would coldly gaze
On such as smile upon us; the heart must
Leap kindly back to kindness, though disgust
Hath wean'd it from all worldlings: thus he felt,
For there was soft remembrance, and sweet trust
In one fond breast, to which his own would melt,[40]
And in its tenderer hour on that his bosom dwelt.

54

And he had learn'd to love,—I know not why,
For this in such as him seems strange of mood,—
The helpless looks of blooming infancy,[41]　　　480
Even in its earliest nurture; what subdued,
To change like this, a mind so far imbued
With scorn of man, it little boots to know;
But thus it was; and though in solitude
Small power the nipp'd affections have to grow,
In him this glowed when all beside had ceased to glow.

55

And there was one soft breast, as hath been said,
Which unto his was bound by stronger ties
Than the church links withal; and, though unwed,
That love was pure, and, far above disguise,　　　490
Had stood the test of mortal enmities
Still undivided, and cemented more
By peril, dreaded most in female eyes;
But this was firm, and from a foreign shore
Well to that heart might his these absent greetings pour!

[40] l. 476 *one fond breast*: an oblique reference to Byron's half-sister Augusta Leigh, by whom Byron had a daughter not long before leaving England.
[41] l. 480 *the helpless looks of blooming infancy*: an oblique reference to Ada.

1

The castled crag of Drachenfels[42]
Frowns o'er the wide and winding Rhine,
Whose breast of waters broadly swells
Between the banks which bear the vine,
And hills all rich with blossomed trees,   500
And fields which promise corn and wine,
And scattered cities crowning these,
Whose far white walls along them shine,
Have strewed a scene, which I should see
With double joy wert *thou* with me!

2

And peasant girls, with deep blue eyes,
And hands which offer early flowers,
Walk smiling o'er this paradise;
Above, the frequent feudal towers
Through green leaves lift their walls of grey,   510
And many a rock which steeply lours,
And noble arch in proud decay,
Look o'er this vale of vintage-bowers;[43]
But one thing want these banks of Rhine,—
Thy gentle hand to clasp in mine!

3

I send the lilies given to me;
Though long before thy hand they touch,
I know that they must withered be,
But yet reject them not as such;
For I have cherish'd them as dear,   520
Because they yet may meet thine eye,
And guide thy soul to mine even here,
When thou behold'st them drooping nigh,

---

[42] ll. 496–535 The castle of Drachenfels stands on the highest summit of 'the Seven Mountains', over the Rhine banks, it is in ruins, and connected with some singular traditions: it is the first in view on the road from Bonn, but on the opposite side of the river; on this bank, nearly facing it, are the remains of another called the Jew's castle, and a large cross commemorative of the murder of a chief by his brother: the number of castles and cities along the course of the Rhine on both sides is very great, and their situations remarkably beautiful.*
[43] l. 513 *vintage-bowers*: poetic locution for vineyards.

And knowst them gathered by the Rhine,
And offered from my heart to thine!

4

The river nobly foams and flows,
The charm of this enchanted ground,
And all its thousand turns disclose
Some fresher beauty varying round;
The haughtiest breast its wish might bound   530
Through life to dwell delighted here;
Nor could on earth a spot be found
To nature and to me so dear,
Could thy dear eyes in following mine
Still sweeten more these banks of Rhine!

5 6

By Coblentz, on a rise of gentle ground,
There is a small and simple pyramid,
Crowning the summit of the verdant mound;
Beneath its base are heroes' ashes hid,
Our enemy's,—but let not that forbid   540
Honour to Marceau! o'er whose early tomb[44]
Tears, big tears, gush'd from the rough soldier's lid,
Lamenting and yet envying such a doom,
Falling for France, whose rights he battled to resume.

5 7

Brief, brave, and glorious was his young career,—
His mourners were two hosts, his friends and foes;
And fitly may the stranger lingering here
Pray for his gallant spirit's bright repose;
For he was Freedom's champion, one of those,
The few in number, who had not o'erstept   550
The charter to chastise which she bestows
On such as wield her weapons; he had kept
The whiteness of his soul, and thus men o'er him wept.[45]

[44] ll. 541–53 *Marceau . . . wept*: François Séverin Desgravins Marceau (1769–96) was wounded on the French side, and later died in the care of the Austrians before whom the French retreated.

[45] The monument of the young and lamented General Marceau (killed by a rifle-ball at Altenkirchen on the last day of the fourth year of the French republic) still remains as described.

58

Here Ehrenbreitstein, with her shattered wall[47, 48]
Black with the miner's blast, upon her height
Yet shows of what she was, when shell and ball
Rebounding idly on her strength did light;
A tower of victory! from whence the flight
Of baffled foes was watch'd along the plain:
But Peace destroy'd what War could never blight,　　　　560

The inscriptions on his monument are rather too long, and not required: his name was enough; France adored, and her enemies admired, both wept over him.—His funeral was attended by the generals and detachments from both armies. In the same grave General Hoche is interred, a gallant man also in every sense of the word, but though he distinguished himself greatly in battle, *he* had not the good fortune to die there; his death was attended by suspicions of poison.

A separate monument (not over his body, which is buried by Marceau's) is raised for him near Andernach, opposite to which one of his most memorable exploits was performed, in throwing a bridge to an island on the Rhine. The shape and style are different from that of Marceau's, and the inscription more simple and pleasing.

The Army of the Sambre and Meuse
　　to its Commander in Chief
　　　　Hoche.

This is all, and as it should be. Hoche was esteemed among the first of France's earlier generals before Buonaparte monopolized her triumphs.—He was the destined commander of the invading army of Ireland.*[46]

[46] Byron's note to l. 553: *Hoche*: General Lazare Hoche (1768–97), celebrated as the general who put down the rising in La Vendée, actually died of consumption.

[47] Ehrenbreitstein, i.e. 'the broad Stone of Honour', one of the strongest fortresses in Europe, was dismantled and blown up by the French at the truce of Leoben.—It had been and could only be reduced by famine or treachery. It yielded to the former, aided by surprise. After having seen the fortifications of Gibraltar and Malta, it did not much strike by comparison, but the situation is commanding. General Marceau besieged it in vain for some time, and I slept in a room where I was shown a window at which he is said to have been standing observing the progress of the siege by moonlight, when a ball struck immediately below it. He was killed not long afterwards at Altenkirchen by a rifleman—it is rather singular that these narrow escapes have in several instances been followed closely by death—at Nuremberg shortly before the battle of Lutzen Gustavus Adolphus had his horse killed under him. Falconer but escaped one Shipwreck to perish by another.—The Prince of Orange died by the more successful attempt by a *third* assassin and Nelson rarely came out of action without a wound till the most fatal and glorious of all—which instead of a scar bequeathed him immortality.*[49]

[48] *Ehrenbreitstein*: Marceau unsuccessfully besieged this fortress in 1795–6, and it was finally taken some time after in 1799, again after a long siege. It was blown up after the peace Treaty of Lunéville in 1801.

[49] Byron's note to l. 554: *Marceau*: Marceau unsuccessfully besieged the fortress 1795–6; *Gustavus Adolphus*: Gustavus II Adolphus, king of Sweden; *Falconer*: William Falconer (1732–09), author of *The Shipwreck* (1762) based on his experience of shipwreck in 1760, was lost at sea in 1769; *Prince of Orange*: William I (1533–84), actually killed by a *second* assassination attempt.

281

And laid those proud roofs bare to Summer's rain—
On which the iron shower for years had pour'd in vain.

59

Adieu to thee, fair Rhine! How long delighted
The stranger fain would linger on his way!
Thine is a scene alike where souls united
Or lonely Contemplation thus might stray;
And could the ceaseless vultures cease to prey
On self-condemning bosoms, it were here,
Where Nature, nor too sombre nor too gay,
Wild but not rude, awful yet not austere,   570
Is to the mellow Earth as Autumn to the year.

60

Adieu to thee again! a vain adieu!
There can be no farewell to scene like thine;
The mind is coloured by thy every hue;
And if reluctantly the eyes resign
Their cherish'd gaze upon thee, lovely Rhine!
'Tis with the thankful glance of parting praise;
More mighty spots may rise—more glaring shine,
But none unite in one attaching maze
The brilliant, fair, and soft,—the glories of old days,   580

61

The negligently grand, the fruitful bloom
Of coming ripeness, the white city's sheen,
The rolling stream, the precipice's gloom,
The forest's growth, and Gothic walls between,
The wild rocks shaped as they had turrets been
In mockery of man's art; and these withal
A race of faces happy as the scene,
Whose fertile bounties here extend to all,
Still springing o'er thy banks, though Empires near them fall.

62

But these recede. Above me are the Alps,   590
The palaces of Nature, whose vast walls
Have pinnacled in clouds their snowy scalps,

And throned Eternity in icy halls
Of cold sublimity, where forms and falls
The avalanche—the thunderbolt of snow!
All which expands the spirit, yet appals,
Gather around these summits, as to show
How Earth may pierce to Heaven, yet leave vain man below.

63

But ere these matchless heights I dare to scan,
There is a spot should not be pass'd in vain,—   600
Morat! the proud, the patriot field! where man[50]
May gaze on ghastly trophies of the slain,
Nor blush for those who conquered on that plain;
Here Burgundy bequeath'd his tombless host,
A bony heap, through ages to remain,
Themselves their monument;—the Stygian coast
Unsepulchred they roam'd, and shriek'd each wandering ghost.[51]

64

While Waterloo with Cannae's carnage vies,[53]
Morat and Marathon twin names shall stand;
They were true Glory's stainless victories,   610
Won by the unambitious heart and hand

[50] *Morat*: battle at which the Swiss successfully defended themselves against the invasion of Charles the Bold, Duke of Burgundy in 1476. Ten thousand Burgundians were killed, and their bones were collected in a famous ossuary, destroyed by the invading French forces in 1798, and what was left was not collected and reburied until 1822.

[51] The chapel is destroyed, and the pyramid of bones diminished to a small number by the Burgundian legion in the service of France, who anxiously effaced this record of their ancestors' less successful invasions. A few still remain notwithstanding the pains taken by the Burgundians for ages, (all who passed that way removing a bone to their own country) and the less justifiable larcenies of the Swiss postillions, who carried them off to sell for knife-handles, a purpose for which the whiteness imbibed by the bleaching of years had rendered them in great request. Of these relics I ventured to bring away as much as may have made the quarter of a hero, for which the sole excuse is, that if I had not, the next passer by might have perverted them to worse uses than the careful preservation which I intend for them.*[52]

[52] Byron's note to l. 607: *the careful preservation which I intend*: Byron sent the bones back to Murray, his publisher.

[53] *Waterloo . . . Marathon*: Waterloo is compared to Cannae (216 BC), Hannibal's great victory over the Romans: in Byron's view they are comparable as battles for imperial domination ('princely cause'). By contrast Morat is compared to Marathon (490 BC) at which the Athenians repelled an invasion by Persia: both of these battles were therefore fought in the cause of republican liberty ('a proud, brotherly, civic band'), and consequently Byron feels they are 'true Glory's stainless victories'.

Of a proud, brotherly, and civic band,
All unbought champions in no princely cause
Of vice-entail'd Corruption; they no land
Doom'd to bewail the blasphemy of laws
Making kings' rights divine, by some Draconic clause.[54, 55]

6 5

By a lone wall a lonelier column rears
A grey and grief-worn aspect of old days,
'Tis the last remnant of the wreck of years,
And looks as with the wild-bewildered gaze   620
Of one to stone converted by amaze,
Yet still with consciousness; and there it stands
Making a marvel that it not decays,
When the coeval pride of human hands,
Levell'd Aventicum, hath strewed her subject lands.[57]

6 6

And there—oh! sweet and sacred be the name!—
Julia—the daughter, the devoted—gave
Her youth to Heaven; her heart, beneath a claim
Nearest to Heaven's, broke o'er a father's grave.[58]
Justice is sworn 'gainst tears, and hers would crave   630
The life she lived in; but the judge was just,
And then she died on him she could not save.

[54] Draco—the author of the first Red Book on record was an Athenian special pleader in great business.—Hippias—the Athenian Bourbon was in the battle of Marathon and did not keep at the respectful distance from danger of the Ghent refugees—but the English and Prussians resembled the Medes and the Persians as little as Blucher and the British General did Datis and Artaphernes and Buonaparte was still more remote in cause and character from Miltiades—and a parallel 'after the manner of Plutarch' might have still existed in the fortunes of the sons of Pisistratus and the reigning doctors of right-divinity.*[56]

[55] l. 616 *Draconic clause*: Draco was the author of the notoriously severe penal code for Athens (624 BC).

[56] Byron's note to l. 616: Byron's list of generals of the classical world is intended to make an ironic commentary on the celebrities of Waterloo; Hippias and Hipparchus died ingloriously or treacherously; and the Prussian General Blücher (1742–1819) and Wellington do not bear comparison with the Prussian generals Datis and Artaphernes, nor Bonaparte with Miltiades.

[57] l. 625 Aventicum (near Morat) was the Roman capital of Helvetia, where Avenches now stands.*

[58] ll. 627–9 *Julia . . . father's grave*: Aulus Caecina captured Aventicum in AD 69 and executed a chief named Julius Alpinus. His daughter's probably apocryphal history and inscription first turns up in the collection of Latin epitaphs published in 1707 supposedly by Janus Gruterus but actually by the forger Paul Wilhelm.

Their tomb was simple, and without a bust,
And held within their urn one mind, one heart, one dust.[59]

67

But these are deeds which should not pass away,
And names that must not wither, though the earth
Forgets her empires with a just decay,
The enslavers and the enslaved, their death and birth;
The high, the mountain-majesty of worth
Should be, and shall, survivor of its woe,   640
And from its immortality look forth
In the sun's face, like yonder Alpine snow,[60]
Imperishably pure beyond all things below.

68

Lake Leman woos me with its crystal face,[62]
The mirror where the stars and mountains view
The stillness of their aspect in each trace
Its clear depth yields of their far height and hue:
There is too much of man here, to look through
With a fit mind the might which I behold;

---

[59] l. 634 Julia Alpinula, a young Aventian priestess, died soon after a vain endeavour to save her father, condemned to death as a traitor by Aulus Caecina. Her epitaph was discovered many years ago;—it is thus—

> Julia Alpinula
> Hic jaceo
> Infelicis patris, infelix proles
> Deae Aventiae Sacerdos;
> Exorare patris necem non potui
> Male mori in fatis ille erat.
> Vixi annos XXIII.

I know of no human composition so affecting as this, nor a history of deeper interest. These are the names and actions which ought not to perish, and to which we turn with a true and healthy tenderness, from the wretched and glittering detail of a confused mass of conquests and battles, with which the mind is roused for a time to a false and feverish sympathy, from whence it recurs at length with all the nausea consequent on such intoxication.*

[60] l. 642 This is written in the eye of Mont Blanc (June 3d, 1816) which even at this distance dazzles mine.

(July 20th). I this day observed for some time the distinct reflection of Mont Blanc and Mont Argentiere in the calm of the lake, which I was crossing in my boat; the distance of these mountains from their mirror is 60 miles.*[61]

[61] Byron's note to l. 642: *in the eye of Mont Blanc*: Byron was staying in the Hotel d'Angleterre at Sécheron until 10th June when he moved to the Villa Diodati.

[62] l. 644 *Leman*: the French name for Lake Geneva.

But soon in me shall Loneliness renew   650
Thoughts hid, but not less cherish'd than of old,
Ere mingling with the herd had penn'd me in their fold.

69

To fly from, need not be to hate, mankind,
All are not fit with them to stir and toil,
Nor is it discontent to keep the mind
Deep in its fountain, lest it overboil
In the hot throng, where we become the spoil
Of our infection, till too late and long
We may deplore and struggle with the coil,
In wretched interchange of wrong for wrong   660
'Midst a contentious world, striving where none are strong.

70

There, in a moment, we may plunge our years
In fatal penitence, and in the blight
Of our own soul, turn all our blood to tears,
And colour things to come with hues of Night,
The race of life becomes a hopeless flight
To those that walk in darkness: on the sea,
The boldest steer but where their ports invite,
But there are wanderers o'er Eternity
Whose bark drives on and on, and anchored ne'er shall be.   670

71

Is it not better, then, to be alone,
And love Earth only for its earthly sake?
By the blue rushing of the arrowy Rhone,
Or the pure bosom of its nursing lake,
Which feeds it as a mother who doth make
A fair but froward infant her own care,
Kissing its cries away as these awake;—
Is it not better thus our lives to wear,
Than join the crushing crowd, doom'd to inflict or bear?

72

I live not in myself, but I become   680
Portion of that around me; and to me,

High mountains are a feeling, but the hum[63]
Of human cities torture: I can see
Nothing to loathe in nature, save to be
A link reluctant in a fleshly chain,
Class'd among creatures, when the soul can flee,
And with the sky, the peak, the heaving plain
Of ocean, or the stars, mingle, and not in vain.

73

And thus I am absorb'd, and this is life:
I look upon the peopled desert past,   690
As on a place of agony and strife,
Where, for some sin, to Sorrow I was cast,
To act and suffer, but remount at last
With a fresh pinion; which I feel to spring,
Though young, yet waxing vigorous, as the blast
Which it would cope with, on delighted wing,
Spurning the clay-cold bonds which round our being cling.

74

And when, at length, the mind shall be all free
From what it hates in this degraded form,
Reft of its carnal life, save what shall be   700
Existent happier in the fly and worm,—
When elements to elements conform,
And dust is as it should be, shall I not
Feel all I see, less dazzling, but more warm?
The bodiless thought? the Spirit of each spot?
Of which, even now, I share at times the immortal lot?

75

Are not the mountains, waves, and skies, a part
Of me and of my soul, as I of them?
Is not the love of these deep in my heart
With a pure passion? should I not contemn   710
All objects, if compared with these? and stem
A tide of suffering, rather than forgo
Such feelings for the hard and worldly phlegm

---

[63] l. 682 *high mountains are a feeling*: an echo from Wordsworth's 'Tintern Abbey', ll. 76–80.

Of those whose eyes are only turn'd below,
Gazing upon the ground, with thoughts which dare not glow?

76

But this is not my theme, and I return
To that which is immediate, and require
Those who find contemplation in the urn,
To look on One, whose dust was once all fire,
A native of the land where I respire[64]   720
The clear air for a while—a passing guest,
Where he became a being,—whose desire
Was to be glorious; 'twas a foolish quest,
The which to gain and keep, he sacrificed all rest.

77

Here the self-torturing sophist, wild Rousseau,
The apostle of affliction, he who threw
Enchantment over passion, and from woe
Wrung overwhelming eloquence, first drew
The breath which made him wretched; yet he knew
How to make madness beautiful, and cast   730
O'er erring deeds and thoughts, a heavenly hue
Of words, like sunbeams, dazzling as they past
The eyes, which o'er them shed tears feelingly and fast.

78

His love was passion's essence—as a tree
On fire by lightning; with ethereal flame
Kindled he was, and blasted, for to be
Thus, and enamoured, were in him the same.
But his was not the love of living dame,
Nor of the dead who rise upon our dreams,
But of ideal beauty, which became   740
In him existence, and o'erflowing teems
Along his burning page, distempered though it seems.

[64] ll. 719–20: Rousseau who was born in Geneva in 1712.

288

79

This breathed itself to life in Júlie, *this*[65]
Invested her with all that's wild and sweet;
This hallowed, too, the memorable kiss[66]
Which every morn his fevered lip would greet,
From hers, who but with friendship his would meet;
But to that gentle touch, through brain and breast
Flash'd the thrill'd spirit's love-devouring heat;
In that absorbing sigh perchance more blest,   750
Than vulgar minds may be with all they seek possest.[67]

80

His life was one long war with self-sought foes,[68]
Or friends by him self-banish'd; for his mind
Had grown Suspicion's sanctuary, and chose
For its own cruel sacrifice, the kind,
'Gainst whom he raged with fury strange and blind.
But he was phrenzied,—wherefore, who may know?
Since cause might be which skill could never find;
But he was phrenzied by disease or woe,
To that worst pitch of all, which wears a reasoning show.   760

81

For then he was inspired, and from him came,
As from the Pythian's mystic cave of yore,[69]
Those oracles which set the world in flame,[70]

[65] l. 743 *Julie:* the heroine of Rousseau's novel *Julie: ou, La Nouvelle Héloïse* (1761).

[66] l. 745 *the memorable kiss:* alluding to Rousseau's *Confessions.*

[67] l. 751 This refers to the account in his 'Confessions' of his passion for the Comtesse d'Houdetot (the mistress of St Lambert) and his long walk every morning for the sake of the single kiss which was the common salutation of French acquaintance.—Rousseau's description of his feelings on this occasion may be considered as the most passionate, yet not impure description and expression of love that ever kindled into words, which after all must be felt, from their very force, to be inadequate to the delineation: a painting can give no sufficient idea of the ocean.*

[68] l. 752 *self-sought foes:* who included Diderot, Grimm, Voltaire, and Hume.

[69] l. 762 *the Pythian's mystic cave:* the oracular shrine of the Greek god Apollo at Delphi to which worshippers made pilgrimage to consult the god on moral and political matters. The god spoke through a woman, the Pythia, in a state of ecstasy or frenzy, who answered questions put to her.

[70] l. 763 *oracles:* alluding to the *Discours* (1750 and 1753) and *Le Contrat Social* (1762), sources of the ideas that influenced the French revolutionaries.

Nor ceased to burn till kingdoms were no more:
Did he not this for France? which lay before
Bowed to the inborn tyranny of years?
Broken and trembling, to the yoke she bore,
Till by the voice of him and his compeers,
Roused up to too much wrath which follows o'ergrown fears?

82

They made themselves a fearful monument! 770
The wreck of old opinions—things which grew
Breathed from the birth of time: the veil they rent,
And what behind it lay, all earth shall view.
But good with ill they also overthrew,
Leaving but ruins, wherewith to rebuild
Upon the same foundation, and renew
Dungeons and thrones, which the same hour re-fill'd,
As heretofore, because ambition was self-will'd.

83

But this will not endure, nor be endured!
Mankind have felt their strength, and made it felt. 780
They might have used it better, but, allured
By their new vigour, sternly have they dealt
On one another; pity ceased to melt
With her once natural charities. But they,
Who in oppression's darkness caved had dwelt,
They were not eagles, nourish'd with the day;
What marvel then, at times, if they mistook their prey?

84

What deep wounds ever closed without a scar?
The heart's bleed longest, and but heal to wear
That which disfigures it; and they who war 790
With their own hopes, and have been vanquish'd, bear
Silence, but not submission: in his lair
Fix'd Passion holds his breath, until the hour
Which shall atone for years; none need despair:
It came, it cometh, and will come,—the power
To punish or forgive—in *one* we shall be slower.

85

Clear, placid Leman! thy contrasted lake,
With the wild world I dwelt in, is a thing
Which warns me, with its stillness, to forsake
Earth's troubled waters for a purer spring.   800
This quiet sail is as a noiseless wing
To waft me from distraction; once I loved
Torn ocean's roar, but thy soft murmuring
Sounds sweet as if a sister's voice reproved,
That I with stern delights should e'er have been so moved.

86

It is the hush of night, and all between
Thy margin and the mountains, dusk, yet clear,
Mellowed and mingling, yet distinctly seen,
Save darken'd Jura, whose capt heights appear
Precipitously steep; and drawing near,   810
There breathes a living fragrance from the shore,
Of flowers yet fresh with childhood; on the ear
Drops the light drip of the suspended oar,
Or chirps the grasshopper one good-night carol more;

87

He is an evening reveller, who makes
His life an infancy, and sings his fill;
At intervals, some bird from out the brakes,
Starts into voice a moment, then is still.
There seems a floating whisper on the hill,
But that is fancy, for the starlight dews   820
All silently their tears of love instil,
Weeping themselves away, till they infuse
Deep into Nature's breast the spirit of her hues.

88

Ye stars! which are the poetry of heaven!
If in your bright leaves we would read the fate
Of men and empires,—'tis to be forgiven,
That in our aspirations to be great,
Our destinies o'erleap their mortal state,
And claim a kindred with you; for ye are

A beauty and a mystery, and create   830
In us such love and reverence from afar,
That fortune, fame, power, life, have named themselves a star.

89

All heaven and earth are still—though not in sleep,
But breathless, as we grow when feeling most;
And silent, as we stand in thoughts too deep:—
All heaven and earth are still: From the high host
Of stars, to the lull'd lake and mountain-coast,
All is concentred in a life intense,
Where not a beam, nor air, nor leaf is lost,
But hath a part of being, and a sense   840
Of that which is of all Creator and defence.

90

Then stirs the feeling infinite, so felt
In solitude, where we are *least* alone,
A truth, which through our being then doth melt
And purifies from self: it is a tone,
The soul and source of music, which makes known
Eternal harmony, and sheds a charm,
Like to the fabled Cytherea's zone,[71]
Binding all things with beauty;—'twould disarm
The spectre Death, had he substantial power to harm.   850

91

Not vainly did the early Persian make
His altar the high places and the peak
Or earth-o'ergazing mountains, and thus take[72]

---

[71] l. 848 *fabled Cytherea's zone*: an allusion to the girdle ('zone') of Aphrodite/Venus, the goddess of love (Cythera was the mythical birthplace of the goddess), which conferred the power to attract love.

[72] l. 853 It is to be recollected, that the most beautiful and impressive doctrines of the Founder of Christianity were delivered, not in the *Temple*, but on the *Mount*.

To waive the question of devotion, and turn to human eloquence,—the most effectual and splendid specimens were not pronounced within walls. Demosthenes addressed the public and popular assemblies. Cicero spoke in the forum. That this added to their effect on the mind of both orator and hearers, may be conceived from the difference between what we read of the emotions then and there produced, and those we ourselves experience in the perusal in the closet. It is one thing to read the *Iliad* at Sigaeum and on the tumuli, or by the springs with

A fit and unwall'd temple, there to seek
The Spirit, in whose honour shrines are weak,
Uprear'd of human hands. Come, and compare
Columns and idol-dwellings, Goth or Greek,
With Nature's realms of worship, earth and air,
Nor fix on fond abodes to circumscribe thy prayer!

92

The sky is changed!—and such a change! Oh night,[73]   860
And storm, and darkness, ye are wondrous strong,
Yet lovely in your strength, as is the light
Of a dark eye in woman! Far along,
From peak to peak, the rattling crags among
Leaps the live thunder! Not from one lone cloud,
But every mountain now hath found a tongue,
And Jura answers, through her misty shroud,
Back to the joyous Alps, who call to her aloud!

93

And this is in the night:—Most glorious night!
Thou wert not sent for slumber! let me be   870

---

mount Ida above, and the plain and rivers and Archipelago around you: and another to trim
your taper over it in a snug library—*this* I know.
    Were the early and rapid progress of what is called Methodism to be attributed to any cause
beyond the enthusiasm excited by its vehement faith and doctrines (the truth or error of which
I presume neither to canvas nor to question) I should venture to ascribe it to the practice of
preaching in the *fields*, and the unstudied and extemporaneous effusions of its teachers.
    The Mussulmans, whose erroneous devotion (at least in the lower orders) is most sincere,
and therefore impressive, are accustomed to repeat their prescribed orisons and prayers where-
ever they may be at the stated hours—of course frequently in the open air, kneeling upon a light
mat (which they carry for the purpose of a bed or cushion as required); the ceremony lasts some
minutes, during which they are totally absorbed, and only living in their supplication; nothing
can disturb them. On me the simple and entire sincerity of these men, and the spirit which
appeared to be within and upon them, made a far greater impression than any general rite
which was ever performed in places of worship, of which I have seen those of almost every persuasion under the sun: including most of our own sectaries, and the Greek, the Catholic, the
Armenian, the Lutheran, the Jewish, and the Mahometan. Many of the negroes, of whom there
are numbers in the Turkish empire, are idolaters, and have free exercise of their belief and its
rites: some of these I had a distant view of at Patras, and from what I could make out of them,
they appeared to be of a truly Pagan description, and not very agreeable to a spectator.*
[73] l. 860 The thunder-storms to which these lines [ll. 860–904] refer occurred on the 13th of
June, 1816, at midnight. I have seen among the Acroceraunian mountains of Chimari several
more terrible, but none more beautiful.*

A sharer in thy fierce and far delight,—
A portion of the tempest and of thee!
How the lit lake shines, a phosphoric sea,
And the big rain comes dancing to the earth!
And now again 'tis black,— and now, the glee
Of the loud hills shakes with its mountain-mirth,
As if they did rejoice o'er a young earthquake's birth.

94

Now, where the swift Rhone cleaves his way between
Heights which appear as lovers who have parted
In hate, whose mining depths so intervene,   880
That they can meet no more, though broken-hearted;
Though in their souls, which thus each other thwarted,
Love was the very root of the fond rage
Which blighted their life's bloom, and then departed:—
Itself expired, but leaving them an age
Of years all winters,—war within themselves to wage.

95

Now, where the quick Rhone thus hath cleft his way,
The mightiest of the storms hath ta'en his stand:
For here, not one, but many, make their play,   890
And fling their thunder-bolts from hand to hand,
Flashing and cast around: of all the band,
The brightest through these parted hills hath fork'd
His lightnings,—as if he did understand,
That in such gaps as desolation work'd,
There the hot shaft should blast whatever therein lurk'd.

96

Sky, mountains, river, winds, lake, lightnings! ye!
With night, and clouds, and thunder, and a soul
To make these felt and feeling, well may be
Things that have made me watchful; the far roll   900
Of your departing voices, is the knoll
Of what in me is sleepless,—if I rest.
But where of ye, oh tempests! is the goal?
Are ye like those within the human breast?
Or do ye find, at length, like eagles, some high nest?

97

Could I embody and unbosom now
That which is most within me,—could I wreak
My thoughts upon expression, and thus throw
Soul, heart, mind, passions, feelings, strong or weak,
All that I would have sought, and all I seek,
Bear, know, feel, and yet breathe—into *one* word,   910
And that one word were Lightning, I would speak;
But as it is, I live and die unheard,
With a most voiceless thought, sheathing it as a sword.

98

The morn is up again, the dewy morn,
With breath all incense, and with cheek all bloom,
Laughing the clouds away with playful scorn,
And living as if earth contain'd no tomb,—
And glowing into day: we may resume
The march of our existence: and thus I,
Still on thy shores, fair Leman! may find room   920
And food for meditation, nor pass by
Much, that may give us pause, if pondered fittingly.

99

Clarens! sweet Clarens, birth-place of deep Love!
Thine air is the young breath of passionate thought;
Thy trees take root in Love; the snows above
The very Glaciers have his colours caught,
And sun-set into rose-hues sees them wrought[74]

[74] l. 927 Rousseau's 'Héloïse', Letter 17, part 4, note. 'Ces montagnes sont si hautes qu'une demi-heure après le soleil couché, leurs sommets sont encore éclairés de ses rayons; dont le rouge forme sur ces cimes blanches *une belle couleur de rose* qu'on apperçoit de fort loin.' [These mountains are so high that for half an hour after the sun has set their summits are still lit with its rays in such a way that the red makes the white peaks a beautiful pink colour which can be seen from a very long way away.]

This applies more particularly to the heights over Meillerie. 'J'allai à Vévay loger à la Clef, et pendant deux jours que j'y restai sans voir personne, je pris pour cette ville un amour oui m'a suivi dans tous mes voyages, et qui m'y a fait établir enfin les héros de mon roman. Je dirois volontiers à ceux qui ont du goût et qui sont sensibles: allez à Vévay – visitez le pays, examinez les sites, promenez-vous sur le lac, et dites si la Nature n'a pas fait ce beau pays pour une Julie, pour une Claire et pour un St Preux; mais ne les y cherchez pas.' *Les Confessions*, livre iv. page 306. Lyons ed. 1706. [I went to Vévay to stay at the Clef, and during the two days that I stayed there without seeing anyone, I conceived for that town a love which has remained with me in

By rays which sleep there lovingly: the rocks,
The permanent crags, tell here of Love, who sought
In them a refuge from the worldly shocks,   930
Which stir and sting the soul with hope that woos, then mocks.

---

all my travels, and which I have at length given to the protagonists of my novel. I would gladly
say to those who have taste and sensibility, go to Vévay – visit the countryside, examine the
sites, walk by the lake, and say whether Nature has not created this beautiful landscape for a
Julie, for a Claire and for a St Preux; but don't look for them there.]

In July, 1816, I made a voyage round the Lake of Geneva; and, as far as my own observations have led me in a not uninterested nor inattentive survey of all the scenes most celebrated by Rousseau in his 'Héloïse', I can safely say, that in this there is no exaggeration. It would be
difficult to see Clarens (with the scenes around it, Vévay, Chillon, Bôveret, St Gingo, Meillerie,
Evian, and the entrances of the Rhône), without being forcibly struck with its peculiar adapta-
tion to the persons and events with which it has been peopled. But this is not all; the feeling
with which all around Clarens, and the opposite rocks of Meillerie is invested, is of a still higher
and more comprehensive order than the mere sympathy with individual passion; it is a sense of
the existence of love in its most extended and sublime capacity, and of our own participation
of its good and of its glory: it is the great principle of the universe, which is there more condensed, but not less manifested; and of which, though knowing ourselves a part, we lose our
individuality, and mingle in the beauty of the whole.

If Rousseau had never written, nor lived, the same associations would not less have belonged
to such scenes. He has added to the interest of his works by their adoption; he has shown his
sense of their beauty by the selection; but they have done that for him which no human being
could do for them.

I had the good fortune (good or evil as it might be) to sail from Meillerie (where we landed
for some time), to St Gingo during a lake storm, which added to the magnificence of all around,
although occasionally accompanied by danger to the boat, which was small and overloaded. It
was over this very part of the lake that Rousseau had driven the boat of St Preux and Madame
Wolmar to Meillerie for shelter during a tempest.

On gaining the shore at St Gingo, I found that the wind had been sufficiently strong to blow
down some fine old chestnut trees on the lower part of the mountains. On the opposite height
of Clarens is a château.

The hills are covered with vineyards, and interspersed with some small but beautiful woods;
one of these was named the 'Bosquet de Julie', and it is remarkable that, though long ago cut
down by the brutal selfishness of the monks of St Bernard (to whom the land appertained), that
the ground might be inclosed into a vineyard for the miserable drones of an execrable superstition, the inhabitants of Clarens still point out the spot where its trees stood, calling it by the
name which consecrated and survived them.

Rousseau has not been particularly fortunate in the preservation of the 'local habitations' he
has given to 'airy nothings'. The Prior of Great St Bernard has cut down some of his woods for
the sake of a few casks of wine, and Buonaparte has levelled part of the rocks of Meillerie in
improving the road to the Simplon. The road is an excellent one, but I cannot quite agree with
a remark which I heard made, that 'La route vaut mieux que les souvenirs' [The road is worth
more than sentimental attachments].*75

75 Byron's note to l. 927 *Claire:* Julie's friend in *La Nouvelle Héloïse; during a tempest: La
Nouvelle Héloïse,* IV, 17; *a chateau:* Château des Crêtes, under whose walls lie the famous
bosquets de Julie.

100

Clarens! by heavenly feet thy paths are trod,—[76]
Undying Love's, who here ascends a throne
To which the steps are mountains; where the god
Is a pervading life and light,—so shown
Not on those summits solely, nor alone
In the still cave and forest: o'er the flower
His eye is sparkling, and his breath hath blown,
His soft and summer breath, whose tender power
Passes the strength of storms in their most desolate hour.   940

101

All things are here of *him*; from the black pines,[77]
Which are his shade on high, and the loud roar
Of torrents, where he listeneth, to the vines
Which slope his green path downward to the shore,
Where the bowed waters meet him, and adore,
Kissing his feet with murmurs; and the wood,
The covert of old trees, with trunks all hoar,
But light leaves, young as joy, stands where it stood,
Offering to him, and his, a populous solitude,

102

A populous solitude of bees and birds,   950
And fairy-form'd and many-coloured things,
Who worship him with notes more sweet than words,
And innocently open their glad wings,
Fearless and full of life: the gush of springs,
And fall of lofty fountains, and the bend
Of stirring branches, and the bud which brings
The swiftest thought of beauty, here extend,
Mingling, and made by Love, unto one mighty end.

103

He who hath loved not, here would learn that lore,
And make his heart a spirit; he who knows   960
That tender mystery, will love the more,

---

[76] l. 932 *Clarens:* celebrated as the setting of Rousseau's *La Nouvelle Héloïse.*
[77] ll. 941–9 *all things . . . solitude:* echoes *La Nouvelle Héloïse,* IV, 17.

For this is Love's recess, where vain men's woes,
And the world's waste, have driven him far from those,
For 'tis his nature to advance or die;
He stands not still, but or decays, or grows
Into a boundless blessing, which may vie
With the immortal lights, in its eternity!

104

'Twas not for fiction chose Rousseau this spot,
Peopling it with affections; but he found
It was the scene which passion must allot   970
To the mind's purified beings; 'twas the ground
Where early Love his Psyche's zone unbound,[77]
And hallowed it with loveliness, 'tis lone,
And wonderful, and deep, and hath a sound,
And sense, and sight of sweetness; here the Rhone
Hath spread himself a couch, the Alps have rear'd a throne.

105

Lausanne! and Ferney! ye have been the abodes[78, 79]
Of names which unto you bequeath'd a name;
Mortals, who sought and found, by dangerous roads,
A path to perpetuity of fame: 980
They were gigantic minds, and their steep aim,
Was, Titan-like, on daring doubts to pile[80]
Thoughts which should call down thunder, and the flame
Of Heaven, again assail'd, if Heaven the while
On man and man's research could deign do more than smile.

106

The one was fire and fickleness, a child,
Most mutable in wishes, but in mind,

[77] l. 972 *Love . . . Psyche's zone:* alluding to the myth of Cupid, the god of love, and his love for Psyche, a mortal.

[78] l. 977 *Lausanne . . . and Ferney:* Gibbon lived in Lausanne from 1783–93, and finished his *Decline and Fall of the Roman Empire* there in 1787; Voltaire lived at Ferney from 1758–77.

[79] l. 977 Voltaire and Gibbon.*

[80] l. 982 *Titan-like:* the Titans and the Giants piled the mountains of Pelion and Ossa on top of each other in an effort to invade heaven and so overthrow Jupiter's reign. The Titans counted among their number Prometheus, a powerful type of political transgression for Byron.

A wit as various,—gay, grave, sage, or wild,—
Historian, bard, philosopher, combined;
He multiplied himself among mankind,   990
The Proteus of their talents: But his own[81]
Breathed most in ridicule,—which, as the wind,
Blew where it listed, laying all things prone,—
Now to o'erthrow a fool, and now to shake a throne.

                        107

The other, deep and slow, exhausting thought,
And hiving wisdom with each studious year,
In meditation dwelt, with learning wrought,
And shaped his weapon with an edge severe,
Sapping a solemn creed with solemn sneer;
The lord of irony,—that master-spell,   1000
Which stung his foes to wrath, which grew from fear,
And doom'd him to the zealot's ready Hell,
Which answers to all doubts so eloquently well.

                        108

Yet, peace be with their ashes,—for by them,
If merited, the penalty is paid;
It is not ours to judge,—far less condemn;
The hour must come when such things shall be made
Known unto all,—or hope and dread allay'd
By slumber, on one pillow,—in the dust,
Which, thus much we are sure, must lie decay'd;   1010
And when it shall revive, as is our trust,
'Twill be to be forgiven, or suffer what is just.

                        109

But let me quit man's works, again to read
His Maker's, spread around me, and suspend
This page, which from my reveries I feed,
Until it seems prolonging without end.
The clouds above me to the white Alps tend,
And I must pierce them, and survey whate'er
May be permitted, as my steps I bend

---

[81] l. 991 *Proteus*: Proteus was a shape-changing Greek god.

To their most great and growing region, where 1020
The earth to her embrace compels the powers of air.

110

Italia! too, Italia! looking on thee,
Full flashes on the soul the light of ages,
Since the fierce Carthaginian almost won thee,[82]
To the last halo of the chiefs and sages;
Who glorify thy consecrated pages;
Thou wert the throne and grave of empires; still,[83]
The fount at which the panting mind assuages
Her thirst of knowledge, quaffing there her fill,
Flows from the eternal source of Roman's imperial hill.[84] 1030

111

Thus far I have proceeded in a theme
Renewed with no kind auspices:—to feel
We are not what we have been, and to deem
We are not what we should be,—and to steel
The heart against itself; and to conceal,
With a proud caution, love, or hate, or aught,—
Passion or feeling, purpose, grief or zeal,—
Which is the tyrant spirit of our thought,
Is a stern task of soul:—No matter,—it is taught.

112

And for these words, thus woven into song, 1040
It may be that they are a harmless wile,—
The colouring of the scenes which fleet along,
Which I would seize, in passing, to beguile
My breast, or that of others, for a while.
Fame is the thirst of youth,—but I am not
So young as to regard men's frown or smile,

---

[82] l. 1024 *the fierce Carthaginian*: Hannibal, who almost succeeded in conquering Rome in the third century BC.

[83] l. 1027 *the throne and grave of empires*: Rome both incorporated the Greek and Persian empires, and conquered the Etruscan and Carthaginian civilizations, before being sacked by the Goths and Lombards.

[84] l. 1030 'Romans', a mistake in the first edition, should read Rome. Possibly Byron has in mind here the Capitoline.

As loss or guerdon of a glorious lot;
I stood and stand alone,—remembered or forgot.

113

I have not loved the world, nor the world me;
I have not flattered its rank breath, nor bow'd   1050
To its idolatries a patient knee,—
Nor coin'd my cheek to smiles,—nor cried aloud
In worship of an echo; in the crowd
They could not deem me one of such; I stood[85]
Among them, but not of them; in a shroud
Of thoughts which were not their thoughts, and still could,
Had I not filed my mind, which thus itself subdued.

114

I have not loved the world, nor the world me,—
But let us part fair foes; I do believe,
Though I have found them not, that there may be   1060
Words which are things,—hopes which will not deceive,
And virtues which are merciful, nor weave
Snares for the failing: I would also deem
O'er others' griefs that some sincerely grieve;[86]
That two, or one, are almost what they seem,—
That goodness is no name, and happiness no dream.

115

My daughter! with thy name this song begun—
My daughter! with thy name thus much shall end—
I see thee not,—I hear thee not,—but none
Can be so wrapt in thee; thou art the friend   1070
To whom the shadows of far years extend:
Albeit my brow thou never should'st behold,
My voice shall with thy future visions blend,
And reach into thy heart,—when mine is cold,—
A token and a tone, even from thy father's mould.

[85] ll. 1054–7 If it be thus, For Banquo's issue I have filed my mind. *Macbeth.**

[86] l. 1064 It is said by Rochefoucault that 'there is always something in the misfortunes of men's best friends not displeasing to them'.*

116

To aid thy mind's development,—to watch
Thy dawn of little joys,—to sit and see
Almost thy very growth,—to view thee catch
Knowledge of objects,—wonders yet to thee!
To hold thee lightly on a gentle knee,   1080
And print on thy soft cheek a parent's kiss,—
This, it should seem, was not reserv'd for me;
Yet this was in my nature:—as it is,
I know not what is there, yet something like to this.

117

Yet, though dull Hate as duty should be taught,
I know that thou wilt love me; though my name
Should be shut from thee, as a spell still fraught
With desolation,—and a broken claim:
Though the grave closed between us,—'twere the same,
I know that thou wilt love me; though to drain   1090
My blood from out thy being, were an aim,
And an attainment,—all would be in vain,—
Still thou would'st love me, still that more than life retain.

118

The child of love,—though born in bitterness,
And nurtured in convulsion,—of thy sire
These were the elements,—and thine no less.
As yet such are around thee,—but thy fire
Shall be more tempered, and thy hope far higher.
Sweet be thy cradled slumbers! O'er the sea,
And from the mountains where I now respire,   1100
Fain would I wast such blessing upon thee,
As, with a sigh, I deem thou might'st have been to me!

Source: Lord Byron, *Childe Harold's Pilgrimage*, 1816, from *Lord Byron: The Major Works*, Jerome J. McGann, ed., *Oxford World's Classics*, Oxford University Press, Oxford and New York, 1986, pp. 104–45. The notes are heavily indebted to Jerome McGann, *Lord Byron: The Complete Poetical Works*, 7 vols, The Clarendon Press Oxford, 1980, vol. 2.

Lord Byron, Cantos I and II.
Preface to *Childe Harold's Pilgrimage*

Published to preface Cantos I and II of *Childe Harold's Pilgrimage* which came out in 1812 and made Byron famous overnight, the preface was expanded with a rejoinder to the reviews in 1813.

A ROMAUNT[87]

L'univers est une espèce de livre, dont on n'a lu que la première page quand on n'a vu que son pays. J'en ai feuilleté un assez grand nombre, que j'ai trouvé également mauvaises. Cet examen ne m'a point été infructueux. Je haïssais ma patrie. Toutes les impertinences des peuples divers, parmi lesquels j'ai vécu, m'ont réconcilié avec elle. Quand je n'aurais tiré d'autre bénéfice de mes voyages que celui-là, je n'en regretterais ni les frais, ni les fatigues.[88]

LE COSMOPOLITE.

PREFACE

The following poem was written, for the most part, amidst the scenes which it attempts to describe. It was begun in Albania; and the parts relative to Spain and Portugal were composed from the author's observations in those countries. Thus much it may be necessary to state for the correctness of the descriptions. The scenes attempted to be sketched are in Spain, Portugal, Epirus, Acarnania, and Greece. There for the present the poem stops: its reception will determine whether the author may venture to conduct his readers to the capital of the East, through Ionia and Phrygia: these two cantos are merely experimental.

A fictitious character is introduced for the sake of giving some connexion to the piece; which, however, no pretension to regularity. It has been suggested to me by friends, on whose opinions I set a high value, that in this fictitious character, 'Childe Harold', I may incur the suspicion

---

[87] *Romaunt*: archaic word for romance, with connotations of medieval verse romance.

[88] '*L'univers est une espèce de livre . . . ni les fatigues*': 'The universe is a sort of book, of which you've only read the first page when you've only seen your own country. I have riffled through a pretty large number of that book's pages, which I have found equally displeasing. Such a study has been by no means unfruitful. I used to loathe my own country. All the sillinesses of the different peoples amongst whom I have lived have reconciled me to her. If I had not got any benefit from my travels other than that, I wouldn't regret either the cost or the trouble.' Louis Charles Fougeret de Monbron, *Le Cosmopolite, ou le Citoyen du Monde* (1753).

303

of having intended some real personage: this I beg leave, once for all, to disclaim—Harold is the child of imagination, for the purpose I have stated. In some very trivial particulars, and those merely local, there might be grounds for such a notion; but in the main points, I should hope, none whatever.

It is almost superfluous to mention that the appellation 'Childe', as 'Childe Waters', 'Childe Childers', etc. is used as more consonant with the old structure of versification which I have adopted. The 'Good Night', in the beginning of the first canto, was suggested by 'Lord Maxwell's Good Night', in the Border Minstrelsy, edited by Mr Scott.

With the different poems which have been published on Spanish subjects, there may be found some slight coincidence in the first part, which treats of the Peninsula, but it can only be casual; as, with the exception of a few concluding stanzas, the whole of this poem was written in the Levant.

The stanza of Spenser, according to one of our most successful poets, admits of every variety. Dr Beattie makes the following observation: 'Not long ago I began a poem in the style and stanza of Spenser, in which I propose to give full scope to my inclination, and be either droll or pathetic, descriptive or sentimental, tender or satirical, as the humour strikes me; for, if I mistake not, the measure which I have adopted admits equally of all these kinds of composition.'—Strengthened in my opinion by such authority, and by the example of some in the highest order of Italian poets, I shall make no apology for attempts at similar variations in the following composition; satisfied that, if they are unsuccessful, their failure must be in the execution, rather than in the design sanctioned by the practice of Ariosto, Thomson, and Beattie.

I have now waited till almost all our periodical journals have distributed their usual portion of criticism. To the justice of the generality of their criticisms I have nothing to object; it would ill become me to quarrel with their very slight degree of censure, when, perhaps, if they had been less kind they had been more candid. Returning, therefore, to all and each my best thanks for their liberality, on one point alone shall I venture an observation. Amongst the many objections justly urged to the very indifferent character of the 'vagrant Childe' (whom, notwithstanding many hints to the contrary, I still maintain to be a fictitious personage), it has been stated, that besides the anachronism, he is very *unknightly*, as the times of the Knights were times of love, honour, and so forth. Now it so happens that the good old times, when 'l'amour du bon vieux tems [*sic*], l'amour antique' [the love of ancient times, classical love] flourished, were the most profligate of all possible centuries. Those who have any doubts on this subject may consult St Palaye, *passim*, and more particularly vol. ii. page 69. The vows of chivalry were no better kept than any other vows whatsoever, and the songs of the Troubadours were not more decent, and certainly were much less refined, than those of Ovid.—The 'Cours d'amour, parlemens d'amour ou de courtesie et de gentilesse' [courts and parliaments of love or of courtesy and gallantry] had much more of love than of courtesy or gentleness.—See Rolland on the same subject with St Palaye.—Whatever other objection may be urged to that most unamiable personage Childe Harold, he was so far perfectly knightly in his attributes—'No waiter, but a knight templar.'—By the by, I fear that Sir Tristram and Sir Lancelot were no better than they should be, although very poetical personages and true knights 'sans peur' [fearless], though not 'sans reproche' [faultless].—If the story of the institution of the 'Garter' be not a fable, the knights of that order have for several centuries borne the badge of a Countess of Salisbury, of indifferent memory. So much for chivalry. Burke need not have regretted that its days are over, though Maria Antoinette was quite as chaste as most of those in whose honours lances were shivered, and knights unhorsed.

Before the days of Bayard, and down to those of Sir Joseph Banks (the most chaste and celebrated of ancient and modern times), few exceptions will be found to this statement, and I fear a little investigation will teach us not to regret these monstrous mummeries of the middle ages.

I now leave 'Childe Harold' to live his day, such as he is; it had been more agreeable, and certainly more easy, to have drawn an amiable character. It had been easy to varnish over his faults, to make him do more and express less, but he never was intended as an example, further than to show that early perversion of mind and morals leads to satiety of past pleasures and disappointment in new ones, and that even the beauties of nature, and the stimulus of travel (except ambition, the most powerful of all excitements) are lost on a soul so constituted, or rather misdirected. Had I proceeded with the Poem, this character would have deepened as he drew to the close; for the outline which I once meant to fill up for him was, with some exceptions, the sketch of a modern Timon, perhaps a poetical Zeluco.

Source: Lord Byron, *Childe Harold's Pilgrimage, Preface to Cantos I and II*, 1812/13, from *Lord Byron: The Major Works*, Jerome J. McGann, ed., *Oxford World's Classics*, Oxford University Press, Oxford and New York, 1986, pp. 79–82.

From a letter sent from Sir Walter Scott to the Earl of Buccleuch

To HIS GRACE THE DUKE OF BUCCLEUCH

[*August* 1815]

MY DEAR LORD DUKE,—I promised to let you hear of my wanderings, however unimportant;

[. . .]

On Wednesday last, I rode over the memorable field of Waterloo, now for ever consecrated to immortality. All the more ghastly tokens of the carnage are now removed the bodies both of men and horses being either burned or buried. But all the ground is still torn with the shot and shells, and covered with cartridges, old hats, and shoes, and various relics of the fray which the peasants have not thought worth removing. Besides, at Waterloo and all the hamlets in the vicinage, there is a mart established for cuirasses; for the eagles worn by the imperial guard on their caps; for casques, swords, carabines, and similar articles. I have bought two handsome cuirasses, and intend them, one for Bowhill, and one for Abbotsford, if I can get them safe over, which Col. Price Gordon has promised to manage for me. I have also, for your Grace, one of the little memorandum books which I picked up on the field, in which every French soldier was obliged to enter his receipts and expenditure, his services, and even his punishments. The field was covered with fragments of these records. I also got a good MS. collection of French songs, probably the work of some young officer, and a croix of the Legion of Honour. I enclose, under another cover, a sketch of the battle, made at Brussels. It is not, I understand, strictly accurate; but sufficiently so to give a good idea of what took place. In fact, it would require twenty separate plans to give an idea of the battle at its various stages. The front, upon which the armies engaged, does not exceed a long mile. Our line, indeed, originally extended half-a-mile further towards the village of Brain-la-Leude;[89] but as the French indicated no disposition to attack in that direction, the troops which occupied that space were gradually concentrated by Lord Wellington, and made to advance till they had reached Hougomont—a sort of château, with a garden and wood attached to it, which was powerfully and effectually maintained by the Guards during the action. This place was particularly interesting. It was a quiet-looking gentleman's house, which had been burnd by the French shells. The

[89] i.e. Braine-l'Alleud.*

defenders, burned out of the villa itself, betook themselves to the little garden, where, breaking loop-holes through the brick walls, they kept up a most destructive fire on the assailants, who had possessed themselves of a little wood which surrounds the villa on one side. In this spot vast numbers had fallen; and, being hastily buried, the smell is most offensive at this moment. Indeed, I felt the same annoyance in many parts of the field; and, did I live near the field, I should be anxious about the diseases which this steaming carnage might occasion. The rest of the ground, excepting this chateau, and a farm-house called La Hay Sainte, early taken, and long held, by the French, because it was too close under the brow of the descent on which our artillery was placed to admit of the pieces being depressed so as to play into it,—the rest of the ground, I say, is quite open, and lies between two ridges, one of which (Mont St. Jean) was constantly occupied by the English; the other, upon which is the farm of La Belle Alliance, was the position of the French. The slopes between are gentle and varied; the ground everywhere practicable for cavalry, as was well experienced on that memorable day. The cuirassiers, despite their arms of proof, were quite inferior to our heavy dragoons. The meeting of the two bodies occasioned a noise, not unaptly compared to the tinkering and hammering of a smith's shop. Generally the cuirassiers came on stooping their heads very low, and giving point; the British frequently struck away their casques while they were in this posture, and then struck at the bare head. Officers and soldiers all fought hand to hand without distinction; and many of the former owed their life to the dexterity at their weapon, and personal strength of body. Shaw, the milling Life-Guardsman, whom your Grace may remember among the Champions of the Fancy, maintained the honour of the fist, and killed or disabled upwards of twenty Frenchmen with his single arm, until he was killed by the assault of numbers. At one place, where there is a sort of precipitous sand or gravel pit, the heavy English cavalry drove many of the cuirassiers over pell-mell, and followed over themselves, like fox-hunters. The conduct of the infantry and artillery was equally, or, if possible, more distinguished, and it was all fully necessary; for, besides that our army was much outnumbered, a great part of the sum-total were for-eigners. Of these, the Brunswickers and Hanoverians behaved very well; the Belgians but sorrily enough. On one occasion, when one regiment fairly ran off, Lord Wellington rode up to them, and said—"My lads, you must be a little blown; come, do take your breath for a moment, and then we'll go back, and try if we can do a little better"; and he actually carried them back to the charge. He was, indeed, upon that date, every-where, and the soul of everything; nor could less than his personal endeavours have supported the spirits of the men through a contest so long, so desperate, and so unequal. At his last attack, Bonaparte brought up 15,000 of his Guard, who had never drawn trigger during the day. It was upon their failure that his hopes abandoned him.

I spoke long with a shrewd Flemish peasant, called John Dacosta, whom he had seized upon as his guide, and who remained beside him the whole day, and afterwards accompanied him in his flight as far as Charleroi. Your Grace may be sure that I interrogated Mynheer Dacosta very closely about what he heard or saw. He guided me to the spot where Bonaparte remained during the latter part of the action. It was in the highway from Brussels to Charleroi, where it runs between two high banks, on each of which was a French battery. He was pretty well sheltered from the English fire; and, though many bullets flew over his head, neither he nor any of his suite were touched. His other stations, during that day, were still more remote from all danger. The story of his having an observatory erected for him is a mistake. There is such a thing, and he repaired to it during the action; but it was built or erected some months before, for the purpose of a trigonometrical survey of the country, by the King of the Netherlands. Bony's last position was nearly fronting a tree where the Duke of Wellington was stationed; there is not more than a quarter of a mile between them; but Bony was well sheltered, and the Duke so much exposed, that the tree is barked in several places by the canon-balls levelled at him. As for Bony, Dacosta says he was very cool during the whole day, and even gay. As the canon-balls flew over them, Dacosta ducked; at which the Emperor laughed, and told him they would hit him all the same. At length, about the time he made his grand and last effort, the re-doubled fire of the Prussian artillery was heard upon his right, and the heads of their columns became visible pressing out of the woods. Aid-de-camp after aid-de-camp came with the tidings of their advance, to which B. only replied, *Attendez, attendez un instant* [wait, wait, a minute], until he saw his troops, *fantassins et cavaliers* [horse and foot], return in disorder from the attack.—He then observed hastily to a general beside him, *Je crois quils sont mêlés* [I think they're beaten]. The person to whom he spoke, hastily raised the spy-glass to his eye; but B., whom the first glance had satisfied of their total discomfiture, bent his face to the ground, and shook his head twice, his complection being then as pale as death. The General then said something, to which Buonaparte answered, *C'est trop tard—sauvons nous* [It's too late – let's save ourselves]. Just at that moment, the allied troops, cavalry and infantry, appeared in full advance on all hands; and the Prussians, operating upon the right flank of the French, were rapidly gaining their rear. Bony, therefore, was compelled to abandon the high-road, which, besides, was choked with dead, with baggage, and with cannon;

and, gaining the open country, kept at full gallop, until he gained, like Johnnie Cope, the van of the flying army.

Source: H. J. C. Grierson, ed., *The Letters of Sir Walter Scott 1815–1817*, Constable and Company Ltd, London, 1933, pp. 78–82.

Letters sent by George Gordon, Lord Byron in the summer of 1816

[TO JOHN CAM HOBHOUSE][90] *Bruxelles—May 1st. 1816*

My dear H[obhous]e—You will be surprized that we are not more "en avant" [advanced] and so am I—but Mr. Baxter's[91] wheels and springs have not done their duty—for which I beg that you will abuse him like a pickpocket (that is—He—the said *Baxter* being the *pickpocket*) and say that I expect a deduction—having been obliged to come out of the way to this place—which was not in my route—for repairs—which however I hope to have accomplished so as to put us in motion in a day or two.—
—We passed through Ghent—Antwerp—and Mechlin—& thence diverged here—having seen all the sights—pictures—docks—basins—& having climbed up steeples &c. & so forth——the first thing—after the flatness & fertility of the country which struck me—was the beauty of the towns—Bruges first—where you may tell Douglas Kinnaird—on entering at Sunset—I overtook a crew of beggarly—looking gentlemen not unlike Oxberry[92]—headed by a Monarch with a Staff the very facsimile of King Clause in the said D[ouglas] K[innaird]'s revived drama.—
—We lost our way in the dark—or rather twilight—not far from Ghent—by the stupidity of the postilion (*one* only by the way to 4 horses) which produced an alarm of intended robbery among the uninitiated—

---

[90] John Cam Hobhouse, long-time friend and contemporary of Byron.
[91] Byron had ordered from Baxter the coachmaker a huge Napoleonic travelling coach before he left England at a cost of £500 (still unpaid).*
[92] William Oxberry (1784–1824) was an actor who had made his debut at Covent Garden and was for some time manager of the Olympic Theatre. In 1816 he played the part of Moses in Sheridan's *School for Scandal* at Drury Lane.*

[. . .]

The way was found again without loss of life or limb:——I thought the learned Fletcher at least would have known better after our Turkish expeditions—and defiles—and banditti—& guards &c. &c. than to have been so valourously alert without at least a better pretext for his superfluous courage. I don't mean to say that they were *frightened* but they were vastly suspicious without any cause.—At Ghent we stared at pictures—& climbed up a steeple 450 steps in altitude—from which I had a good view & notion of these "paese bassi." [Low Countries]—— Next day we broke down—by a damned wheel (on which Baxter should be broken) pertinaciously refusing it's stipulated rotation—this becalmed us at Lo-Kristi—(2 leagues from Ghent)—& obliged us to return for repairs—At Lo Kristi I came to anchor in the house of a Flemish Blacksmith (who was ill of a fever for which Dr. Dori[93] physicked him—I dare say he is dead by now) and saw somewhat of Lo-Kristi— Low-country—low life—which regaled us much—besides it being a Sunday—all the world were in their way to Mass—& I had the pleasure of seeing a number of very ordinary women in extraordinary garments:—we found the "Contadini" however very goodnatured & obliging though not at all useful.——At Antwerp we pictured— churched—and steepled again—but the principal Street and *bason* pleased me most—poor dear Bonaparte!!!—and the foundries &c.—as for Rubens—I was glad to see his tomb on account of that ridiculous description (in Smollett's P[eregrine] Pickle)[94] of Pallet's absurdity at his monument—but as for his works—and his superb "tableaux"—he seems to me (who by the way know nothing of the matter) the most glaring—flaring—staring—harlotry imposter that ever passed a trick upon the senses of mankind—it is not nature—it is not art—with the exception of some linen (which hangs over the cross in one of his pictures) which to do it justice looked like a very handsome table cloth—I never saw such an assemblage of florid night-mares as his canvas contains—his portraits seem clothed in pulpit cushions.——On the way to Mechlin— a wheel—& a *spring* too gave way—that is—the one went—& the other would not go—so we came off here to get into dock—I hope we shall sail shortly.——On to Geneva.—Will you have the goodness—to get at my account at Hoares—(my bankers) I believe there must be a balance in my favour—as I did not draw a great deal previously to going:—whatever there may be over the two thousand five hundred—they can send by you to me in a further credit when you come out:—I wish you to enquire (for

---

[93] Dr John William Polidori, whom Byron had hired as a personal physician.*
[94] Tobias Smollet, *The Adventures of Peregrine Pickle*, 1784.

fear any tricks might be played with my drafts) my bankers books left with you—will show you exactly what I have drawn—and you can let them have the book to make out the remainder of the account. All I have to urge to Hanson—or to our friend Douglas K[innaird]—is to *sell* if possible.——All kind things to Scrope—and the rest—

ever yrs. most truly & obligedly
B

P.S.—If you hear of my child—let me know any good of her health—& well doing.—Will you bring out πασανιας[95] (Taylor's ditto) when you come—I shall bring to for you at Geneva—don't forget to urge Scrope into our crew—we will buy females and found a colony—provided Scrope does not find those ossified barriers to "the forefended place"—which cost him such a siege at Brighthelmstone—write at your leisure—or "ipse veni"[come in person].——

[TO AUGUSTA LEIGH]   *Bruxelles—May 1st. 1816*

My Heart——We are detained here for some petty carriage repairs—having come out of our way to the Rhine on purpose—after passing through Ghent—Antwerp—and Mechlin.—I have written to you twice—once from Ostend—and again from Ghent—I hope most truly that you will receive my letters—not as important in themselves—but because you wish it—& so do I.—It would be difficult for me to write anything amusing—this country has been so frequently described—& has so little for description—though a good deal for observation—that I know not what to say of it—& one don't like talking only of oneself.—We saw at Antwerp the famous basons of Bonaparte for his navy—which are very superb—as all his undertakings were—& as for churches—& pictures—I have stared at them till my brains are like a guide-book:—the last (though it is heresy to say so) don't please me at all—I think Rubens a very great dauber—and prefer Vandyke a hundred times over—(but then I know nothing about the matter) Rubens' women have all red gowns and red shoulders—to say nothing of necks—of which they are more liberal than charming—it may all be very fine—and I suppose it must be Art—for—I'll swear—'tis not Nature.——As the low Countries did not make part of my plan (except as a route) I feel a little anxious to get out of them—level roads don't suit me—as thou knowest—it must be up hill or down—& then I am more au fait.—Imagine to yourself a succession of avenues with a Dutch Spire at the end of each—and you see the road;—an accompaniment of highly cultivated

---

[95] Pausanias's *Description of Greece* was one of the books listed as among Byron's possessions when he died in Missolonghi.*

farms on each side intersected with small canals or ditches—and sprinkled with very neat & clean cottages—a village every two miles—and you see the country——not a rise from Ostend to Antwerp—a molehill would make the inhabitants think that the Alps had come here on a visit—it is a perpetuity of plain & an eternity of *pavement* (on the *road*) but it is a country of great apparent comfort—and of singular though *tame* beauty—and were it not out of my way—I should like to survey it less cursorily.—The towns are wonderfully fine.——The approach to Brussels is beautiful—and there is a fine palace to the right in coming.[96]

[TO JOHN CAM HOBHOUSE]   *Carlsruhe—May 16th. 1816*

My dear Hobhouse—We are this far by the Rhenish route on our way to Switzerland—where I shall wait to hear of your intentions as to junction before I go to Italy.——I have written to you three times—and mention the number—in case of any non-arrival of epistles.—We were obliged to diverge from Anvers & Mechlin to Brussels—for some wheel repairs—& in course seized the opportunity to visit Mont St. Jean &c. where I had a gallop over the field on a Cossac horse (left by some of the Don gentlemen at Brussels) and after a tolerably minute investigation— returned by Soignies—having purchased a quantity of helmets sabres &c all of which are consigned to the care of a Mr. Gordon at B[russe]ls (an old acquaintance) who desired to forward them to Mr. Murray—in whose keeping I hope to find them safe some day or other.——Our route by the Rhine has been beautiful—& much surpassing my expectation— though very much answering in it's outlines to my previous conceptions.——The Plain at Waterloo is a fine one—but not much after Marathon & Troy—Cheronea—& Platea.——Perhaps there is something of prejudice in this—but I detest the cause & the victors—& the victory—including Blucher & the Bourbons.——From Bonn to Coblenz—& Coblenz again to Bingen & Mayence—nothing can exceed the prospects at every point—not even—any of the old scenes—though this is in a different style:—what it most reminded me of were parts of Cintra—& the valley which leads from Delvinachi—by Libochabo and Argyrocastro (on the opposite mountains) to Tepaleni—the last resemblance struck even the learned Fletcher—who seems to thrive upon his present expedition & is full of comparisons & preferences of the present to the last—particularly in the articles of provision & Caravanseras.—— Poor Polidori[97] is devilish ill—I do not know with what—nor does he— but he seems to have a slight constitution—& is seriously laid up—if he

---

[96] The manuscript ends here at the end of the page. One or more pages seem to be missing.*
[97] Byron's travelling companion, Dr Polidori.

does not get well soon—he will be totally unfit for travelling—his complaints are headaches & feverishness:—all the rest are well—for the present—nor has he had any patients except a Belgian Blacksmith (at Lo Kristi a village where our wheels stuck) and himself.—At Cologne I had a ludicrous adventure—the host of our hotel mistook a German Chambermaid—whose red cheeks & white teeth had made me venture upon her carnally—for his wife—& stood swearing at the door like a Squadron of Cavalry—to the amusement of [or] consternation of all his audience—till the mystery was developed by his wife walking out of her own room—& the girl out of mine.—We have seen all the sights—churches & so forth—& at Coblentz crossed the Rhine—and scrambled up the fortress of Ehrenbreitstein now a ruin—we also saw on the road the sepulchres—& monuments of Generals Marceau & Hoche & went up to examine them—they are simple & striking—but now much neglected if not to say defaced by the change of times & this cursed aftercrop of rectilignes & legitimacy.—At Manheim we crossed the Rhine & keep on this side to avoid the French segment of Territory at Strasburg—as we have not French passports—& no desire to view a degraded country—& oppressed people.—This town (a very pretty one) is the seat of the court of the Grand Duke of Baden:—tomorrow I mean to proceed (if Polidori is well enough) on our journey.—At Geneva I expect to hear from you—tell me of Scrope and his intentions—and of all or any things or persons—saving and except *one* subject—which I particularly beg never to have mentioned again—unless as far as regards my *child*—& my *child only*.—If Scrope comes out—tell him there are some "light wines" which will bring to his recollection "the day of Pentecost" & other branches of his vinous thirty nine articles.—I have solaced myself moderately with such "flaggons of Rhenish" as have fallen in my way—but without our Yorick—they are nothing.—I hope your book of letters[98] is not slack in sale—and I can't see why Ridgway should not pay "a few paouands" for the 2d. Edition unless it be that I did not pay him his bill & that he thinks therefore *you* should.——I trust that you will give *Spooney* a jog as to selling & so forth—& tell my Potestas (Kinnaird) to come the committee over him.—I suppose poor K[innaird] will be devilishly bothered with his Drury Lane speech this year—how does Mathurin's play go on—or rather go off—of course the prologue has fallen to your lot—& the Comedy eh?—I hope you executed the ten thousand petty commissions I saddled you withal—— pray remember me to all the remembering—& not less to the superb Murray—who is

[98] Hobhouse had published in 1815 his *Letters by an Englishman Resident at Paris during the Last Reign of Napoleon* (2 vols).*

now enjoying inglorious ease at his green table—& wishing for some-body to keep him in hot water.——Wishing you all prosperity—I am ever

yrs. most truly
BYRON

[TO JOHN CAM HOBHOUSE] *Secheron—May 26th. 1816*

My dear Hobhouse—*No* letter from *you*—is this miscarriage by the way?—or are you coming?—Never mind which—as there is no remedy —but I shall wait here till I hear from you:—All the other epistles I expected have arrived.—There is an epistle from Hoares who tell me they have given in an account to you of my banking concerns:—I hope you saw or will see (as I believe I locked up my draft book in my desk & you cannot get to it) the *drafts* at Hoares—which I drew immediately previous to my departure—as the holders might possibly take advantage of my absence to alter or play tricks with them—they being Servants or tradesmen—& not much used to resist temptation— I put this as a pos-sibility—which it is best to ascertain and avoid—& you & I know of human nature & so forth—not to trust to anything but one's optics & *these only* in very *clear* weather.——Hoares will shew you them—as they always keep them in case of accidents—& it would be a satisfaction to me to know you have looked over them—as I could not do so myself— —Perhaps you have written to me by way of France—& *there* letters are rather more carefully investigated than delivered.——I wrote to you three times from Flanders—& once from Bonn—and once from Carl-sruhe—the Rhine from Bonn to Mayence is the perfection of *mixed* Beauty;—from Basle to Geneva we were five days—arriving here last night—Nothing has disappointed me on my way or out of it—except not hearing from you—but I trust to see you & the "forefender" Scrope according to compact—and do not like to begin my Alpine scrambles without you.——We went over the site of Aventicum—where there is some beautiful Mosaic of some extent & preservation—a few inscrip-tions—a column or two *down*—several scattered shafts—& one solitary pillar in the midst of a field—the last of its family—besides extensive traces of wall & amphitheatre.—From Morat I brought away the leg and wing of a Burgundian:—the descendants of the vanquished—when last here in the service of France buried or carried away the greater part of the heap—except what the Swiss had made into *knife-handles*—but there are still a few left—and with some of these relics I made free though for a less sordid purpose.——I do not like boring you with descriptions of what I hope you will see—and shall only say that all my expectations

314

have been gratified—& there are things—not inferior to what we have seen elsewhere—& one or two superior—such as Mont Blanc—& the Rhine.——Polidori has been ill—but is much better—a little experience will make him a very good traveller—if his health can stand it.—In the hope of seeing you soon—I shall scribble no further—I believe the best way is to write frequently & briefly—both on account of *weight*—& the *chance* of letters reaching their destination—*you* must excuse repetitions (as uncertainty induces them) and amongst others the *repetition* of my being

very much & ever yrs.
BYRON

P.S.—Remembrances to all—particularly to Kinn[air]d—Hunt—& Davies.—P.S. I have written to Mrs. Leigh—but pray let her know when you hear—as she will be glad of it.——

[. . .]

[TO JOHN CAM HOBHOUSE]   *Evian—June 23d. 1816*

My dear H[obhous]e/—Despite of this date—address as usual to the Genevese Poste—which awaits your answers as I await your arival—with that of Scrope—whose pocket appears (by your late letter of revolutions at the Union) to have become as "light" as his "wines"—though I suppose on the whole he is still worth at least 50–000 pds—being what is called here a "Millionaire" that is in Francs & such Lilliputian coinage. I have taken a very pretty villa in a vineyard—with the Alps behind—& Mt. Jura and the Lake before—it is called Diodati—from the name of the Proprietor—who is a descendant of the critical & illustrissimi Diodati—and has an agreeable house which he lets at a reasonable rate per season or annum as suits the lessée—when you come out—don't go to an Inn—not even to Secheron—but come on to head-quarters—where I have rooms ready for you—and Scrope—and all "appliances & means to boot".—Bring with you also for me some bottles of *Calcined Magnesia*—a new *Sword cane*—procured by Jackson—he alone knows the sort—(my last tumbled into this lake—) some of Waite's *red* tooth-powder—& tooth-brushes—a Taylor's *Pawrsanias*—and—I forget the other things.—Tell Murray I have a 3d. Canto of Childe Harold finished—it is the longest of the three—being one hundred & eleven Stanzas—I shall send it by the first plausible conveyance.—At the present writing I am on my way on a water-tour round the Lake Leman[99] and am

---

[99] Although he doesn't mention it, Byron was accompanied by Shelley on this trip, which inspired his *Prisoner of Chillon* and the stanzas on Rousseau in the third canto of *Childe Harold.**

thus far proceeded in a pretty open boat which I bought & navigate—it is an English one & was brought lately from Bordeaux—I am on shore for the Night—and have just had a row with the Syndic of this town who wanted my passports which I left at Diodati—not thinking they would be wanted except in grand route—but it seems this is Savoy and the dominion of his Cagliari Majesty whom we saw at his own Opera—in his own city—in 1809—however by dint of references to Geneva—& other corroborations—together with being in a very ill humour—Truth has prevailed—wonderful to relate they actually take one's word for a fact—although it is credible and indubitable.—Tomorrow we go to Meillerie—& Clarens—& Vevey—with Rousseau in hand—to see his scenery—according to his delineation in his Heloise now before me.— The views have hitherto been very fine—but I should conceive less so than those of the remainder of the lake.——All your letters (that is *two*) have arrived—thanks & greetings:—

yrs ever most truly
B

P.S.—I left the Doctor at Diodati—he sprained his ancle. P.S. Will you particularly remember to bring me a largish bottle of the strongest *Pot Ash*—as before—Mr. Le Man[n] will furnish it—that Child and Childish Dr. Pollydolly contrived to find it broken, or to break it at Carlsruhe— so that I am in a fuss—the Genevese make it badly—it effervesces in the Sulphuric acid, and it ought not—bring me some of a more quiescent character.

[TO JOHN MURRAY]   *Ouchy nr. Lausanne—June 27th. 1816*

Dear Sir—I am thus far (kept by stress of weather) on my way back to Diodati (near Geneva) from a voyage in my boat round the lake—& I enclose you a sprig of *Gibbon's Acacia* & some rose leaves from his garden—which with part of his house I have just seen—you will find honourable mention in his life made of this "Acacia" when he walked out on the night of concluding his history,—The garden—& *summer house* where he composed are neglected—& the last utterly decayed— but they still show it as his "Cabinet" & seem perfectly aware of his memory.—My route—through Flanders—& by the Rhine to Switzer-land was all I expected & more.——I have traversed all Rousseau's ground—with the Heloise before me—& am struck to a degree with the force & accuracy of his descriptions—& the beauty of their reality:— Meillerie—Clarens—& Vevey—& the Chateau de Chillon are places of which I shall say little—because all I could say must fall short of the impressions they stamp.——Three days ago—we were most nearly wrecked in a Squall off Meillerie—& driven to shore—I ran no risk being so near the rocks and a good swimmer—but our party were wet—& incommoded a good deal:—the wind was strong enough to blow down some trees as we found at landing—however all is righted & right—& we are thus far on return.——Dr. Polidori is not here—but at Diodati—left behind in hospital with a sprained ancle acquired in tumbling from a wall—he can't jump.——I shall be glad to hear you are well—& have received for me certain helms & swords sent from Waterloo—which I rode over with pain & pleasure.——I have finished a third Canto of Childe Harold (consisting of one hundred & seventeen stanzas (longer than either of the two former)—& in some parts—it may be—better—but of course on that *I* cannot determine.—I shall send it by the first safe-looking opportunity.—

ever very truly yrs.
B

Source: Leslie A. Marchand, ed., '*So late into the night*', *Byron's Letters and Journals*, vol. 5, John Murray, London, 1976, pp. 72–82.

Sir Walter Scott, *The Field of Waterloo*, 1815

Sir Walter Scott's poem was written following an early visit to the field of Waterloo, and set the agenda for the majority of subsequent poetic treatments of the victory. It is emphatically an establishment poem, from its dedication to royalty through to its conventional quasi-official statements. Notes marked with an asterisk are Scott's own.

The Field of Waterloo:

A POEM.

'Though Valois braved young Edward's gentle hand,
And Albert rush'd on Henry's way-worn band,
With Europe's chosen sons, in arms renown'd,
Yet not on Vere's bold archers long they look'd,
Nor Audley's squires nor Mowbray's yeomen brook'd,—
They saw their standard fall, and left their monarch bound.'

AKENSIDE.

TO

HER GRACE

THE DUCHESS OF WELLINGTON,

PRINCESS OF WATERLOO,

THE FOLLOWING VERSES

ARE MOST RESPECTFULLY INSCRIBED

BY

THE AUTHOR.

It may be some apology for the imperfections of this poem, that it was composed hastily, and during a short tour upon the Continent, when the Author's labours were liable to frequent interruption; but its best apology is, that it was written for the purpose of assisting the Waterloo Subscription.
ABBOTSFORD, 1815.

I.

Fair Brussels, thou art far behind,
Though, lingering on the morning wind,
   We yet may hear the hour
Peal'd over orchard and canal,
With voice prolong'd and measured fall,
   From proud Saint Michael's tower;
Thy wood, dark Soignies, holds us now,
Where the tall beeches' glossy bough
   For many a league around,
With birch and darksome oak between,
Spreads deep and far a pathless screen
   Of tangled forest ground.
Stems planted close by stems defy
The adventurous foot—the curious eye
   For access seeks in vain;
And the brown tapestry of leaves,
Strew'd on the blighted ground, receives
   Nor sun, nor air, nor rain.
No opening glade dawns on our way,
No streamlet, glancing to the ray,
   Our woodland path has cross'd;
And the straight causeway which we tread

318

Prolongs a line of dull arcade,
Unvarying through the unvaried shade
　　Until in distance lost.

II.

A brighter, livelier scene succeeds;
In groups the scattering wood recedes,
Hedge-rows, and huts, and sunny meads,
　　And corn-fields glance between;
The peasant, at his labour blithe,
Plies the hook'd staff and shorten'd scythe.[100]
　　But when these ears were green,
Placed close within destruction's scope,
Full little was that rustic's hope
　　Their ripening to have seen!
And, lo, a hamlet and its fane—
Let not the gazer with disdain
　　Their architecture view;
For yonder rude ungraceful shrine
And disproportion'd spire are thine,
　　Immortal WATERLOO!

III.

Fear not the heat, though full and high
The sun has scorch'd the autumn sky,
And scarce a forest straggler now
To shade us spreads a greenwood bough;
These fields have seen a hotter day
Than e'er was fired by sunny ray.
Yet one mile on—yon shatter'd hedge
Crests the soft hill whose long smooth ridge
　　Looks on the field below,
And sinks so gently on the dale,
That not the folds of Beauty's veil
　　In easier curves can flow.
Brief space from thence the ground again,

---

[100] *The peasant, at his labour blithe*
　　Plies the hook'd staff and shorten'd scythe.
　The reaper in Flanders carries in his left hand a stick with an iron hook, with which he collects as much grain as he can cut at one sweep with a short scythe, which he holds in his right hand. They carry on this double process with great spirit and dexterity.*

Ascending slowly from the plain,
　　Forms an opposing screen,
Which with its crest of upland ground
Shuts the horizon all around.
　　The soften'd vale between
Slopes smooth and fair for courser's tread;—
Not the most timid maid need dread
To give her snow-white palfrey head
　　On that wide stubble-ground;
Nor wood, nor tree, nor bush is there,
Her course to intercept or scare,
　　Nor fosse nor fence is found,
Save where, from out her shatter'd bowers,
Rise Hougomont's dismantled towers.

IV.

Now, see'st thou aught in this lone scene
Can tell of that which late hath been?—
　　A stranger might reply,
'The bare extent of stubble-plain
Seems lately lighten'd of its grain;
And yonder sable tracks remain
Marks of the peasant's ponderous wain,
　　When harvest-home was nigh.
On these broad spots of trampled ground,
Perchance the rustics danced such round
　　As Teniers loved to draw;
And where the earth seems scorch'd by flame.
To dress the homely feast they came,
And toil'd the kerchief'd village dame
　　Around her fire of straw.'

v.

So deem'st thou; so each mortal deems,
Of that which is from that which seems:
　　But other harvest here,
Than that which peasant's scythe demands,
Was gather'd in by sterner hands,
　　With bayonet, blade, and spear.
No vulgar crop was theirs to reap,
No stinted harvest thin and cheap!

Heroes before each fatal sweep
  Fell thick as ripen'd grain;
And ere the darkening of the day,
Piled high as autumn shocks, there lay
The ghastly harvest of the fray,
  The corpses of the slain.

VI.

Ay, look again: that line, so black
And trampled, marks the bivouac;
You deep-graved ruts the artillery's track,
  So often lost and won;
And close beside, the harden'd mud
Still shows where, fetlock-deep in blood,
The fierce dragoon through battle's flood
  Dash'd the hot war-horse on.
These spots of excavation tell
The ravage of the bursting shell;
And feel'st thou not the tainted steam,
That reeks against the sultry beam,
  From yonder trenched mound?
The pestilential fumes declare
That Carnage has replenish'd there
  Her garner-house profound.

VII.

Far other harvest-home and feast,
Than claims the boor from scythe released,
  On these scorch'd fields were known!
Death hover'd o'er the maddening rout,
And, in the thrilling battle-shout,
Sent for the bloody banquet out
  A summons of his own.
Through rolling smoke the Demon's eye
Could well each destined guest espy,
Well could his ear in ecstasy
  Distinguish every tone
That fill'd the chorus of the fray—
From cannon-roar and trumpet-bray,
From charging squadrons' wild hurra,
From the wild clang that mark'd their way—

Down to the dying groan
And the last sob of life's decay
   When breath was all but flown.

VIII.

Feast on, stern foe of mortal life,
Feast on! but think not that a strife,
With such promiscuous carnage rife,
   Protracted space may last;
The deadly tug of war at length
Must limits find in human strength,
   And cease when these are past.
Vain hope! that morn's o'erclouded sun
Heard the wild shout of fight begun
   Ere he attain'd his height,
And through the war-smoke, volumed high,
Still peals that unremitted cry,
   Though now he stoops to night.
For ten long hours of doubt and dread,
Fresh succours from the extended head
Of either hill the contest fed;
   Still down the slope they drew,
The charge of columns paused not,
Nor ceased the storm of shell and shot;
   For all that war could do
Of skill and force was proved that day,
And turn'd not yet the doubtful fray
   On bloody Waterloo.

IX.

Pale Brussels! then what thoughts were thine;[101]
When ceaseless from the distant line
   Continued thunders came!
Each burgher held his breath to hear
These forerunners of havoc near,
   Of rapine and of flame.
What ghastly sights were thine to meet,
When rolling through thy stately street,

---

[101] *Pale Brussels! then what thoughts were thine.*
   It was affirmed by the prisoners of war, that Bonaparte had promised his army, in case of victory, twenty-four hours' plunder of the city of Brussels.*

The wounded show'd their mangled plight
In token of the unfinish'd fight,
And from each anguish-laden wain
The blood-drops laid thy dust like rain!
How often in the distant drum
Heard'st thou the fell Invader come,
While Ruin, shouting to his band,
Shook high her torch and gory brand!—
Cheer thee, fair City! From yon stand,
Impatient, still his outstretch'd hand
    Points to his prey in vain,
While maddening in his eager mood,
And all unwont to be withstood,
    He fires the fight again.

        x.

'On! on!' was still his stern exclaim;[102]
'Confront the battery's jaws of flame!
    Rush on the levell'd gun!
My steel-clad cuirassiers, advance!
Each Hulan forward with his lance!
My Guard, my Chosen, charge for France,
    France and Napoleon!'
Loud answer'd their acclaiming shout,
Greeting the mandate which sent out

---

[102] *'On! On!' was still his stern exclaim.*

The characteristic obstinacy of Napoleon was never more fully displayed than in what we may be permitted to hope will prove the last of his fields. He would listen to no advice, and allow of no obstacles. An eyewitness has given the following account of his demeanour towards the end of the action:—

'It was near seven o'clock; Bonaparte, who till then had remained upon the ridge of the hill whence he could best behold what passed, contemplated with a stern countenance the scene of this horrible slaughter. The more that obstacles seemed to multiply, the more his obstinacy seemed to increase. He became indignant at these unforeseen difficulties; and, far from fearing to push to extremities an army whose confidence in him was boundless, he ceased not to pour down fresh troops, and to give orders to march forward—to charge with the bayonet—to carry by storm. He was repeatedly informed, from different points, that the day went against him, and that the troops seemed to be disordered; to which he only replied,—"*En-avant! En-avant!*" '

'One general sent to inform the Emperor that he was in a position which he could not maintain, because it was commanded by a battery, and requested to know at the same time, in what way he should protect his division from the murderous fire of the English artillery. "Let him storm the battery," replied Bonaparte, and turned his back on the aide-de-camp who brought the message.'—*Relation de la Bataille de Mont St. Jean. Par un Témoin Oculaire.* Paris 1815, 8vo, p. 51.*

Their bravest and their best to dare
The fate their leader shunn'd to share.[103]
But HE, his country's sword and shield,
Still in the battle-front reveal'd
Where danger fiercest swept the field,
　　Came like a beam of light;
In action prompt, in sentence brief,
'Soldiers, stand firm,' exclaim'd the Chief,
　　'England shall tell the fight!'[104]

XI.

On came the whirlwind, like the last
But fiercest sweep of tempest-blast—
On came the whirlwind! steel-gleams broke
Like lightning through the rolling smoke;
　　The war was waked anew;
Three hundred cannon-mouths roard loud,
And from their throats, with flash and cloud,
　　Their showers of iron threw.
Beneath their fire, in full career,
Rush'd on the ponderous cuirassier,

---

[103] *The fate their leader shunn'd to share.*

　It has been reported that Bonaparte charged at the head of his guards, at the last period of this dreadful conflict. This, however, is not accurate. He came down indeed to a hollow part of the high road, leading to Charleroi, within less than a quarter of a mile of the farm of La Haye Sainte, one of the points most fiercely disputed. Here he harangued the guards, and informed them that his preceding operations had destroyed the British infantry and cavalry, and that they had only to support the fire of the artillery, which they were to attack with the bayonet. This exhortation was received with shouts of *Vive l'Empereur*, which were heard over all our line, and led to an idea that Napoleon was charging in person. But the guards were led on by Ney; nor did Bonaparte approach nearer the scene of action than the spot already mentioned, which the rising banks on each side rendered secure from all such balls as did not come in a straight line. He witnessed the earlier part of the battle from places yet more remote, particularly from an observatory which had been placed there by the King of the Netherlands, some weeks before, for the purpose of surveying the country. It is not meant to infer from these particulars that Napoleon showed, on that memorable occasion, the least deficiency in personal courage; on the contrary, he evinced the greatest composure and presence of mind during the whole action. But it is no less true that report has erred in ascribing to him any desperate efforts of valour for recovery of the battle; and it is remarkable that during the whole carnage, none of his suite were either killed or wounded, whereas scarcely one of the Duke of Wellington's personal attendants escaped unhurt.*

[104] *England shall tell the fight!*—

　In riding up to a regiment which was hard pressed, the Duke called to the men, 'Soldiers, we must never be beat—what will they say in England?' It is needless to say how this appeal was answered.*

The lancer couch'd his ruthless spear,
And hurrying as to havoc near,
   The cohorts' eagles flew.
In one dark torrent, broad and strong,
The advancing onset roll'd along,
Forth harbinger'd by fierce acclaim,
That, from the shroud of smoke and flame,
Peal'd wildly the imperial name.

XII.

But on the British heart were lost,
The terrors of the charging host;
For not an eye the storm that view'd
Changed its proud glance of fortitude,
Nor was one forward footstep staid,
As dropp'd the dying and the dead.
Fast as their ranks the thunders tear,
Fast they renew'd each serried square,
And on the wounded and the slain,
Closed their diminish'd files again,
Till from their line, scarce spears' lengths three,
Emerging from the smoke they see
Helmet, and plume, and panoply;
   Then waked their fire at once!
Each musketeer's revolving knell
As fast, as regularly fell,
As when they practise to display
Their discipline on festal day;
   Then down went helm and lance!
Down were the eagle banners sent,
Down reeling steeds and riders went,
Corslets were pierced, and pennons rent,
   And, to augment the fray,
Wheel'd full against their staggering flanks,
The English horsemen's foaming ranks
   Forced their resistless way.
Then to the musket-knell succeeds
The clash of swords, the neigh of steeds;
As plies the smith his clanging trade,[105]

---

[105] *As plies the smith his clanging trade.*
A private soldier of the 95th regiment compared the sound which took place immediately

Against the cuirass rang the blade;
And while amid their close array
The well-served cannon rent their way,
And while amid their scatter'd band
Raged the fierce rider's bloody brand,
Recoil'd in common rout and fear
Lancer and guard and cuirassier,
Horsemen and foot, a mingled host,
Their leaders fall'n, their standards lost.

XIII.

Then, WELLINGTON, thy piercing eye
This crisis caught of destiny;
    The British host had stood
That morn 'gainst charge of sword and lance
As their own ocean-rocks hold stance,
But when thy voice had said, 'Advance!'
    They were their ocean's flood.
O thou, whose inauspicious aim
Hath wrought thy host this hour of shame,
Think'st thou thy broken bands will bide
The terrors of yon rushing tide?
Or will thy Chosen brook to feel
The British shock of levell'd steel,[106]
    Or dost thou turn thine eye
Where coming squadrons gleam afar,

---

upon the British cavalry mingling with those of the enemy, to '*a thousand tinkers at work mending pots and kettles.*'*

[106] *The British shock of levell'd steel.—*

No persuasion or authority could prevail upon the French troops to stand the shock of the bayonet. The Imperial Guards, in particular, hardly stood till the British were within thirty yards of them, although the French author, already quoted, has put into their mouths the magnanimous sentiment, 'The Guards never yield—they die.' The same author has covered the plateau, or eminence, of St. Jean, which formed the British position, with redoubts and retrenchments which never had an existence. As the narrative, which is in many respects curious, was written by an eye-witness, he was probably deceived by the appearance of a road and ditch which run along part of the hill. It may be also mentioned, in criticising this work, that the writer mentions the Château of Hougomont to have been carried by the French, although it was resolutely and successfully defended during the whole action. The enemy, indeed, possessed themselves of the wood by which it is surrounded, and at length set fire to the house itself; but the British (a detachment of the Guards, under the command of Colonel Macdonnell, and afterwards of Colonel Home) made good the garden, and thus preserved, by their desperate resistance, the post which covered the return of the Duke of Wellington's right flank.*

And fresher thunders wake the war,
   And other standards fly?
Think not that in yon columns, file
Thy conquering troops from Distant Dyle—
   Is Blucher yet unknown?
Or dwells not in thy memory still,
(Heard frequent in thine hour of ill)
What notes of hate and vengeance thrill
   In Prussia's trumpet tone?
What yet remains? shall it be thine
To head the relics of thy line
   In one dread effort more!
The Roman lore thy leisure loved,
And thou canst tell what fortune proved
   That Chieftain, who, of yore,
Ambition's dizzy paths essay'd,
And with the gladiators' aid
   For empire enterprised:
He stood the cast his rashness play'd,
Left not the victims he had made,
Dug his red grave with his own blade
And on the field he lost was laid,
   Abhorr'd—but not despised.

XIV.

But if revolves thy fainter thought
On safety, howsoever bought,
Then turn thy fearful rein and ride,
Though twice ten thousand men have died
   On this eventful day,
To gild the military fame
Which thou, for life, in traffic tame
   Wilt barter thus away.
Shall future ages tell this tale
Of inconsistence faint and frail?
And art thou he of Lodi's bridge,
Marengo's field, and Wagram's ridge!
   Or is thy soul like mountain-tide,
That, swell'd by winter storm and shower,
Rolls down in turbulence of power,
   A torrent fierce and wide;
Reft of these aids, a rill obscure,

Shrinking unnoticed, mean and poor,
  Whose channel shows display'd
The wrecks of its impetuous course,
But not one symptom of the force
  By which these wrecks were made!

XV.

Spur on thy way! since now thine ear
Has brook'd thy veterans' wish to hear,
  Who, as thy flight they eyed,
Exclaim'd, while tears of anguish came,
Wrung forth by pride, and rage, and shame,
  'O that he had but died!'
But yet, to sum this hour of ill,
Look, ere thou leavest the fatal hill,
  Back on yon broken ranks
Upon whose wild confusion gleams
The moon, as on the troubled streams
  When rivers break their banks,
And, to the ruin'd peasant's eye,
Objects half seen roll swiftly by,
  Down the dread current hurl'd:
So mingle banner, wain, and gun,
Where the tumultuous flight rolls on
Of warriors, who, when morn begun,
  Defied a banded world.

XVI.

List! frequent to the hurrying rout
The stern pursuers' vengeful shout
Tells that upon their broken rear
Rages the Prussian's bloody spear.
  So fell a shriek was none,
When Beresina's icy flood
Redden'd and thaw'd with flame and blood,
And, pressing on thy desperate way,
Raised oft and long their wild hurra,
  The children of the Don.
Thine ear no yell of horror cleft
So ominous, when, all bereft
Of aid, the valiant Polack left—

Ay, left by thee—found soldier's grave
In Leipsic's corpse-encumber'd wave.
Fate, in those various perils past,
Reserved thee still some future cast;
On the dread die thou now hast thrown,
Hangs not a single field alone,
Nor one campaign; thy martial fame,
Thy empire, dynasty, and name,
   Have felt the final stroke;
And now, o'er thy devoted head
The last stern vial's wrath is shed,
   The last dread seal is broke.

XVII.

Since live thou wilt, refuse not now
Before these demagogues to bow,
Late objects of thy scorn and hate,
Who shall thy once imperial fate
Make wordy theme of vain debate
Or shall we say thou stoop'st less low
In seeking refuge from the foe
Against whose heart, in prosperous life,
Thine hand hath ever held the knife!
   Such homage hath been paid
By Roman and by Grecian voice,
And there were honour in the choice,
   If it were freely made.
Then safely come: in one so low,
So lost, we cannot own a foe;
Though dear experience bid us end
In thee we ne'er can hail a friend.
Come, howsoe'er: but do not hide
Close in thy heart that germ of pride,
Erewhile, by gifted bard espied,
   That 'yet imperial hope';
Think not that for a fresh rebound,
To raise ambition from the ground,
   We yield thee means or scope.
In safety come: but ne'er again
Hold type of independent reign;
   No islet calls thee lord,
We leave thee no confederate band,

No symbol of thy lost command,
To be a dagger in the hand
   From which we wrench'd the sword.

XVIII.

Yet even in yon sequester'd spot
May worthier conquest be thy lot
   Than yet thy life has known;
Conquest, unbought by blood or harm,
That needs nor foreign aid nor arm,
   A triumph all thine own.
Such waits thee when thou shalt control
Those passions wild, that stubborn soul,
   That marr'd thy prosperous scene:
Hear this from no unmoved heart,
Which sighs, comparing what thou art
   With what thou might'st have been!

XIX.

Thou, too, whose deeds of fame renew'd
Bankrupt a nation's gratitude,
To thine own noble heart must owe
More than the meed she can bestow.
For not a people's just acclaim,
Not the full hail of Europe's fame,
Thy Prince's smiles, thy State's decree,
The ducal rank, the garter'd knee,—
Not these such pure delight afford
As that, when hanging up thy sword,
Well may'st thou think, 'This honest steel
Was ever drawn for public weal;
And, such was rightful Heaven's decree,
Ne'er sheathed unless with victory!'

XX.

Look forth once more with soften'd heart,
Ere from the field of same we part;
Triumph and sorrow border near,
And joy oft melts into a tear.
Alas! what links of love that morn
Has war's rude hand asunder torn!

For ne'er was field so sternly fought,
And ne'er was conquest dearer bought.
Here piled in common slaughter sleep
Those whom affection long shall weep:
Here rests the sire, that ne'er shall strain
His orphans to his heart again;
The son, whom on his native shore
The parent's voice shall bless no more;
The bridegroom, who has hardly press'd
His blushing consort to his breast;
The husband, whom through many a year
Long love and mutual faith endear.
Thou canst not name one tender tie,
But here dissolved its relics lie!
O! when thou see'st some mourner's veil
Shroud her thin form and visage pale;
Or mark'st the matron's bursting tears
Stream when the stricken drum she hears;
Or see'st how manlier grief, suppress'd,
Is labouring in a father's breast,—
With no enquiry vain pursue
The cause, but think on Waterloo!

XXI.

Period of honour as of woes,
What bright careers 'twas thine to close!
Mark'd on thy roll of blood what names
To Briton's memory, and to Fame's,
Laid there their last immortal claims!
Thou saw'st in seas of gore expire
Redoubted Picton's soul of fire,
Saw'st in the mingled carnage lie
All that of Ponsonby could die,
De Lancey change Love's bridal-wreath
For laurels from the hand of Death,
Saw'st gallant Miller's failing eye
Still bent where Albion's banners fly,
And Cameron in the shock of steel
Die like the offspring of Lochiel;
And generous Gordon 'mid the strife
Fall while he watch'd his leader's life.
Ah! though her guardian angel's shield

Fenced Britain's hero through the field,
Fate not the less her power made known,
Through his friends' hearts to pierce his own!

XXII.

Forgive, brave Dead, the imperfect lay!
Who may your names, your numbers, say?
What high-strung harp, what lofty line,
To each the dear-earn'd praise assign,
From high-born chiefs of martial fame
To the poor soldier's lowlier name?
Lightly ye rose that dawning day,
From your cold couch of swamp and clay,
To fill, before the sun was low,
The bed that morning cannot know.
Oft may the tear the green sod steep,
And sacred be the heroes' sleep,
   Till time shall cease to run;
And ne'er beside their noble grave,
May Briton pass and fail to crave
A blessing on the fallen brave
   Who fought with Wellington!

XXIII.

Farewell, sad Field! whose blighted face
Wears desolation's withering trace;
Long shall my memory retain
Thy shatter'd huts and trampled grain,
With every mark of martial wrong,
That scathe thy towers, fair Hougomont!
Yet though thy garden's green arcade
The marksman's fatal post was made,
Though on thy shatter'd beeches fell
The blended rage of shot and shell,
Though from thy blacken'd portals torn,
Their fall thy blighted fruit-trees mourn,
Has not such havoc brought a name
Immortal in the rolls of fame?
Yes, Agincourt may be forgot,
And Cressy be an unknown spot,
   And Blenheim's name be new;

But still in story and in song,
For many an age remember'd long,
Shall live the towers of Hougomont,
    And field of Waterloo.

STERN tide of human Time! that know'st not rest,
But, sweeping from the cradle to the tomb,
Bear'st ever downward on thy dusky breast
Successive generations to their doom;
While thy capacious stream has equal room
For the gay bark where pleasure's streamers sport,
And for the prison-ship of guilt and gloom,
The fisher-skiff, and barge that bears a court,
Still wafting onward all to one dark silent port;—

Stern tide of Time! through what mysterious change
Of hope and fear have our frail barks been driven!
For ne'er before, vicissitude so strange
Was to one race of Adam's offspring given.
And sure such varied change of sea and heaven
Such unexpected bursts of joy and woe,
Such fearful strife as that where we have striven,
Succeeding ages ne'er again shall know,
Until the awful term when thou shalt cease to flow!

Well hast thou stood, my Country, the brave fight
Hast well maintain'd through good report and ill;
In thy just cause and in thy native might,
And in Heaven's grace and justice constant still;
Whether the banded prowess, strength, and skill
Of half the world against thee stood array'd,
Or when, with better views and freer will,
Beside thee Europe's noblest drew the blade,
Each emulous in arms the Ocean Queen to aid.

Well art thou now repaid; though slowly rose
And struggled long with mists thy blaze of fame,
While like the dawn that in the orient glows
On the broad wave its earlier lustre came;
Then eastern Egypt saw the growing flame,
And Maida's myrtles gleam'd beneath its ray,
Where first the soldier, stung with generous shame,
Rivall'd the heroes of the wat'ry way,
And wash'd in foemen's gore unjust reproach away.

Now, Island Empress, wave thy crest on high,
And bid the banner of thy patron flow,
Gallant Saint George, the flower of Chivalry,
For thou hast faced, like him, a dragon foe,
And rescued innocence from overthrow,
And trampled down, like him, tyrannic might,
And to the gazing world mayst proudly show
The chosen emblem of thy sainted Knight,
Who quell'd devouring pride, and vindicated right.

Yet 'mid the confidence of just renown,
Renown dear-bought, but dearest thus acquired,
Write, Britain, write the moral lesson down:
'Tis not alone the heart with valour fired,
The discipline so dreaded and admired,
In many a field of bloody conquest known;
Such may by fame be lured, by gold be hired;
'Tis constancy in the good cause alone,
Best justifies the meed thy valiant sons have won.

Source: J. Logie Robertson, ed., *The Poetical Works of Sir Walter Scott*, Oxford University Press, London, New York and Toronto, 1904, pp. 619–29.

Jean-Jacques Rousseau, *Confessions* (completed 1770, published posthumously 1782)

Already well-known as an Enlightenment radical political theorist and sentimental novelist before his death, Rousseau became an important figure for romantic writers of the next generation after his death courtesy of his autobiography, the *Confessions*. Arguably the first exercise in modern autobiography, and remarkable for its interest in psychological self-analysis and its astonishing sexual frankness, the *Confessions* provided a model for the exhaustive analysis of the self characteristic of works as otherwise diverse as William Wordsworth's *The Prelude*, and Byron's *Childe Harold's Pilgrimage III*. Here he describes the genesis of his novel, *La Nouvelle Héloïse*, an important text for Byron's poem.

334

[. . .]

How could it be that, with a naturally expansive nature for which to live was to love, I had not hitherto found a friend entirely my own, a true friend – I who felt so truly formed to be a friend? How could it be that with such inflammable feelings, with a heart entirely moulded for love, I had not at least once burned with love for a definite object? Devoured by a need to love that I had never been able to satisfy, I saw myself coming to the gates of old age, and dying without having lived.

These melancholy but moving reflections drove me back upon myself with a regret that was not without its own pleasure. It seemed to me that fate owed me something she had never given me. To what purpose had she sent me into the world with delicate faculties, if they were to remain to the end unused? This consciousness of my internal worth gave me a feeling of injustice, which afforded me some form of compensation and caused me to weep tears that pleased me as they flowed.

[. . .]

Whatever the intensity of this intoxication [the intoxicating memory of youthful love-sickness], however, it was not sufficient to make me forget my age and situation, to flatter me that I could still arouse love, or to make me try at last to communicate this devouring but barren flame by which ever since my childhood I had felt my heart to be consumed in vain.

[. . .]

What then did I do? My reader has already guessed, if he has paid the least attention to my progress so far. The impossibility of attaining the real persons precipitated me into the land of chimeras; and seeing nothing that existed worthy of my exalted feelings, I fostered them in an ideal world which my creative imagination soon peopled with beings after my own heart. Never was this resource more opportune, and never did it prove more fertile. In my continual ecstasies I intoxicated myself with draughts of the most exquisite sentiments that have ever entered the heart of a man. Altogether ignoring the human race, I created for myself societies of perfect creatures celestial in their virtue and in their beauty, and of reliable, tender, and faithful friends such as I had never found, here below. I took such pleasure in thus soaring into the empyrean in the midst of all the charms that surrounded me, that I spent countless hours and days at it, losing all memory of anything else. No sooner had I eaten a hasty morsel than I was impatient to escape and run into my woods once more. When I was about to set out for my enchanted world and saw wretched mortals appearing to hold me down to earth, I could neither restrain nor conceal my annoyance. Indeed I lost control of myself and gave them so rude a reception that it might almost have been called brutal. This merely increased my reputation for misanthropy, whereas it would have gained me quite a contrary one if people had been more able to read my heart.

[. . . Rousseau details illness and troubles that interrupt his imaginary idyll.]

All these distractions should have worked a radical cure for my fantastic amours, and this was perhaps a means offered me by Heaven for preventing their fatal consequences. But my unlucky star prevailed, and no sooner did I begin to recover than my heart, my head and my feet resumed the same paths. I say the same, but only in certain respects; for my ideas were a little less exalted and this time remained upon earth. But they made so exquisite a choice among all the charming things of every kind that could be found there that it was not much less chimerical than the chimerical world I had deserted. I imagined love and friendship, the two idols of my heart, in the most ravishing of forms, and took delight in adorning them with all the charms of the sex I had always adored. I imagined two women friends rather than two of my own sex, since although examples of such friendships are rarer they are also more beautiful. I endowed them with analogous but different characters; with features if not perfect yet to my taste, and radiant with kindliness and sensibility. I made one dark, the other fair; one lively, the other gentle; one sensible, the other weak, but so touching in her weakness that virtue itself seemed to gain by it. I gave one of them a lover to whom the other was a tender friend and even something more; but I allowed of no rivalry or quarrels or jealousy because I find it hard to imagine any painful feelings, and I did not wish to discolour my charming picture with anything degrading to Nature. Being captivated by my two charming models, I identified myself as far as I could with the lover and friend. But I made him young and pleasant, whilst endowing him also with the virtues and faults that I felt in myself.

In order to place my characters in a suitable setting, I passed the loveliest places I had seen in my travels one after another in review. But I found no woodland fresh enough, no countryside moving enough to suit me. The valleys of Thessaly would have satisfied me, if I had seen them; but my imagination was tired of inventing, and wanted some real locality to serve as a basis, and to create for the inhabitants I intended to place there the illusion of real existence. I thought for some time of the Borromean Islands, the delicious sight of which had enraptured me; but I found too much ornament and artifice about them for my inhabitants. I needed a lake, however, and finally I chose that lake around which my heart has never ceased to wander. I fixed on that part of its shores, which my wishes long ago chose as my dwelling-place in that imaginary state of bliss which is all that fate has allowed me. My poor Mamma's[107] birth-place had still a special attraction for me. Its contrasting features, the richness and variety of its landscape, the magnificence and majesty of the whole, which charms the senses, moves the heart, and elevates the soul, finally determined me, and I established my young pupils at Vevey. That is as much as I imagined at the first inspiration; the rest was only added subsequently.

I confined myself for a long time to so vague a plan because it was suf-ficient to fill my imagination with pleasant objects, and my heart with those feelings on which it loves to feed. This fiction, by constant repeti-tion, finally assumed greater consistency and took a fixed and definite shape in my brain. It was then that the whim seized me to set down on paper some of the situations that it suggested to me and, by recalling all that I had felt in my youth, to give some sort of expression to my desire to love which I had never been able to satisfy, and which I now felt was devouring me.

Source: J. M. Cohen, trans., *The Confessions of Jean-Jacques Rousseau* (1782), Penguin Books, London, first published 1953, reprinted 1987, pp. 396–401.

Sir Walter Scott, from his review of Byron's *Childe Harold's Pilgrimage, III,* in the *Quarterly Review*

Dated October 1816, issued February 1817, XVI, 172–208

We have felt ourselves very much affected by the perusal of these poems, nor can we suppose that we are singular in our feelings. [. . .] It has been, [. . .] reserved for our own time to produce one distinguished example of the Muse having descended upon a bard of a wounded spirit, and lent

---

[107] *Mamma*: Rousseau's pet-name for his long-term mistress, Louise de Warens.

her lyre to tell, and we trust to soothe, afflictions of no ordinary description, afflictions originating probably in that singular combination of feeling which has been called the poetical temperament, and which has so often saddened the days of those on whom it has been conferred. If ever a man could lay claim to that character in all its strength and all its weakness, with its unbounded range of enjoyment, and its exquisite sensibility of pleasure and of pain, it must certainly be granted to Lord Byron. Nor does it require much time or a deep acquaintance with human nature to discover why these extraordinary powers should in many cases have contributed more to the wretchedness than to the happiness of their possessor.

The 'imagination all compact,' which the greatest poet who ever lived has assigned as the distinguishing badge of his brethren, is in every case a dangerous gift. It exaggerates, indeed, our expectations, and can often bid its possessor hope, where hope is lost to reason: but the delusive pleasure arising from these visions of imagination, resembles that of a child whose notice is attracted by a fragment of glass to which a sun-beam has given momentary splendour. He hastens to the spot with breathless impatience, and finds the object of his curiosity and expectation is equally vulgar and worthless. Such is the man of quick and exalted powers of imagination. His fancy over-estimates the object of his wishes, and pleasure, fame, distinction, are alternately pursued, attained, and despised when in his power. Like the enchanted fruit in the palace of a sorcerer, the objects of his admiration lose their attraction and value as soon as they are grasped by the adventurer's hand, and all that remains is regret for the time lost in the chase, and astonishment at the hallucination under the influence of which it was undertaken. The disproportion between hope and possession which is felt by all men, is thus doubled to those whom nature has endowed with the power of gilding a distant prospect by the rays of imagination. These reflexions, though trite and obvious, are in a manner forced from us by the poetry of Lord Byron, by the sentiments of weariness of life and enmity with the world which they so frequently express—and by the singular analogy which such sentiments hold with incidents of his life so recently before the public. The works before us contain so many direct allusions to the author's personal feelings and private history, that it becomes impossible for us to divide Lord Byron from his poetry, or to offer our criticism upon the continuation of *Childe Harold*, without reverting to the circumstances in which the commencement of that singular and original work first appeared . . .

[. . .]

The family misfortunes which have for a time lost Lord Byron to his native land have neither chilled his poetical fire, nor deprived England of its benefit. The Third Canto of *Childe Harold* exhibits, in all its strength and in all its peculiarity, the wild, powerful and original vein of poetry which, in the preceding cantos, first fixed the public attention upon the author. If there is any difference, the former seem to us to have been rather more sedulously corrected and revised for publication, and the present work to have been dashed from the author's pen with less regard to the subordinate points of expression and versification. Yet such is the deep and powerful strain of passion, such the original tone and colouring of description, that the want of polish in some of its minute parts rather adds to than deprives the poem of its energy. It seems, occasionally, as if the consideration of mere grace was beneath the care of the poet, in his ardour to hurry upon the reader the 'thoughts that glow and words that burn;' and that the occasional roughness of the verse corresponded with the stern tone of thought, and of mental suffering which it expresses.

[. . .]

Versification, in the hands of a master-bard, is as frequently correspondent to the thoughts it expresses as to the action it describes, and the 'line labours and the words move slow' under the heavy and painful thought; wrung, as it were, from the bosom.

[. . .]

He [the Pilgrim] arrives on Waterloo,—a scene where all men, where a poet especially, and a poet such as Lord Byron, must needs pause, and amid the quiet simplicity of whose scenery is excited a moral interest, deeper and more potent even than that which is produced by gazing upon the sublimest efforts of Nature in her most romantic recesses.

That Lord Byron's sentiments do not correspond with ours is obvious, and we are sorry for both our sakes. For our own—because we have lost that note of triumph with which his harp would otherwise have rung over a field of glory such as Britain never reaped before; and on Lord Byron's account,—because it is melancholy to see a man of genius duped by the mere cant of words and phrases, even when facts are most broadly confronted with them. If the poet has mixed with original, wild, and magnificent creations of his imagination, prejudices which he could only have caught by the contagion which he most professes to despise, it is he himself must be the loser. If his lofty muse has soared in all her brilliancy over the field of Waterloo without dropping even one leaf of laurel on the head of Wellington, his merit can dispense even with the praise of Lord Byron. And as, when the images of Brutus were excluded from the triumphal procession, his memory became only the more powerfully imprinted on the souls of the Romans,—the name of the British hero will be but more eagerly recalled to remembrance by the very lines in which his praise is forgotten.

We would willingly avoid mention of the political opinions hinted at by Childe Harold, and more distinctly expressed in other poems of Lord Byron;—the more willingly, as we strongly suspect that these effusions are rather the sport of whim and singularity, or at best the suggestion of sudden starts of feeling and passion, than the expressions of any serious or fixed opinion . . . For to compare Waterloo to the battle of Cannæ, and speak of the blood which flowed on the side of the vanquished as lost in the cause of freedom, is contrary not only to plain sense and general opinion, but to Lord Byron's own experience, and to the testimony of that experience which he has laid before the public. Childe Harold, in his former Pilgrimage, beheld in Spain the course of the 'tyrant and of the tyrant's slaves'. He saw 'Gaul's vulture with her wings unfurled', and indignantly expostulated with Fate on the impending destruction of the patriotic Spaniards.

> And must they fall,—the young, the proud, the brave,
>   To swell one bloated Chief's unwholesome reign,
> No step between submission and a grave,
>   The rise of rapine, and the fall of Spain!

Childe Harold saw the scenes which he celebrates,—and does he now compare to the field of Cannæ the plain of Waterloo, and mourn over the fall of the tyrant and the military satraps and slaves whose arms built his power, as over the fall of the cause of liberty? We know the ready answer which will be offered by the few who soothe their own prejudices, or seek to carry their own purposes by maintaining this extravagant proposition. They take a distinction: Buonaparte, according to their creed, fell a tyrant in 1814, and revived a deliverer in 1815. A few months' residence in the Isle of Elba had given him time for better thoughts, and had mortified within his mind that gorging ambition for which Russia was not too great, nor Hamburgh too small a morsel; which neither evaporated under the burning sun of Egypt nor was chilled by the polar snows; which survived the loss of millions of soldiers and an incalculable tract of territory, and burned as fiercely during the conferences of Chatillon, when the despot's fate was trembling in the scales, as at those of Tilsit, when that of his adversary had kicked the beam. All the experience which Europe had bought by oceans of blood and years of degradation ought, according to these gentlemen, to have been forgotten upon the empty professions of one whose word, whensoever or wheresoever pledged, never bound him an instant when interest or ambition required a breach of it. Buonaparte assured the world he was changed in temper, mind and disposition; and his old agent and minister (Fouché of Nantes) was as ready to give his security as Bardolph was to engage for Falstaff.

When Gil Blas found his old comrades in knavery, Don Raphael and Ambrose de Lamela, administrating the revenues of a Carthusian convent, he shrewdly conjectured that the treasure of the holy fathers was in no small danger, and grounded his suspicion on the old adage *Il ne faut pas mettre à la cave un ivrogne qui à renoncé au vin.*[108] But Europe—when France had given the strongest proof of her desire to recover what she termed her glory, by expelling a king whose reign was incompatible with foreign wars, and recalling Napoleon to whom conquest was as the very breath of his nostrils—Europe, most deserving, had she yielded to such arguments, to have been crowned with 'the diadem, hight foolscap', is censured for having exerted her strength to fix her security, and confuting with her own warlike weapons those whose only law was arms, and only argument battle. We do not believe there lives any one who can seriously doubt the truth of what we have said. If, however, there were any simple enough to expect to hail Freedom restored by the victorious arms of Buonaparte, their mistake (had Lord Wellington not saved them from its consequences) would have resembled that of poor Slender, who, rushing to the embraces of Anne Page, found himself unexpectedly in the gripe of a lubberly post-master's boy. But probably no one was foolish enough to nourish such hopes, though there are some—their number is few—whose general opinions concerning the policy of Europe are so closely and habitually linked with their party prejudices at home, that they see in the victory of Waterloo only the triumph of Lord Castlereagh; and could the event have been reversed, would have thought rather of the possible change of seats in St. Stephen's, than of the probable subjugation of Europe. Such were those who, hiding perhaps secret hopes with affected despondence, lamented the madness which endeavoured to make a stand against the Irresistible whose military calculations were formed on plans far beyond the comprehension of all other minds; and such are they who, confuted by stubborn facts, now affect to mourn over the consequences of a victory which they had pronounced impossible. But, as we have already hinted, we cannot trace in Lord Byron's writings any systematic attachment to a particular creed of politics, and he appears to us to seize the subjects of public interest upon the side in which they happen to present themselves for the moment, with this qualification, that he usually paints them on the shaded aspect, perhaps that their tints may harmonize with the sombre colours of his landscape. Dangerous as prophecies are, we could almost hazard a prediction that, if Lord Byron enjoys that length of life which we desire for his sake and our own, his future writings may probably shew that he thinks better of

---

[108] 'You must not put a reformed drunkard in the wine-cellar.'*

the morals, religion, and constitution of his country, than his poems have hitherto indicated. Should we fail in a hope which we cherish fondly, the disgrace of false prophecy must rest with us, but the loss will be with Lord Byron himself.

[. . .]

With kinder feelings to Lord Byron in person and reputation no one could approach him than ourselves: we owe it to the pleasure which he has bestowed upon us, and to the honour he has done to our literature. We have paid our warmest tribute to his talents—it is their due. We will touch on the uses for which he was invested with them—it is our duty; and happy, most happy, should we be, if, in discharging it, we could render this distinguished author a real service. We do not assume the office of harsh censors;—we are entitled at no time to do so towards genius, least of all in its hour of adversity; and we are prepared to make full allowance for the natural effect of misfortune upon a bold and haughty spirit.

[. . .]

But this mode of defiance may last too long, and hurry him who indulges it into further evils; and to this point our observations tend. The advice ought not to be contemned on account of the obscurity of those by whom it is given:—the roughest fisherman is an useful pilot when a gallant vessel is near the breakers; the meanest shepherd may be a sure guide over a pathless heath, and the admonition which is given in well meant kindness should not be despised, even were it tendered with a frankness which may resemble a want of courtesy.

If the conclusion of Lord Byron's literary career were to be such as these mournful verses have anticipated—if this darkness of the spirit, this scepticism concerning the existence of worth, of friendship, of sincerity, were really and permanently to sink like a gulph between this distinguished poet and society, another name will be added to the illustrious list to whom Preston's caution refers.

> Still wouldst thou write?—to tame thy youthful fire
> Recall to life the masters of the lyre;
> Lo every brow the shade of sorrow wears,
> And every wreath is stained with dropping tears!

But this is an unfair picture. It is not the temper and talents of the poet, but the use to which he puts them, on which his happiness or misery is grounded. A powerful and unbridled imagination is, we have already said, the author and architect of its own disappointments. Its fascinations, its exaggerated pictures of good and evil, and the mental distress to which they give rise, are the natural and necessary evils attending on

that quick susceptibility of feeling and fancy incident to the poetical temperament. But the Giver of all talents, while he has qualified them each
with its separate and peculiar alloy, has endowed the owner with the
power of purifying and refining them. But, as if to moderate the arro-
gance of genius, it is justly and wisely made requisite, that he must regulate and tame the fire of his fancy, and descend from the heights to
which she exalts him, in order to obtain ease of mind and tranquillity.
The materials of happiness, that is of such degree of happiness as is consistent with our present state, lie around us in profusion. But the man of
talents must stoop to gather them, otherwise they would be beyond the
reach of the mass of society, for whose benefit, as well as for his, Provi-
dence has created them. There is no royal and no poetical path to contentment and heart's-ease: that by which they are attained is open to all
classes of mankind, and lies within the most limited range of intellect. To
narrow our wishes and desires within the scope of our powers of attainment; to consider our misfortunes, however peculiar in their character,
as our inevitable share in the patrimony of Adam; to bridle those irrita-
ble feelings, which ungoverned are sure to become governors; to shun
that intensity of galling and self-wounding reflection which our poet has
so forcibly described in his own burning language:

> ———————I have thought
> Too long and darkly, till my brain became,
> In its own eddy, boiling and o'erwrought,
> A whirling gulf of phantasy and flame—

—to stoop, in short, to the realities of life; repent if we have offended,
and pardon if we have been trespassed against; to look on the world less
as our foe than as a doubtful and capricious friend, whose applause we
ought as far as possible to deserve, but neither to court nor contemn—
such seem the most obvious and certain means of keeping or regaining
mental tranquillity

[. . .]

We are compelled to dwell upon this subject: for future ages, while our
language is remembered, will demand of this why Lord Byron was
unhappy? We retort this query on the noble poet himself while it is called
'to-day'. He does injustice to the world, if he imagines he has left it exclusively filled with those who rejoice in his sufferings. If the voice of consolation be in cases like his less loudly heard than that of reproach or
upbraiding, it is because those who long to conciliate, to advise, to medi-
ate, to console, are timid in thrusting forward their sentiments, and fear
to exasperate where they most seek to soothe; while the busy and offi-
cious intrude, without shame or sympathy, and embitter the privacy of

affliction by their rude gaze and importunate clamour. But the pain which such insects can give only lasts while the wound is raw. Let the patient submit to the discipline of the soul enjoined by religion, and recommended by philosophy, and the scar will become speedily insensible to their stings. Lord Byron may not have loved the world, but the world has loved him, not perhaps with a wise or discriminating affection, but as well as it is capable of loving any one. And many who do not belong to the world, as the word is generally understood, have their thoughts fixed on Lord Byron, with the anxious wish and eager hope that he will bring his powerful understanding to combat with his irritated feelings, and that his next efforts will shew that he has acquired the peace of mind necessary for the free and useful exercise of his splendid talents.

I decus, i nostrum, melioribus utere fatis.[109]

Source: Andrew Rutherford, ed., *Lord Byron: The Critical Heritage*, Routledge, London, 1995, pp. 84–6, 91–7.

---

[109] 'Go, glory of our race, and enjoy a happier fate.'*

PART IV
The exotic and oriental

The Royal Pavilion at Brighton

In 1783 the young Prince of Wales and future George IV first visited Brighton, beginning a love-affair with the resort that would make it fashionable for the next forty-odd years. The Royal Pavilion, after successive incarnations completed in 1823 to the designs of John Nash, stands there as a monument to a princely fantasy of the exotic and an exemplum of Regency design's take on the East.

The extracts in this section are designed to provide some literary sidelights on the Regency romance with the East. The first is taken from Maria Edgeworth's novel *The Absentee* (1812). *The Absentee* was for Edgeworth's contemporaries probably her most important novel, influencing amongst others Sir Walter Scott, largely because it is the first 'national' novel fully recognizable as such. It forms part of the group of her so-called 'Irish novels' which deal principally with the relations between the Anglo-Irish Protestant Ascendancy families and London on the one hand and the native, Catholic Irish on the other. *The Absentee* satirises 'absenteeism', the practice of milking estates held in Ireland for income whilst living in London, which gave rise to the impoverishment of the land and its people through irresponsible management by unscrupulous agents. Hence the opening satire on the Anglo-Irish Lady Clonbrony determined to make her mark as a metropolitan socialite in London, regardless of expense and largely unconscious of the contempt of the ladies of the *ton*. Of interest here is the description of the fashion for the exotic in interior décor, and Edgeworth's disdain for it as socially irresponsible because so randomly eclectic.

Another version of the East, equally eclectic but emphatically less domesticated, is provided by Thomas De Quincey, friend and admirer of William Wordsworth, autobiographer, essayist and journalist, in his *Confessions of an English Opium-Eater* (1822). An exercise in autobiography, it proceeds by documenting how traumatic youthful experiences are transmuted in later life into dreams through the heightening agency of opium, taken as laudanum, the only available analgesic at the time. In this extract, De Quincey describes how an earlier visit of a non-English speaking

Malay to his cottage in the Lake District revivifies in his opium-enhanced dreams. The Malay acts as a conduit into a fantastical and nightmarish confederation of Asiatic images drawn from De Quincey's varied and arcane reading. The difference between Edgeworth's version of the Orient and De Quincey's is in part a 'romantic' difference: if Edgeworth's East is on the frontier of the ridiculous, De Quincey's is the territory of the sublime.

Drafted in 1798 but not published until 1816 at the urging of Byron, 'Kubla Khan' is one of the most famous and mystifying poems in the English language. Not the least mystifying element is its view of the East in the person of Kubla Khan, the Mongolian empire-builder who over-ran China from the North. Formally, it is a 'fragment' poem, insisting on its own unfinished state (see the poem's preface); in this it conforms to contemporary taste for the ruinous as more hospitable to the Romantic imagination. William Hazlitt, essayist and critic, published an essay in *The London Magazine* for June 1821, the bulk of which is devoted to a literary controversy between Byron and William Bowles, a poet and belles-lettrist, over the merits of Alexander Pope, the early eighteenth-century poet who authored *The Rape of The Lock*. The argument centres upon whether art is superior to nature or vice versa. Hazlitt's position is quintessentially Romantic, preferring the primitive or ruinous in art, which both leave room for the exercise of the viewer's or reader's imagination and feelings, and it is in this spirit that he criticises the Pavilion.

Maria Edgeworth, *The Absentee*

FULL of what he had heard, and impatient to obtain farther information respecting the state of his father's affairs, lord Colambre hastened home; but his father was out, and his mother was engaged with Mr. Soho, directing, or rather being directed, how her apartments should be fitted up for her gala. As lord Colambre entered the room, he saw his mother, miss Nugent, and Mr. Soho, standing at a large table, which was covered with rolls of paper, patterns, and drawings of furniture: Mr. Soho was speaking in a conceited, dictatorial tone, asserting that there was no "colour in nature for that room equal to *the belly-o'-the fawn*;" which *belly-o'-the fawn* he so pronounced, that lady Clonbrony understood it to be *la belle uniforme*, and, under this mistake, repeated and assented to the assertion, till it was set to rights, with condescending superiority, by the upholsterer. This first architectural upholsterer of the age, as he styled himself, and was universally admitted to be by all the world of fashion, then, with full powers given to him, spoke *en maître*. The whole face of things must be changed. There must be new hangings, new draperies, new cornices, new candelabras, new every thing!—

"The upholsterer's eye, in fine frenzy rolling,
Glances from ceiling to floor, from floor to ceiling;
And, as imagination bodies forth
The form of things unknown, the upholsterer's pencil
Turns them to shape, and gives to airy nothing
A local habitation and a NAME."[1]

Of the value of a NAME no one could be more sensible than Mr. Soho.

"Your la'ship sees[2]—this is merely a scratch of my pencil. Your la'-ship's sensible—just to give you an idea of the shape, the form of the thing. You fill up your angles[3] here with *encoinières*[4]—round your walls with the *Turkish tent drapery*—a fancy of my own—in apricot cloth, or crimson velvet, suppose, or, *en flute*,[5] in crimson satin draperies, fanned and riched with gold fringes, *en suite*[6]—intermediate spaces, Apollo's heads with gold rays—and here, ma'am, you place four *chancelières*,[7] with chimeras[8] at the corners, covered with blue silk and silver fringe, elegantly fanciful—with my STATIRA CANOPY here—light blue silk draperies—aërial tint,[9] with silver balls—and for seats here, the

---

[1] *"The upholsterers' eye ... NAME.":* parody of *A Midsummer Night's Dream*, v. i. 12–17:
   The poet's eye, in a fine frenzy rolling,
   Doth glance from heaven to earth, from earth to heaven;
   And as imagination bodies forth
   The forms of things unknown, the poet's pen
   Turns them to shapes and gives to airy nothing
   A local habitation and a name.
The satirical substitution of upholsterer for poet leads on to themes—local habitation and the significance of names—which acquire a realistic significance in the novel.*

[2] *Your la'ship sees . . .:* Soho's rhodomontade, as Edgeworth calls it, is a display case of trade jargon used to flatter Lady Clonbrony. While the descriptions of decor for each room may not have been excessively fanciful given the contemporary taste for the exotic, the collective effect is grotesquely excessive.*

[3] *angles:* corners.*

[4] *encoinières:* pieces of furniture made with an angle to fit into a corner.*

[5] *en flute:* fluted, in ruffles.*

[6] *en suite:* in harmony.*

[7] *chancelières:* footmuffs; cushions (or perhaps boxes) furred on the inside and with an opening on one side.*

[8] *chimeras:* grotesque monsters composed of parts of various animals.*

[9] *aërial tint:* atmospheric blue.*

SERAGLIO[10] OTTOMANS, superfine scarlet—your paws[11] griffin—golden—and golden tripods, here, with antique cranes—and oriental alabaster tables here and there—quite appropriate, your la'ship feels.

"And let me reflect. For the next apartment, it strikes me—as your la'-ship don't value expence—*the Alhambra[12] hangings*—my own thought entirely—Now, before I unrol them, lady Clonbrony, I must beg you'll not mention I've shown them. I give you my sacred honour, not a soul has set eye upon the Alhambra hangings except Mrs. Dareville, who stole a peep; I refused, absolutely refused, the duchess of Torcaster—but I can't refuse your la'ship—So see, ma'am—(unrolling them)—scagliola[13] porphyry[14] columns supporting the grand dome—entablature,[15] silvered and decorated with imitative bronze ornaments: under the entablature, a *valance in pelmets*, of puffed scarlet silk, would have an unparalleled grand effect, seen through the arches—with the TRE-BISOND[16] TRELLICE PAPER, would make a *tout ensemble*, novel beyond example. On that trebisond trellice paper, I confess, ladies, I do pique myself.[17]

"Then, for the little room, I recommend turning it temporarily into a Chinese pagoda, with this *Chinese pagoda paper*, with the *porcelain border*, and josses,[18] and jars, and beakers, to match; and I can venture to promise one vase of pre-eminent size and beauty.—O, indubitably! if your la'ship prefers it, you can have the *Egyptian hieroglyphic paper*, with the *ibis border* to match!—The only objection is, one sees it every-where—quite antediluvian—gone to the hotels even; but, to be sure, if your la'ship has a fancy—at all events, I humbly recommend, what her grace of Torcaster longs to patronize, my MOON CURTAINS, with candlelight draperies. A demi-saison[19] elegance this—I hit off yesterday—and—True, your la'ship's quite correct—out of the common completely. And, of course, you'd have the *sphynx candelabras*, and the phœnix

---

[10] *SERAGLIO*: Turkish apartments reserved for wives and concubines.*

[11] *your paws*: here, Soho's string of exotic technical names and devices suddenly admits the familiar possessive adjective—this is part of his condescending attitude towards Lady Clonbrony—which has the satiric effect of linking her to the composite monsters or griffins whose paws are really indicated.*

[12] *Alhambra*: palace of Moorish kings at Granada.*

[13] *scagliola*: (from the Italian), plaster work designed to imitate types of stone.*

[14] *porphyry*: deep red and white stone, associated with the orient.*

[15] *entablature*: the part of an architectural order (or series of mouldings) which is above the column, including architrave, frieze, and cornice.*

[16] *TREBISOND*: (modern-day Trabizon), a Turkish city.*

[17] *pique myself*: pride myself on.*

[18] *josses*: Chinese figures of deities.*

[19] *demi-saison*: style intermediate between past and coming season of fashion.*

argands[20] O! nothing else lights now, ma'am!—Expence!—Expence of the whole!—Impossible to calculate here on the spot!—but nothing at all worth your ladyship's consideration!"

At another moment, lord Colambre might have been amused with all this rhodomontade, and with the airs and voluble conceit of the orator; but, after what he had heard at Mr. Mordicai's, this whole scene struck him more with melancholy than with mirth. He was alarmed by the prospect of new and unbounded expence; provoked, almost past enduring, by the jargon and impertinence of this upholsterer; mortified and vexed to the heart, to see his mother the dupe, the sport of such a coxcomb.

"Prince of puppies!—Insufferable!—My own mother!" lord Colambre repeated to himself, as he walked hastily up and down the room.

"Colambre, won't you let us have your judgment—your *teeste*?" said his mother.

"Excuse me, ma'am—I have no taste, no judgment, in these things."

[. . .]

THE opening of her gala, the display of her splendid reception rooms, the Turkish tent, the Alhambra, the pagoda, formed a proud moment to lady Clonbrony. Much did she enjoy, and much too naturally, notwithstanding all her efforts to be stiff and stately, much too naturally did she show her enjoyment of the surprise excited in some and affected by others on their first entrance.

One young, very young lady expressed her astonishment so audibly as to attract the notice of all the bystanders. Lady Clonbrony, delighted, seized both her hands, shook them, and laughed heartily; then, as the young lady with her party passed on, her ladyship recovered herself, drew up her head, and said to the company near her, "Poor thing! I hope I covered her little *naïveté* properly. How NEW she must be!"

Then, with well practised dignity, and half subdued self complacency of aspect, her ladyship went gliding about—most importantly busy, introducing my lady *this* to the sphynx candelabra, and my lady *that* to the Trebisond trellice; placing some delightfully for the perspective of the Alhambra; establishing others quite to her satisfaction on seraglio ottomans; and honouring others with a seat under the statira canopy. Receiving and answering compliments from successive crowds, of select friends, imagining herself the mirror of fashion, and the admiration of the whole world, lady Clonbrony was, for her hour, as happy certainly as ever woman was in similar circumstances.

---

[20] *argands*: lamps with cylindrical wick, invented in 1782.*

Her son looked at her, and wished that this happiness could last. Naturally inclined to sympathy, lord Colambre reproached himself for not feeling as gay at this instant as the occasion required. But the festive scene, the blazing lights, the "universal hubbub,"[21] failed to raise his spirits. As a dead weight upon them hung the remembrance of Mordicai's denunciations; and, through the midst of this eastern magnificence, this unbounded profusion, he thought he saw future domestic misery and ruin to those he loved best in the world.

[. . .]

[. . .] How transient are all human joys, especially those of vanity! Even on this long meditated, this long desired, this gala night, lady Clonbrony found her triumph incomplete—inadequate to her expectations. For the first hour all had been compliment, success, and smiles; presently came the *buts*, and the hesitated objections, and the "damning with faint praise"[22] all *that* could be borne—every body has his taste—and one person's taste is as good as another's; and while she had Mr. Soho to cite, lady Clonbrony thought she might be well satisfied. But she could not be satisfied with colonel Heathcock, who, dressed in black, had stretched his "fashionable length of limb" under the statira canopy, upon the snow-white swan down couch. When, after having monopolised attention, and been the subject of much bad wit, about black swans and rare birds, and swans being geese and geese being swans, the colonel condescended to rise, and, as Mrs. Dareville said, to vacate his couch—that couch was no longer white—the black impression of the colonel remained on the sullied snow.

"Eh, now! really didn't recollect I was in black," was all the apology he made. Lady Clonbrony was particularly vexed that the appearance of the statira canopy should be spoiled before the effect had been seen by lady Pococke, and lady Chatterton, and lady G——, lady P——, and the duke of V——, and a party of superlative fashionables, who had promised *to look in upon her*, but who, late as it was, had not yet arrived. They came in at last. But lady Clonbrony had no reason to regret for their sake the statira couch. It would have been lost upon them, as was every thing else which she had prepared with so much pains and cost to

---

[21] "*universal hubbub*": Milton, *Paradise Lost*, ii. 951. In her notes to Mary Leadbeater's *Cottage Dialogues* (1811) Edgeworth glosses 'hubbub' as a Miltonic word, and cites this line. In fact, hubbub dates back to the sixteenth century (Holinshed and Spenser) when it seems to have been a term for what was thought a characteristically Irish cry, cf. Barnaby Rich's *The Irish Hubbub: or the English Hue and Cry* (1617).*

[22] "*damning with faint praise*": the phrase dates back at least as far as William Wycherley (1640?–1716): see the prologue to *The Plain Dealer*: 'And with faint praises one another damn'.*

excite their admiration. They came resolute not to admire. Skilled in the art of making others unhappy, they just looked round with an air of apathy.—"Ah! you've had Soho!—Soho has done wonders for you here!—Vastly well!—Vastly well!—Soho's very clever in his way!"

Others of great importance came in, full of some slight accident that had happened to themselves, or their horses, or their carriages; and, with privileged selfishness, engrossed the attention of all within their sphere of conversation. Well, lady Clonbrony got over all this, and got over the history of a letter about a chimney that was on fire, a week ago, at the duke of V——'s old house, in Brecknockshire. In gratitude for the smiling patience with which she listened to him, his grace of V——fixed his glass to look at the Alhambra, and had just pronounced it to be "Well!—Very well!" when the dowager lady Chatterton made a terrible discovery—a discovery that filled lady Clonbrony with astonishment and indignation—Mr. Soho had played her false! What was her mortification, when the dowager assured her that these identical Alhambra hangings had not only been shown by Mr. Soho to the duchess of Torcaster, but that her grace had had the refusal of them, and had actually criticised them, in consequence of sir Horace Grant, the great traveller's objecting to some of the proportions of the pillars—Soho had engaged to make a new set, vastly improved, by sir Horace's suggestions, for her grace of Torcaster.

[. . .]

All who secretly envied or ridiculed lady Clonbrony enjoyed this scene. The Alhambra hangings, which had been in one short hour before the admiration of the world, were now regarded by every eye with contempt, as *cast* hangings, and every tongue was busy declaiming against Mr. Soho; every body declared, that from the first, the want of proportion "struck them, but that they would not mention it till others found it out."

People usually revenge themselves for having admired too much, by afterwards despising and depreciating without mercy—in all great assemblies the perception of ridicule is quickly caught, and quickly too revealed. Lady Clonbrony, even in her own house, on her gala night, became an object of ridicule,—decently masked, indeed, under the appearance of condolence with her ladyship, and of indignation against "that abominable Mr. Soho!"

[. . .]

Some hits, sufficiently palpable,[23] however, are recorded for the advantage of posterity. When lady Clonbrony led her to look at the Chinese pagoda, the lady [Mrs. Dareville] paused, with her foot on the threshold,

---

[23] *Some hits, sufficiently palpable*: again *Hamlet*; see V. ii. 295: 'A hit, a very palpable hit'.*

as if afraid to enter this porcelain Elysium, as she called it—Fool's Paradise, she would have said; and, by her hesitation, and by the half pronounced word, suggested the idea,—"None but belles without petticoats can enter here," said she, drawing her clothes tight round her; "fortunately, I have but two, and lady Langdale has but one." Prevailed upon to venture in, she walked on with prodigious care and trepidation, affecting to be alarmed at the crowd of strange forms and monsters by which she was surrounded.

"Not a creature here that I ever saw before in nature!—Well, now I may boast I've been in a real Chinese pagoda!"

"Why yes, every thing is appropriate here, I flatter myself," said lady Clonbrony.

"And how good of you, my dear lady Clonbrony, in defiance of bulls and blunders,[24] to allow us a comfortable English fireplace and plenty of Newcastle coal in China![25] And a white marble—no! white velvet hearthrug painted with beautiful flowers—O! the delicate, the *useful* thing!"

Vexed by the emphasis on the word *useful*, lady Clonbrony endeavoured to turn off the attention of the company. "Lady Langdale, your ladyship's a judge of china—this vase is an unique, I am told."

"I am told," interrupted Mrs. Dareville, "this is the very vase in which B——, the nabob's father, who was, you know, a China captain, smuggled his dear little Chinese wife and all her fortune out of Canton—positively, actually put the lid on, packed her up, and sent her off on shipboard!—True! true! upon my veracity! I'll tell you my authority!"

With this story, Mrs. Dareville drew all attention from the jar, to lady Clonbrony's infinite mortification.

Lady Langdale at length turned to look at a vast range of china jars.

"Ali Baba and the forty thieves!" exclaimed Mrs. Dareville: "I hope you have boiling oil ready!"

Lady Clonbrony was obliged to laugh, and to vow that Mrs. Dareville was uncommon pleasant to-night—"But now," said her ladyship, "let me take you to the Turkish tent."

Having with great difficulty got the malicious wit out of the pagoda and into the Turkish tent, lady Clonbrony began to breathe more freely; for here she thought she was upon safe ground:—"Every thing, I flatter myself," said she, "is correct, and appropriate, and quite picturesque"—

[24] *bulls and blunders*: an insistent identification of Lady Clonbrony as Irish is effected through 'bulls', thought to be a distinctively Irish form of verbal error. Edgeworth and her father wrote an extensive study of language, *Essay on Irish Bulls*, in 1802.*

[25] *English fireplace . . . in China*, perhaps this prepares the way for Edgeworth's very subversive allusion to a pamphlet, 'An Intercepted Letter from China.*

The company, dispersed in happy groups, or reposing on seraglio ottomans, drinking lemonade and sherbet—beautiful Fatimas[26] admiring, or being admired—"Every thing here quite correct, appropriate, and picturesque," repeated Mrs. Dareville.

Source: Maria Edgeworth, *The Absentee*, W. J. McCormack and Kim Walker, eds, *Oxford World's Classics*, Oxford University Press, Oxford and New York, 1988, pp. 12–14, 27–8, 33–7.

Thomas De Quincey, *Confessions of an English Opium-Eater*, 1822

May, 1818.

The Malay has been a fearful enemy for months. I have been every night, through his means, transported into Asiatic scenes. I know not whether others share in my feelings on this point; but I have often thought that if I were compelled to forego England, and to live in China, and among Chinese manners and modes of life and scenery, I should go mad. The causes of my horror lie deep; and some of them must be common to others. Southern Asia, in general, is the seat of awful images and associations. As the cradle of the human race, it would alone have a dim and reverential feeling connected with it. But there are other reasons. No man can pretend that the wild, barbarous, and capricious superstitions of Africa, or of savage tribes elsewhere, affect him in the way that he is affected by the ancient, monumental, cruel, and elaborate religions of Indostan,[27] &c. The mere antiquity of Asiatic things, of their institutions, histories, modes of faith, &c. is so impressive, that to me the vast age of the race and name overpowers the sense of youth in the individual. A young Chinese seems to me an antediluvian man renewed. Even Englishmen, though not bred in any knowledge of such institutions, cannot but shudder at the mystic sublimity of *castes* that have flowed apart, and refused to mix, through such immemorial tracts of time; nor can any man fail to be awed by the names of the Ganges, or the Euphrates. It contributes much to these feelings, that southern Asia is, and has been for thousands of years, the part of the earth most swarm-

---

[26] *Fatimas*: the prophet Mohammed's daughter was Fatimah (600–32), one of the four perfect women of Islam.

[27] *Indostan*: Hindostan, or India as it is now known.

ing with human life; the great *officina gentium*.[28] Man is a weed in those regions. The vast empires also, into which the enormous population of Asia has always been cast, give a further sublimity to the feelings associated with all oriental names or images. In China, over and above what it has in common with the rest of southern Asia, I am terrified by the modes of life, by the manners, and the barrier of utter abhorrence, and want of sympathy, placed between us by feelings deeper than I can analyze. I could sooner live with lunatics, or brute animals. All this, and much more than I can say, or have time to say, the reader must enter into before he can comprehend the unimaginable horror which these dreams of oriental imagery, and mythological tortures, impressed upon me. Under the connecting feeling of tropical heat and vertical sun-lights, I brought together all creatures, birds, beasts, reptiles, all trees and plants, usages and appearances, that are found in all tropical regions, and assembled them together in China or Indostan. From kindred feelings, I soon brought Egypt and all her gods under the same law. I was stared at, hooted at, grinned at, chattered at, by monkeys, by paroquets, by cockatoos. I ran into pagodas: and was fixed, for centuries, at the summit, or in secret rooms; I was the idol; I was the priest; I was worshipped; I was sacrificed. I fled from the wrath of Brama through all the forests of Asia: Vishnu hated me: Seeva laid wait for me. I came suddenly upon Isis and Osiris:[29] I had done a deed, they said, which the ibis and the crocodile trembled at. I was buried, for a thousand years, in stone coffins, with mummies and sphynxes, in narrow chambers at the heart of eternal pyramids. I was kissed, with cancerous kisses, by crocodiles; and laid, confounded with all unutterable slimy things, amongst reeds and Nilotic mud.

I thus give the reader some slight abstraction of my oriental dreams, which always filled me with such amazement at the monstrous scenery, that horror seemed absorbed, for a while, in sheer astonishment. Sooner or later, came a reflux of feeling that swallowed up the astonishment, and left me, not so much in terror, as in hatred and abomination of what I saw. Over every form, and threat, and punishment, and dim sightless incarceration, brooded a sense of eternity and infinity that drove me into an oppression as of madness. Into these dreams only, it was, with one or two slight exceptions, that any circumstances of physical horror entered. All before had been moral and spiritual terrors. But here the main agents were ugly birds, or snakes, or crocodiles; especially the last. The cursed crocodile became to me the object of more horror than almost all the rest. I was compelled to live with him; and (as was always the case almost

---

[28] *officina gentium*: the workshop of peoples.

[29] *Brahma . . . Vishnu . . . Siva . . . Isis and Osiris*: the first three are Hindu deities, the last two the Egyptian goddess and god (consorts) of death and rebirth.

in my dreams) for centuries. I escaped sometimes, and found myself in Chinese houses, with cane tables, &c. All the feet of the tables, sophas, &c. soon became instinct with life: the abominable head of the crocodile, and his leering eyes, looked out at me, multiplied into a thousand repetitions: and I stood loathing and fascinated. And so often did this hideous reptile haunt my dreams, that many times the very same dream was broken up in the very same way: I heard gentle voices speaking to me (I hear every thing when I am sleeping); and instantly I awoke: it was broad noon; and my children were standing, hand in hand, at my bedside; come to show me their coloured shoes, or new frocks, or to let me see them dressed for going out. I protest that so awful was the transition from the damned crocodile, and the other unutterable monsters and abortions of my dreams, to the sight of innocent *human* natures and of infancy, that, in the mighty and sudden revulsion of mind, I wept, and could not forbear it, as I kissed their faces.

Source: Grevel Lindop, ed., *Works of Thomas de Quincey*, 18 vols, Pickering and Chatto, London, 2000, *Confessions of an English Opium Eater*, 1821/1822, vol. 2, pp. 70–2.

Samuel Taylor Coleridge, *Kubla Khan*

OF THE FRAGMENT OF KUBLA KHAN

The following fragment is here published at the request of a poet of great and deserved celebrity,[30] and as far as the Author's own opinions are concerned, rather as a psychological curiosity, than on the ground of any supposed *poetic* merits.

In the summer of the year 1797,[31] the Author, then in ill health, had retired to a lonely farm-house between Porlock and Linton,[32] on the Exmoor confines of Somerset and Devonshire. In consequence of a slight indisposition, an anodyne[33] had been prescribed, from the effects of

---

[30] ll. 2–3 [Poet of great and deserved celebrity] Lord Byron. Byron's enthusiasm for the poem was recorded by Thomas Medwin (*Conversations of Lord Byron*, ed., Lovell 178).*

[31] l. 6 [summer of the year 1797] the ms dates the composition in "the fall of the year 1797".*

[32] l. 7 [a lonely farm-house between Porlock and Linton] identified as Ash Farm: or as Broomstreet Farm, which is 2 miles from Culbone church.*

[33] l. 8 [indisposition . . . anodyne] the indisposition is dysentery, and the anodyne is opium.*

which he fell asleep in his chair at the moment that he was reading the following sentences,[34] or words of the same substance, in "Purchas's Pilgrimage:" "Here the Khan Kubla commanded a palace to be built, and a stately garden thereunto. And thus ten miles of fertile ground were inclosed with a wall." The author continued for about three hours in a profound sleep, at least of the external senses, during which time he has the most vivid confidence, that he could not have composed less than from two to three hundred lines; if that indeed can be called composition in which all the images rose up before him as *things*, with a parallel production of the correspondent expressions, without any sensation or consciousness of effort. On awaking he appeared to himself to have a distinct recollection of the whole, and taking his pen, ink, and paper, instantly and eagerly wrote down the lines that are here preserved. At this moment he was unfortunately called out by a person on business from Porlock, and detained by him above an hour, and on his return to his room, found to his no small surprise and mortification, that though he still retained some vague and dim recollection of the general purpose of the vision, yet, with the exception of some eight or ten scattered lines and images, all the rest had passed away like the images on the surface of a stream into which a stone has been cast, but, alas! without the after restoration of the latter:

> Then all the charm
> Is broken—all that phantom-world so fair
> Vanishes, and a thousand circlets spread,
> And each mis-shape the other. Stay awhile,
> Poor youth! who scarcely dar'st lift up thine eyes—
> The stream will soon renew its smoothness, soon
> The visions will return! And lo, he stays,
> And soon the fragments dim of lovely forms
> Come trembling back, unite, and now once more
> The pool becomes a mirror.

Yet from the still surviving recollections in his mind, the Author has frequently purposed to finish for himself what had been originally, as it were, given to him. Αὔριον ἄδιον ᾄσω[35] but the to-morrow is yet to come.

---

[34] l. 10 The sentence in Purchas's *Pilgrimage* (1617) "In *Xamdu* did *Cublai Can* build a stately Palace, encompassing sixteene miles of plaine ground with a wall, wherein are fertile Meddowes, pleasant springs, delightfull Streames, and all sorts of beasts of chase and game, and in the middest thereof a sumptuous house of pleasure, which may be remoued from place to place."*

[35] l. 40 Αὔριον ἄδιον ᾄσω] Theocritus *Idyll* l. 145 (var) tr "Tomorrow I shall sing more sweetly."*

In Xanadu did KUBLA KHAN
A stately pleasure-dome decree:
Where ALPH,[36] the sacred river, ran
Through caverns measureless to man
 Down to a sunless sea.   5
So twice five miles of fertile ground
With walls and towers were girdled round;
And here were gardens bright with sinuous rills
Where blossom'd many an incense-bearing tree;
And here were forests ancient as the hills,   10
Enfolding sunny spots of greenery.

But oh that deep romantic chasm which slanted
Down the green hill athwart a cedarn cover!
A savage place! as holy and inchanted
As e'er beneath a waning moon was haunted   15
By woman wailing for her demon-lover!
And from this chasm, with ceaseless turmoil seething,
As if this earth in fast thick pants were breathing,
A mighty fountain momently was forced:
Amid whose swift half-intermitted Burst   20
Huge fragments vaulted like rebounding hail,
Or chaffy grain beneath the thresher's flail:
And mid these dancing rocks at once and ever
It flung up momently the sacred river.
Five miles meandering with a mazy motion   25
Through wood and dale the sacred river ran,
Then reached the caverns measureless to man,
And sank in tumult to a lifeless ocean:
And 'mid this tumult Kubla heard from far
Ancestral voices prophesying war!   30

 The shadow of the dome of pleasure
 Floated midway on the waves;
 Where was heard the mingled measure
 From the fountain and the caves.
 It was a miracle of rare device,   35
 A sunny pleasure-dome with caves of ice!

---

[36] [ALPH] The possible implications of the name include the Nile, the Alpheus (which after various disappearances underground was said to cross the Adriatic and emerge as the fountain Arethusa), and the initial letter of the Greek alphabet, with its suggestion of the origin of language. Such implications do not exclude one another or others.*

A damsel with a dulcimer
In a vision once I saw:
It was an Abyssinian maid
And on her dulcimer she play'd,   40
Singing of Mount Abora.[37]
Could I revive within me
Her symphony and song,
To such a deep delight 'twould win me,
That with music loud and long,   45
I would build that dome in air,
That sunny dome! those caves of ice!
And all who heard should see them there,
And all should cry, Beware! Beware!
His flashing eyes, his floating hair!   50
Weave a circle round him thrice,
And close your eyes with holy dread:
For he on honey-dew hath fed,
And drank the milk of Paradise.

Source: J. C. C. Mays, ed., *The Collected Works of Samuel Taylor Coleridge; Poetical Works, Vol. I*, Princeton University Press, Princeton, 2001, pp. 511–14.

William Hazlitt, essay in *The London Magazine*, June 1821

A Ruin is poetical. Because it is a work of art, says Lord Byron. No, but because it is a work of art o'erthrown. In it we see, as in a mirror, the life, the hopes, the labour of man defeated, and crumbling away under the slow hand of time; and all that he has done reduced to nothing, or to a useless mockery. Or as one of the bread-and-butter poets[38] has described the same thing a little differently, in his tale of Peter Bell[39] the potter,—

---

[37] *Abora*: possibly the false *Abyssinian* paradise described in *Milton's Paradise Lost*.

[38] *one of the bread-and-butter poets*: William Wordsworth, so-called here for his preference for simple style and domestic subject-matter.

[39] *Peter Bell*: Wordsworth's poem of the same title.

'——The stones and tower
Seem'd fading fast away
From human thoughts and purposes,
To yield to some transforming power,
And blend with the surrounding trees.'

If this is what Lord Byron means by artificial objects and interests [viewed as a possible subject for poetry], there is an end of the question, for he will get no critic, no school to differ with him. But a fairer instance would be a snug citizen's box by the road-side, newly painted, plastered and furnished, with every thing in the newest fashion and gloss, not an article the worse for wear, and a lease of one-and-twenty years to run, and then let us see what Lord Byron, or his friend and 'host of Human Life' will make of it, compared with the desolation, and the waste of all these comforts, arts, and elegances. Or let him take—not the pyramids of Egypt, but the pavilion at Brighton, and make a poetical description of it in prose or verse. We defy him. The poetical interest, in his Lordship's transposed cases, arises out of the imaginary interest. But the truth is, that where art flourishes and attains its object, imagination droops, and poetry along with it. It ceases, or takes a different and ambiguous shape; it may be elegant, ingenious, pleasing, instructive, but if it aspires to the semblance of a higher interest, or the ornaments of the highest fancy, it necessarily becomes burlesque, as for instance, in the Rape of the Lock. As novels end with marriage, poetry ends with the consummation and success of art. And the reason (if Lord Byron would attend to it) is pretty obvious. Where all the wishes and wants are supplied, anticipated by art, there can be no strong cravings after ideal good, nor dread of unimaginable evils; the sources of terror and pity must be dried up: where the hand has done every thing, nothing is left for the imagination to do or to attempt: where all is regulated by conventional indifference, the full workings, the involuntary, uncontrollable emotions of the heart cease: property is not a poetical, but a practical prosaic idea, to those who possess and clutch it; and cuts off others from cordial sympathy; but nature is common property, the unenvied idol of all eyes, the fairy ground where fancy plays her tricks and feats; and the passions, the workings of the heart (which Mr. Bowles very properly distinguishes from manners, inasmuch as they are not in the power of the will to regulate or satisfy) are still left as a subject for something very different from didactic or mock-heroic poetry. By *art* and *artificial*, as these terms are applied to poetry or human life, we mean those objects and feelings which depend for their subsistence and perfection on the will and arbitrary conventions of man and society; and by nature, and natural subjects, we mean those objects which exist in the universe at large, without, or in spite of, the interference of human power and contrivance, and those interests and affections which are not amenable to the human will. That we are to exclude art, or the operation of the human will, from poetry altogether, is what we do not affirm; but we mean to say, that where this operation is the most complete and manifest, as in the creation of given objects, or regulation of certain feelings, there the spring of poetry, *i.e.* of passion and imagination, is proportionably and much impaired. We are masters of Art, Nature is our master; and it is to this greater power that we find working above, about, and within us, that the genius of poetry bows and offers up its highest homage. If the infusion of art were not a natural disqualifier for poetry, the most artificial objects and manners would be the most poetical: on the contrary, it is only the rude beginnings, or the ruinous decay of objects of art, or the simplest modes of life and manners, that admit of, or harmonize kindly with, the tone and language of poetry.

[. . .]

What is the difference between the feeling with which we contemplate a gas-light in one of the squares, and the crescent moon beside it, but this—that though the brightness, the beauty perhaps, to the mere sense, is the same or greater; yet we know that when we are out of the square we shall lose sight of the lamp, but that the moon will lend us its tributary light wherever we go; it streams over green valley or blue ocean alike; it is hung up in air, a part of the pageant of the universe; it steals with gradual, softened state into the soul, and hovers, a fairy apparition over our existence! It is this which makes it a more poetical object than a patent-lamp, or a Chinese lanthorn, or the chandelier at Covent-garden, brilliant as it is, and which, though it were made ten times more so, would still only dazzle and scorch the sight so much the more; it would not be attended with a mild train of reflected glory; it would 'denote no foregone conclusion,' would touch no chord of imagination or the heart; it would have nothing romantic about it.—A man can make any thing, but he cannot make a sentiment! It is a thing of inveterate prejudice, of old association, of common feelings, and so is poetry, as far as it is serious. A 'pack of cards,' a silver bodkin, a paste buckle, 'may be imbued' with as much mock poetry as you please, by lending false associations to it; but real poetry, or poetry of the highest order, can only be produced by unravelling the real web of associations, which have been wound round any subject by nature, and the unavoidable conditions of humanity.

[. . .]

'How far that little candle throws its beams!
So shines a good deed in a naughty world.'

The image here is one of artificial life; but it is connected with natural circumstances and romantic interests, with darkness, with silence, with distance, with privation, and uncertain danger: it is common, obvious, without pretension or boast, and therefore the poetry founded upon it is natural, because the feelings are so. It is not the splendour of the candle itself, but the contrast to the gloom without,—the comfort, the relief it holds out from afar to the benighted traveller,—the conflict between nature and the first and cheapest resources of art, that constitutes the romantic and imaginary, that is, the poetical interest, in that familiar but striking image. There is more art in the lamp or chandelier; but for that very reason, there is less poetry. A light in a watch-tower, a beacon at sea, is sublime for the same cause; because the natural circumstances and associations set it off; it warns us against danger, it reminds us of common calamity, it promises safety and hope: it has to do with the broad feelings and circumstances of human life, and its interest does not assuredly turn upon the vanity or pretensions of the maker or proprietor of it. This sort of art is co-ordinate with nature, and comes into the first-class of poetry, but no one ever dreamt of the contrary. The features of nature are great leading land-marks, not near and little, or confined to a spot, or an individual claimant; they are spread out everywhere the same, and are of universal interest. The true poet has therefore been described as

'Creation's tenant, he is nature's heir.'

What has been thus said of the man of genius might be said of the man of no genius. The spirit of poetry, and the spirit of humanity are the same. The productions of nature are not locked up in the cabinets of the curious, but spread out on the green lap of earth. The flowers return with the cuckoo in the spring: the daisy for ever looks bright in the sun; the rainbow still lifts its head above the storm to the eye of infancy or age—

'So was it when my life began;
So it is now I am a man,
So shall it be till I grow old and die;'

but Lord Byron does not understand this, for he does not understand Mr. Wordsworth's poetry, and we cannot make him. His Lordship's nature, as well as his poetry, is something arabesque and outlandish.

Source: P. P. Howe, ed., *The Complete Works of William Hazlitt in Twenty-One Volumes*, London and Toronto, 1933, vol. 19, pp. 73–6.

Contemporary reactions to the Royal Pavilion at Brighton

The Royal Pavilion at Brighton provoked reactions ranging from the scornful to the admiring among contemporaries. There follows an assortment of remarks on the Prince Regent's fantasy palace by both 'insiders' and 'outsiders'.

1. From Anthony Pasquin, *The New Brighton Guide* . . ., 6th edn, London, 1796, p. 16:

a nondescript monster in building, and appears like a mad-house, or a house run mad, as it has neither beginning, middle, nor end . . .

2. Thomas Creevey reminiscing about visits in 1805, from *The Creevey Papers*, ed. John Gore, 1963, London, The Folio Society, 1970, p. 39:

I suppose the Courts or houses of Princes are all alike in one thing, viz., that in attending them you lose your liberty. After one month was gone by, you fell naturally and of course into the ranks, and had to reserve your observations till you were asked for them. These royal invitations are by no means calculated to reconcile one to a Court. To be sent for half an hour before dinner, or perhaps in the middle of one's own, was a little too humiliating to be very agreeable.

3. From a letter from Lady Bessborough to Granville Leveson Gower on her visit to the Pavilion in 1805. *Lord Granville Leveson Gower . . . Private Correspondence 1781–1821*, ed. Castalia Countess Grenville, 2 vols, London, Murray, 1916, vol. II, p. 120:

Today I have been going all over the Pavilion, which is really beautiful in its way. I did not think the strange Chinese shapes and columns could have looked so well. It is like Concetti in poetry, in outré and false taste, but for the kind of thing as perfect as it can be, and the Prince says he had it so because at the time there was such an outcry against French things, etc., that he was afraid of his furniture being accused of jacobinism.

4. From Mary Lloyd, *Brighton: A Poem* . . ., London, 1809, p. 42:

Around the beauteous lawn, gay buildings rise,
  There the Pavilion woos admiring eyes; . . .
    Within, the lovely edifice is grac'd
    With every beauty of inventive taste;
  And as each scene admiring we explore,
It seems enchantment all, some magic bower . . .

5. From R[ichard] Sickelmore, *An Epitome of Brighton, Topographical and Descriptive . . .*, Brighton, 1815, p. 44. Sickelmore describes the Chinese interiors in detail and concludes by asserting that they afford

the most pleasing testimony, that John Bull, with suitable encouragement, has it within the scope of his own powers to excel all the boasted frippery ornaments of the Continent.

6. The Comtesse de Boigne (of a slightly earlier incarnation of the Pavilion in 1817 when it was still filled with real Chinese things), from *Memoirs of the Comtesse de Boigne*, ed. Charles Nicollaud, 4 vols, London, Heinemann, 1907, II (1815–19), p. 248:

[The Pavilion] was indeed a masterpiece of bad taste. The most heterogeneous magnificence had been gathered at vast expense from the four quarters of the globe and piled beneath the eight or ten cupolas of this ugly and eccentric palace, the several parts of which displayed not the slightest architectural unity . . . The inside was no better arranged than the outside, and art was certainly conspicuous by its absence. After these observations, criticism was disarmed. The comforts and pleasures of life were equally well understood in this palace, and when the spectator had satisfied his artistic conscience by criticising the association of so many strange curiosities, much amusement might be found in considering their elaboration and their extravagant elegance.

7. *Brighton; or, The Steyne. A Satirical Novel*, 2nd edn. London, 1818, pp. 86–7, of the interior viewed as a guest at an evening party:

It was night; or rather, intrusive day was excluded; odours burned in all directions; a thousand lamps glittered in the regal hall; . . . the table groaned under the weight of massy plate and delicious viands; rich and expensive wines flowed like rivers to slack [sic] the fevered lip of intemperance. A stranger would here have considered himself in the age of gold . . . the beholder must have thought there could be no misery, no want, in that land which bore so great a chief.

8. John Wilson Croker, from his journal entry for December 1818, in *The Correspondence and Diaries of the late Rt Honourable John Wilson Croker*, ed. Louis J. Jennings, 3 vols, London, 1884, vol. 1, p. 122:

. . . an absurd waste of money, and will be a ruin in half a century or sooner.

9. From William Hone, *The Joss and His Folly*, 1820:

The queerest of all the queer sights I've set sight on;
Is, the *what d'ye – call't thing*, here, the FOLLY at Brighton.
The outside – huge teapots, all drill'd round with holes,
Relieved by extinguishers, sticking on poles:
The inside – all tea-things, and dragons and bells,
The show rooms – all show, the sleeping rooms – cells.

But the *grand* Curiosity's not to be seen—
The owner himself – an old fat MANDARIN . . .

10. Princess Lieven writing to Metternich, October 27, 1820:

How can one describe such a piece of architecture? The style is a mixture of
Moorish, Tartar, Gothic, and Chinese and all in stone and iron. It is a whim
which has already cost £700,000, and it is still not fit to live in.

11. From John Evans, *Recreation for the Young and the Old. An Excursion to Brighton, with an Account of the Royal Pavilion*, Chiswick, 1821, pp. 40–1, 41, 44–5:

England has been reproached by travellers for a want of palaces on a scale commensurate with the grandeur of its monarchy . . . the PAVILION is only a royal
winter residence, but in proportion to its extent, it may be said to exceed any
other of the palaces in the kingdom.

Of the exterior:

. . . besides the Pagoda spires at both ends of the edifice, intermediate ornaments
of a circular form have been added. It is said to be an imitation of the *Kremlin*
in Moscow, the ancient capital of the Russian Empire. It was amusing to hear
the conjectures of the spectators relative to these ornaments, while they were
constructing – some comparing them to large Spanish onions; and others likening them to distillery utensils, or to inverted balloons! Most persons appeared
very sagacious in ascertaining their form and use, whilst a few individuals modestly confessed that they were so dissimilar from anything that had been ever
seen in this part of the world as to surpass comprehension!

Of the interior:

It is scarcely in the power of words to convey an accurate idea of its rich and
glowing magnificence. The aerial imagery of fancy, and the embellishments of
fertile invention, profusely described in 'The Thousand and One Nights,' and
the popular tales of magic, involving the enchanted palaces of the *Genii*, fall
short, in splendour of detail, to the scene of imposing grandeur, and the beautiful combination and effect of myriads of glittering objects . . .

In conclusion:

In the scene of radiant and imposing splendour here displayed, it has been His
Majesty's wish to give encouragement to every branch of the arts, and especially
to British manufactures; . . . Every thing here and throughout the Palace is
almost entirely the work of British materials and British hands; it combines a
whole, in which the high and cultivated taste of a *Patriot Monarch* forms a
strong feature, as diffusing its rays and illuminating national talents to the liberal and just support of national worth and industry, that merits, and must
obtain, the admiration of the world.

12. From George Colman, *The Gewgaw; or, Brighton Toy, A Caricature Poem*, London, 1822 or 1824, pp. 7–9:

such a trifle—
Contrived the *purse* and *mint* to rifle

help me form a rhyming jumble–
Though its style be ne'er so humble,
Touching of a certain pile
At which so many often smile
While others whisper, think and say
"What thousands here are thrown away," –
And Folly, with her eyes, besets
Its turrets, tow'rs, and minarets,
Exclaiming "La! what pretty things
Are formed to please the eyes of Kings,
And make them happy, night and day,
Would stern *Reflection* keep away–
And not disturb their banquet rout,
With aching head and burning gout;
But let them spend their earthly hours
In Pleasure's lap – strew'd o'er with flow'rs–
Enjoying, ev'ry day and night,
The sweetest sweets of each delight–
That ev'ry sensual bliss affords".

13. Anonymous Whig MP (June 1816) on the Prince's expenditure on the Pavilion:

that squanderous and lavish profusion which in a certain quarter resembled more the pomp and magnificence of a Persian satrap, seated in the splendour of Oriental state, than the sober dignity of a British Prince, seated in the bosom of his subjects.

14. *The Times*, 1830:

In the tawdry childishness of Carlton House and the mountebank Pavilion, or cluster of pagodas at Brighton, His Royal Highness afforded an infallible earnest of what might one day be expected from His Majesty when the appetite for profusion and the contempt for all that deserves the name of architecture should have reached their full maturity . . .

15. William Cobbett, *Rural Rides*, ed. G. D. H. and Margaret Cole, 3 vols, London, Peter Davies, 1930, I, p. 68:

Brighton is a very pleasant place . . . The *Kremlin*, the very name of which has so long been a subject of laughter all over the country, lies in a gorge of the valley, and amongst the old houses of the town. The grounds, which cannot, I think, exceed a couple or three acres, are surrounded by a wall neither lofty nor good-looking. Above this rise some trees, bad in sorts, stunted in growth, and dirty with smoke. As to the 'palace' as the Brighton newspapers call it, the apartments appear to be all on the ground floor; and when you see the thing from a distance, you think you see a parcel of *cradle-spits*, of various dimensions, sticking up out of the mouths of so many squat decanters. Take a square box, the sides of which are three feet and a half, and the height a foot and a half. Take a large Norfolk-turnip, cut off the green of the leaves, leave the stalks 9 inches long, tie these round with a string three inches from the top, and put the turnip in the middle of the top of the box. Then take four turnips half the size, treat them the same way, and put them on the corners of the box. Then take a considerable number of bulbs of the crown-imperial, the narcissus, the hyacinth, the tulip, the crocus, and others; let the leaves of each have sprouted to about an inch, more or less according to the size of the bulb; put all these, pretty promiscuously but pretty thickly, on the top of the box. Then stand off and look at your architecture. There! That's '*a Kremlin*'! Only you must cut some church-looking windows in the sides of the box. As to what you ought to put *into* the box, that is a subject far above my cut. (10th June, 1822)

The Journal of Eugène Delacroix

The French Romantic artist Eugène Delacroix travelled to Morocco in 1832, in the party of the Comte de Mornay, a French diplomat. The French had seized Algeria in 1830 and wished to establish friendly relations with Algeria's neighbour, Morocco, ruled at the time by the Sultan Muley-abd-el-Rahman. Delacroix became acquainted with Mornay through the Parisian circles in which he moved. The six-month journey to Morocco was to prove a crucial stage in the artist's development. He returned to France with eight albums of drawings and annotated sketches. Already well established as a painter of flamboyant, oriental and exotic subjects (mostly taken from other artists and writers), Delacroix was nevertheless keen to assert his allegiance to classical sources of inspiration. The journey to Morocco allowed him to encounter at first hand new, vivid effects of colour and light. It also reinforced his love of antique simplicity, which he discerned in the drapery, poses and contours of local people. The following extract consists of notes accompanying the sketches in his albums and demonstrates the careful, precise observation of colours and forms that informed later paintings such as *The Jewish Wedding* (1837?–41).

The Jewish wedding, extract from *The Journal of Eugène Delacroix*

Tuesday, February 21.

The Jewish wedding.[1] The Moors and the Jews at the entrance. The two musicians. The violinist, his thumb in the air, the under side of the other hand very much in the shadow, light behind, the haik on his head transparent in places; white sleeves, shadowy background. The violinist;

[1] The scene described here inspired Delacroix's painting, exhibited at the Salon of 1841, *The Jewish Wedding*.

seated on his heels and on his gelabia.[2] Blackness between the two musicians below. The body of the guitar on the knee of the player; very dark
toward the belt, red vest, brown ornaments, blue behind his neck.
Shadow from his left arm (which is directly in front of one) cast on the
haik over his knee. Shirtsleeves rolled up showing his arms up to the
biceps; green woodwork at his side; a wart on his neck, short nose.

At the side of the violinist, pretty Jewish woman; vest, sleeves, gold
and amaranth. She is silhouetted halfway against the door, half-way
against the wall; nearer the foreground, an older woman with a great
deal of white, which conceals her almost entirely. The shadows full of
reflections; white in the shadows.

A pillar cutting out, dark in the foreground. The women to the left in
lines one above the other like flower pots. White and gold dominate,
their handkerchiefs are yellow. Children on the ground in front.

At the side of the guitarist, the Jew who plays the tambourine. His face
is a dark silhouette, concealing part of the hand of the guitarist. The
lower part of his head cuts out against the wall. The tip of a gelabia
under the guitarist. In front of him, with legs crossed, the young Jew who
holds the plate. Gray garment. Leaning against his shoulder a young
Jewish child about ten years old.

Against the door of the stairway, Prisciada; purplish handkerchief on
her head and under her throat. Jews seated on the steps; half seen against
the door, strong light on their noses, one of them standing straight up on
the staircase; a cast shadow with reflections clearly marked on the wall,
the reflection a light yellow.

Above, Jewesses leaning over the balcony rail. One at the left, bare-
headed, very dark, clear-cut against the wall, lit by the sun. In the corner,
the old Moor with his beard on one side; shaggy haik, his turban placed
low on the forehead, gray beard against the white haik. The other Moor,
with a shorter nose, very masculine, turban sticking out. One foot out of
the slipper, sailor's vest and sleeves the same.

Tangier. After the return from Meknez.

Went to the house of Abraham[3] with M. de Praslin[4] and M. d'Haussonville.[5] The girl with the little kerchief on her head; her dress. The

---

[2] 'gelabia' (or 'jellaba'): loose cloak with hood.

[3] Abraham ben-Chimol, an interpreter at the French Consulate who introduced Delacroix
into the Jewish community.

[4] The Duke of Choiseul-Praslin (1805–47), attaché at the French Embassy in Madrid.

[5] Count Joseph d'Haussonville (1809–84), secretary at the French Embassy in Madrid. Like
Choiseul-Praslin, he was passing through Tangier.

13 Eugène Delacroix, *A Jewish Wedding in Morocco*, 1837?–41, exhibited at the Salon of 1841, oil on canvas, 105 x 140.5 cm, Musée du Louvre, Paris. The Bridgeman Art Library.

Negroes who came to dance at the consulate and through the city. Woman in front of them covered with a haik[6] and bearing a staff with a cloth at the end to collect money. A touch of fever about the 16th of April. On the 20th took a walk. My first outing with M. D.[7] and M. Freyssinet[8] along the waterfront. The black man bathing the black horse; the Negro as black and as shiny as the horse.

Tangier, April 28.

Yesterday, April 27th, there passed under our windows a procession with music; drums and oboes, it was for a young boy who had just finished his school and who was being escorted about with ceremony. He was surrounded by his comrades who sang, and by his parents and teachers. People came out of the shops and houses to compliment him. He was enveloped in a burnous, etc.

[6] Piece of cloth in which men and women draped themselves.
[7] This probably refers to M. Desgranges, the king's interpreter, attaché to the ambassadorial party of the Comte de Mornay.
[8] Freycinet was attached to the Dutch Consulate in Tangier. The original French text here gives 'à la Marine' which may mean 'at the Naval Offices' rather than 'on the waterfront'.

At times of distress, the children come out with their school tablets and carry them with solemnity. These tablets are of wood coated with clay. They write with reeds and a sort of sepia which can easily be wiped off. This people is wholly antique. This exterior life and these carefully closed houses: the women withdrawn, etc. The other day, quarrel with sailors who wanted to enter a Moorish house. A Negro threw his wooden shoe in their faces, etc.

Abou,[9] the general who conducted us, was seated the other day on the doorstep; our kitchen boy was seated on the bench. He bent over to the side only the least bit so as to let us pass. There is something democratic in such offhand manners. The big men of the country will squat down in the sun on a street corner and chat together, or stretch out in the shop of some merchant.

Source: Walter Pach, ed. and trans., *The Journal of Eugène Delacroix*, Jonathan Cape, London, 1933 [1822–1863], pp. 106–7, 121.

[9] Ben Abou, head of the military escort.

Index